The Society of puBlication deSignerS / 2009

44th puBlication deSign annual

2

CRAIG CUTLER   HORACIO SALINAS   LOU VEGA   RIGGARDO VECCHIO

CRAIG CUTLER
CRAIG MCDEAN
CRISWELL LAPPIN
CRYSTAL PHILLIPS
CYBELE GRANDJEAN
CYNTHIA A. HOFFMAN
CYNTHIA SEARIGHT
D.W. PINE
DAKOTA KECK
DALE STEPHANOS
DAMIAN HEINISCH
DAN FORBES
DAN REVITTE
DAN SAELINGER
DAN WINTERS
DANA PRITTS
DANIEL-ADEL
DANIEL MÖLLER-GROTE
DANNY CLINCH
DANNY FISHER
DANNY WILCOX-FRAZIER
DARHIL CROOKS
DARIN LEDFORD
DARROW
DAVIA SMITH
DAVID ATTIE
DAVID ARKY
DAVID ROWMAN
DAVID CARTHAS
DAVID CLUGSTON
DAVID CURCURITO
DAVID GRIFFIN
DAVID GRAY
DAVID HARRIS
DAVID HILTON
DAVID LEVENTI
DAVID LA SPINA
DAVID M. BRINLEY
DAVID MCKENNA
DAVID ROEMER
DAVID SCHLOW
DAVID SEBBAH
DAVID SIMS
DAVID SPERANZA
DAVID WHITMORE
DAVID ZIMMER

HORACIO SALINAS
HOWARD CAO
HUGH KRETSCHMER
HYE JIN LEE
IAN ALLEN
IAN ROBINSON
IAN BROWN
ILAN RUBIN
INGO ARNDT
I-NI CHEN
IVYLISE SIMONES
IXEL OSARIO
J.C. DE MARCOS
J.D. CUBAN
J.R. AREBALO JR.
JACK UNRUH
JACKIE DASHEVSKY
JACKIE MCCAFFREY
JACKIE NICKERSON
JACLYN STEINBERG
JACOB HUULLAINEN
JAQUELINE MUNZ
JAIMEY EASLER
JAKE CHESSUM
JAKE LEFEBURE
JAKOB CARLSEN
JAMES DAY
JAMES DUNLINSON
JAMES NACHTWEY
JAMES VICTORE
JAMES WOJCIK
JAMESON SIMPSON
JAMIE BARTOLACCI
JAMIE CHUNG
JAN STROMME
JANA MEIER
JAN WELTERS
JANINE ARROYO FONSECA
JARRED FORD
JASON GNEWIKOW
JASON GROW

LOU VEGA
LOUIS-CHARLES TIAR
LUCAS ALLEN
LUKE BEST
LUKE HAYMAN
LUKE WILLIAMS
MACIEK KOBIELSKI
MADS FREUND-BRUNSE
MAELI-HOLLMAN
MAIRA KALMAN
MAISIE TODD
MANUELLO PAGANELLI
MARIA LILIANA GONZÁLEZ
MARC ALARY
MARC ASNIN
MARC HOM
MARC KAUFMAN
MARC STEINMETZ
MARCUS BROOKS
MARCUS PIGGOTI
MARCY RYAN
MARGARET SWART
MARIA DEL CARMEN MERCADO
MARIAN BANTJES
MARIANA SASSO ROJAS
MARIANO VIVANCO
MARILYN MINTER
MARINA GARNIER
MARINO ZUILICH
MARIO SORRENTI
MARISSA BOURKE
MARK HEITHOFF
MARK MANN
MARK MICHAELSON
MARK SANDERS
MARK SELIGER
MARK SHAW
MARLA KAPLAN
MARNE-MAYER
MARSHALL MCKINNEY
MARTHA RICH
MARTIN KUENSTING
MARTIN SCHOELLER
MARTIN WATTENBERG
MARTIN KILLMAN
MARTIN WOODTLI
MARTINE FOUGERON
MARVIN ORELLANA
MARY ELLEN MARK
MASA
MASSIMO GAMMACURTA
MATT ZARTAIN
MATT WILLEY
MATTHEW BATES
MATTHEW COOK
MATTHEW ERICSON
MATTHEW FROST
MATTHEW LENNING
MATTHEW KALMAN
MATTHEW ROLSTON
MATTHEW SPORZYNSKI
MAURICIO ALEJO
MAX AGUILERA-HELLWEG

RIGGARDO VECCHIO
RICHARD FERRETTI
RICHARD PHIBBS
RICHARD PIERCE
RICHARD SANDLER
RICHIE SWANN
RICK FRIEDMAN
RICKY MOLLOY
RINA STONE
RITA SALGUEIRO
ROB DILESO
ROB HANEY
ROB HEWITT
ROB HOWARD
ROBBIE COOPER
ROBERT BEST
ROBERT CLARK
ROBERT FESTINO
ROBERT MAXWELL
ROBERT NEWMAN
ROBERT PERINO
ROBERT POLIDORI
ROBERT PRIEST
ROBERT TRACHTENBERG
ROBERT VARGAS
ROBERTO PARADO
ROCKWELL HARWOOD
RODRIGO CASTILLO BONNER
RODRIGO CORRAL
RODRIGO SAIAS
RODRIGO SANCHEZ
ROMAN LUBA
ROMULO YANES
RON GALELLA
RON HAVIV
RON PLYMAN
RONALD J. CALA
RONY ALWIN
RORY WALSH
ROSIE GAINSBOROUGH
ROXANNE LOWIT
RUSSEL ESTES
RUVEN AFANADOR
RYAN CADIZ
SAM KAPLAN
SAM WEBER
SAMUEL SOLOMON
SANDRA FREJ
SARA MCKAY
SARAH WILLIAMS
SARAH CWYNAR
SARAH GARCEA
SARAH VINAS
SARAH WILSON
SASHA CUTTER
SCOTT HALL
SEAN CAPONE
SEAN JOHNSTON
SEAN KENNEDY SANTOS
SEBASTIÃO SALGADO
SERGE BLOCH
SETH WENIG
SHANE LUITJENS
SIMON EMMETT
SIMON SOORY

Bottom-left contributors column

/CONTRIBUTORS/
AARON GOODMAN
AARON KOBLIN
ABBEY KUSTER-PROKELL
ABBY CLAWSON LOW
ABI HUYNH
ABRIL Y DE LA CARRERA
ADAM BILLYEALD
ADAM BOOKBINDER
ADAM LOGAN FULRATH
ADAM SAVITCH
ADAM SIMPSON
ADHEMAS BATISTA
AGNÈS DHERBEYS
ALAN MAHON
ALBERTO GARCÍA-ALIX
ALEC HOLST
ALEC GHEZ
ALEX GROSSMAN
ALEX MARTINEZ
ALEXANDRA CARR
ALICE ALVES
ALICE CHO
AMBER TERRANOVA
AMY FEITELBERG
ALLISON CHIN
AMANDA COX
AMID CAPECI
AMY BERKLEY
AMY HOPPY
AMY ROSENFELD
AMY SHROADS
ANDERS OVERGAARD

Publications (bottom axis)

WIRED
W
VISAO
VIBE
VANITY FAIR
U OF T MAGAZINE
UD &SE
TWIN CITIES METRO
TV GUIDE MAGAZINE
TIME OUT NEW YORK
TIME INTERNATIONAL
TIME
THIS OLD HOUSE
THE VILLAGE VOICE
THE NEW YORKER
THE NEW YORK TIMES UPFRONT
THE NEW YORK TIMES MAGAZINE
THE NEW YORK TIMES BOOK REVIEW
THE NEW YORK TIMES
THE FADER
THE ATLANTIC
TEXAS MONTHLY
STANFORD MAGAZINE
SPORTS ILLUSTRATED
SPIN
SKI
SHUFTI
SHOPSMART!
SELF
SEED
SAMVIRKE
RUNNER'S WORLD
ROOM
ROLLING STONE
REAL SIMPLE
PSYCHOLOGY TODAY
PROTO
PRINT
POPULAR MECHANICS
PLAY
PLATINO
PEOPLE
OUTSIDE
OUT
ONEARTH
NYLON
NOX
NEWSWEEK
NEW YORK
NATIONAL GEOGRAPHIC ADVENTURE
NATIONAL GEOGRAPHIC
MOVIEMAKER
MORE
MONEY
MINNESOTA MONTHLY
METROPOLITAN HOME
METROPOLIS
METROPOLI
MEN'S JOURNAL
MEN'S HEALTH
MEDICINE AT MICHIGAN
MAXIM
MARTHA STEWART LIVING
MADRIZ

COVER AND BOOK DESIGN
TODD ALBERTSON & TOM BROWN
WEAPON OF CHOICE

CONTRIBUTING DESIGN
DIAN HOLTON
LESLEY QUITMEIER
JENNIFER ROBERTS

COVER PHOTOGRAPH
FREDRIK BRODEN

/(PUBLICATIONS/
(T)HERE
2008 HRC ANNUAL REPORT
AARP SEGUNDA JUVENTUD
AARP THE MAGAZINE
AMERICAN CRAFT
AMERICAN WAY
ARCHITECT
ARCHITECTURAL
ATLANTA MAGAZINE
BACKPACKER
BARCELONA
BAY
BEST LIFE
BICYCLING
BILLBOARD
BLACK INK
BLENDER
BODY + SOUL
BON
BON APPÉTIT
BUSINESS WEEK
CALIFORNIA
CHICAGO
CHICAGO
CONDÉ NAST PORTFOLIO
CONDÉ NAST TRAVELER
CONTRIBUTE
COOKIE
CULTURE + TRAVEL
D2
DEPARTURES
DETAILS
DOMINO
DWELL
EARNSHAW'S
EGOISTA
ELLE
ELLE
ELLE (UK)
ELLE DÉCOR
ENTERTAINMENT WEEKLY
ESPN THE MAGAZINE
ESQUIRE
EVERYDAY WITH RACHAEL RAY
FAST COMPANY
FIELD & STREAM
FOOD & WINE
FOOTWEAR PLUS
FORTUNE
FOUNDATION
FOUR SEASONS MAGAZINE
FUTU MAGAZINE
GARDEN & GUN
GEO
GEO
GLAMOUR
GO
GOLF DIGEST INDEX
GOLF DIGEST
GOOD
GOURMET
GOURMET
GQ
GREEN SOURCE
GREEN GUIDE
HANA HOU!
HAWAII SKIN DIVER
HHMI BULLETIN
ILLUMINATION
INC.
INKED
INSTITUTIONAL INVESTOR

judge/

2009 CHAIR

2009 CHAIR
2009 CHAIR
2009 CHAIR

CHAIR EMERITUS
CHAIR EMERITUS

CHAIR EMERITUS
CHAIR EMERITUS

CHAIR EMERITUS

CAPTAIN

CAPTAIN

CAPTAIN
CAPTAIN

CAPTAIN

CAPTAIN

CAPTAIN
CAPTAIN

CAPTAIN

CAPTAIN
CAPTAIN

CAPTAIN

CAPTAIN
CAPTAIN
CAPTAIN

CAPTAIN
CAPTAIN
CAPTAIN
CAPTAIN

CAPTAIN
CAPTAIN

CAPTAIN
CAPTAIN

CAPTAIN
CAPTAIN
CAPTAIN

/FROM TOP, LEFT TO RIGHT/ Co-Chair NATHALIE KIRSHEH, ART DIRECTOR: W / Co-Chair JUDITH PUCKETT-RINELLA, SENIOR PHOTO EDITOR: T, THE NEW YORK TIMES STYLE MAGAZINE / Co-Chair Emeritus DIRK BARNETT, CREATIVE DIRECTOR: MAXIM / Co-Chair Emeritus SCOTT DADICH, CREATIVE DIRECTOR: WIRED / Captain FLORIAN BACHLEDA, CREATIVE DIRECTOR: FB DESIGN / Captain DEBRA BISHOP, CREATIVE DIRECTOR: MORE / Captain KEN DELAGO, DESIGN DIRECTOR: GOLF DIGEST / Captain GERALDINE HESSLER, DESIGN DIRECTOR: GLAMOUR / Captain BRANDON KAVULLA, DESIGN DIRECTOR: MEN'S HEALTH / Captain EDWARD LEIDA, DESIGN DIRECTOR: W / Captain WYATT MITCHELL, DESIGN DIRECTOR: WIRED / Captain ROBERT NEWMAN, THE MAN AT ROBERT NEWMAN DESIGN / Captain ROBERT PERINO, DESIGN DIRECTOR: FORTUNE / Captain INA SALTZ, PRINCIPAL: SALTZ DESIGN /NOT PICTURED/ Magazine of the Year Chair BRUCE RAMSAY, ART DIRECTOR / On-line Chair JEREMY LACROIX, CREATIVE DIRECTOR: CBS INTERACTIVE / Competition Captain NANCY STAMATOPOULOS, ART DIRECTOR: SUPERMARKET NEWS

/FROM TOP,LEFT TO RIGHT/ MATTHEW BATES, DESIGN DIRECTOR: BACKPACKER / APRIL BELL, ASSOCIATE ART DIRECTOR: MONEY / GAIL BICHLER, DEPUTY ART DIRECTOR: THE NEW YORK TIMES MAGAZINE / PHIL BICKER, CREATIVE DIRECTOR: THE FADER / CASS BIRD, PHOTOGRAPHER / KYLE BLUE, DESIGN DIRECTOR: DWELL / NIELS BØJE ZIEGLER, EDUCATOR / EDIT DESIGNER: DANISH SCHOOL OF MEDIA AND JOURNALISM / SHAWN BRYDGES, PARTNER: BRYDGES MCKINNEY / SCOTT BUSCHKUHL, CREATIVE DIRECTOR: HINTERLAND STUDIO / DAVID CARTHAS, PHOTO DIRECTOR / CHRISTOPHER CHEW, ART DIRECTOR: MCGRAW-HILL / LEE CLOWER, PHOTOGRAPHER / PASCAL DANGIN, FOUNDER: BOX STUDIOS / JEFFREY DOCHERTY, ART DIRECTOR / ELIZABETH DOYLE, PHOTO EDITOR / LISA ELIN, PHOTO DIRECTOR: MEN'S FITNESS / SYLVIA FARAGO, PHOTO DIRECTOR

2009 JUDGE   2009 JUDGE   2009 JUDGE   2009 JUDGE   2009 JUDGE

2009 JUDGE   2009 JUDGE   2009 JUDGE   2009 JUDGE

2009 JUDGE   2009 JUDGE   2009 JUDGE

2009 JUDGE   2009 JUDGE   2009 JUDGE   2009 JUDGE   2009 JUDGE

2009 JUDGE   2009 JUDGE   2009 JUDGE   2009 JUDGE   2009 JUDGE   2009 JUDGE

2009 JUDGE   2009 JUDGE   2009 JUDGE   2009 JUDGE   2009 JUDGE   2009 JUDGE

2009 JUDGE   2009 JUDGE   2009 JUDGE   2009 JUDGE   2009 JUDGE   2009 JUDGE

/FROM TOP, LEFT TO RIGHT/ CHRISTOPHER GRIFFITH, PHOTOGRAPHER / SCOTT HALL, PHOTO EDITOR: T, THE NEW YORK TIMES STYLE MAGAZINE / DARRICK HARRIS, PHOTO EDITOR: COOKIE / LUKE HAYMAN, PARTNER: PENTAGRAM / STEVEN HOFFMAN, PARTNER: HOFFMAN NOLI DESIGN / VANESSA HOLDEN, EDITOR: MARTHA STEWART WEDDINGS / JOSEPH HUTCHINSON, ART DIRECTOR: ROLLING STONE / ANTON IOUKHNOVETS, ART DIRECTOR: GQ / NEIL JAMIESON, ART DIRECTOR: FIELD & STREAM ANDRE JOINTE, ART DIRECTOR: DETAILS / KORY KENNEDY, DESIGN DIRECTOR: RUNNER'S WORLD / KATE LARKWORTHY, PRINCIPAL: KATE LARKWORTHY ARTIST REPRESENTATION / DRAGOS LEMNEI, ART DIRECTOR / TIM LEONG, DESIGN DIRECTOR: COMPLEX / JEREMY LESLIE, CREATIVE DIRECTOR: JOHN BROWN PUBLISHING, EDITOR: MAGCULTURE.COM / KATHLEEN MCGOWAN, ART DIRECTOR: BARNEYS

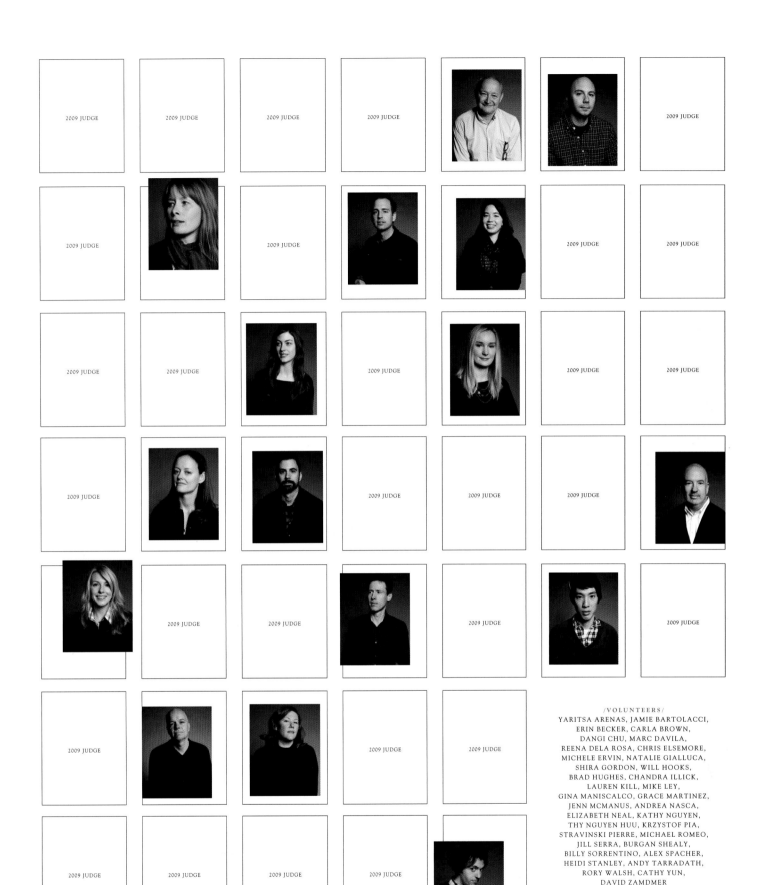

2009 JUDGE · 2009 JUDGE · 2009 JUDGE · 2009 JUDGE · 2009 JUDGE

2009 JUDGE · 2009 JUDGE · 2009 JUDGE · 2009 JUDGE · 2009 JUDGE

2009 JUDGE · 2009 JUDGE · 2009 JUDGE · 2009 JUDGE · 2009 JUDGE

2009 JUDGE · 2009 JUDGE · 2009 JUDGE · 2009 JUDGE · 2009 JUDGE

2009 JUDGE · 2009 JUDGE · 2009 JUDGE · 2009 JUDGE

2009 JUDGE · 2009 JUDGE · 2009 JUDGE · 2009 JUDGE

2009 JUDGE · 2009 JUDGE · 2009 JUDGE · 2009 JUDGE

/VOLUNTEERS/
YARITSA ARENAS, JAMIE BARTOLACCI,
ERIN BECKER, CARLA BROWN,
DANGI CHU, MARC DAVILA,
REENA DELA ROSA, CHRIS ELSEMORE,
MICHELE ERVIN, NATALIE GIALLUCA,
SHIRA GORDON, WILL HOOKS,
BRAD HUGHES, CHANDRA ILLICK,
LAUREN KILL, MIKE LEY,
GINA MANISCALCO, GRACE MARTINEZ,
JENN MCMANUS, ANDREA NASCA,
ELIZABETH NEAL, KATHY NGUYEN,
THY NGUYEN HUU, KRZYSTOF PIA,
STRAVINSKI PIERRE, MICHAEL ROMEO,
JILL SERRA, BURGAN SHEALY,
BILLY SORRENTINO, ALEX SPACHER,
HEIDI STANLEY, ANDY TARRADATH,
RORY WALSH, CATHY YUN,
DAVID ZAMDMER

/PHOTOGRAPHS/
HILARY WALSH

/FROM TOP, LEFT TO RIGHT/ RAYMOND MEIER, PHOTOGRAPHER / CHRIS MUELLER, DEPUTY ART DIRECTOR: VANITY FAIR / CATRIONA NI AOLAIN, DIRECTOR OF PHOTOGRAPHY: ESPN THE MAGAZINE / TOM O'QUINN, DEPUTY ART DIRECTOR: BON APPÉTIT / MICHELE OUTLAND, ART DIRECTOR / JENNIFER PASTORE, PHOTO DIRECTOR: TEEN VOGUE / KRISTA PRESTEK, PHOTO EDITOR: GQ / EMMA REEVES, PHOTO DIRECTOR: TAR / JEFFREY SALCITO, ART DIRECTOR: LAIRD & PARTNERS / BERNARD SCHARF, CREATIVE DIRECTOR: DEPARTURES / EVA SPRING, ART DIRECTOR / GARY STEWART, DESIGN DIRECTOR: TENNIS / JO-EY TANG, PHOTO DIRECTOR: OUT / BLAKE TAYLOR, CREATIVE DIRECTOR: INC. / LISA VOSPER, PHOTO EDITOR / JAN WILKER, PARTNER: KARLSSONWILKER, INC. /NOT PICTURED/ HUBERT JOCHAM, TYPOGRAPHER

RICCARDO VECCHIO
RICHARD SANDLER
ROB HEWITT
ROB HOWARD
ROBERT FESTINO
ROBERT MAXWELL
ROBIN PLATZER
ROCKWELL HARWOOD
RODRIGO CORRAL
RON GALELLA
ROXANNE LOWIT
SARAH FILIPPI
SCOTT HALL
SCOTT DADICH
SEAN MCCABE
SERGE BLOCH
SHARON SUH
SIAN KENNEDY

LUISE STRAUSS
MAILI HOLIMAN
MARGARET SWART
MARINA GARNIER
MARIO SORRENTI
MARK KING
MARTHA RICH
MARVIN ORELLANA
MASA
MATTHEW LENNING

IAN ALLEN
JAKE CHESSUM
JAMIE CHUNG
JANET FROELICH
JARRED FORD
JASON GNEWIKOW
JASON LEE
JAY MAISEL
JEFF RIEDEL
JENNIFER TASTORE
JERI HEIDEN
JESSE LEE
JOANNA MILTER
JODY QUON
JOEL HOLLAND
JOHN BALDESSARI

CRAIG CUTLER
CRISSIE ABBOTT
DAN FORBES
DAN WINTERS
DANIEL SALO
D ARROW
DAVID GHAR
DAVID LEVENTI
DAVID SEBBAH
DAVID SIMS
DAVIES+STARR
DELGIS CANAHUATE
DENNIS FREEDMAN
DONNA FERRATO
DORA SOMOSI
DRUE WAGNER
EDWARD KEATING
EDWARD LEIDA
ELIZABETH SPIRIDAKIS
EMILY CRAWFORD
EMILY ROSENBERG

ALEX GHEZ
ANDRE JOINTE
ANNA GOLDWATER ALEXANDER
ANTON IOUKHNOVETS
AREM DUPLESSIS
ARTHUR MOUNT
BAILEY FRANKLIN
BARBARA KRUGER

W
WIRED

THE NEW YORK TIMES MAGAZINE

IT

NEW YORK

magazine of the year

STEVEN KLEIN

THOMAS ALBERTY
THOMAS ALLEN

TOBY KAUFMANN

TOM O'QUINN
TOM SCHIERLITZ

TURE LILLEGRAVEN
TYRON DUKES

VICTOR KRUMMENACHER
VICTOR SCHRAGER

WALTER C. BAUMANN

WYATT MITCHELL

ZANA WOODS

MITCHELL FEINBERG
NADIA VELLAM
NANCY HARRIS ROUEMY
NATALIE MATUTSCHOVSKY
NATHALIE KIRSHEH

NICOLAS FELTON
NIGEL COX
NOAH KALINA

PATRICIA HEAL

PATRICK MCMULLAN
PATRICK THOMAS

PAUL MCDONOUGH

PETER ARKLE

RANDY MINOR

REBECCA LOUTSCH

JOSÉ PICAYO
JUDITH PUCKET RINELLA
JULIA MOBURG

JUSTIN O'NEILL
KANG KIM

KATIE VAN SYCKLE
KATHY RYAN

KIRA POLLACK

KRISTA PRESTEK

LAURA KONRAD

LEO JUNG
LEVI BROWN

LIZ MATTHEWS

FRED WOODWARD

GAIL BICHLER

GINA MANISCALCO

GLUEKIT

HALI-TARA FELDMAN

HANNAH WHITAKER
HANS GISSINGER

HARRY BENSON

HENRY LEUTWYLER
HILARY FITZGIBBONS
HILARY GREENBAUM

HITOMI SATO

BRIAN FINKE
BRIAN REA

CARL DETORRES
CAROL HAYES
CAROLINE JACKSON
CAROLYN RAUCH

CATHERINE GILMORE-BARNES
CATHERINE LEDNER

CHANDRA GLICK

CHELSEA CARDINAL

CHRIS DIXON

CHRIS SEGEDY

CHRISTIAN WEBER

CHRISTINE PARK
CHRISTOPH NIEMANN

CHRISTOPHER MARTINEZ

CHRISTY SHEPPARD

CLINTON CARGILL

CORY JACOBS

GQ

DETAILS

CULTURE + TRAVEL

BON APPÉTIT

/PUBLICATIONS/

WIRED—PALM

SEARCH SECRETS!
How to Google Better /
BLASTOFF!
DIY Rockets Conquer Space /
PEOPLE POWER!
The Facebook Underground

WIRED

The Future of Food How Science Will Solve the Next Global Crisis

A WIRED ATLAS

GADGET LUST!
141 NEW PRODUCTS, TESTED & RATED

COUNTING CALORIES | NOV.2008

001

/001/ **WIRED**
CREATIVE DIRECTOR: SCOTT DADICH / DESIGN DIRECTOR: WYATT MITCHELL / ART DIRECTORS: CARL DETORRES, MAILI HOLIMAN
ASSOCIATE ART DIRECTORS: CHRISTY SHEPPARD, MARGARET SWART / DESIGNERS: WALTER C. BAUMANN, VICTOR KRUMENNACHER / SENIOR PHOTO EDITOR: ZANA WOODS
PHOTO EDITOR: CAROLYN RAUCH / DEPUTY PHOTO EDITOR: ANNA GOLDWATER ALEXANDER / PHOTO ASSISTANTS: SARAH FILIPPI, MARK KING, DANIEL SALO
PUBLISHER: CONDÉ NAST PUBLICATIONS, INC. / CATEGORY: MAGAZINE OF THE YEAR

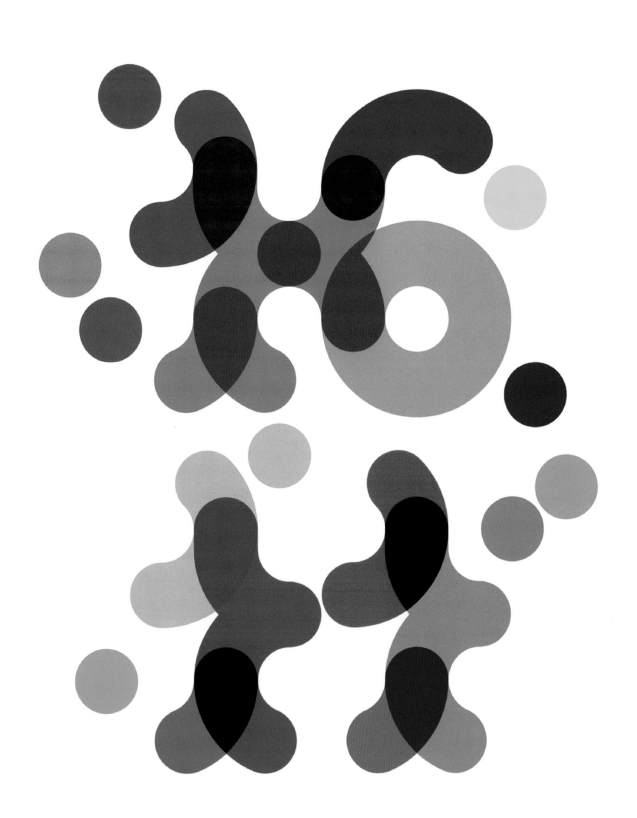

FEATURES | 16.11

TYPOGRAPHY BY **Fanette Mellier**

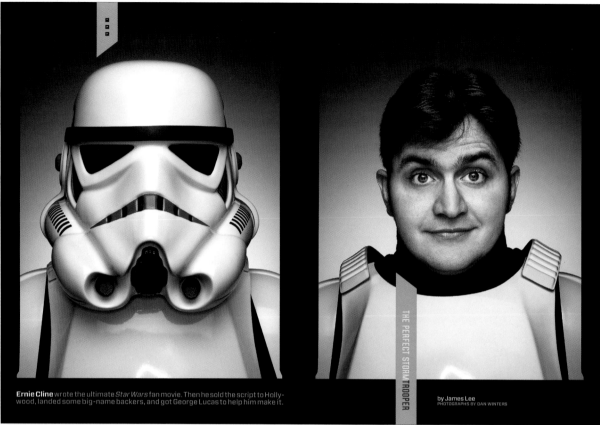

Ernie Cline wrote the ultimate *Star Wars* fan movie. Then he sold the script to Hollywood, landed some big-name backers, and got George Lucas to help him make it.

THE PERFECT STORMTROOPER

by James Lee
PHOTOGRAPHS BY DAN WINTERS

001

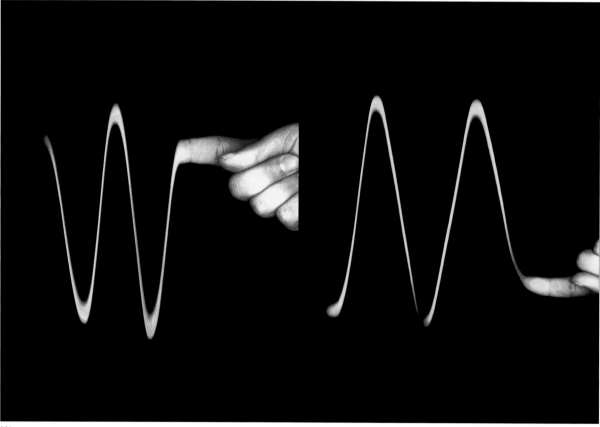

001

/001/ **WIRED**
CREATIVE DIRECTOR: SCOTT DADICH / DESIGN DIRECTOR: WYATT MITCHELL / ART DIRECTORS: CARL DETORRES, MAILI HOLIMAN
ASSOCIATE ART DIRECTORS: CHRISTY SHEPPARD, MARGARET SWART / DESIGNERS: WALTER C. BAUMANN, VICTOR KRUMENNACHER / SENIOR PHOTO EDITOR: ZANA WOODS
PHOTO EDITOR: CAROLYN RAUCH / DEPUTY PHOTO EDITOR: ANNA GOLDWATER ALEXANDER / PHOTO ASSISTANTS: SARAH FILIPPI, MARK KING, DANIEL SALO
PUBLISHER: CONDÉ NAST PUBLICATIONS, INC. / CATEGORY: MAGAZINE OF THE YEAR

THE SECRET HISTORY OF THE iPHONE

WIRED

WTF?! | FEB.2008

WHY THINGS SUCK!

THE 33 THINGS THAT MAKE US CRAZY

TRAFFIC
JUNK MAIL
BOOZE
PRINTERS
SPAM FILTERS
AIR TRAVEL
KNEES
WHITEBOARDS
BATTERIES
COPIERS
CREDIT CARDS
TOMATOES
WEB VIDEO
AND MORE...

WITH HELP DESK DIVA

SARAH SILVERMAN

THE LOST
FILES
OF THE
EAST GERMAN
SPY STATE

PAGE 126

TECH SUPPORT

wired-16.04

WIRED

ORIGINAL SIN | Apr.2008

How Apple Wins by Breaking All the Rules

Eco Hype: ZAP's No-Show Green Cars

What's Next: Top 9 Biz Trends

Eureka! Epic Moments In Tech

Evil/Genius

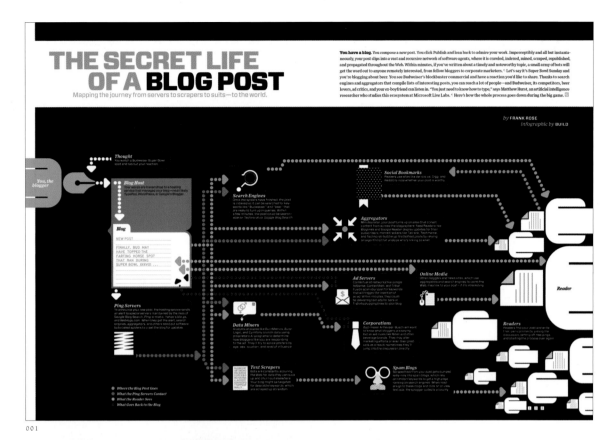

001

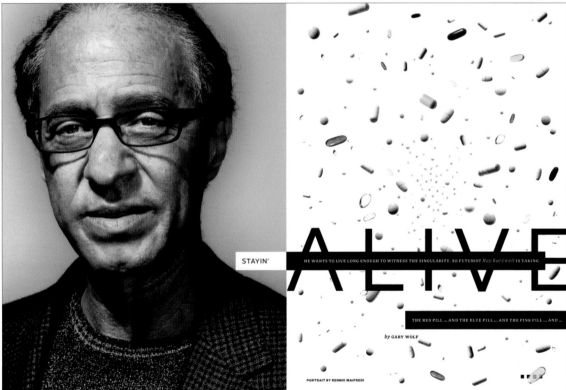

001

/001/ **WIRED**
CREATIVE DIRECTOR: SCOTT DADICH / DESIGN DIRECTOR: WYATT MITCHELL / ART DIRECTORS: CARL DETORRES, MAILI HOLIMAN
ASSOCIATE ART DIRECTORS: CHRISTY SHEPPARD, MARGARET SWART / DESIGNERS: WALTER C. BAUMANN, VICTOR KRUMENNACHER / SENIOR PHOTO EDITOR: ZANA WOODS
PHOTO EDITOR: CAROLYN RAUCH / DEPUTY PHOTO EDITOR: ANNA GOLDWATER ALEXANDER / PHOTO ASSISTANTS: SARAH FILIPPI, MARK KING, DANIEL SALO
PUBLISHER: CONDÉ NAST PUBLICATIONS, INC. / CATEGORY: MAGAZINE OF THE YEAR

*HERE COMES THE SUMMER!

39 PAGES OF THE CLOTHES YOU NEED TO STAY COOL

LOOK SHARP + LIVE SMART

*SHIA LaBEOUF CRACKS THE WHIP ON INDIANA JONES

LEAVE NO HERO BEHIND >HOW ONE AMAZING TEAM IS FINDING AMERICA'S LONG-LOST SOLDIERS

FIRE UP! >THE GQ GUIDE TO GRILLING PAGE 138

IS THIS THE MOST AWESOME RECESSION EVER OR WHAT? 20 GREAT WAYS TO ENJOY THE CRASH

+

HOW TO STOCK YOUR SUMMER BAR

GET A SAFE TAN

BECOME THE LEAD SINGER OF JOURNEY

GQ ● COM → SEE SEXY VIDEOS OF THE WOMEN YOU LOVE

002

/002/ GQ
DESIGN DIRECTOR: FRED WOODWARD / ART DIRECTOR: ANTON IOUKHNOVETS / DESIGNERS: THOMAS ALBERTY, DRUE WAGNER, CHELSEA CARDINAL, DELGIS CANAHUATE, ROB HEWITT / DIRECTOR OF PHOTOGRAPHY: DORA SOMOSI / PHOTO EDITORS: KRISTA PRESTEK, JUSTIN O'NEILL, JESSE LEE, EMILY ROSENBERG, JOLANTA BIELAT, TOBY KAUFMANN / CREATIVE DIRECTOR, FASHION: JIM MOORE / EDITOR-IN-CHIEF: JIM NELSON / PUBLISHER: CONDÉ NAST PUBLICATIONS INC. / ISSUES: JUNE 2008, NOVEMBER 2008, DECEMBER 2008 / CATEGORY: MAGAZINE OF THE YEAR

T#ANK ↑G0D f0R ↓TH£ R€¢€$ $I0N !

How to cash in, feel superior, explore the world, and find your inner peace in the coming economic end-times

Zohar Lazar

167 / GQ

The

(Hot-Dog-Vending, Knife-Fighting, Break-Dancing, Spielberg-Wooing)

Adventures Of Young Shia LaBeouf

By Kevin Conley
Photographs
By Peggy Sirota

PAGE
.132
GQ.COM
JUNE 2008

Eight races, eight gold medals, seven world records. Michael Paterniti visits with the unstoppable force who needs no introduction

MICHAEL PHELPS
Golden Boy ●

002

★ A PHOTOGRAPHIC PORT FOLIO OF THE CANDIDATES,
OPERATIVES, HANDLERS,   HUSTLERS, TRUE BELIEVERS,
AND WARRIORS WHO BRO   UGHT YOU THE MOST EPIC
PRESIDENTIAL CAMPAIGN   OF OUR LIFETIME

PHOTOGRAPHS BY **JEFF RIEDEL**

002

/002/ **GQ**
DESIGN DIRECTOR: FRED WOODWARD / ART DIRECTOR: ANTON IOUKHNOVETS / DESIGNERS: THOMAS ALBERTY, DRUE WAGNER, CHELSEA CARDINAL, DELGIS CANAHUATE, ROB HEWITT / DIRECTOR OF PHOTOGRAPHY: DORA SOMOSI / PHOTO EDITORS: KRISTA PRESTEK, JUSTIN O'NEILL, JESSE LEE, EMILY ROSENBERG, JOLANTA BIELAT, TOBY KAUFMANN / CREATIVE DIRECTOR, FASHION: JIM MOORE / EDITOR-IN-CHIEF: JIM NELSON / PUBLISHER: CONDÉ NAST PUBLICATIONS INC. / ISSUES: JUNE 2008, NOVEMBER 2008, DECEMBER 2008 / CATEGORY: MAGAZINE OF THE YEAR

GQ

LOOK SHARP + LIVE SMART

Starring

**LEONARDO
DiCAPRIO**

**JON
HAMM**

**BARACK
OBAMA**

**THE
BOSTON
CELTICS**

**GENERAL
PETRAEUS**

**GORDON
RAMSAY**

**AARON
ECKHART**

**SEAN
PENN**

**JAMES
FRANCO**

**JOHN
MALKOVICH**

**RAFAEL
NADAL**

+

**OUR
CONTINUING
OBSESSION
WITH**
**MEGAN
FOX**

→ | Upgrade your style in 30 days. See page TK.

002

MICHAEL
PHELPS
MAKES A
SPLASH IN OUR
MEN
OF
THE
YEAR
ISSUE

The Most
Amazing
Rescue
Story We've
Heard in
Years

GET THE
MOST BANG
FOR YOUR
BUCK
THE BEST
STUFF
OF 2008

FESTIVE HOLIDAY DESSERTS
THAT SPARKLE WITH THE FLAVORS
OF THE SEASON

By Claudia Fleming / Photography by Kenji Toma

Desserts That Dazzle

*

/003/ **BON APPÉTIT**
DESIGN DIRECTOR: MATTHEW LENNING / ART DIRECTOR: ROBERT FESTINO / DESIGNERS: ROBERT FESTINO, REBECCA LOUTSCH, CHRISTINE PARK, TOM O'QUINN
ILLUSTRATORS: CHRISTOPH NIEMANN, ARTHUR MOUNT, MASA, MARTHA RICH, SERGE BLOCH, BRIAN REA, JASON LEE, JOEL HOLLAND
DIRECTOR OF PHOTOGRAPHY: LIZ MATHEWS / PHOTO EDITORS: BAILEY FRANKLIN, SHARON SUH, ANGELA MISTRO
PHOTOGRAPHERS: CRAIG CUTLER, JAMIE CHUNG, JOSÉ PICAYO, MISHA GRAVENOR, SIAN KENNEDY, TOM SCHIERLITZ, DAN FORBES, KENJI TOMA, BRIAN FINKE,
PATRICIA HEAL, ELINOR CARUCCI, NIGEL COX, TURE LILLEGRAVEN, HANS GISSINGER, MITCHELL FEINBERG, VICTOR SCHRAGER, JAKE CHESSUM, LEVI BROWN,
CHRISTIAN WEBER / EDITOR-IN-CHIEF: BARBARA FAIRCHILD / PUBLISHER: CONDÉ NAST PUBLICATIONS, INC. / CATEGORY: MAGAZINE OF THE YEAR

**ONE DESSERT,
TWO WAYS**
SERVE THE GINGERBREAD
TRIFLE WITH CANDIED
KUMQUATS AND WINE-
POACHED CRANBERRIES
IN A LARGE DISH FOR A
STUNNING CENTERPIECE
OR LAYER THE INGREDIENTS
IN PRETTY GLASSES FOR
INDIVIDUAL SERVINGS
(RECIPE ON PAGE 121).

/004/ **NEW YORK**
DESIGN DIRECTOR: CHRIS DIXON / ART DIRECTOR: RANDY MINOR / DESIGNERS: CHRIS DIXON, RANDY MINOR, HITOMI SATO, KATIE VAN SYCKLE, CAROL HAYES,
HILARY FITZGIBBONS, CAROLINE JACKSON / ILLUSTRATORS: PATRICK THOMAS, BARBARA KRUGER, GLUEKIT, RODRIGO CORRAL, DARROW, CHIP KIDD, THOMAS ALLEN,
JOHN BALDESSARI, PETER ARKLE, SEAN MCCABE, JASON GNEWIKOW, RICCARDO VECCHIO, NICOLAS FELTON, CHRISSIE ABBOTT
DIRECTOR OF PHOTOGRAPHY: JODY QUON / PHOTOGRAPHERS: HENRY LEUTWYLER, ROBERT MAXWELL, JEFF RIEDEL, TOM SCHIERLITZ, DAVIES+STARR, JAKE CHESSUM,
KANG KIM, CATHERINE LEDNER, EDWARD KEATING, DAVID LEVENTI, DAN WINTERS, DONNA FERRATO, ROB HOWARD, HARRY BENSON, RICHARD SANDLER, JAY MAISEL,
HANNAH WHITAKER, PAUL MCDONOUGH, DAVID GHAR, TYRON DUKES, RON GALELLA, ROBIN PLATZER, ROXANNE LOWIT, MARINA GARNIER, PATRICK MCMULLAN,
NOAH KALINA, JERI HEIDEN / EDITOR-IN-CHIEF: ADAM MOSS / PUBLISHER: NEW YORK MAGAZINE HOLDINGS, LLC / CATEGORY: MAGAZINE OF THE YEAR

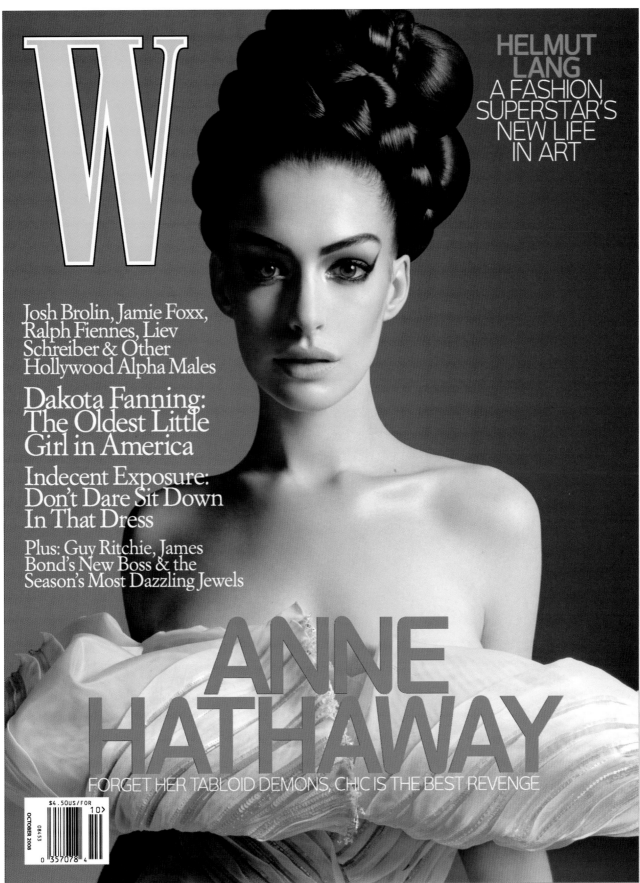

W

HELMUT
LANG
A FASHION
SUPERSTAR'S
NEW LIFE
IN ART

Josh Brolin, Jamie Foxx,
Ralph Fiennes, Liev
Schreiber & Other
Hollywood Alpha Males

Dakota Fanning:
The Oldest Little
Girl in America

Indecent Exposure:
Don't Dare Sit Down
In That Dress

Plus: Guy Ritchie, James
Bond's New Boss & the
Season's Most Dazzling Jewels

ANNE HATHAWAY
FORGET HER TABLOID DEMONS, CHIC IS THE BEST REVENGE

$4.50US/FOR 10>
OCTOBER 2008
08453
0 357078 4

005

/005/ **W**

CREATIVE DIRECTOR: DENNIS FREEDMAN / DESIGN DIRECTOR: EDWARD LEIDA / ART DIRECTOR: NATHALIE KIRSHEH
DESIGNERS: LAURA KONRAD, GINA MANISCALCO / PHOTO EDITOR: NADIA VELLAM / PHOTOGRAPHERS: STEVEN KLEIN, MARIO SORRENTI, DAVID SIMS
PUBLISHER: CONDÉ NAST PUBLICATIONS INC. / CATEGORY: MAGAZINE OF THE YEAR

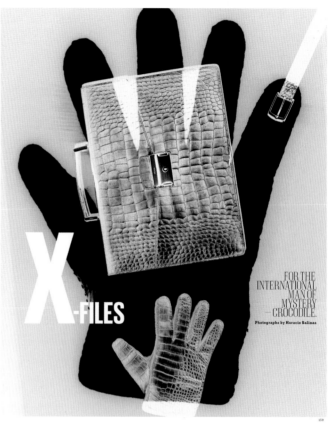

X-FILES

FOR THE
INTERNATIONAL
MAN OF
MYSTERY —
CROCODILE.

Photographs by Horacio Salinas

SPY CRAFT BALLY EMBOSSED PORTFOLIO,
$450. GO TO BALLY.COM. HERMÈS WALLET,
$2,800. GO TO HERMES.COM. TOD'S
CARRY-ON BAG, $34,000. GO TO TODS.COM.
(OPPOSITE) PRADA BLACK BRIEFCASE,
$11,600. GO TO PRADA.COM. TRAFALGAR BLACK
BELT, $295. GO TO TRAFALGARSTORE.COM.
TOM FORD BLACK GLOVE, $3,230 A PAIR.
GO TO TOMFORD.COM.
FASHION EDITOR: BRUCE PASK.

006

CHIC-A-BOO
PICK UP THE
LOBSTER PHONE.
THE SEASON'S
SURREAL REVEAL
IS CALLING.

Photographs by Paolo Roversi

006

/006/ T, THE NEW YORK TIMES STYLE MAGAZINE
CREATIVE DIRECTOR: JANET FROELICH / SENIOR ART DIRECTOR: DAVID SEBBAH / SENIOR DESIGNER: ELIZABETH SPIRIDAKIS
ART DIRECTOR: CHRISTOPHER MARTINEZ / DIRECTOR OF PHOTOGRAPHY: KATHY RYAN / SENIOR PHOTO EDITOR: JUDITH PUCKETT-RINELLA
PHOTO EDITORS: SCOTT HALL, JENNIFER PASTORE / EDITOR-IN-CHIEF: STEFANO TONCHI / PUBLISHER: THE NEW YORK TIMES / CATEGORY: MAGAZINE OF THE YEAR

Screens Goddess

Jennifer Aniston could watch herself
on a TV, a movie screen, an iPhone or a laptop.
But mostly she tunes herself out —
while everyone else tunes her in.
Interview by Lynn Hirschberg

PHOTOMONTAGE BY RUVEN AFANADOR
SET DESIGN BY CHARLOTTE MALMLOF

60

61

007

Crowded House

A firm based in Rotterdam
solves the problem of too many people on too small
a planet by tunneling down,
packing tight and making pigs fly.
By Darcy Frey

PHOTOGRAPH BY JULIAN FAULHABER

In the fall of 2002, a young Dutch architect named Winy Maas came to Yale to give a lecture on designing and building the 21st-century city, the challenges of which he illustrated by showing a 30-second video that could have been shot above any American metropolitan airport: a view of the tops of several buildings and then, as the camera rose, more and more buildings, more roads and bridges and asphalt lots, until an ugly concrete skin of low-rise development spread to all horizons. Maas was not the first architect to protest the unsightly sprawl that humans have left over much of the earth's surface, but he may have been the first to suggest that we preserve what's left of our finite planetary space by creating "vertical suburbs" — stacking all those quarter-acre plots into high-rise residential towers, each with its own hanging, cantilevered yard. "Imagine: It's Saturday afternoon, and all the barbecues are running," Maas said, unveiling his

Urban Flight: WoZoCos, a housing complex for Amsterdamers 55 and older.

54

007

/007/ **THE NEW YORK TIMES MAGAZINE**
CREATIVE DIRECTOR: JANET FROELICH / ART DIRECTOR: AREM DUPLESSIS / DEPUTY ART DIRECTOR: GAIL BICHLER
DESIGNERS: AREM DUPLESSIS, GAIL BICHLER, LEO JUNG, NANCY HARRIS ROUEMY, HILARY GREENBAUM, CATHERINE GILMORE-BARNES, JULIA MOBURG, IAN ALLEN
DIRECTOR OF PHOTOGRAPHY: KATHY RYAN / PHOTO EDITORS: KIRA POLLACK, JOANNA MILTER, CLINTON CARGILL, LUISE STAUSS, STACEY BAKER, MARVIN ORELLANA
EDITOR-IN-CHIEF: GERRY MARZORATI / PUBLISHER: THE NEW YORK TIMES / CATEGORY: MAGAZINE OF THE YEAR

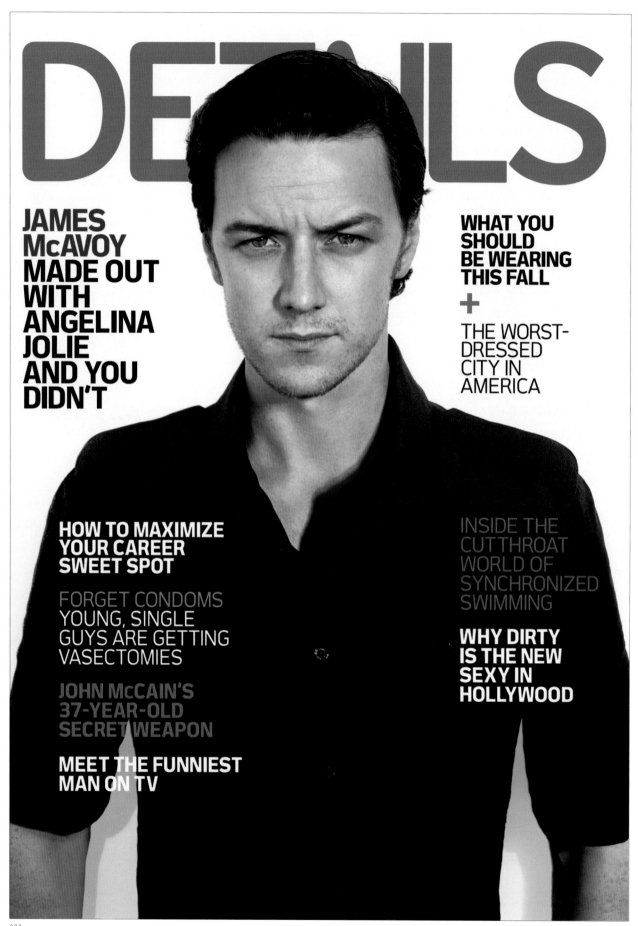

DET**A**ILS

JAMES
McAVOY
MADE OUT
WITH
ANGELINA
JOLIE
AND YOU
DIDN'T

WHAT YOU
SHOULD
BE WEARING
THIS FALL

+

THE WORST-
DRESSED
CITY IN
AMERICA

HOW TO MAXIMIZE
YOUR CAREER
SWEET SPOT

FORGET CONDOMS
YOUNG, SINGLE
GUYS ARE GETTING
VASECTOMIES

JOHN McCAIN'S
37-YEAR-OLD
SECRET WEAPON

MEET THE FUNNIEST
MAN ON TV

INSIDE THE
CUTTHROAT
WORLD OF
SYNCHRONIZED
SWIMMING

WHY DIRTY
IS THE NEW
SEXY IN
HOLLYWOOD

008

/008/ **DETAILS**
CREATIVE DIRECTOR: ROCKWELL HARWOOD / ART DIRECTOR: ANDRE JOINTE / DESIGNERS: CHRIS SEGEDY, JARRED FORD
PHOTO EDITORS: ALEX GHEZ, CHANDRA GLICK / SENIOR PHOTO EDITOR: HALI TARA FELDMAN / EDITOR-IN-CHIEF: DANIEL PERES
PUBLISHER: CONDÉ NAST PUBLICATIONS / CATEGORY: MAGAZINE OF THE YEAR

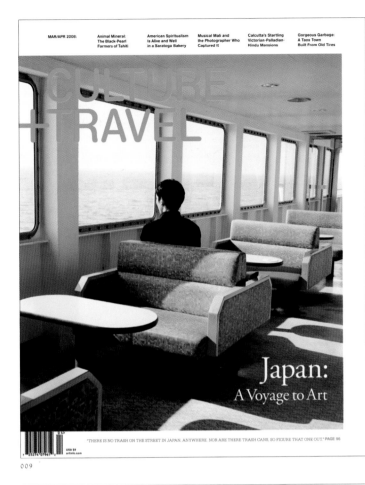

CULTURE +TRAVEL

Japan: A Voyage to Art

"THERE IS NO TRASH ON THE STREET IN JAPAN. ANYWHERE. NOR ARE THERE TRASH CANS. SO FIGURE THAT ONE OUT." PAGE 96

USA $9
artinfo.com

009

stuffu happens: crossing japan to soak in a hot-tub art installation, a bohemian trio debates the aesthetic permeating all things, from gyoza to goths to gardens.
by joshuah bearman. photographs by takashi yasumura

009

¡GOL!

009

Santiago Calatrava's City of Arts and Sciences helped put his hometown on the map.

AN ORANGE REVOLUTION: COPA, PAELLA, CALATRAVA, RITA. FROM ITS ARCHITECTURE TO ITS LESBIAN MAYOR, VALENCIA IS JUICED.
BY ANYA VON BREMZEN
PHOTOGRAPHS BY JASON FULFORD

76 | Culture+Travel | Culture+Travel 77

009

/009/ CULTURE + TRAVEL
CREATIVE DIRECTOR: EMILY CRAWFORD / DIRECTOR OF PHOTOGRAPHY: CORY JACOBS / PHOTO EDITOR: NATALIE MATUTSCHOVSKY
PUBLISHER: LOUISE BLOUIN MEDIA /CATEGORY: MAGAZINE OF THE YEAR

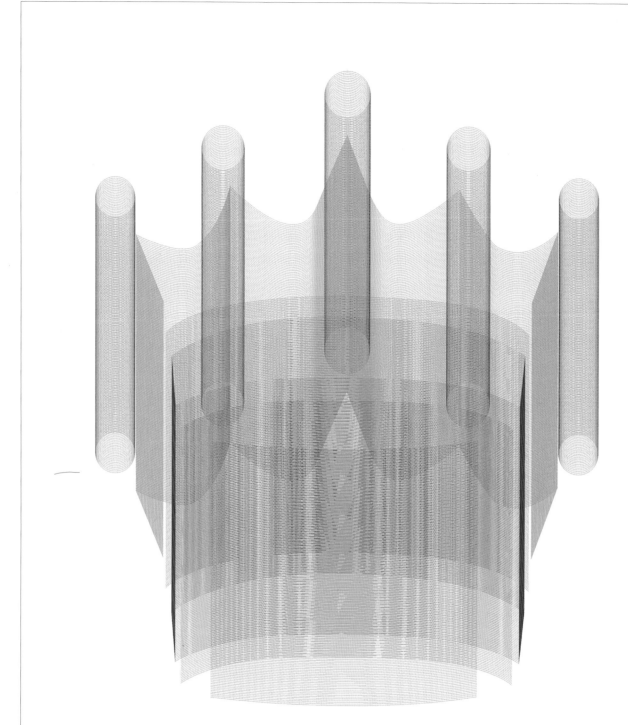

Queen Anne

DESPITE HER HIGHLY PUBLICIZED PERSONAL TRIALS,
ANNE HATHAWAY IS EMERGING WITH MORE CONFIDENCE BOTH IN HER ROLES AND IN HER LIFE.
BY DANIELLE STEIN
PHOTOGRAPHED BY MARIO SORRENTI
STYLED BY **CAMILLA NICKERSON**

010

/010/ **W**
DESIGN DIRECTOR: EDWARD LEIDA / ART DIRECTOR: NATHALIE KIRSHEH
DESIGNER: NATHALIE KIRSHEH / PHOTOGRAPHER: MARIO SORRENTI
PUBLISHER: CONDÉ NAST PUBLICATIONS INC. / ISSUE: OCTOBER 2008
CATEGORY: MEMBERS' CHOICE

W Profile

/CONTRIBUTORS/

ABBEY KUSTER-PROKELL
ABBY CLAWSON LOW
ABI HUYNH

ADAM BILLYEALD

ADAM LOGAN FULRATH
ADAM SAVITCH

ADHEMAS BATISTA

ALEC HOLST
ALEX GHEZ
ALEX GROSSMAN

ALEXANDRA CARR
ALICE ALVES
ALICE CHO
AMBER TERRANOVA
AMY FEITELBERG
ALLISON CHIN

AMY KLOBENZER
AMY BERKLEY
AMY HOPPY

ANDERS OVERGAARD
ANDI BEHRMAN
ANDRAOS AND WOOD
ANDRE JOINTE
ANDRE WOLFF

ANDREAS SERRANO
ANDREAS SIODIN
ANDREW BETTLES

ANDREW MCPHERSON

ANDREW RAE
ANDRZEJ JANERKA
ANDY ANDERSON
ANDY FRIEDMAN

ANNA GOLDWATER ALEXANDER
ANGEL BECERRIL

ANNA WOLF
ANNE BRCN
ANNICK ROBBERFIELD

ANTHONY COTSIFAS
ANTONI TOUKHMOVEIS
ANTONIN KRATOCHVIL
AREM DUPLESSIE
BAILEY FRANKLIN

BARBARA KRUGER

BEN STECHSCHULTE
BEN THOMA

CRAIG CUTLER
CRAIG MCDEAN

D.W. PINE

DAMIAN HEINISCH
DAN FORBES

DAN SAELINGER
DAN WINTERS

DANNY FISHER

DARHIL CROOKS
DARIN LEDFORD

DAVID CARTHAS

DAVID CURCURITO
DAVID GRIFFIN
DAVID GRAY

DAVID LA SPINA

DAVID SEBBAH
DAVID SIMS
DAVID SPERANZA
DAVID WHITMORE
DAVIES+STARR
DEAN CHALKLEY

DEAN MARKADAKIS
DEANNA LOWE
DEANNE CHEUK
DEBBIE KIM
DEBRA BISHOP
DELGIS CANAHUATE

DENISE SEE
DENNIS FREEDMAN

DEVIN PEDZWATER
DEVRIEL WEEKES
DEAN HOLTON

DIANE FIELDS

DIRK BARNETT
DOGO
DON'T WAKE ME UP

DORA SOMOSI

DRU DONOVAN
DRUE WAGNER

EAMO
EDEL RODRIGUEZ

EDWARD BURTYNSKY

EDWARD LEIDA
EDWARD LEVINE

ELISHEA NICHOLSON
ELIZABETH SPIRIDAKIS
ELIZABETH YOUNG
EILEEN VON UNWERTH

ELSA MEHARY
ELVIS CRUZ
EMILY CM ANDERSON
EMILY CRAWFORD
EMILY GRUZ
EMIR DUPLER

HORACIO SALINAS
HOWARD CAO

HYE JIN LEE
IAN LEE
IAN ALLEN
IAN ROBINSON
IAN BROWN

I-NI CHEN
IVYLISE SIMONES

J.D. CUBAN
J.R. AREBALO JR.

JACKIE DASHEVSKY

JACKIE NICKERSON
JACLYN STEINBERG
JACOB HUURINAINEN
JACQUELINE MUNZ

JAKE CHESSUM

JAMES DAY
JAMES DUNLINSON
JAMES NACHTWEY
JAMES VICTORE

JAMES WOJCIK
JAMESON SIMPSON
JAMIE BARTOLACCI
JAMIE CHUNG

JAN WELTERS
JANA MEIER
JANET FROEHLICH
JANINE ARROYO FONSECA

JASON BELL

JASON GROW
JASON HIJRIDA
JASON LANCASTER
JASON LEE

JASON MISCHKA

JASON SELDON
JASON TREAT

JEAN-LUC BERNARD

JEFF DOCHERTY

JEFF RIEDEL

JEFFREY DOCHERTY
JEFFREY FELIMUS

JENN MCMANUS
JENNA BROUSE

JENNIFER LEE

JESSICA ANJOLA
JESSICA NELSON

JILL GREENBERG
JILLIAN TAMAKI
JOANNA MILTER
JODY QUON
JOE KIMBERLING
JOE MARIANEK
JOE PUGLIESE
JOE ZEFF
JOEL HOLLAND
JOEL STERNFELD
JODI PICKMAN

JOHN BENNETT FITTS
JOHN DIXON

JOHN GRIMWADE

LOU VEGA

LUCAS ALLEN
LUKE BEST
LUKE HAYMAN
LUKE WILLIAMS
MACE FLEEGER
MACIEK KOBIELSKI
MADS FREUND BRUNSE
MAILI HOLIMAN

MAISIE TODD

MARC ALARY
MARC ASNIN
MARC HOM

MARÍA DEL CARMEN MERCADO
MARIAN BANTJES
MARIANA SASSO ROJAS
MARIANO VIVANCO

MARIO SORRENTI
MARISSA BOURKE
MARK HEITHOFF

MARK SANDERS
MARK SELIGER
MARK SHAW

MARNE MAYER
MARSHALL MCKINNEY
MARTHA RICH
MARTIN KLIMAS
MARTIN SCHOELLER
MARTIN VALLIN

MARTIN WOODTLI

MARVIN ORELLANA

MASA

MATT SARTAIN
MATT WILLEY

MATTHEW LENNING

MATTHEW ROLSTON

MAURICIO ALEJO

MAX BECHERER
MAXINE DAVIDOWITZ

MELISSA VENTOSA MARTIN
MERT ALAS
MICHAEL BIERUT
MICHAEL BRALEY
MICHAEL BRIAN
MICHAEL DIGIACOMO
MICHAEL ELMENBECK
MICHAEL LAWTON
MICHAEL LEWIS
MICHAEL MULLER
MICHAEL NORSENG
MICHAEL PANGILINAN
MICHAEL SCHMELLING
MICHAEL SCHNAIDT

MICHAEL THOMPSON
MICHEL HADDI

MIKAEL DAHL
MIKE LEY
MIKE MCGREGOR

RICCARDO VECCHIO
RICHARD FERRETTI
RICHARD PHIBBS

RICHIE SWANN
RICK FRIEDMAN
RICKY MOLLOY

ROB DILESO
ROB HANEY
ROB HEWITT

ROBBIE COOPER

ROBERT CLARK
ROBERT FESTINO

ROBERT NEWMAN
ROBERT PERINO

ROBERT PRIEST

ROBERT VARGAS

ROCKWELL HARWOOD
RODRIGO CASTILLO BONNER
RODRIGO CORRAL

RODRIGO SANCHEZ

RONALD J. CALA
RORY ALWIN
RORY WALSH
ROSIE GAINSBOROUGH

RUVEN AFANADOR
RYAN CADIZ

RYAN THACKER

SAM RICHARDS
SAM WEBER

SANDRA FREIJ

SARA MCKAY
SARAH WILLIAMS
SARAH CWYNAR
SARAH GARCEA
SARAH VINAS

SCOTT HALL
SCOTT DADICH
SCOTT SCHUMAN
SCOTT STOWELL
SEAN CAPONE

SERGE LEBLON
SERGE SIEDLITZ

SERIFCAN OZCAN

SETH WENIG
SHANE LUITJENS
SHANNON GREENGREEN
SHANNON SAWTELLE
SHAUN BARON
SI SCOTT

SIAN KENNEDY

SIMEN SKYER
SIMON CORRY
SIMON EMMETT
SIUNG TJIA

SONI KHATRI

SPENCER JONES

WIRED
W
VISAO
VIBE
UD &SE
U OF T MAGAZINE
TWIN CITIES METRO
TIME OUT NEW YORK
TIME
THE VILLAGE VOICE
THE NEW YORK TIMES MAGAZINE
THE ATLANTIC
TEXAS MONTHLY
T
SPIN
SEED
ROLLING STONE
REAL SIMPLE
PSYCHOLOGY TODAY
PRINT
POPULAR MECHANICS
PLAY
PLATINO
PEOPLE
OUTSIDE
OUT
ONEARTH
NEW YORK
NATIONAL GEOGRAPHIC ADVENTURE
NATIONAL GEOGRAPHIC
MORE
MOVIEMAKER
MINNESOTA MONTHLY
METROPOLITAN HOME
METROPOLITAN
METROPOLIS
METROPOLI
MEN'S HEALTH
MARTHA STEWART LIVING
MADRIZ
LOS ANGELES

DeSign/

STEVE HASLIP

STEVE STANFORD
STEVEN BRAHMS
STEVEN E. BANKS
STEVEN KLEIN

STEVEN SMITH
STEVEN WILSON
STINA PERSSON
STRAVINSKI PIERRE
SUCHA BECKY

SUSANA SOARES
SUSANNE BAMBERGER
SUSANNE DUCKER

T.J. TUCKER

TERRY RICHARDSON
TETSUYA NAGATO
THE DESIGN DEPT/COPENHAGEN
THERESA GRIGGS
THOMAS ALBERTY

THOMAS HANNICH

THOMAS MACDONALD

TIM OLIVER
TIM WALKER

TISH KING

TITOUAN LAMAZOU

TODD ALBERTSON

TOM BROWN
TOM LOWE
TOM MUELLER

TOM SCHIERLITZ

TONI FRANÇOIS
TONY KIM

TORSTEN HOGH RASMUSSEN
TRACY EVERDING
TRAVIS RATHBONE
TREVETT MCCANDLISS
TURE LILLEGRAVEN

VASCO FERREIRA
VERN EVANS

VICTOR KRUMMENACHER

VICTORIA HELY-HUTCHINSON
VIK MUNIZ

VINCENT LAFORET
VIVAN SUNDARAM

WALTER C. BAUMANN
WALTER CALAHAN

WILBERT GUTIÉRREZ

WILLIAMS + HIRAKAWA
WIN MCNAMEE
WYATT MITCHELL
YURI KOZYREV
ZACHARY SCOTT
ZANA WOODS
ZOHAR LAZAR

JONAS REKER
JONATHAN BRUCE WILLIAMS

JONATHON KAMTOR
JONROTMAN

JOSÉ FERNANDEZ

JOSÉ PICAYO
JOSEPH HUTCHINSON
JOSH COCHRAN

JUDITH PUCKET-RINELLA
JÜRGEN TELLER

JULIA MOBURG
JULIANA SOHN
JULIE VANDENOEVER

JÜRGEN BEY
JUSTIN STEPHENS
JUSTIN WOOD

KAMO

KANG KIM

KAREEM BLACK

KARTEAN LEVINE

KARLSSONWILKER
KARSTEN SCHMIDT
KATE HOLLENBACK
KATE ILTIS

KATHY RYAN
KAZUNARI TAJIMA
KEIR NOVESKY
KEITH D'MELLO

KEN DELAGO
KENJI TOMA
KENNETH CAPPELLO
KEVIN BANNA
KEVIN CHRISTY
KEVIN MAZUR
KEVIN VAN AELST
KIRA POLLACK
KIM GOUGENHEIM
KIRBY RODRIGUEZ
KNICKERBOCKER DESIGN

KRISTIN MULZER
KRISTINA DIMATTEO

KYLE BEAN

LAMSWEERDE & MATADIN
LARRY SULTAN

LAURA KONRAD

LAURA STRÖM

LAURIE FRANKEL
LEANN MUELLER

LENDON FLANAGAN
LEO JUNG

LINDSAY BALLANT
LINSEY LAIDLAW
LISA HUBBARD
LISA BERMAN
LISA LIMER
LISA MAIONE

LIVIA CORONA
LIZ MACFARLANE

LORIN BROWN
LOU BEACH

PAOLA KUDACKI
PAOLO PELLEGRIN
PAOLO ROVERSI
PATRICIA HEAL

PATRICK BOLECEK

PAUL RITTER

PAUL WEEKS
PEGGY SIROTA
PETER ARKLE

PETER HERBERT

PETER YANG

PHILLIPE APELOIG
PHILIP TOLEDANO
PHOEBE FLYNN RICH
PIERRE BJORK
PLAMEN PETKOV
PLATON
PUM LEFEBURE

QUENTIN NARDI

R.O. BLECHMAN

RAMI MOGHADAM
RANDAL FORD
RANDY MINOR
RATIONAL BEAUTY
RAYMOND MEIER
REBECCA LOUTSCH

RENNIO MAIFREDI

MÓNICA MANZANO
MONTSE BERNAL
NADAV-KANDER

NANCY CAMPBELL
NANCY HARRIS ROUEMY

NATASHA TIBBOTT

NAPE WILLIAMS
NATHALIE KIRSHEH

NATHANIEL GOLDBERG
NEIL JAMIESON
NICHOLAS-BENNER

NICK DEWAR

NICK VOGELSON
NICK WAPLINGTON

NICOLETTE BERTHELOT
NIGEL-COX

NIKOLAS KOENIG
NOAH KALINA

NOLI NOVAK

O. RUFUS LOVETT
OFFICE

ERIKA LARSEN
ERIKA OLIVEIRA
ERIN BENNER
ERIN JANG

FABIEN BARON
FENDI

FERNANDA VIÉGAS

FIGEL-PENA

FIRSTBORN
FLOCHE
FLORENTINO PAMINTUAN
FLORIAN BACHLEDA
FLOTO+WARNER

FRANCESCO CARROZZINI

FRANÇOIS HALARD

FRANK W. OCKENFELS
FRED WOODWARD
FREDRIK BRODEN
FRITZ HOFMANN
GABRIEL BOBADILLA

GAIL GHEZZI
GAVIN-BOND
GENTL & HYERS
GEOF KERN

GEORGE AWDE
GEORGE KARABOTSOS
GEORGE PITTS
GERALDINE HESSLER

GILLIAN LAUB
GINA MANISCALCO

GLUEKIT

GRACE LEE
GRACE MARTINEZ

GREG-DUNCAN

GREG MILLER
GREG MONFRIES
GREGG SEGAL
GREG POND

GUDMUNDUR INGI ULFASRRON

GUN LARSON

GYONGY LAKY
HAL WOLVERTON
HANK HUANG
HANNAH MCCAUGHEY

HANS GISSINGER

HEATHER JONES

HEDI SLIMANE

HENRIK HALVARSSON

HENRY JANSEN
HENRY LEUTWYLER
HILARY FITZGIBBONS
HILARY GREENBAUM

HITOMI SATO

HOLLY LINDEM

BRANDON KAVULLA
BRENDA-MILLS
BRENT HUMPHREYS
BRIAN ANSTEY
BRIANNY

BRIAN JOHNSON
BRIAN REA

BRIGITTE LACOMBE
BROOKS KRAFT

BRUCE GILDEN

BRYAN CHRISTIE DESIGN

BRYAN JASHE

BRYAN SHEFFIELD
BRYCE DUFFY
BUILD

CALEB BENNETT

CAMERON WITTIG
CARA BARER
CARL DETORRES

CAROL HAYES

CAROLYN RAUCH

CASEY TIERNEY

CATHERINE HAWTHORN
CATRIONA NIAGLAIN

CEDRIC ANGELES

CHAD GRIFFITH
CHAD HUNT
CHAD PITMAN

CHALKLEY CALDERWOOD
CHANDRA GLICK

CHELSEA CARDINAL
CHRIS BUCK

CHRIS DIXON
CHRIS EHRMAN

CHRIS JORDAN
CHRIS MCPHERSON

CHRIS SEGEDY

CHRISTIAN COINBERGH

CHRISTINE BOWER-WRIGHT
CHRISTINE PARK
CHRISTOPH NJEMANN
CHRISTOPHER ANDERSON
CHRISTOPHER BAKER
CHRISTOPHER GRIFFITH
CHRISTOPHER KIM
CHRISTOPHER MARTINEZ

CHRISTOPHER MORABITO
CHRISTOPHER MORRIS
CHRISTOPHER SILAS NEAL
CHRISTOPHER STURMAN

CHRISTY SHEPPARD

CINDY HOFFMAN
CLAIRE DAWSON

CLAUDIA DE ALMEIDA
CLINTON CARGILL
CLIFFORD CHENG
COLIN TUNSTALL
COOLIFE
COPPI BARBIERI
CORY JACOBS

/011/ **WIRED**
CREATIVE DIRECTOR: SCOTT DADICH / DESIGN DIRECTOR: WYATT MITCHELL / ART DIRECTORS: MAILI HOLIMAN, CARL DETORRES
ASSOCIATE ART DIRECTORS: CHRISTY SHEPPARD, MARGARET SWART / DESIGNERS: WALTER C. BAUMANN, VICTOR KRUMMENACHER / SENIOR PHOTO EDITOR: ZANA WOODS
PHOTO EDITOR: CAROLYN RAUCH / DEPUTY PHOTO EDITOR: ANNA GOLDWATER ALEXANDER / PHOTO ASSISTANTS: SARAH FILIPPI, MARK KING, DANIEL SOLO
PUBLISHER: CONDÉ NAST PUBLICATIONS, INC. / ISSUE: NOVEMBER 2008 / CATEGORY: DESIGN: ENTIRE ISSUE

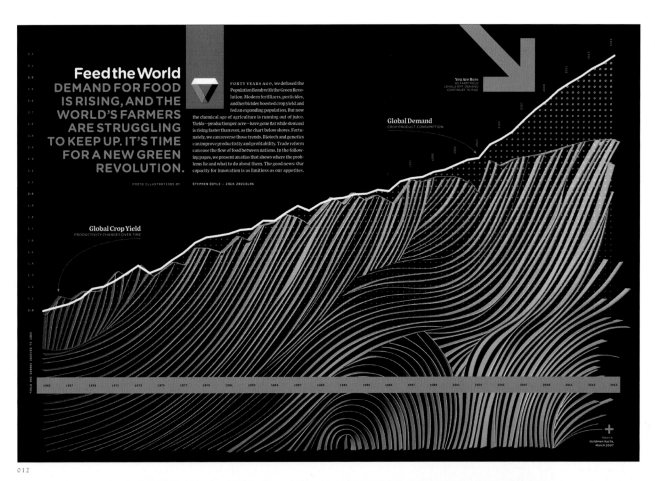

Feed the World

DEMAND FOR FOOD IS RISING, AND THE WORLD'S FARMERS ARE STRUGGLING TO KEEP UP. IT'S TIME FOR A NEW GREEN REVOLUTION.

PHOTO ILLUSTRATIONS BY   STEPHEN DOYLE · ZACK ZAVISLAK

FORTY YEARS AGO, we defused the Population Bomb with the Green Revolution. Modern fertilizers, pesticides, and herbicides boosted crop yield and fed an expanding population. But now the chemical age of agriculture is running out of juice. Yields—production per acre—have gone flat while demand is rising faster than ever, as the chart below shows. Fortunately, we can reverse those trends. Biotech and genetics can improve productivity and profitability. Trade reform can ease the flow of food between nations. In the following pages, we present an atlas that shows where the problems lie and what to do about them. The good news: Our capacity for innovation is as limitless as our appetites.

You Are Here
AS FARM YIELD
LEVELS OFF DEMAND
CONTINUES TO RISE

Global Demand
CROP PRODUCT CONSUMPTION

Global Crop Yield
PRODUCTIVITY CHANGES OVER TIME

Source
Goldman Sachs,
March 2007

012

CATFISH

MEAT ISN'T THE ONLY SOURCE OF PROTEIN. AS THE OCEANS GET TAPPED OUT, U.S. FISH FARMERS ARE RAISING 350 MILLION OF THIS BOTTOM FEEDER EVERY YEAR.

Energy
The water in the catfish
pens needs to be circulated
and oxygenated artificially.
PER FISH · U.S.
ELECTRICITY
8.2 kWh · 2.9 billion kWh
GASOLINE
0.4 gallon · 13.3 million gallons
DIESEL FUEL
0.23 gallon · 82.1 million gallons

Nutrition
The vitamin E helps the fish flesh
stand up better to freezing and storage
PER FISH · U.S.

A	0.0003 ounce	3 tons
B12	0.000009 ounce	0.1 ton
C	0.05 ounce	500 tons
D	0.0009 ounce	10 tons
E	0.05 ounce	500 tons
FOLIC ACID	0.002 ounce	22 tons
PANTOTHENIC ACID	0.01 ounce	150 tons
PYRIDOXINE	0.004 ounce	50 tons
RIBOFLAVIN	0.005 ounce	60 tons
THIAMIN	0.002 ounce	25 tons

PRODUCTS
LOTS OF FISH SLURRY—AND THOUSANDS OF TONS OF NUGGETS AND PET FOOD.
TOTAL ANNUAL U.S. CATFISH
OUTPUT: 220,404 TONS

Fat for omega-3 production
7,716 TONS

Fillets
86,572 TONS

Mincemeat
(surimi, fishmeal,
and pet food)
27,713 TONS

IN   **OUT**

Nuggets
7,272 TONS

Steaks
3,076 TONS

Waste
18,589 TONS

Nutrition
Catfish oil, sprayed onto catfish
feed pellets, keeps dust down.
PER FISH · U.S.

CATFISH OIL	13.6 ounces	150,034 tons
CORN GRAIN	13 pounds	2.3 million tons
COTTONSEED MEAL	5.7 pounds	1 million tons
DICALCIUM PHOSPHATE	9.1 ounces	100,023 tons
MEAT/BONE/BLOOD	2.3 pounds	400,091 tons
MENHADEN MEAL	2.3 pounds	400,091 tons
SOYBEAN MEAL	20.7 pounds	3.7 million tons
WHEAT MIDDLINGS	11.3 pounds	2 million tons

Materials
Many catfish ponds are 10 to
20 acres, built of earthen berms
6 feet high and 16 feet wide.
U.S. OVERALL
ANTIBIOTICS
57,990 tons
SOIL
162.5 million cubic feet
WATER
743.2 billion gallons

Whole fish
66,345 TONS

BY ALEXIS MADRIGAL

Sources: FAO Fisheries Department, LSU Ag Center;
Mississippi State University; Oklahoma State
University; Southern Regional Aquaculture Center

012

/012/ **WIRED**
CREATIVE DIRECTOR: SCOTT DADICH / DESIGN DIRECTOR: WYATT MITCHELL / ART DIRECTORS: MAILI HOLIMAN, CARL DETORRES
DESIGNERS: MAILI HOLIMAN, CARL DETORRES, VICTOR KRUMMENACHER, WALTER C. BAUMANN, SCOTT DADICH
ILLUSTRATOR: STEPHEN DOYLE / PHOTO EDITOR: CAROLYN RAUCH / PHOTOGRAPHER: ZACHARY ZAVISLAK
PUBLISHER: CONDÉ NAST PUBLICATIONS, INC. / ISSUE: NOVEMBER 2008 / CATEGORY: DESIGN: FEATURE: SERVICE (STORY)

CORN

99 PERCENT OF THE U.S. CORN CROP IS THE STARCHY, TOUGH PLANT WE ALSO KNOW AS MAIZE. THE STUFF ON YOUR PLATE— SWEET CORN—IS A HIGH-SUGAR VARIANT.

Energy

It takes 0.05 gallon of diesel to make a bushel of corn—from which you can make 2.7 gallons of ethanol.

PER EAR • U.S. OVERALL

DIESEL FUEL
0.0576 fl. oz. • 65.9 million gallons

FIELD CORN

Nutrition

Deficiencies in phosphorus and potassium result in diminished crop yield.

PER EAR • U.S. OVERALL

NITROGEN	0.2 ounce	13.9 billion pounds
PHOSPHATE	0.05 ounce	4.8 billion pounds
POTASH	0.04 ounce	4 billion pounds
LIME	0.6 ounce	53 billion pounds
WATER	31.4 gallons	46.1 trillion gallons

IN

SWEET CORN

Nutrition

Nitrogen-containing fertilizer has to be managed carefully to avoid contaminating groundwater.

PER EAR • U.S. OVERALL

FERTILIZER	1 ounce	473.6 million pounds
AMMONIA NITRATE	0.3 ounce	126.3 million pounds
LIME	1.3 ounces	625.1 million pounds
WATER	26.1 gallons	205.8 billion gallons

Energy

Herbicides mean fewer weeds, which means less tilling, which means using less fossil fuel.

PER EAR • U.S. OVERALL

DIESEL FUEL
0.08448 fl. oz. • 5.2 million gallons

Sources: **Argonne National Laboratory; Auburn University; Iowa Corn Growers Association; Iowa State University; National Corn Growers Association; Nebraska Corn Board; North Carolina State University**

013

/013/ **WIRED**
CREATIVE DIRECTOR: SCOTT DADICH / DESIGN DIRECTOR: WYATT MITCHELL / ART DIRECTORS: MAILI HOLIMAN, CARL DETORRES / DESIGNERS: MAILI HOLIMAN, CARL DETORRES, VICTOR KRUMMENACHER, WALTER C. BAUMANN, SCOTT DADICH / ILLUSTRATOR: STEPHEN DOYLE / PHOTO EDITOR: CAROLYN RAUCH / PHOTOGRAPHER: ZACHARY ZAVISLAK / PUBLISHER: CONDÉ NAST PUBLICATIONS, INC. / ISSUE: NOVEMBER 2008 / CATEGORY: DESIGN: FEATURE: TRAVEL/FOOD/STILL LIFE (STORY)

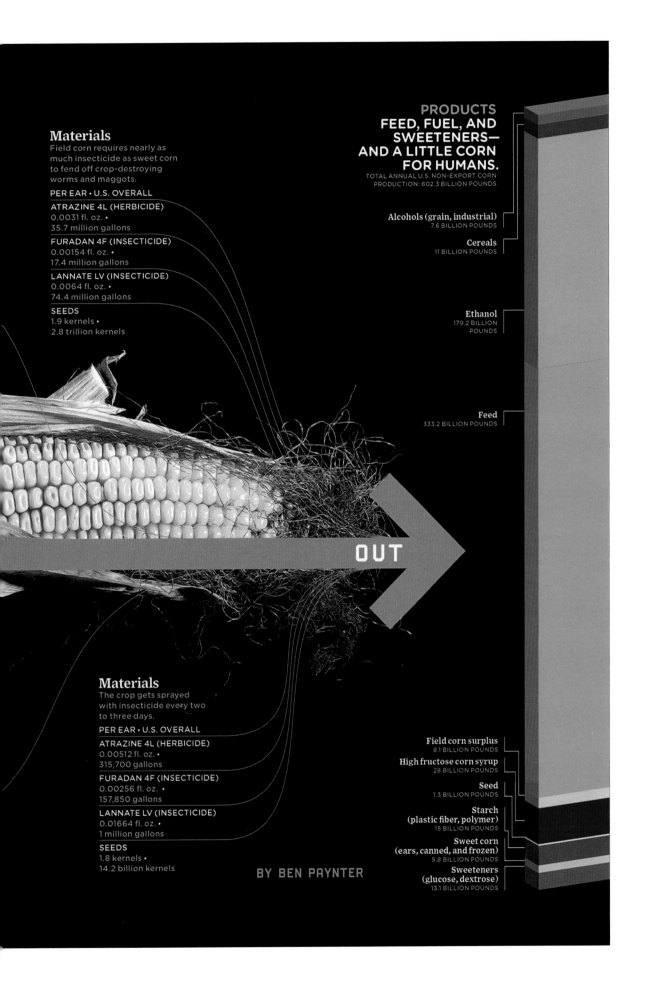

Materials

Field corn requires nearly as much insecticide as sweet corn to fend off crop-destroying worms and maggots.

PER EAR · U.S. OVERALL

ATRAZINE 4L (HERBICIDE)
0.0031 fl. oz. ·
35.7 million gallons

FURADAN 4F (INSECTICIDE)
0.00154 fl. oz. ·
17.4 million gallons

LANNATE LV (INSECTICIDE)
0.0064 fl. oz. ·
74.4 million gallons

SEEDS
1.9 kernels ·
2.8 trillion kernels

PRODUCTS
FEED, FUEL, AND SWEETENERS— AND A LITTLE CORN FOR HUMANS.

TOTAL ANNUAL U.S. NON-EXPORT CORN
PRODUCTION: 602.3 BILLION POUNDS

Alcohols (grain, industrial)
7.6 BILLION POUNDS

Cereals
11 BILLION POUNDS

Ethanol
179.2 BILLION POUNDS

Feed
333.2 BILLION POUNDS

OUT

Materials

The crop gets sprayed with insecticide every two to three days.

PER EAR · U.S. OVERALL

ATRAZINE 4L (HERBICIDE)
0.00512 fl. oz. ·
315,700 gallons

FURADAN 4F (INSECTICIDE)
0.00256 fl. oz. ·
157,850 gallons

LANNATE LV (INSECTICIDE)
0.01664 fl. oz. ·
1 million gallons

SEEDS
1.8 kernels ·
14.2 billion kernels

BY BEN PAYNTER

Field corn surplus
8.1 BILLION POUNDS

High fructose corn syrup
28 BILLION POUNDS

Seed
1.3 BILLION POUNDS

Starch (plastic fiber, polymer)
15 BILLION POUNDS

Sweet corn (ears, canned, and frozen)
5.8 BILLION POUNDS

Sweeteners (glucose, dextrose)
13.1 BILLION POUNDS

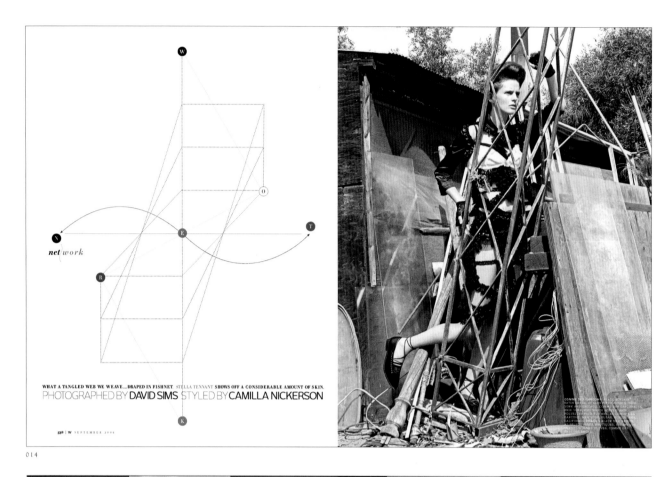

WHAT A TANGLED WEB WE WEAVE....DRAPED IN FISHNET, STELLA TENNANT SHOWS OFF A CONSIDERABLE AMOUNT OF SKIN.
PHOTOGRAPHED BY DAVID SIMS STYLED BY CAMILLA NICKERSON

014

ROCKETHEADS!
BY PRESTON LERNER
PHOTOGRAPHS BY J. BENNETT FITTS

FOR THE NEXT GIANT LEAP IN SPACECRAFT DESIGN, FORGET ABOUT NASA. THE ACTION IS IN THE NEVADA DESERT, WHERE A HANDFUL OF ROCKETEERS ARE TRYING TO BLAST THEIR HOMEBREW MISSILES INTO THE BEYOND.

015

/014/ **W**
DESIGN DIRECTOR: EDWARD LEIDA / ART DIRECTOR: NATHALIE KIRSHEH
PHOTOGRAPHER: DAVID SIMS / PUBLISHER: CONDÉ NAST PUBLICATIONS INC.
ISSUE: SEPTEMBER 2008 / CATEGORY: DESIGN: FEATURE: FASHION/BEAUTY
(SINGLE/SPREAD)

/015/ **WIRED**
CREATIVE DIRECTOR: SCOTT DADICH / DESIGN DIRECTOR: WYATT MITCHELL
ART DIRECTOR: CARL DETORRES / DESIGNERS: WALTER C. BAUMANN, CARL
DETORRES / PHOTO EDITOR: CAROLYN RAUCH / PHOTOGRAPHER: JOHN BENNETT
FITTS / PUBLISHER: CONDÉ NAST PUBLICATIONS, INC. / ISSUE: NOVEMBER 2008
CATEGORY: DESIGN: FEATURE: TRAVEL/FOOD/STILL LIFE (SINGLE/SPREAD)

/016/ **NEW YORK**
DESIGN DIRECTOR: CHRIS DIXON / ART DIRECTOR: RANDY MINOR / DESIGNER: CHRIS DIXON / ILLUSTRATOR: BARBARA KRUGER
DIRECTOR OF PHOTOGRAPHY: JODY QUON / PHOTOGRAPHER: HENRY LEUTWYLER / EDITOR-IN-CHIEF: ADAM MOSS
PUBLISHER: NEW YORK MAGAZINE HOLDINGS, LLC / ISSUE: MARCH 24, 2008 / CATEGORY: DESIGN: COVER

A COCONUT
CAKE TO LOVE
p. 110

FAMILY DINNER
TUSCAN
CHICKEN p. 96

PASTA PARTY
FOR 8 p. 192

bon appétit

MAY 2008

THE
TRAVEL
ISSUE

world's
best recipes

MEXICO
BBQ PORK
TACOS

MOROCCO
LAMB TAGINE

PARIS
STEAK
FRITES p. 38

ITALY
PIZZA BIANCA

MALAYSIA
SHRIMP
NOODLES

TEST-DRIVE
THE
**SHARPEST
KNIVES**
ON
EARTH
p. 50

HOW TO
**CHEESE
SOUFFLÉ**
SUPER EASY
p. 122

A DELICIOUS
**BISTRO
MENU**
p. 154

EURO
RESTAURANT
BARGAINS
p. 54

bonappétit.com

$3.99US $4.99FOR
05>

08432

0 319465 2

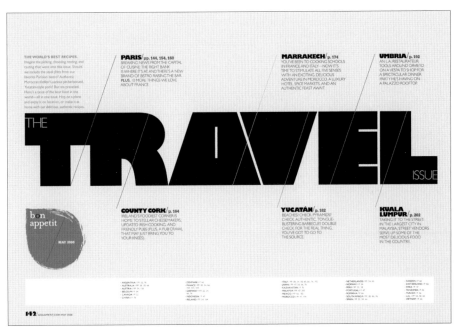

/017/ **BON APPÉTIT**
DESIGN DIRECTOR: MATTHEW LENNING / ART DIRECTOR: ROBERT FESTINO / DESIGNERS: REBECCA LOUTSCH, TOM BROWN, HANK HUANG
ILLUSTRATORS: JOEL HOLLAND, CHRISTOPH NIEMANN, JILLIAN TAMAKI / PHOTO EDITORS: LIZ MATHEWS, SHARON SUH, BAILEY FRANKLIN
PHOTOGRAPHERS: CRAIG CUTLER, TOM SCHIERLITZ, PLAMEN PETKOV, LISA HUBBARD, ANNA WOLF, CEDRIC ANGELES, LISA LIMER,
JEAN-LUC BERNARD, TURE LILLEGRAVEN / EDITOR-IN-CHIEF: BARBARA FAIRCHILD / PUBLISHER: CONDÉ NAST PUBLICATIONS, INC.
ISSUE: MAY 2008 / CATEGORY: REDESIGN: AFTER ISSUE

018

/018/ **GQ**
DESIGN DIRECTOR: FRED WOODWARD / DESIGNER: ROB HEWITT / DIRECTOR OF PHOTOGRAPHY: DORA SOMOSI / PHOTOGRAPHER: HORACIO SALINAS
EDITOR-IN-CHIEF: JIM NELSON / PUBLISHER: CONDÉ NAST PUBLICATIONS INC. / ISSUE: JULY 2008 / CATEGORY: DESIGN: FEATURE: SERVICE (SINGLE/SPREAD)

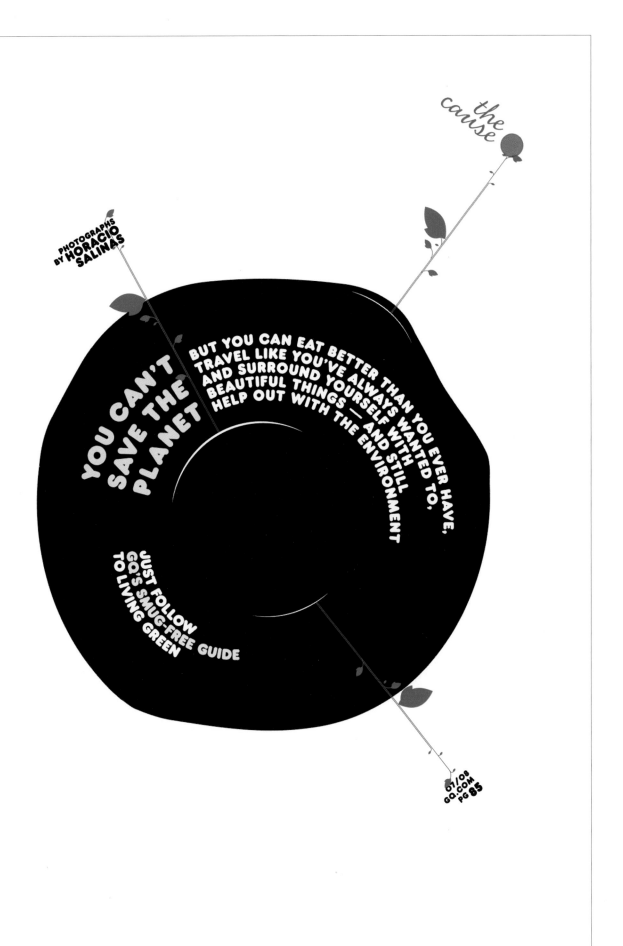

the cause

PHOTOGRAPHS BY HORACIO SALINAS

YOU CAN'T SAVE THE PLANET BUT YOU CAN EAT BETTER THAN YOU EVER HAVE, TRAVEL LIKE YOU'VE ALWAYS WANTED TO, AND SURROUND YOURSELF WITH BEAUTIFUL THINGS — AND STILL HELP OUT WITH THE ENVIRONMENT

JUST FOLLOW GQ'S SMUG-FREE GUIDE TO LIVING GREEN

07/08
GQ.COM
PG 85

Snake charm
THE MAKEUP ARTIST SHARON DOWSETT FIRST DEFINES THE EYE WITH A SOFT KOHL PENCIL, LIKE ESTÉE LAUDER ARTIST'S EYE PENCIL IN SLATE WRITER, $19. BLENDING IT INTO A DARK SHADOW. A TRANSLUCENT POWDER (E.G., YVES SAINT LAURENT SEMI-LOOSE POWDER NATURAL RADIANCE, $56) IS BRUSHED ON THE LID, FOLLOWED BY M.A.C.'S CARBON EYE SHADOW, $15, TO ADD SHINE TO THE CREASE. SHE APPLIES ELIZABETH ARDEN'S EIGHT HOUR DREAM, FOLLOWED BY MAKE UP FOR EVER WATERPROOF LENGTHENING MASCARA IN BLACK, $30.

dream states
WHERE THE EYE COLLIDES WITH THE NATURAL ORDER
Photographs by COPPI BARBIERI

019

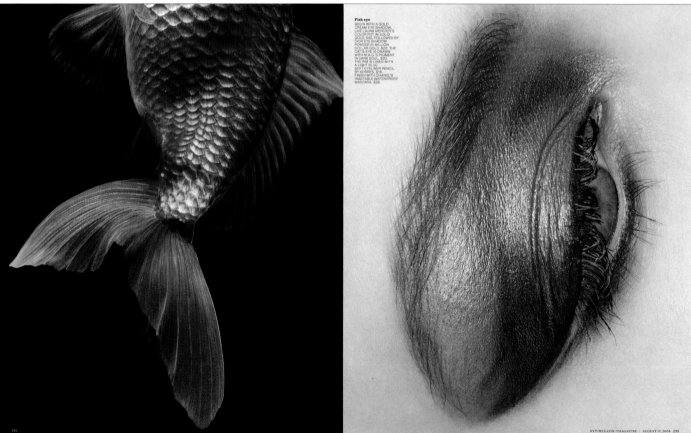

Fish eye
BEGIN WITH A GOLD CREAM EYE SHADOW, LIKE LAURA MERCIER'S COLOR POT IN SOLID GOLD, $32, FOLLOWED BY DIOR EYE SHADOW POWDER IN MILLION DOLLAR GOLD, $25. THE CAT'S-EYE IS DRAWN WITH M.A.C.'S PIGMENT IN DARK SOUL, $20. THE RIM IS LINED WITH A LIGHT BLUE SOFT EYELINER PENCIL BY KORRES, $18. FINISH WITH CHANEL'S INIMITABLE WATERPROOF MASCARA, $28.

NYTIMES.COM/TMAGAZINE | AUGUST 17, 2008 232

019

/019/ **T, THE NEW YORK TIMES STYLE MAGAZINE**
CREATIVE DIRECTOR: JANET FROELICH / SENIOR ART DIRECTOR: DAVID SEBBAH / ART DIRECTOR: CHRISTOPHER MARTINEZ / SENIOR DESIGNER: ELIZABETH SPIRIDAKIS
DIRECTOR OF PHOTOGRAPHY: KATHY RYAN / PHOTO EDITOR: SCOTT HALL / PHOTOGRAPHER: COPPI BARBIERI / EDITOR-IN-CHIEF: STEFANO TONCHI
PUBLISHER: THE NEW YORK TIMES / ISSUE: AUGUST 17, 2008 / CATEGORY: DESIGN: FEATURE: FASHION/BEAUTY (STORY)

Cities are more energy-efficient than suburbs, exurbs, or rural communities.

020

Cooling a home in Arizona produces 93 percent fewer CO₂ emissions than warming a house in New England.

020

/020/ **WIRED**
CREATIVE DIRECTOR: SCOTT DADICH / DESIGN DIRECTOR: WYATT MITCHELL / ART DIRECTOR: CARL DETORRES / DESIGNERS: SCOTT DADICH, CARL DETORRES
PHOTO EDITOR: CAROLYN RAUCH / PUBLISHER: CONDÉ NAST PUBLICATIONS, INC. / ISSUE: JUNE 2008 / CATEGORY: DESIGN: FEATURE: NEWS/REPORTAGE (STORY)

021

/021/ **MOVIEMAKER**
ART DIRECTOR: ROB HEWITT, CURIOUS OUTSIDER / DESIGNER: ROB HEWITT / ILLUSTRATOR: EMMANUEL POLANCO / STUDIO: CURIOUS OUTSIDER
EDITOR-IN-CHIEF: TIMOTHY RHYS / PUBLISHER: MOVIEMAKER LLC / CLIENT: MOVIEMAKER / ISSUE: OCTOBER 2008 / CATEGORY: DESIGN: SINGLE/SPREAD/STORY

The Horror Within
An Interview with Dario Argento
BY BRYAN REESMAN
ILLUSTRATION BY EMMANUEL POLANCO

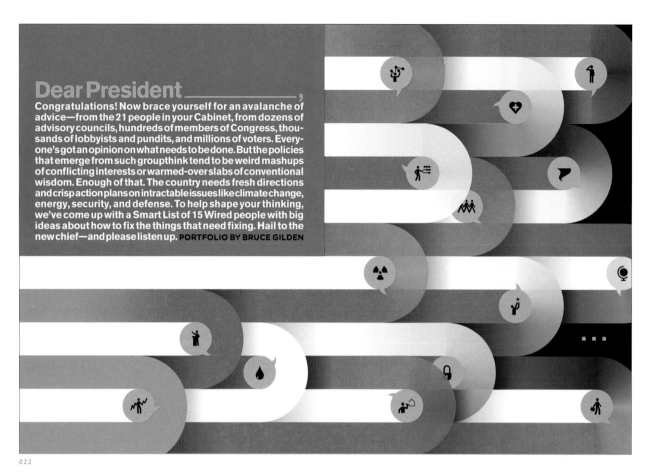

Dear President _____,

Congratulations! Now brace yourself for an avalanche of advice—from the 21 people in your Cabinet, from dozens of advisory councils, hundreds of members of Congress, thousands of lobbyists and pundits, and millions of voters. Everyone's got an opinion on what needs to be done. But the policies that emerge from such groupthink tend to be weird mashups of conflicting interests or warmed-over slabs of conventional wisdom. Enough of that. The country needs fresh directions and crisp action plans on intractable issues like climate change, energy, security, and defense. To help shape your thinking, we've come up with a Smart List of 15 Wired people with big ideas about how to fix the things that need fixing. Hail to the new chief—and please listen up. **PORTFOLIO BY BRUCE GILDEN**

022

Director, Global Governance Initiative, New America Foundation   The Smart List

Parag Khanna
Embrace the Post-American Age

Wise up about what parts of the world matter —and what parts don't. And guess what? India doesn't really matter.

Here's one view of America circa 2008: The US is a modern-day Roman Empire—overstretched, underperforming, slowly crumbling into history's dustbin. Here's Parag Khanna's view: Nonsense. The geopolitical woziness Americans are feeling isn't decline. It's realignment. In his book *The Second World: Empires and Influence in the New Global Order*, Khanna, 31, describes a planet dominated by a trio of superpowers: the US, China, and Europe. In this tripolar era, America's fate depends on tough national choices, not lame historical analogies. If the US wises up—by tightening trade and energy ties to the rest of the hemisphere, pursuing economic innovation at home, and establishing a "diplomatic-industrial complex"—it can grow stronger even as the globe becomes less red, white, and blue. « Khanna himself is a peripatetic emblem of this post-American world. Born in India, he lived as a child in

United Arab Emirates, and attended high school in the US and Germany. He earned two degrees from Georgetown University's School of Foreign Service. Then he punched his ticket at places that might earn him early admission at the Trilateral Commission: the Council on Foreign Relations, the Brookings Institution, and the World Economic Forum. "I think I'm the only person who went to Davos seven times by the age of 30," the smooth-talking wunderwonk says. "I'm not sure that's a good thing." « From Canada to Uzbekistan, Khanna identifies the unexpected flash points, overstated threats, and hidden opportunities the next US president might confront. —DANIEL H. PINK

8 Regions to Watch

Mexico and Canada
Integrate, don't isolate

America's oil comes from a volatile region half a world away. That's lunacy, Khanna says. "An energy partnership with Mexico, Canada, Venezuela, and Brazil could make the US much less dependent on oil from the Middle East." That's also why building a wall along our southern border is foolish. "We should treat Mexico like Europe treats Turkey—integrating, elevating, and partnering with it."

Colombia
Partner up

Bogotá is as close to Miami as Phoenix is to San Francisco. "We should invest here," Khanna says. "Colombia now exports mostly flowers and drugs. We can do better than that."

Egypt
Make friends fast

Egypt is smoldering. The people are restless after 27 years of the Mubarak dynasty, and the country is ripe for revolt. We should "make friends, quickly, with other power centers in the country, including the Muslim Brotherhood."

Iran
Regime change will lead to love

Khanna's recommendation: "Make the West irresistible to Iranians." The US president should deliver a speech directly to the Iranian people that offers them a deal: They can have, in Khanna's words, "everything they want in terms of Western investment in energy, freer trade, diplomatic recognition, and increased cultural and student exchanges—if they oust President Ahmadinejad."

Uzbekistan
Dangerous—and too long ignored

Khanna says this is the most important country no one ever talks about. Sitting at the heart of the ancient Silk Road, Uzbekistan is the only state that borders all the other -stan nations, whose volatility and strategic significance intensify each day. It's also the most populous and industrialized nation in energy-rich central Asia and pivotal to a stable Afghanistan and region. The challenge: dealing with an autocratic regime that's not especially fond of human rights.

China and India
The panda matters more

The race isn't even close. "India will never rival China," Khanna says. "India accounts for less than 2 percent of the global economy. It's not a superpower." Meantime, China's ever-accelerating "neo-mercantilist" freight train won't be slowed by demands for such democratic niceties as transparency or free expression. "The communist leadership is the most powerful emperor China has ever had. The Chinese people have a preference for stability over another revolution."

Russia
Overrated

On the surface, Russia glitters: It ranks second only to the US in billionaires; Moscow has a larger Prada store than Milan. And the country's army can still spank the neighbors. But Russia is in "demographic free fall," Khanna says, and faces alarming rates of tuberculosis and other health problems. Meanwhile, Chinese immigration is blurring the border. In the long run, this bear is going to spend a lot of time in hibernation.

INFOGRAPHICS BY **Department of Information Design at Copenhagen**   OCT 2008

022

/022/ **WIRED**
CREATIVE DIRECTOR: SCOTT DADICH / DESIGN DIRECTOR: WYATT MITCHELL / ART DIRECTOR: CARL DETORRES / DESIGNERS: CARL DETORRES, WALTER C. BAUMANN
ILLUSTRATOR: THE DEPARTMENT FOR INFORMATION DESIGN AT COPENHAGEN / PHOTO EDITOR: CAROLYN RAUCH / PHOTOGRAPHER: BRUCE GILDEN
PUBLISHER: CONDÉ NAST PUBLICATIONS, INC. / ISSUE: OCTOBER 2008 / CATEGORY: DESIGN: FEATURE: NON-CELEBRITY PROFILE (STORY)

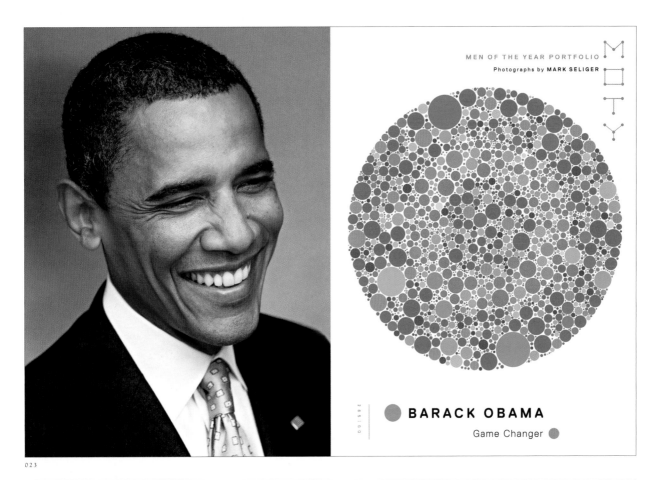

MEN OF THE YEAR PORTFOLIO
Photographs by MARK SELIGER

BARACK OBAMA

Game Changer

023

Eight races, eight gold medals, seven world records. Michael Paterniti visits with the unstoppable force who needs no introduction

MICHAEL PHELPS

Golden Boy

023

/023/ **GQ**
DESIGN DIRECTOR: FRED WOODWARD / DESIGNER: ANTON IOUKHNOVETS / DIRECTOR OF PHOTOGRAPHY: DORA SOMOSI / PHOTOGRAPHER: MARK SELIGER
CREATIVE DIRECTOR, FASHION: JIM MOORE / EDITOR-IN-CHIEF: JIM NELSON / PUBLISHER: CONDÉ NAST PUBLICATIONS INC. / ISSUE: DECEMBER 2008
CATEGORY: DESIGN: FEATURE: CELEBRITY/ENTERTAINMENT PROFILE (STORY)

/024/ **GQ**
DESIGN DIRECTOR: FRED WOODWARD
DESIGNER: THOMAS ALBERTY
DIRECTOR OF PHOTOGRAPHY: DORA SOMOSI
PHOTO EDITOR: JUSTIN O'NEILL
PHOTOGRAPHER: JILL GREENBERG
EDITOR-IN-CHIEF: JIM NELSON
PUBLISHER: CONDÉ NAST PUBLICATIONS INC.
ISSUE: FEBRUARY 2008
CATEGORY: DESIGN: FEATURE: NEWS/REPORTAGE
(SINGLE/SPREAD)

/025/ **W**
DESIGN DIRECTOR: EDWARD LEIDA
ART DIRECTOR: NATHALIE KIRSHEH
DESIGNER: NATHALIE KIRSHEH
PHOTOGRAPHER: MARIO SORRENTI
PUBLISHER: CONDÉ NAST PUBLICATIONS INC.
ISSUE: OCTOBER 2008
CATEGORY: DESIGN: FEATURE: CELEBRITY/
ENTERTAINMENT PROFILE (SINGLE/SPREAD)

/026/ **PLAY, THE NEW YORK TIMES
SPORT MAGAZINE**
CREATIVE DIRECTOR: JANET FROELICH
ART DIRECTOR: ROB HEWITT
DESIGNER: ROB HEWITT
DIRECTOR OF PHOTOGRAPHY: KATHY RYAN
PHOTO EDITOR: KIRA POLLACK
PHOTOGRAPHER: LARRY SULTAN
EDITOR-IN-CHIEF: MARK BRYANT
PUBLISHER: THE NEW YORK TIMES
ISSUE: SEPTEMBER 2008
CATEGORY: DESIGN: FEATURE:
NON-CELEBRITY PROFILE (SINGLE/SPREAD)

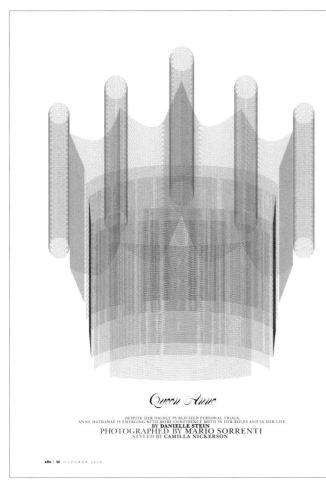

Queen Anne

DESPITE HER HIGHLY PUBLICIZED PERSONAL TRIALS,
ANNE HATHAWAY IS EMERGING WITH MORE CONFIDENCE BOTH IN HER ROLES AND IN HER LIFE.
BY DANIELLE STEIN
PHOTOGRAPHED BY MARIO SORRENTI
STYLED BY CAMILLA NICKERSON

ALAS, POOR' ZITO

HE HAD THE BEST CURVEBALL IN THE GAME, AND THEN, INEXPLICABLY, HE DIDN'T.

WHAT WENT WRONG REMAINS A MYSTERY.

THE ONGOING METAPHYSICAL CRISIS OF **BARRY ZITO**, BASEBALL'S PRINCE OF CONFUSION.

BY **PAT JORDAN**
PHOTOGRAPH BY LARRY SULTAN

36

Esquire CONTENTS

December 2008 / vol. 150 / no. 6

B 2008

Our seventh annual celebration of the innovators, renegades, heart surgeons, and jungle explorers who are leading the way to a better tomorrow.

{ continued on page 22 }

ON THE COVER: VINCE VAUGHN PHOTOGRAPHED EXCLUSIVELY FOR ESQUIRE BY JAKE CHESSUM. PRODUCED BY EMILY ROTH FOR PRODUCIT. STYLING BY ALIX HESTER FOR THE GERSH AGENCY. GROOMING BY CHERYL NICK. PROP STYLING BY FI CAMPBELL JOHNSON. TWO-BUTTON WOOL SUIT BY BOSS BLACK; COTTON SHIRT AND SILK TIE BY HUGO BOSS; LEATHER BELT BY ALLEN EDMONDS.

/027/ **ESQUIRE**
DESIGN DIRECTOR: DAVID CURCURITO / ART DIRECTOR: DARHIL CROOKS / ASSOCIATE ART DIRECTOR: ERIN JANG / DESIGN ASSISTANT: SONI KHATRI
DIRECTOR OF PHOTOGRAPHY: MICHAEL NORSENG / PHOTO EDITOR: ALISON UNTERREINER / EDITOR-IN-CHIEF: DAVID GRANGER / PUBLISHER:
THE HEARST CORPORATION-MAGAZINES DIVISION / ISSUES: MAY 2008, JUNE 2008, JULY 2008, DECEMBER 2008 / CATEGORY: DESIGN: SECTION (SERIES OF PAGES)

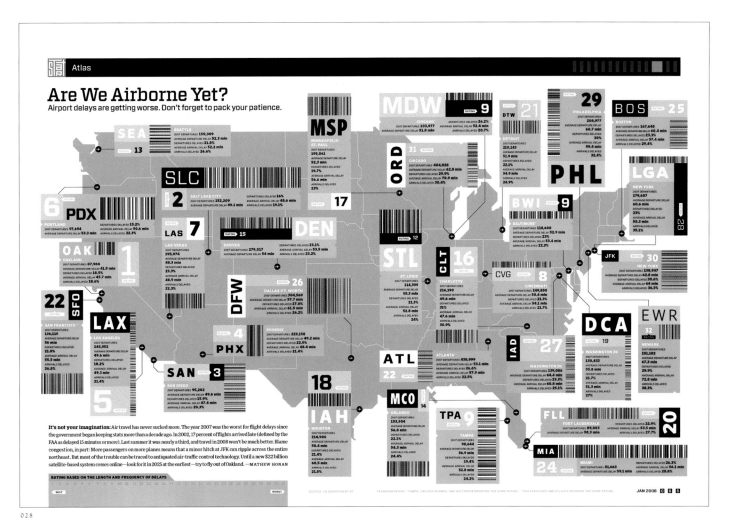

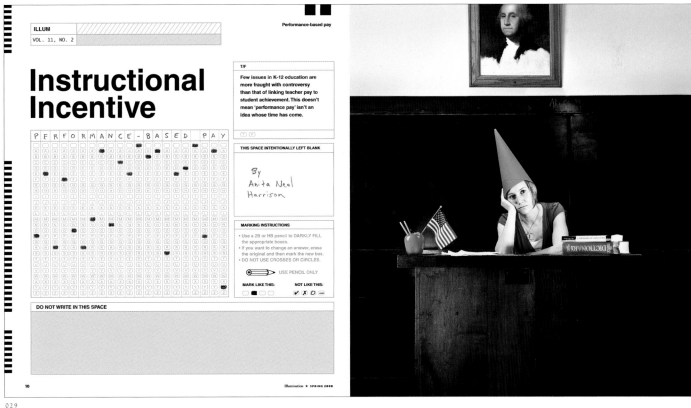

/028/ **WIRED**
CREATIVE DIRECTOR: SCOTT DADICH / DESIGN DIRECTOR: WYATT MITCHELL
ART DIRECTOR: CARL DETORRES / PUBLISHER: CONDÉ NAST PUBLICATIONS, INC.
ISSUE: JANUARY 2008 / CATEGORY: DESIGN: SECTION (SINGLE/SPREAD)

/029/ **ILLUMINATION**
ART DIRECTOR: BLAKE DINSDALE / DESIGNER: BLAKE DINSDALE /
PHOTOGRAPHER: NICHOLAS BENNER / EDITOR-IN-CHIEF: CHARLES REINEKE
PUBLISHER: UNIVERSITY OF MISSOURI / ISSUE: SPRING 2008
CATEGORY: DESIGN: SINGLE/SPREAD/STORY

Randall Patterson: College Kids Who Opt Out of Sex **Ilan Greenberg:** Making Sure the Olympics Are Politicized

The New York Times Magazine

MARCH 30, 2008

The End of Republican America?

Karl Rove had a plan
to realign American politics for generations.
Now G.O.P. leaders are
struggling to prevent another 1964.

By Benjamin Wallace-Wells

030

/030/ THE NEW YORK TIMES MAGAZINE
CREATIVE DIRECTOR: JANET FROELICH / ART DIRECTOR: AREM DUPLESSIS / DEPUTY ART DIRECTOR: GAIL BICHLER
DESIGNER: LEO JUNG / DIRECTOR OF PHOTOGRAPHY: KATHY RYAN / PHOTO EDITOR: DAVID CARTHAS / PHOTOGRAPHER: ANDREW BETTLES
EDITOR-IN-CHIEF: GERRY MARZORATI / PUBLISHER: THE NEW YORK TIMES / ISSUE: MARCH 30, 2008 / CATEGORY: DESIGN: COVER

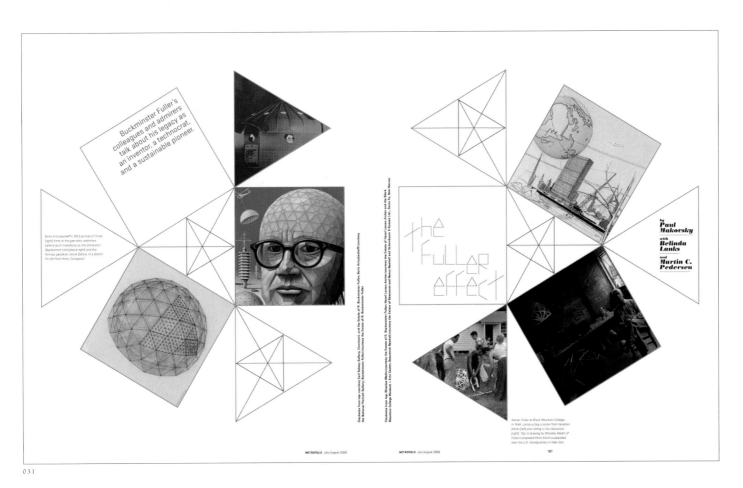

Buckminster Fuller's colleagues and admirers talk about his legacy as an inventor, a technocrat, and a sustainable pioneer.

Paul Makovsky
with Belinda Lanks
and Martin C. Pedersen

the Fuller effect

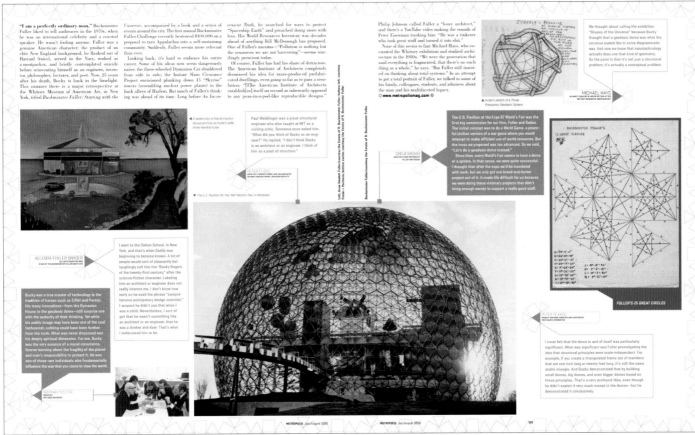

"I am a perfectly ordinary man," Buckminster Fuller liked to tell audiences in the 1970s, when he was an international celebrity and a coveted speaker. He wasn't fooling anyone. Fuller was a genuine American character: the product of an elite New England background, he flunked out of Harvard (twice), served in the Navy, worked as a meatpacker, and briefly contemplated suicide before reinventing himself as an engineer, inventor, philosopher, lecturer, and poet. Now, 25 years after his death, Bucky is back in the limelight. This summer there is a major retrospective at the Whitney Museum of American Art, in New York, titled *Buckminster Fuller: Starting with the*

Universe, accompanied by a book and a series of events around the city. The first annual Buckminster Fuller Challenge recently bestowed $100,000 on a proposal to turn Appalachia into a self-sustaining community. Suddenly, Fuller seems more relevant than ever.

Looking back, it's hard to embrace his entire career. Some of his ideas now seem dangerously naive: the three-wheeled Dymaxion Car shuddered from side to side; the Instant Slum Clearance Project envisioned plunking down 15 "Skyrise" towers (resembling nuclear power plants) in the back alleys of Harlem. But much of Fuller's thinking was ahead of its time. Long before *An Incon-*

venient Truth, he searched for ways to protect "Spaceship Earth" and preached doing more with less. His World Resources Inventory was decades ahead of anything Bill McDonough has proposed. One of Fuller's maxims—"Pollution is nothing but the resources we are not harvesting"—seems startlingly prescient today.

Of course, Fuller has had his share of detractors. The American Institute of Architects completely dismissed his idea for mass-produced prefabricated dwellings, even going so far as to pass a resolution: "[T]he American Institute of Architects establishe[s] itself on record as inherently opposed to any peas-in-a-pod-like reproducible designs."

Philip Johnson called Fuller a "lousy architect," and there's a YouTube video making the rounds of Peter Eisenman trashing him: "He was a tinkerer who took great stuff and turned it into shit."

None of this seems to faze Michael Hays, who co-curated the Whitney exhibition and studied architecture in the 1980s. "We were the generation that said everything was fragmented, that there's no such thing as a whole," he says. "But Fuller still insisted on thinking about total systems." In an attempt to get a total portrait of Fuller, we talked to some of his family, colleagues, students, and admirers about the man and his multifaceted legacy.

www.metropolismag.com

FULLER'S 25 GREAT CIRCLES

/031/ METROPOLIS
CREATIVE DIRECTOR: CRISWELL LAPPIN / ART DIRECTOR: DUNGJAI UNGANTHAIKAN / DESIGNER: LISA MAIONE / PHOTO EDITOR: SARAH PALMER
PUBLISHER: BELLEROPHON PUBLICATIONS / ISSUE: JULY/AUGUST 2008 / CATEGORY: DESIGN: FEATURE: NON-CELEBRITY PROFILE (STORY)

WIRED·JG.OG

15th Anniversary: Our Greatest Hits & Misses

WIRED

Attention Environmentalists: Keep your SUV. Forget organics. Go nuclear. Screw the spotted owl.

If you're serious about global warming, only one thing matters: Cutting carbon. That means facing some inconvenient truths.

Plus:
What We'll	Spies and	Farewell,
Miss About	Sabotage	Battlestar
Bill Gates	at Ferrari	Galactica

GIVE A HOOT | JUN.2008

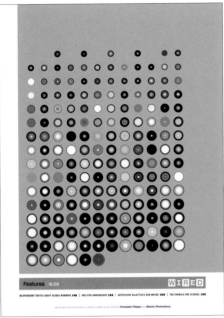

032

032

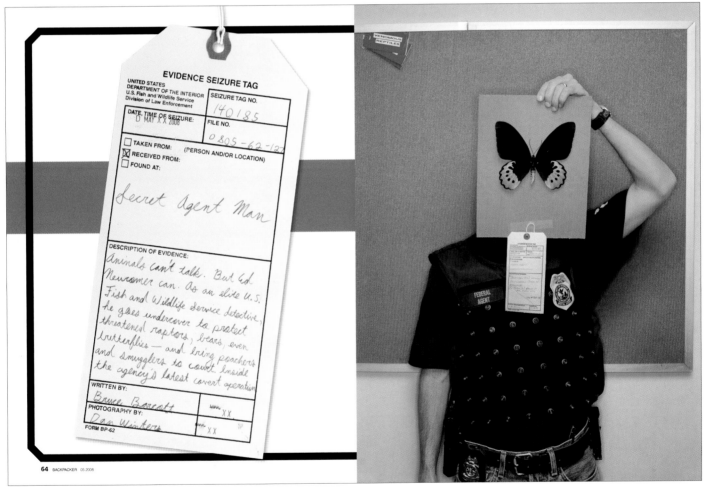

033

/032/ WIRED
CREATIVE DIRECTOR: SCOTT DADICH / DESIGN DIRECTOR: WYATT MITCHELL
ASSOCIATE ART DIRECTORS: CHRISTY SHEPPARD, MARGARET SWART
ART DIRECTORS: MAILI HOLIMAN, CARL DETORRES / DESIGNERS:
WALTER C. BAUMANN, VICTOR KRUMENNACHER / SENIOR PHOTO EDITOR:
ZANA WOODS / PHOTO EDITOR: CAROLYN RAUCH / DEPUTY PHOTO EDITOR:
ANNA GOLDWATER ALEXANDER / PHOTO ASSISTANTS: SARAH FILIPPI,
DANIEL SALO / PUBLISHER: CONDÉ NAST PUBLICATIONS, INC.
ISSUE: JUNE 2008 / CATEGORY: DESIGN: ENTIRE ISSUE

/033/ BACKPACKER
DESIGN DIRECTOR: MATTHEW BATES / DESIGNERS: MATTHEW BATES,
JACKIE MCCAFFREY, TED ALVAREZ / PHOTO EDITOR: JULIA VANDENOEVER
PHOTOGRAPHER: DAN WINTERS / PUBLISHER: ACTIVE INTEREST MEDIA
ISSUE: MAY 2008 / CATEGORY: DESIGN: FEATURE: NON-CELEBRITY PROFILE
(SINGLE/SPREAD)

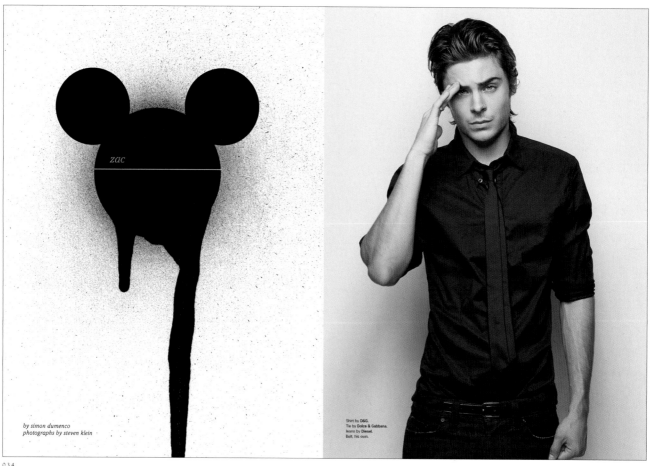

by simon dumenco
photographs by steven klein

Shirt by D&G.
Tie by Dolce & Gabbana.
Jeans by Diesel.
Belt, his own.

034

1

2

THE
FRAME
GAME

GOLF-THEMED
ART IS HOTTER
THAN EVER.
HERE'S WHAT'S
IN DEMAND—
AND WHY

3

BY MICHAEL
CALLAHAN
ILLUSTRATIONS
BY JAMESON
SIMPSON

4

035

/034/ **DETAILS**
CREATIVE DIRECTOR: ROCKWELL HARWOOD / ART DIRECTOR: ANDRE JOINTE
DESIGNER: ROCKWELL HARWOOD / PHOTO EDITORS: ALEX GHEZ, CHANDRA GLICK
SENIOR PHOTO EDITOR: HALI TARA FELDMAN / PHOTOGRAPHER: STEVEN KLEIN
EDITOR-IN-CHIEF: DANIEL PERES / PUBLISHER: CONDÉ NAST PUBLICATIONS
ISSUE: JANUARY/FEBRUARY 2008 / CATEGORY: DESIGN: FEATURE: CELEBRITY/
ENTERTAINMENT PROFILE (SINGLE/SPREAD)

/035/ **GOLF DIGEST INDEX**
DESIGN DIRECTOR: KEN DELAGO / DESIGNER: MARNE MAYER
ILLUSTRATOR: JAMESON SIMPSON / PUBLISHER: CONDÉ NAST PUBLICATIONS INC.
ISSUE: SPRING 2008 / CATEGORY: DESIGN: FEATURE: SERVICE (SINGLE/SPREAD)

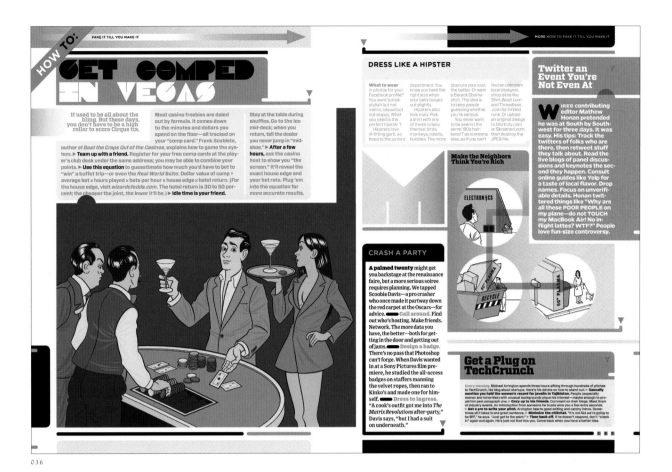

HOW TO: FAKE IT TILL YOU MAKE IT | MORE HOW TO FAKE IT TILL YOU MAKE IT

GET COMPED IN VEGAS

It used to be all about the bling. But these days, you don't have to be a high roller to score Cirque fix.

author of *Beat the Craps Out of the Casinos*, explains how to game the system. ▶ Team up with a friend. Register for your free comp cards at the player's club desk under the same address; you may be able to combine your points. ▶ Use this equation to guesstimate how much you'd have to bet to "win" a buffet trip—or even the *Real World Suite*: Dollar value of comp = average bet x hours played x bets per hour x house edge x hotel return. (For the house edge, visit *wizardofodds.com*. The hotel return is 30 to 50 percent; the cheaper the joint, the lower it'll be.) ▶ Idle time is your friend.

Most casino freebies are doled out by formula. It comes down to the minutes and dollars you spend on the floor—all tracked on your "comp card." Frank Scoblete,

Stay at the table during shuffles. Go to the loo mid-deck; when you return, tell the dealer you never jump in "mid-shoe." ▶ After a few hours, ask the casino host to show you "the screen." It'll reveal the exact house edge and your bet rate. Plug 'em into the equation for more accurate results.

DRESS LIKE A HIPSTER

What to wear in photos for your Facebook profile? You want to look stylish but not metro, casual but not sloppy. What you need is the perfect hipster T. Hipsters love ill-fitting garb; so head to the juniors' department. You know you have the right size when your belly bulges out slightly. Hipsters also love irony. Pick a shirt with any of these cutesy themes: birds, monkeys, robots, bubbles. The more obscure your icon, the better. Or wear a Barack Obama shirt. The idea is to keep people guessing whether you're serious. You never went to be seen in the same '80s hairband T as someone else, so if you can't find an unknown local designer, shop sites like Shirt.Woot.com and Threadless .com for limited runs. Or upload an original design to Shirtcity.com or Skreened.com, then destroy the JPEG file.

Make the Neighbors Think You're Rich

ELECTRONICS

CRASH A PARTY

A palmed twenty might get you backstage at the renaissance faire, but a more serious soiree requires planning. We tapped Scoobie Davis—a pro crasher who once made it partway down the red carpet at the Oscars—for advice. ■ Call around. Find out who's hosting. Make friends. Network. The more data you have, the better—both for getting in the door and getting out of jams. ■ Design a badge. There's no pass that Photoshop can't forge. When Davis wanted in at a Sony Pictures film premiere, he studied the all-access badges on staffers manning the velvet ropes, then ran to Kinko's and made one for himself. ■ Dress to ingress. "A cook's outfit got me into *The Matrix Revolutions* after-party," Davis says, "but I had a suit on underneath."

Twitter an Event You're Not Even At

WIRED contributing editor Mathew Honan pretended he was at South by Southwest for three days. It was easy. His tips: Track the twitters of folks who are there, then retweet stuff they talk about. Read the live blogs of panel discussions and keynotes the second they happen. Consult online guides like Yelp for a taste of local flavor. Drop names. Focus on unverifiable details. Honan twittered things like "Why are all these POOR PEOPLE on my plane—do not TOUCH my MacBook Air! No in-flight lattes? WTF?" People love fun-size controversy.

Get a Plug on TechCrunch

Every morning, Michael Arrington spends three hours sifting through hundreds of pitches to TechCrunch, his blog about startups. Here's his advice on how to stand out: ▶ Casually mention you hold the women's record for javelin in Tajikistan. People (especially women and minorities) with unusual backgrounds pique his interest—maybe enough to propel him past paragraph one. ▶ Cozy up to his friends. Comment on their blogs. Meet them at industry events. An introduction from someone he trusts wins you a few extra seconds. ▶ Get a pen to write your pitch. Arrington hearts good writing and catchy intros. Sometimes all it takes is one great sentence. ▶ Minimize the chitchat. "It's not like we're going to be BFF," he says. "Just get to the point." ▶ Then back off. If he doesn't respond, don't "check in" again and again. He's just not that into you. Come back when you have a better idea.

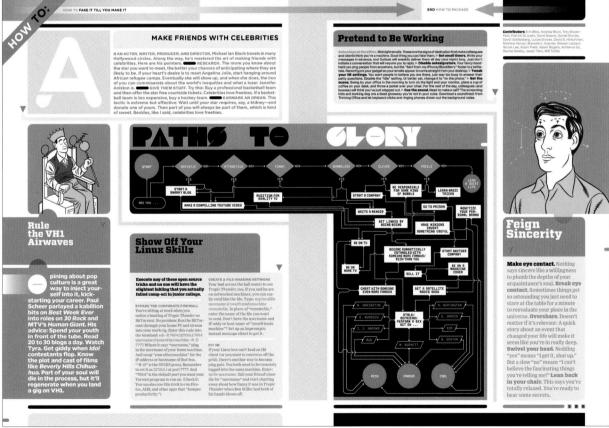

HOW TO: FAKE IT TILL YOU MAKE IT | END HOW TO PACKAGE

MAKE FRIENDS WITH CELEBRITIES

S AN ACTOR, WRITER, PRODUCER, AND DIRECTOR, Michael Ian Black travels in many Hollywood circles. Along the way, he's mastered the art of making friends with celebrities. Here are his pointers. ■ RESEARCH. The more you know about the star you want to meet, the better your chances of anticipating where they are likely to be. If your heart's desire is to meet Angelina Jolie, start hanging around African refugee camps. Eventually she will show up, and when she does, the two of you can commiserate about the world's inequities and what a loser Jennifer Aniston is. ■ GIVE THEM STUFF. Try this: Buy a professional basketball team and then offer the star free courtside tickets. Celebrities love freebies. If a basketball team is too expensive, buy a hockey team. ■ EARMARK AN ORGAN. This tactic is extreme but effective: Wait until your star requires, say, a kidney—and donate one of yours. Then part of you will always be part of them, which is kind of sweet. Besides, like I said, celebrities love freebies.

Pretend to Be Working

Saturdays at the office. Midnight emails. These are the signs of dedication that make colleagues and clients think you're a machine. Good thing you can fake them. ▶ Set email timers. Write your messages in advance, and Outlook will sneakily deliver them all day (and night) long. Just don't initiate a conversation that will require you to reply. ▶ Disable autosignature. Your fancy handheld can ping people from anywhere, but the "Sent from my iPhone/BlackBerry" footer is a tattletale. Reconfigure your gadget so your emails appear to come straight from your desktop. ▶ Tweak your IM settings. You want people to believe you are there, just way too busy to answer their petty questions. Disable the "idle" setting. Or better yet, change it to "on the phone." ▶ Set the scene. Swing by your office in the morning to turn on the light and your monitor, place a cup of coffee on your desk, and throw a jacket over your chair. For the rest of the day, colleagues (and bosses) will think you've just stepped out. ▶ Cue the sound. Need to make a call? The screaming kids and barking dog are a dead giveaway you're not in your cube. Download a soundtrack from Thriving Office and let keyboard clicks and ringing phones drown out the background noise.

Contributors Erin Biba, Andrew Blum, Troy Brownfield, Patrick Di Justo, David Downs, Daniel Dumas, David Goldenberg, Lucas Graves, David S. Hirschman, Mathew Honan, Brandon I. Koerner, Steven Leckart, Nicole Lee, Adam Pash, Adam Rogers, Adrienne So, Rachel Swaby, Jason Tanz, Will Tuttle

PATHS TO GLORY

Rule the VH1 Airwaves

pining about pop culture is a great way to inject yourself into it, kickstarting your career. Paul Scheer parlayed a kabillion bits on *Best Week Ever* into roles on *30 Rock* and MTV's *Human Giant*. His advice: Spend your youth in front of the tube. Read 20 to 30 blogs a day. Watch Tyra. Get giddy when *Idol* contestants flop. Know the plot and cast of films like *Beverly Hills Chihuahua*. Part of your soul will die in the process, but it'll regenerate when you land a gig on VH1.

Show Off Your Linux Skillz

Execute any of these open source tricks and no one will have the slightest inkling that you actually failed comp-sci in junior college.

BYPASS THE CORPORATE FIREWALL You're sitting at work when you notice a bootleg of *Tropic Thunder* on BitTorrent. No problem: Run the BitTorrent through your home PC and stream into your work rig. Enter this code into the terminal: ssh -R 7654:127.0.0.1:7654 username@yourothermachine -N -D 7777. Where it says "username," put in the username of your home machine. And swap "yourothermachine" for the IP address or hostname of that box. "-N-D" is the SOCKS proxy. Remember to set it as 127.0.0.1 at port 7777. And "7654" is the default port you want your Torrent program to run on. (Check it: You can also use this trick to run Firefox, AIM, and other apps that "humper productivity.")

CREATE A FILE-SHARING NETWORK Your bud across the hall wants to see *Tropic Thunder*, too. If you and he are on networked machines, you can easily swindle him the file. Type: scp localfile username@yourfriendsmachine:remotefile. In place of "remotefile," enter the name of the file you want to send. Don't have the username and IP addy or host name of "yourfriendsmachine"? Set up an impromptu instant message client to get it.

DIY IM If your Linux box can't load an IM client (or you want to converse off the grid), there's another way to become ping pals. You both need to be remotely logged into the same machine. Enter: write username. Sub your friend's handle for "username" and start chatting away about how funny it was in *Tropic Thunder* when Ben Stiller had both of his hands blown off.

Feign Sincerity

Make eye contact. Nothing says sincere like a willingness to plumb the depths of your acquaintance's soul. Break eye contact. Sometimes things get so astounding you just need to stare at the table for a minute to reevaluate your place in the universe. Overshare. Doesn't matter if it's relevant: A quick story about an event that changed your life will make it seem like you're in really deep. Swivel your head. Nodding "yes" means "I get it, shut up." But a slow "no" means "I can't believe the fascinating things you're telling me!" Lean back in your chair. This says you're totally relaxed. You're ready to hear some secrets.

/036/ **WIRED**
CREATIVE DIRECTOR: SCOTT DADICH / DESIGN DIRECTOR: WYATT MITCHELL / ART DIRECTOR: CARL DETORRES
DESIGNERS: CARL DETORRES, WALTER C. BAUMANN / ILLUSTRATOR: NICK DEWAR / PHOTO EDITOR: CAROLYN RAUCH
PHOTOGRAPHER: PLATON / PUBLISHER: CONDÉ NAST PUBLICATIONS, INC. / ISSUE: SEPTEMBER 2008
CATEGORY: DESIGN: FEATURE: SERVICE (STORY)

The New York Times Magazine / APRIL 20, 2008

THE GREEN ISSUE

ACT	EAT	*INVENT*	LEARN	LIVE	*MOVE*	BUILD
46	52	54	61	62	68	72

Some Bold Steps to Make Your Carbon Footprint Smaller

LETTERING BY GYONGY LAKY   PHOTOGRAPHS BY DWIGHT ESCHLIMAN   GROWING-FOREST ILLUSTRATIONS BY ANDREW RAE

45

/037/ THE NEW YORK TIMES MAGAZINE
CREATIVE DIRECTOR: JANET FROELICH / ART DIRECTOR: AREM DUPLESSIS / DEPUTY ART DIRECTOR: GAIL BICHLER / DESIGNERS: GAIL BICHLER, AREM DUPLESSIS,
IAN ALLEN, HILARY GREENBAUM, LEO JUNG, JULIA MOBURG, JEFF DOCHERTY, SARA MCKAY / ILLUSTRATORS: GYONGY LAKY, ANDREW RAE, MARC ALARY, R.O. BLECHMAN,
KEVIN CHRISTY, STEVE STANFORD / DIRECTOR OF PHOTOGRAPHY: KATHY RYAN / PHOTO EDITOR: CLINTON CARGILL / EDITOR-IN-CHIEF: GERRY MARZORATI
PUBLISHER: THE NEW YORK TIMES /ISSUE: APRIL 20, 2008 / CATEGORY: DESIGN: FEATURE: NEWS/REPORTAGE (STORY)

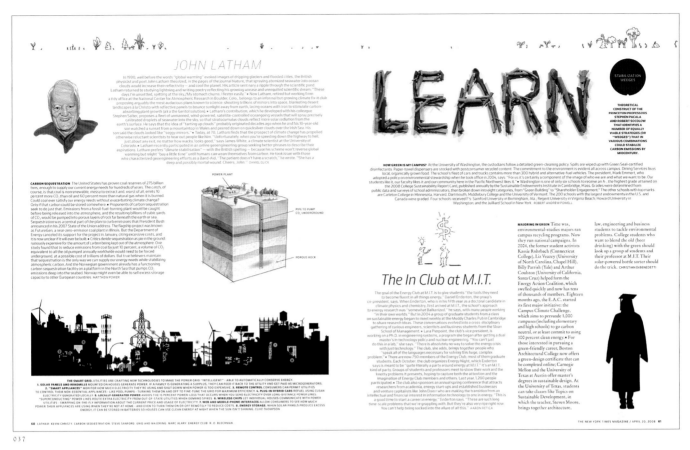

037

038

039

/038/ T, THE NEW YORK TIMES STYLE MAGAZINE
CREATIVE DIRECTOR: JANET FROELICH / SENIOR ART DIRECTOR: DAVID SEBBAH
ART DIRECTOR: CHRISTOPHER MARTINEZ / SENIOR DESIGNER: ELIZABETH
SPIRIDAKIS / PHOTOGRAPHER: KAZUNARI TAJIMA / ARTWORK BY KAMO
EDITOR-IN-CHIEF: STEFANO TONCHI / PUBLISHER: THE NEW YORK TIMES
ISSUE: APRIL 13, 2008 / CATEGORY: DESIGN: FEATURE: TRAVEL/FOOD/STILL LIFE
(SINGLE/SPREAD)

/039/ GQ
DESIGN DIRECTOR: FRED WOODWARD / DESIGNER: THOMAS ALBERTY
DIRECTOR OF PHOTOGRAPHY: DORA SOMOSI / EDITOR-IN-CHIEF: JIM NELSON
PUBLISHER: CONDÉ NAST PUBLICATIONS INC. / ISSUE: DECEMBER 2008
CATEGORY: DESIGN: SECTION (SINGLE/SPREAD)

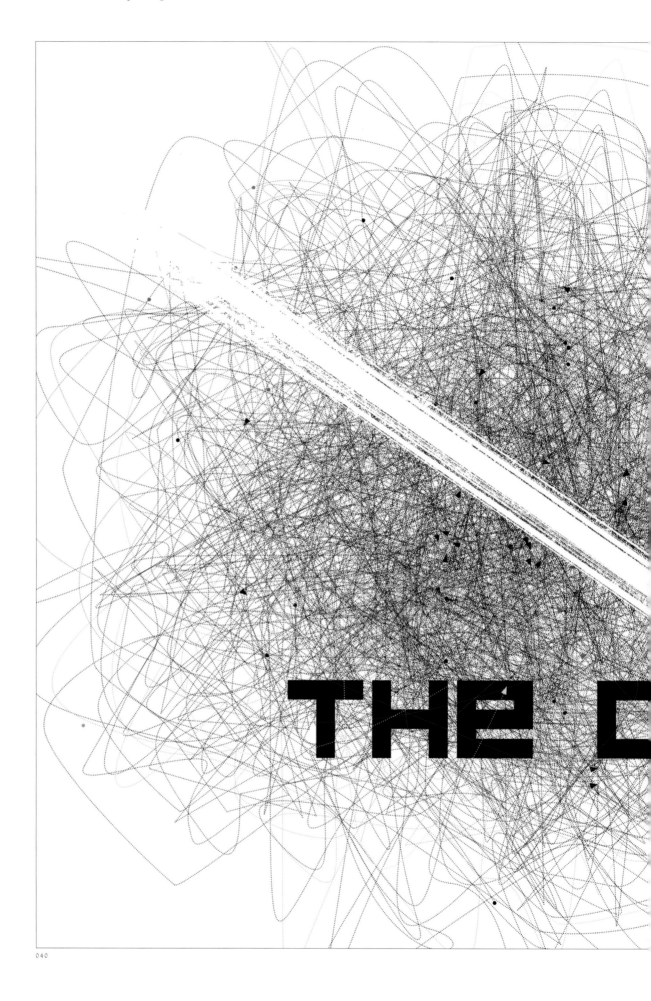

/040/ **WIRED**
CREATIVE DIRECTOR: SCOTT DADICH / DESIGN DIRECTOR: WYATT MITCHELL / ART DIRECTOR: CARL DETORRES / DESIGNER: CARL DETORRES
PUBLISHER: CONDÉ NAST PUBLICATIONS, INC. / ISSUE: JANUARY 2008 / CATEGORY: DESIGN: FEATURE: NEWS/REPORTAGE (SINGLE/SPREAD)

THEY CALL IT ~~SCRAPING~~ — *WHEN WEB COMPANIES AUTOMATICALLY HARVEST INFORMATION FROM THE LIKES OF YAHOO, GOOGLE, AND CRAIGSLIST. NOW THE INTERNET ESTABLISHMENT IS CLAMPING DOWN.*

DATA WARS

BY JOSH MCHUGH

041

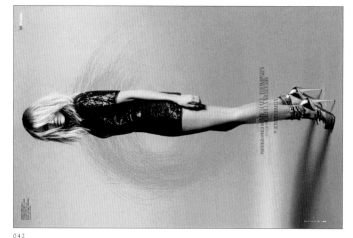

042

042

/041/ **W**
DESIGN DIRECTOR: EDWARD LEIDA / ART DIRECTOR: NATHALIE KIRSHEH
PHOTOGRAPHER: DAVID SIMS / PUBLISHER: CONDÉ NAST PUBLICATIONS INC.
ISSUE: MARCH 2008 / CATEGORY: DESIGN: FEATURE: FASHION/BEAUTY
(SINGLE/SPREAD)

/042/ **W**
DESIGN DIRECTOR: EDWARD LEIDA / ART DIRECTOR: NATHALIE KIRSHEH
DESIGNER: NATHALIE KIRSHEH / PHOTOGRAPHER: MICHAEL THOMPSON
PUBLISHER: CONDÉ NAST PUBLICATIONS INC. / ISSUE: MAY 2008
CATEGORY: DESIGN: FEATURE: CELEBRITY/ENTERTAINMENT PROFILE (STORY)

THINKING LIKE AN ENGINEER

by Benjamin Lester | illustration by Josh Cochran

Scientists are applying the tools and approaches of engineering to solve some practical problems and fathom the basic nature of things.

043

WHEN YOU FIRST LOOK AT IT, it's hard to tell what exactly is going on. Properly attired 18th-century gentlemen lunge from different angles toward the cup, perhaps to challenge whose ball is away, perhaps to follow the path of a putt. Around the men are some 50 spectators—some engaged, some seemingly bored, all stylishly dressed—surveying or ignoring the moment to varying degrees. Painted in oil by the Scottish artist Charles Lees in 1847, "The Golfers: A Grand Match Played Over the Links of St. Andrews on the day of the Annual Meeting of the Royal and Ancient Golf Club," is the most sought-after work ever to depict the game. "It's probably the most famous painting in golf," says Dale Concannon, the author of 17 books on golf and an art collector in Stratford-upon-Avon, England.

044

044

/043/ **HHMI BULLETIN**
DESIGN DIRECTOR: MICHAEL BRALEY / DESIGNER: JENNIFER LEE
ILLUSTRATOR: JOSH COCHRAN / STUDIO: VSA PARTNERS / PUBLISHER:
HOWARD HUGHES MEDICAL INSTITUTE / CLIENT: HOWARD HUGHES MEDICAL
INSTITUTE / ISSUE: AUGUST 2008 / CATEGORY: DESIGN: SINGLE/SPREAD/STORY

/044/ **GOLF DIGEST INDEX**
DESIGN DIRECTOR: KEN DELAGO / DESIGNER: MARNE MAYER
ILLUSTRATOR: JAMESON SIMPSON / PUBLISHER: CONDÉ NAST PUBLICATIONS INC.
ISSUE: SPRING 2008 / CATEGORY: DESIGN: SINGLE/SPREAD/STORY

045

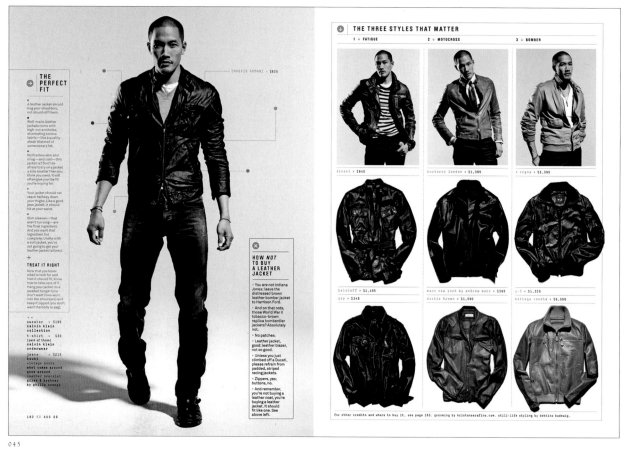

045

/045/ **GQ**
DESIGN DIRECTOR: FRED WOODWARD / DESIGNER: ANTON IOUKHNOVETS / DIRECTOR OF PHOTOGRAPHY: DORA SOMOSI
PHOTO EDITOR: JESSE LEE / PHOTOGRAPHERS: ERIC RAY DAVIDSON, TOM SCHIERLITZ / EDITOR-IN-CHIEF: JIM NELSON
PUBLISHER: CONDÉ NAST PUBLICATIONS INC. / ISSUE: AUGUST 2008 / CATEGORY: DESIGN: FEATURE: FASHION/BEAUTY (STORY)

046

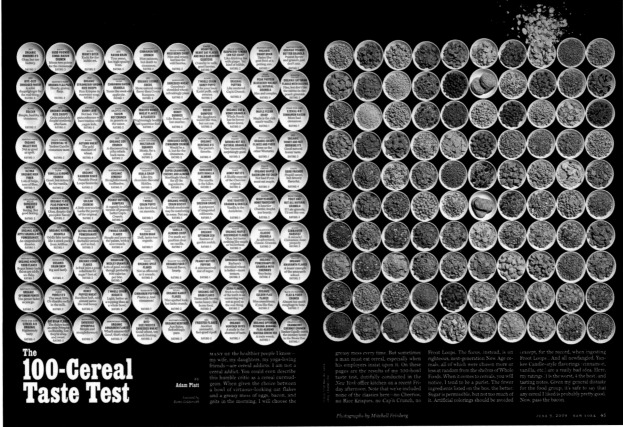

046

/046/ **NEW YORK**
DESIGN DIRECTOR: CHRIS DIXON / ART DIRECTOR: RANDY MINOR / DESIGNER: RANDY MINOR / DIRECTOR OF PHOTOGRAPHY: JODY QUON
PHOTOGRAPHERS: MITCHELL FEINBERG, BEN STECHSCHULTE / EDITOR-IN-CHIEF: ADAM MOSS / PUBLISHER: NEW YORK MAGAZINE HOLDINGS, LLC
ISSUE: MAY 9, 2008 / CATEGORY: DESIGN: FEATURE: TRAVEL/FOOD/STILL LIFE (STORY)

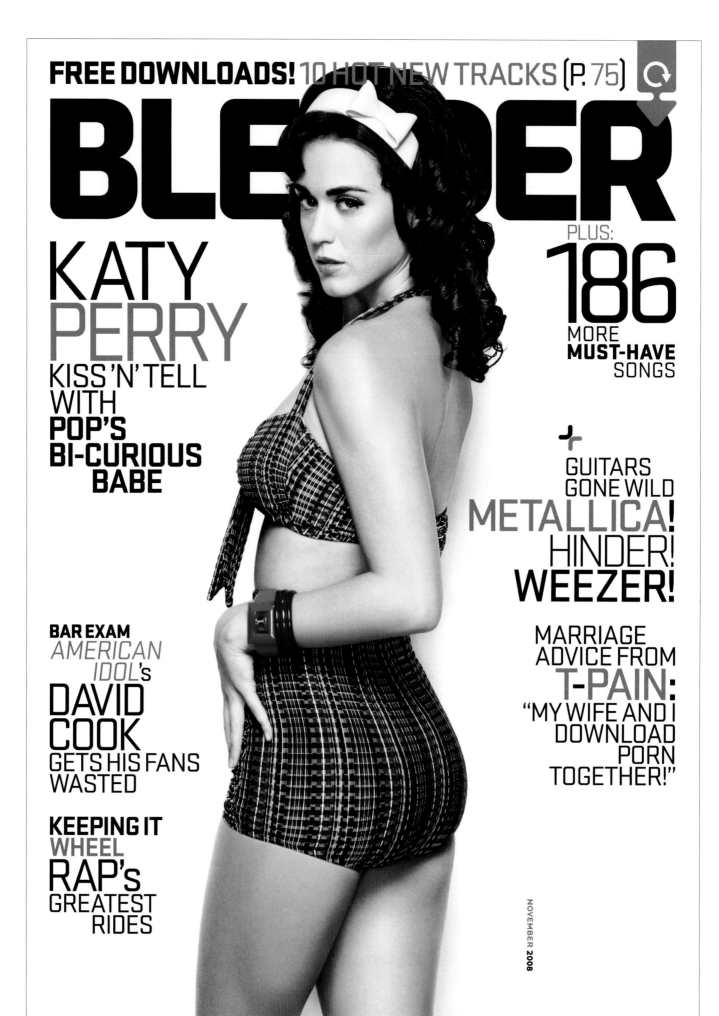

FREE DOWNLOADS! 10 HOT NEW TRACKS (P. 75)

BLENDER

KATY PERRY

KISS 'N' TELL WITH **POP'S BI-CURIOUS BABE**

PLUS: 186 MORE **MUST-HAVE** SONGS

GUITARS GONE WILD METALLICA! HINDER! WEEZER!

MARRIAGE ADVICE FROM **T-PAIN:** "MY WIFE AND I DOWNLOAD PORN TOGETHER!"

BAR EXAM AMERICAN IDOL's **DAVID COOK** GETS HIS FANS WASTED

KEEPING IT WHEEL **RAP's** GREATEST RIDES

NOVEMBER 2008

047

047

048

048

/047/ BLENDER
CREATIVE DIRECTOR: DIRK BARNETT / ART DIRECTORS: ROBERT VARGAS,
CLAUDIA DE ALMEIDA / DESIGNERS: DIRK BARNETT, ROBERT VARGAS,
CLAUDIA DE ALMEIDA / ILLUSTRATORS: AUGUST HEFFNER, EAMO,
JAMESON SIMPSON, ANDY FRIEDMAN, JASON LEE, DON'T WAKE ME UP
DIRECTOR OF PHOTOGRAPHY: DAVID CARTHAS / PHOTO EDITORS:
CHRIS EHRMANN, RORY WALSH / PHOTOGRAPHERS: BEN WATTS, RENNIO
MAIFREDI, MARTIN SCHOELLER, TURE LILLEGRAVEN, KENNETH CAPPELLO,
WILLIAMS+HIRAKAWA / EDITOR-IN-CHIEF: JOE LEVY / PUBLISHER: ALPHAMEDIA
GROUP / ISSUE: NOVEMBER 2008 / CATEGORY: REDESIGN: AFTER ISSUE

/048/ BLENDER
CREATIVE DIRECTOR: DIRK BARNETT / ART DIRECTORS: ROBERT VARGAS,
CLAUDIA DE ALMEIDA / DESIGNERS: ROBERT VARGAS, ALICE CHO
ILLUSTRATOR: DON'T WAKE ME UP / DIRECTOR OF PHOTOGRAPHY:
DAVID CARTHAS / PHOTO EDITOR: RORY WALSH / EDITOR-IN-CHIEF: JOE LEVY
PUBLISHER: ALPHAMEDIA GROUP / ISSUE: NOVEMBER 2008
CATEGORY: DESIGN: SECTION (SERIES OF PAGES)

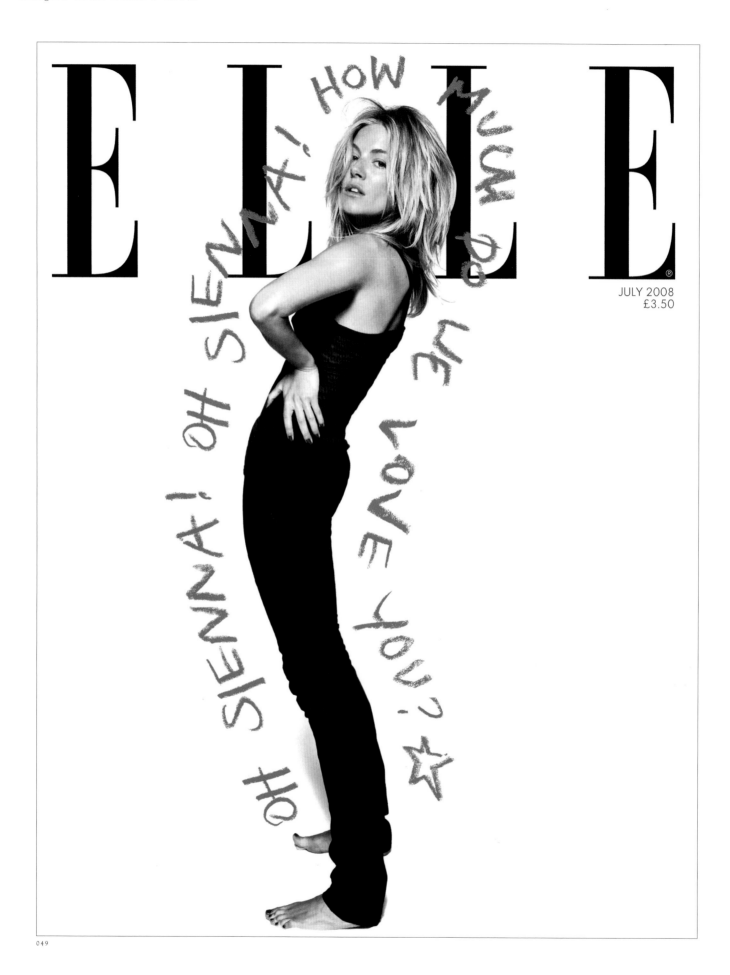

049

/049/ **ELLE (UK)**
CREATIVE DIRECTOR: MARISSA BOURKE / PHOTOGRAPHER: JAN WELTERS / EDITOR-IN-CHIEF: LORRAINE CANDY
PUBLISHER: HACHETTE FILIPACCHI MAGAZINES, INC. / ISSUE: JULY 2008 / CATEGORY: DESIGN: COVER

YEAR-END DOUBLE ISSUE

NEW YORK ®

DECEMBER 22–29, 2008

REASONS TO LOVE NEW YORK

(Especially Right Now)

/050/ NEW YORK
DESIGN DIRECTOR: CHRIS DIXON / ART DIRECTOR: RANDY MINOR / DESIGNER: CHRIS DIXON / ILLUSTRATORS: RODRIGO CORRAL DESIGN
WITH BEN WISEMAN AND TRACY MORFORD / DIRECTOR OF PHOTOGRAPHY: JODY QUON / EDITOR-IN-CHIEF: ADAM MOSS
PUBLISHER: NEW YORK MAGAZINE HOLDINGS, LLC / ISSUE: DECEMBER 22-29, 2008 / CATEGORY: DESIGN: COVER

051

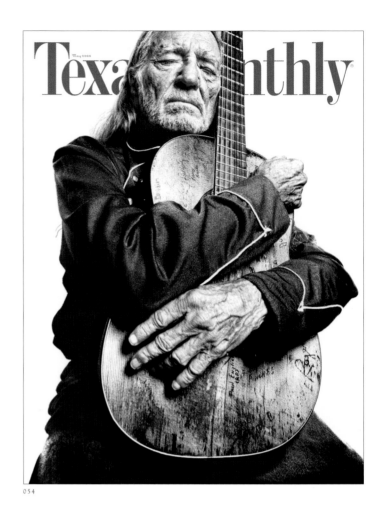

054

052

053

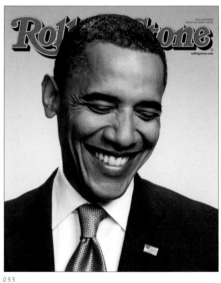

055

/051/ **TIME**
CREATIVE DIRECTOR: ARTHUR HOCHSTEIN
DESIGN DIRECTOR: HAL WOLVERTON / ART DIRECTOR: BEN THOMA
DESIGNER: PATRICK BOLECEK / PROJECT DIRECTOR: JOSÉ CABACO
STUDIO: EURORSCG / EDITOR-IN-CHIEF: JOHN HUEY / PUBLISHER: TIME INC.
ISSUE: MAY 12, 2008 / CATEGORY: DESIGN: COVER

/052/ **TIME**
ART DIRECTORS: ARTHUR HOCHSTEIN, CINDY HOFFMAN
DESIGNER: KARLSSON WILKER / CHIEF PICTURE EDITOR: ALICE GABRINER
EDITOR-IN-CHIEF: JOHN HUEY / PUBLISHER: TIME INC.
ISSUE: DECEMBER 22, 2008 / CATEGORY: DESIGN: COVER

/053/ **TIME**
ART DIRECTOR: ARTHUR HOCHSTEIN / CHIEF PICTURE EDITOR: ALICE GABRINER
PHOTOGRAPHER: SPENCER JONES / EDITOR-IN-CHIEF: JOHN HUEY
PUBLISHER: TIME INC. / ISSUE: JULY 7, 2008 / CATEGORY: DESIGN: COVER

/054/ **TEXAS MONTHLY**
ART DIRECTOR: T.J. TUCKER / DESIGNER: T.J. TUCKER
PHOTO EDITOR: LESLIE BALDWIN / PHOTOGRAPHER: PLATON
PUBLISHER: EMMIS COMMUNICATIONS CORP. / ISSUE: MAY 2008
CATEGORY: DESIGN: COVER

/055/ **ROLLING STONE**
ART DIRECTOR: JOSEPH HUTCHINSON / DESIGNER: JOSEPH HUTCHINSON
DIRECTOR OF PHOTOGRAPHY: JODI PECKMAN / PHOTOGRAPHER: PETER YANG
PUBLISHER: WENNER MEDIA / ISSUE: JULY 10-24, 2008 / CATEGORY: DESIGN: COVER

056

058

057

059

060

/056/ **NEW YORK**
DESIGN DIRECTOR: CHRIS DIXON / ART DIRECTOR: RANDY MINOR
DESIGNER: CHRIS DIXON / DIRECTOR OF PHOTOGRAPHY: JODY QUON
PHOTOGRAPHERS: BAOBA IMAGES, GETTY IMAGES
EDITOR-IN-CHIEF: / ADAM MOSS
PUBLISHER: NEW YORK MAGAZINE HOLDINGS, LLC
ISSUE: OCTOBER 27, 2008 / CATEGORY: DESIGN: COVER

/057/ **NEW YORK**
DESIGN DIRECTOR: CHRIS DIXON / ART DIRECTOR: RANDY MINOR
DESIGNER: CHRIS DIXON / DIRECTOR OF PHOTOGRAPHY: JODY QUON
PHOTOGRAPHER: MITCHELL FEINBERG / EDITOR-IN-CHIEF: ADAM MOSS
PUBLISHER: NEW YORK MAGAZINE HOLDINGS, LLC / ISSUE: JUNE 9, 2008
CATEGORY: DESIGN: COVER

/058/ **NEW YORK**
DESIGN DIRECTOR: CHRIS DIXON / ART DIRECTOR: RANDY MINOR
DESIGNER: CHRIS DIXON / DIRECTOR OF PHOTOGRAPHY: JODY QUON
PHOTOGRAPHER: TOM SCHIERLITZ / EDITOR-IN-CHIEF: ADAM MOSS
PUBLISHER: NEW YORK MAGAZINE HOLDINGS, LLC
ISSUE: JANUARY 14, 2008 / CATEGORY: DESIGN: COVER

/059/ **NEW YORK**
DESIGN DIRECTOR: CHRIS DIXON / ART DIRECTOR: RANDY MINOR / DESIGNER:
CHRIS DIXON / DIRECTOR OF PHOTOGRAPHY: JODY QUON / PHOTOGRAPHER: SETH
WENIG, AP / EDITOR-IN-CHIEF: ADAM MOSS / PUBLISHER: NEW YORK MAGAZINE
HOLDINGS, LLC / ISSUE: SEPTEMBER 29, 2008 / CATEGORY: DESIGN: COVER

/060/ **BUSINESS WEEK**
CREATIVE DIRECTOR: ANDREW HORTON / PHOTO EDITOR: RONNIE WEIL
PHOTOGRAPHERS: BRENDAN SMIALOWSKI, WIN MCNAMEE / PUBLISHER: MCGRAW-
HILL COMPANIES / ISSUE: OCTOBER 27, 2008 / CATEGORY: DESIGN: COVER

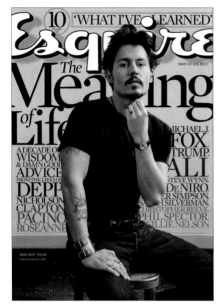

061

062

World's Greatest Bird Sculptor
The Best of New Orleans
Elvis Costello's Southern Attraction

GARDEN&GUN
SOUL *of the* NEW SOUTH

DEC. 2008/JAN. 2009

The Hidden Bahamas
30 New Reasons to Head South, Way South

The Natchez Trace by Motorcycle

How to Love a Woman's Dog
by Rick Bragg

The Great Camellia Experiment

Damn Good Duck Gumbo

A green turtle gets a lift on Andros Island

GARDENANDGUN.COM

063

/061/ **ESQUIRE**
DESIGN DIRECTOR: DAVID CURCURITO
ART DIRECTOR: DARHIL CROOKS
ASSOCIATE ART DIRECTOR: ERIN JANG
DESIGN ASSISTANT: SONI KHATRI
DIRECTOR OF PHOTOGRAPHY: MICHAEL NORSENG
PHOTO EDITOR: ALISON UNTERREINER
PHOTOGRAPHER: MARC HOM
EDITOR-IN-CHIEF: DAVID GRANGER
PUBLISHER: THE HEARST CORPORATION-
MAGAZINES DIVISION
ISSUE: JANUARY 2008
CATEGORY: DESIGN: COVER

/062/ **ESPN THE MAGAZINE**
CREATIVE DIRECTOR: SIUNG TJIA
DESIGNER: SIUNG TJIA
DIRECTOR OF PHOTOGRAPHY: CATRIONA NI AOLAIN
PHOTO EDITOR: NANCY WEISMAN
PHOTOGRAPHER: MICHAEL MULLER
EDITOR-IN-CHIEF: GARY BELSKY
PUBLISHER: ESPN, INC.
ISSUE: AUGUST 11, 2008
CATEGORY: DESIGN: COVER

/063/ **GARDEN & GUN**
ART DIRECTOR: MARSHALL MCKINNEY
DESIGNER: RICHIE SWANN
DIRECTOR OF PHOTOGRAPHY:
MAGGIE BRETT KENNEDY
PHOTOGRAPHER: ANDY ANDERSON
ISSUE: DECEMBER 2008/JANUARY 2009
CATEGORY: DESIGN: COVER

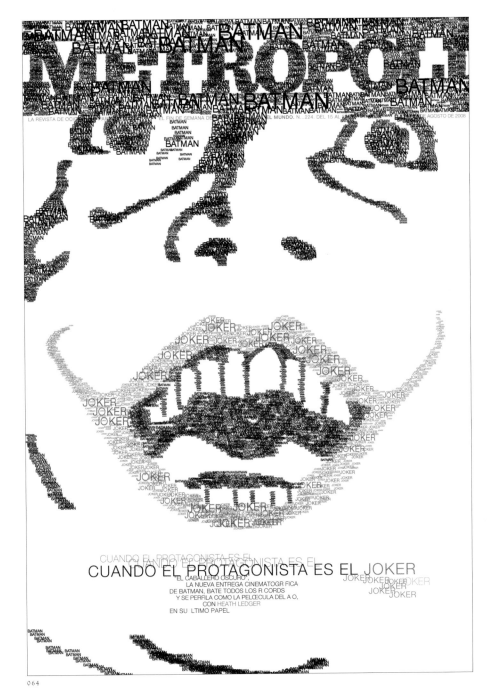

064

065

066

/064/ **METROPOLIS**
CREATIVE DIRECTOR: RODRIGO SÁNCHEZ
ART DIRECTOR: RODRIGO SÁNCHEZ
DESIGNER: RODRIGO SÁNCHEZ
PUBLISHER: UNIDAD EDITORIAL S.A.
ISSUE: AUGUST 15, 2008
CATEGORY: DESIGN: COVER

/065/ **METROPOLIS**
CREATIVE DIRECTOR: RODRIGO SÁNCHEZ
ART DIRECTOR: RODRIGO SÁNCHEZ
DESIGNER: RODRIGO SÁNCHEZ
PHOTOGRAPHER: ANGEL BECERRIL
PUBLISHER: UNIDAD EDITORIAL S.A.
ISSUE: NOVEMBER 14, 2008
CATEGORY: DESIGN: COVER

/066/ **TIME OUT NEW YORK**
DESIGN DIRECTOR: ADAM LOGAN FULRATH
ILLUSTRATOR: ANDRAOS AND WOOD
PUBLISHER: TIME OUT NEW YORK PARTNERS, L.P.
ISSUE: JUNE 12-18, 2008
CATEGORY: DESIGN: COVER

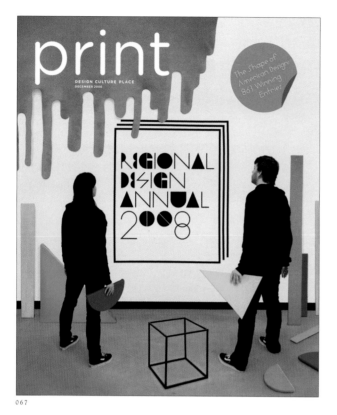

067

069

068

070

/067/ **PRINT**
ART DIRECTOR: KRISTINA DIMATTEO
ASSOCIATE ART DIRECTOR: LINDSAY BALLANT / ILLUSTRATOR: GLUEKIT
EDITOR-IN-CHIEF: JOYCE RUTTER KAYE / PUBLISHER: F & W MEDIA
ISSUE: DECEMBER 2008 / CATEGORY: DESIGN: COVER

/068/ **PRINT**
ART DIRECTOR: KRISTINA DIMATTEO
ASSOCIATE ART DIRECTOR: LINDSAY BALLANT
ILLUSTRATOR: KARSTEN SCHMIDT / EDITOR-IN-CHIEF: JOYCE RUTTER KAYE
PUBLISHER: F & W MEDIA / ISSUE: AUGUST 2008 / CATEGORY: DESIGN: COVER

/069/ **PRINT**
ART DIRECTOR: KRISTINA DIMATTEO
ASSOCIATE ART DIRECTOR: LINDSAY BALLANT / ILLUSTRATOR: STINA PERRSON
EDITOR-IN-CHIEF: JOYCE RUTTER KAYE / PUBLISHER: F & W MEDIA
ISSUE: APRIL 2008 / CATEGORY: DESIGN: COVER

/070/ **PRINT**
ART DIRECTOR: KRISTINA DIMATTEO
ASSOCIATE ART DIRECTOR: LINDSAY BALLANT / ILLUSTRATOR: GREG DUNCAN
EDITOR-IN-CHIEF: JOYCE RUTTER KAYE / PUBLISHER: F & W MEDIA
ISSUE: OCTOBER 2008 / CATEGORY: DESIGN: COVER

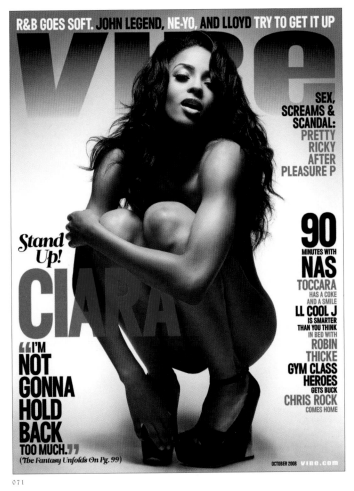

071

073

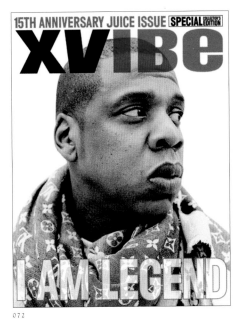

072

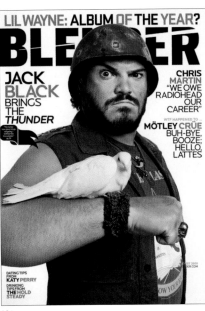

074

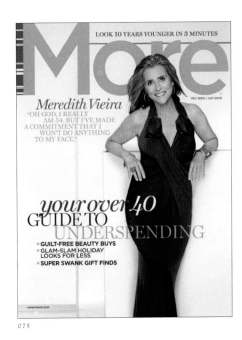

075

/071/ **VIBE**
ART DIRECTOR: MARK SHAW / PHOTO EDITOR: ROBYN FOREST
PHOTOGRAPHER: SIMON EMMETT / PUBLISHER: VIBE MEDIA GROUP LLC
ISSUE: OCTOBER 2008 / CATEGORY: DESIGN: COVER

/072/ **VIBE**
ART DIRECTOR: MARK SHAW / PHOTO EDITOR: ROBYN FOREST
PHOTOGRAPHER: LEANN MUELLER / PUBLISHER: VIBE MEDIA GROUP LLC
ISSUE: SEPTEMBER 2008 / CATEGORY: DESIGN: COVER

/073/ **ENTERTAINMENT WEEKLY**
DESIGN DIRECTOR: BRIAN ANSTEY / DIRECTOR OF PHOTOGRAPHY: LISA BERMAN
MANAGING EDITOR: RICK TETZELI / PUBLISHER: TIME INC. / ISSUE: OCTOBER 3,
2008 / CATEGORY: DESIGN: COVER

/074/ **BLENDER**
CREATIVE DIRECTOR: DIRK BARNETT / DESIGNER: DIRK BARNETT
DIRECTOR OF PHOTOGRAPHY: AMY HOPPY / PHOTOGRAPHER: GAVIN BOND
EDITOR-IN-CHIEF: JOE LEVY / PUBLISHER: ALPHAMEDIA GROUP
ISSUE: AUGUST 2008 / CATEGORY: DESIGN: COVER

/075/ **MORE**
CREATIVE DIRECTOR: DEBRA BISHOP / DESIGNER: DEBRA BISHOP
DIRECTOR OF PHOTOGRAPHY: KAREN FRANK / PHOTO EDITORS: DAISY CAJAS,
NATALIE GIALLUCA / PHOTOGRAPHER: MATTHEW ROLSTON
PUBLISHER: MEREDITH CORPORATION / ISSUE: DECEMBER 2008/JANUARY 2009
CATEGORY: DESIGN: COVER

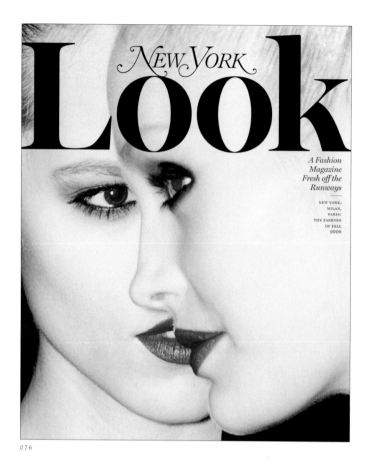

076

078

077

079

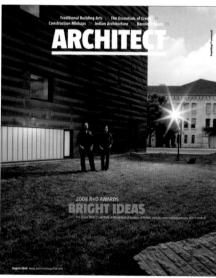

080

/076/ **LOOK NEW YORK**
DESIGN DIRECTOR: CHRIS DIXON / ART DIRECTOR: RANDY MINOR
DESIGNER: CHRIS DIXON / DIRECTOR OF PHOTOGRAPHY: JODY QUON
PHOTOGRAPHER: CHRISTOPHER ANDERSON/MAGNUM / EDITOR-IN-CHIEF:
ADAM MOSS / PUBLISHER: NEW YORK MAGAZINE HOLDINGS, LLC
ISSUE: FALL FASHION 2008 / CATEGORY: DESIGN: COVER

/077/ **REAL SIMPLE**
DESIGN DIRECTOR: ELLENE WUNDROK / DIRECTOR OF PHOTOGRAPHY: CASEY
TIERNEY / PHOTO EDITOR: ALLISON BONNANO / PHOTOGRAPHER: LUCAS ALLEN
PUBLISHER: TIME INC. / ISSUE: DECEMBER 2008 / CATEGORY: DESIGN: COVER

/078/ **KEY, THE NEW YORK TIMES REAL ESTATE MAGAZINE**
CREATIVE DIRECTOR: JANET FROELICH / ART DIRECTOR: JEFF GLENDENNING
DESIGNER: JEFF GLENDENNING / DIRECTOR OF PHOTOGRAPHY: KATHY RYAN
PHOTO EDITOR: JOANNA MILTER / PHOTOGRAPHER: THOMAS HANNICH
ARTWORK BY JURGEN BEY / EDITOR-IN-CHIEF: GERRY MARZORATI
PUBLISHER: THE NEW YORK TIMES / ISSUE: SPRING 2008
CATEGORY: DESIGN: COVER

/079/ **SPIN**
DESIGN DIRECTOR: DEVIN PEDZWATER / ART DIRECTOR: IAN ROBINSON
DESIGNER: LIZ MACFARLANE / DIRECTOR OF PHOTOGRAPHY: MICHELLE EGIZIANO
PHOTO EDITORS: GAVIN STEVENS, JENNIFER EDMONDSON / PHOTOGRAPHER:
HEDI SLIMANE / PUBLISHER: SPIN MEDIA LLC / ISSUE: FEBRUARY 2008
CATEGORY: DESIGN: COVER

/080/ **ARCHITECT**
ART DIRECTOR: AUBREY ALTMANN / DESIGNER: MARCY RYAN
PHOTOGRAPHER: NOAH KALINA / PUBLISHER: HANLEY WOOD
ISSUE: AUGUST 2008 / CATEGORY: DESIGN: COVER

081

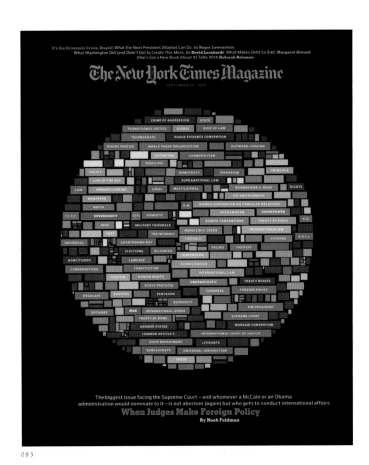

083

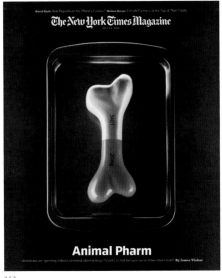

082

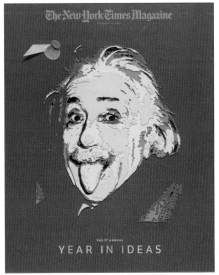

084

085

/081/ **THE NEW YORK TIMES MAGAZINE**
CREATIVE DIRECTOR: JANET FROELICH / ART DIRECTOR: AREM DUPLESSIS
DEPUTY ART DIRECTOR: GAIL BICHLER / DESIGNER: AREM DUPLESSIS
DIRECTOR OF PHOTOGRAPHY: KATHY RYAN / PHOTO EDITOR: KIRA POLLACK
PHOTOGRAPHER: RUVEN AFANADOR / EDITOR-IN-CHIEF: GERRY MARZORATI
PUBLISHER: THE NEW YORK TIMES / ISSUE: NOVEMBER 23, 2008
CATEGORY: DESIGN: COVER

/082/ **THE NEW YORK TIMES MAGAZINE**
CREATIVE DIRECTOR: JANET FROELICH / ART DIRECTOR: AREM DUPLESSIS
DEPUTY ART DIRECTOR: GAIL BICHLER / DESIGNER: GAIL BICHLER
DIRECTOR OF PHOTOGRAPHY: KATHY RYAN / PHOTO EDITOR: DAVID CARTHAS
PHOTOGRAPHER: ZACHARY SCOTT / EDITOR-IN-CHIEF: GERRY MARZORATI
PUBLISHER: THE NEW YORK TIMES / ISSUE: JULY 13, 2008
CATEGORY: DESIGN: COVER

/083/ **THE NEW YORK TIMES MAGAZINE**
CREATIVE DIRECTOR: JANET FROELICH / ART DIRECTOR: AREM DUPLESSIS
DEPUTY ART DIRECTOR: GAIL BICHLER / DESIGNER: AREM DUPLESSIS
ILLUSTRATORS: IAN ALLEN, AREM DUPLESSIS / EDITOR-IN-CHIEF: GERRY
MARZORATI / PUBLISHER: THE NEW YORK TIMES / ISSUE: SEPTEMBER 28, 2008
CATEGORY: DESIGN: COVER

/084/ **THE NEW YORK TIMES MAGAZINE**
CREATIVE DIRECTOR: JANET FROELICH / ART DIRECTOR: AREM DUPLESSIS
DEPUTY ART DIRECTOR: GAIL BICHLER / DESIGNER: LEO JUNG
DIRECTOR OF PHOTOGRAPHY: KATHY RYAN / PHOTO EDITOR: JOANNA MILTER
PHOTOGRAPHER: VIK MUNIZ / EDITOR-IN-CHIEF: GERRY MARZORATI
PUBLISHER: THE NEW YORK TIMES / ISSUE: DECEMBER 14, 2008
CATEGORY: DESIGN: COVER

/085/ **THE NEW YORK TIMES MAGAZINE**
CREATIVE DIRECTOR: JANET FROELICH / ART DIRECTOR: AREM DUPLESSIS
DEPUTY ART DIRECTOR: GAIL BICHLER / DESIGNERS: CATHERINE GILMORE-
BARNES, AREM DUPLESSIS / DIRECTOR OF PHOTOGRAPHY: KATHY RYAN
PHOTO EDITOR: JOANNA MILTER / PHOTOGRAPHER: MARTIN KLIMAS
EDITOR-IN-CHIEF: GERRY MARZORATI / PUBLISHER: THE NEW YORK TIMES
ISSUE: OCTOBER 12, 2008 / CATEGORY: DESIGN: COVER

086

088

090

087

089

091

/086/ **GOURMET**
CREATIVE DIRECTOR: RICHARD FERRETTI
ART DIRECTORS: RICHARD FERRETTI,
ERIKA OLIVEIRA
DESIGNER: RICHARD FERRETTI
PHOTO EDITOR: AMY KOBLENZER
PHOTOGRAPHER: JOHN KERNICK
EDITOR-IN-CHIEF: RUTH REICHL
PUBLISHER: CONDÉ NAST PUBLICATIONS, INC.
ISSUE: JANUARY 2008
CATEGORY: DESIGN: COVER

/087/ **GOURMET**
CREATIVE DIRECTOR: RICHARD FERRETTI
ART DIRECTORS: RICHARD FERRETTI,
ERIKA OLIVEIRA
DESIGNER: RICHARD FERRETTI
PHOTO EDITOR: AMY KOBLENZER
PHOTOGRAPHER: JOHN KERNICK
EDITOR-IN-CHIEF: RUTH REICHL
PUBLISHER: CONDÉ NAST PUBLICATIONS, INC.
ISSUE: AUGUST 2008
CATEGORY: DESIGN: COVER

/088/ **GOLF DIGEST**
DESIGN DIRECTOR: KEN DELAGO
DESIGNER: KEN DELAGO
PHOTO EDITOR: CHRISTIAN IOOSS
PHOTOGRAPHER: MARC HOM
PUBLISHER: CONDÉ NAST PUBLICATIONS INC.
ISSUE: NOVEMBER 2008
CATEGORY: DESIGN: COVER

/089/ **UD & SE**
DESIGN DIRECTOR: TORSTEN HOGH RASMUSSEN
PHOTOGRAPHER: RICKY MOLLOY
PUBLISHER: DSB
ISSUE: DECEMBER 2008
CATEGORY: DESIGN: COVER

/090/ **BON APPÉTIT**
DESIGN DIRECTOR: MATTHEW LENNING
DESIGNER: MATTHEW LENNING
PHOTO EDITOR: BAILEY FRANKLIN
PHOTOGRAPHER: TOM SCHIERLITZ
EDITOR-IN-CHIEF: BARBARA FAIRCHILD
PUBLISHER: CONDÉ NAST PUBLICATIONS, INC.
ISSUE: DECEMBER 2008
CATEGORY: DESIGN: COVER

/091/ **BON APPÉTIT**
DESIGN DIRECTOR: MATTHEW LENNING
ART DIRECTOR: ROBERT FESTINO
PHOTO EDITOR: LIZ MATHEWS
PHOTOGRAPHER: CRAIG CUTLER
EDITOR-IN-CHIEF: BARBARA FAIRCHILD
PUBLISHER: CONDÉ NAST PUBLICATIONS, INC.
ISSUE: MAY 2008
CATEGORY: DESIGN: COVER

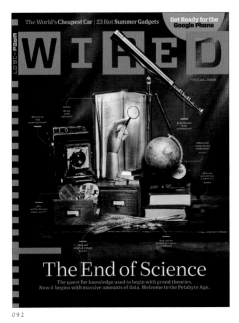

092

094

096

093

095

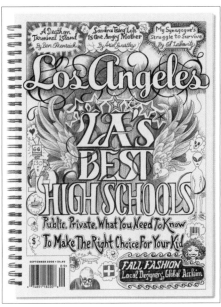

097

/092/ **WIRED**
CREATIVE DIRECTOR: SCOTT DADICH
DESIGN DIRECTOR: WYATT MITCHELL
DESIGNERS: SCOTT DADICH, WALTER C. BAUMANN
PHOTO EDITOR: CAROLYN RAUCH
PHOTOGRAPHER: PLAMEN PETKOV
PUBLISHER: CONDÉ NAST PUBLICATIONS, INC.
ISSUE: JULY 2008
CATEGORY: DESIGN: COVER

/093/ **WIRED**
CREATIVE DIRECTOR: SCOTT DADICH
DESIGN DIRECTOR: WYATT MITCHELL
DESIGNER: SCOTT DADICH
ILLUSTRATOR: BRYAN CHRISTIE
PUBLISHER: CONDÉ NAST PUBLICATIONS, INC.
ISSUE: APRIL 2008
CATEGORY: DESIGN: COVER

/094/ **GQ**
DESIGN DIRECTOR: FRED WOODWARD
DESIGNER: THOMAS ALBERTY
DIRECTOR OF PHOTOGRAPHY: DORA SOMOSI
PHOTOGRAPHER: MARK SELIGER
CREATIVE DIRECTOR, FASHION: JIM MOORE
EDITOR-IN-CHIEF: JIM NELSON
PUBLISHER: CONDÉ NAST PUBLICATIONS INC.
ISSUE: DECEMBER 2008
CATEGORY: DESIGN: COVER

/095/ **GQ**
DESIGN DIRECTOR: FRED WOODWARD
DESIGNER: THOMAS ALBERTY
DIRECTOR OF PHOTOGRAPHY: DORA SOMOSI
PHOTOGRAPHER: PEGGY SIROTA
CREATIVE DIRECTOR, FASHION: JIM MOORE
EDITOR-IN-CHIEF: JIM NELSON
PUBLISHER: CONDÉ NAST PUBLICATIONS INC.
ISSUE: AUGUST 2008
CATEGORY: DESIGN: COVER

/096/ **GOOD**
DESIGN DIRECTOR: SCOTT STOWELL
DESIGNER: RYAN THACKER
ILLUSTRATOR: RYAN THACKER
STUDIO: OPEN
PUBLISHER: GOOD WORLDWIDE, INC.
CLIENT: GOOD
ISSUE: SEPTEMBER/OCTOBER 2008
CATEGORY: DESIGN: COVER

/097/ **LOS ANGELES**
ART DIRECTOR: JOE KIMBERLING
DESIGNER: DEBBIE KIM
ILLUSTRATOR: MARIAN BANTJES
EDITOR-IN-CHIEF: KIT RACHLIS
PUBLISHER: EMMIS COMMUNICATIONS CORP.
ISSUE: SEPTEMBER 2008
CATEGORY: DESIGN: COVER

IT'S WHAT YOUR RIGHT ARM'S FOR | WE DO IT YOUR WAY
WE KEEP YOUR PROMISES | HEAD FOR THE BORDER
| ONE LEG AT A TIME
WE'RE NUMBER TWO. WE TRY HARDER | WOT A LOT I GOT
FINGER-LICKIN' GOOD
WHILE IN EUROPE, PICK UP AN UGLY EUROPEAN
A LITTLE DAB'LL DO YA
CLEANS ROUND THE BEND | GEE, I WISH I HAD A NICKEL
JUST IMAGINE | LIVE TODAY. TOMORROW WILL COST MORE
| ONLY 1 OUT OF 25 MEN IS COLOR BLIND. THE OTHER 24 JUST DRESS THAT WAY
STOPS HALITOSIS!
TASTE AS GOOD AS IT SMELLS | MAKE YOURSELF HEARD
WE SELL MORE CARS THAN FORD, CHRYSLER, CHEVROLET, AND BUICK COMBINED
LIMITED EDITION OF UNLIMITED IDEAS
PURE GENIUS | IT IS. ARE YOU?
| PREPARE TO WANT ONE
SOFT, STRONG AND VERY LONG | THINK DIFFERENT
IT'S SO BIG, YOU'VE GOTTA GRIN TO GET IT IN |
HELLO BOYS | BLOW SOME MY WAY
THE GENUINE ARTICLE | COME TO WHERE THE FLAVOR IS

098

DESIGN WITH WHISPERS

JM

Jasper Morrison projektuje zwyczajne przedmioty dla każdego, lekkie, o łagodnej linii, naprowadzające do używania. Wyglądają tak, jakby nikt ich nie projektował. Jasper Morrison designs light, fronting everyday products for everyone's use. The objects look as if they weren't designed at all.

098

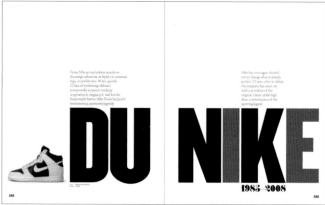

DU NIKE
1985–2008

Firma Nike po raz kolejny wyszła ze słusznego założenia, że lepiej nie zmieniać tego, co perfekcyjne. W tym sposób 23 lata od rynkowego debiutu postanowiła wypuścić rewizję oryginalnych, stających się nad kostką klasycznych butów Nike Dunk będących reminiscencją sportowej legendy.

Nike has once again decided not to change what is already perfect. 23 years after its debut, the company has came out with a re-edition of the original, classic ankle-high shoe, a reminiscence of the sporting legend.

098

RUN
AWAY
BRANDs

TEST — HELENA CHMIELEWSKA-SZLAJFER

Marka, której wizerunek wymknął się odgórnym ustaleniom specjalistów, to spełnienie najgorszych marketingowych snów. Co więcej, przytrafiło się to niejednej z tych o zbyt wielkim, jak się okazało, apetycie na masowy rynek A brand image that has escaped the control of specialists is marketing's worst nightmare. What's more, it has happened to more than one brand with too big of an appetite for the market

132
133

098

/098/ **FUTU MAGAZINE**
DESIGN DIRECTOR: MATT WILLEY / DESIGNER: MATT WILLEY / STUDIO: STUDIO8 DESIGN
EDITOR-IN-CHIEF: MARTYNA BEDNARSKA-CWIEK / PUBLISHER: PUBLISHING & DESIGN GROUP
CLIENT PUBLISHING & DESIGN GROUP / ISSUE: AUTUMN/WINTER 2008 / CATEGORY: DESIGN: ENTIRE ISSUE

099

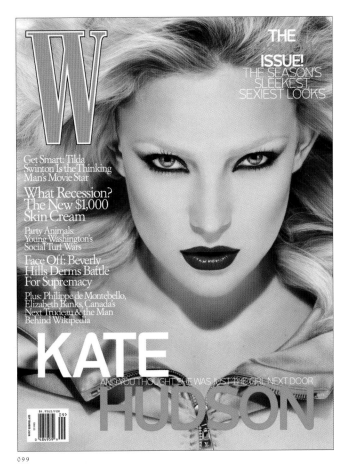

099

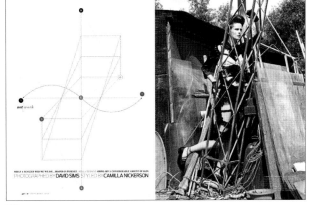

099

099

/099/ W
CREATIVE DIRECTOR: DENNIS FREEDMAN / DESIGN DIRECTOR: EDWARD LEIDA / ART DIRECTOR: NATHALIE KIRSHEH / DESIGNERS: LAURA KONRAD,
GINA MANISCALCO / PHOTO EDITOR: NADIA VELLAM / PHOTOGRAPHERS: JACKIE NICKERSON, DAVID SIMS, MERT ALAS, MARCUS PIGGOTT
PUBLISHER: CONDÉ NAST PUBLICATIONS INC. / ISSUE: SEPTEMBER 2008 / CATEGORY: DESIGN: ENTIRE ISSUE

100

100

101

101

102

102

/100/ **GQ**
DESIGN DIRECTOR: FRED WOODWARD
ART DIRECTOR: ANTON IOUKHNOVETS
DESIGNERS: THOMAS ALBERTY,
DRUE WAGNER, CHELSEA CARDINAL,
DELGIS CANAHUATE, ROB HEWITT
ILLUSTRATOR: ZOHAR LAZAR
DIRECTOR OF PHOTOGRAPHY: DORA SOMOSI
PHOTO EDITORS: KRISTA PRESTEK,
JUSTIN O'NEILL, JESSE LEE, EMILY ROSENBERG,
JOLANTA BIELAT, TOBY KAUFMANN
EDITOR-IN-CHIEF: JIM NELSON
PUBLISHER: CONDÉ NAST PUBLICATIONS INC.
ISSUE: AUGUST 2008
CATEGORY: DESIGN: ENTIRE ISSUE

/101/ **GQ**
DESIGN DIRECTOR: FRED WOODWARD
ART DIRECTOR: ANTON IOUKHNOVETS
DESIGNERS: THOMAS ALBERTY, DRUE WAGNER,
CHELSEA CARDINAL, DELGIS CANAHUATE,
ROB HEWITT, MICHAEL PANGILINAN
DIRECTOR OF PHOTOGRAPHY: DORA SOMOSI
PHOTO EDITORS: KRISTA PRESTEK,
JUSTIN O'NEILL, JESSE LEE, EMILY ROSENBERG,
JOLANTA BIELAT, TOBY KAUFMANN
CREATIVE DIRECTOR, FASHION: JIM MOORE
EDITOR-IN-CHIEF: JIM NELSON
PUBLISHER: CONDÉ NAST PUBLICATIONS INC.
ISSUE: APRIL 2008
CATEGORY: DESIGN: ENTIRE ISSUE

/102/ **GQ**
DESIGN DIRECTOR: FRED WOODWARD
ART DIRECTOR: ANTON IOUKHNOVETS
DESIGNERS: THOMAS ALBERTY, DRUE WAGNER,
CHELSEA CARDINAL, DELGIS CANAHUATE,
ROB HEWITT, EVE BINDER
DIRECTOR OF PHOTOGRAPHY: DORA SOMOSI
PHOTO EDITORS: KRISTA PRESTEK,
JUSTIN O'NEILL, JESSE LEE, EMILY ROSENBERG,
JOLANTA BIELAT, TOBY KAUFMANN
CREATIVE DIRECTOR, FASHION: JIM MOORE
EDITOR-IN-CHIEF: JIM NELSON
PUBLISHER: CONDÉ NAST PUBLICATIONS INC.
ISSUE: JANUARY 2008
CATEGORY: DESIGN: ENTIRE ISSUE

103

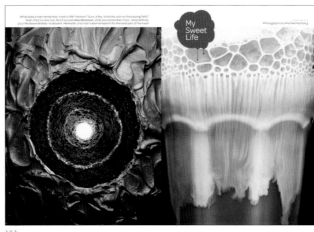

383

103

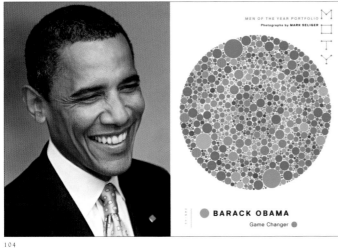

BARACK OBAMA
Game Changer

104

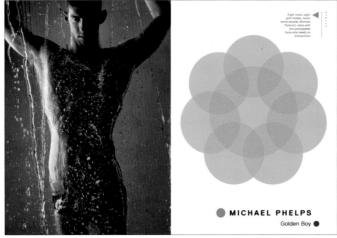

MICHAEL PHELPS
Golden Boy

104

/103/ **GQ**
DESIGN DIRECTOR: FRED WOODWARD
ART DIRECTOR: ANTON IOUKHNOVETS
DESIGNERS: THOMAS ALBERTY, DRUE WAGNER, CHELSEA CARDINAL,
DELGIS CANAHUATE, ROB HEWITT
ILLUSTRATORS: JOHN RITTER, ZOHAR LAZAR, PETER ARKLE, KNICKERBOCKER DESIGN
DIRECTOR OF PHOTOGRAPHY: DORA SOMOSI
PHOTO EDITORS: KRISTA PRESTEK, JUSTIN O'NEILL, JESSE LEE,
EMILY ROSENBERG, JOLANTA BIELAT, TOBY KAUFMANN
PHOTOGRAPHERS: INEZ VAN LAMSWEERDE & VINOODH MATADIN,
TOM SCHIERLITZ, GEOF KERN, HORACIO SALINAS, NATHANIEL GOLDBERG,
GILLIAN LAUB, JAMES NACHTWEY, ANDERS OVERGAARD, NADAV KANDER,
ELLEN VON UNWERTH, MITCHELL FEINBERG
CREATIVE DIRECTOR, FASHION: JIM MOORE
EDITOR-IN-CHIEF: JIM NELSON
PUBLISHER: CONDÉ NAST PUBLICATIONS INC. / ISSUE: JULY 2008
CATEGORY: DESIGN: ENTIRE ISSUE

/104/ **GQ**
DESIGN DIRECTOR: FRED WOODWARD
ART DIRECTOR: ANTON IOUKHNOVETS
DESIGNERS: THOMAS ALBERTY, DRUE WAGNER,
CHELSEA CARDINAL, DELGIS CANAHUATE
DIRECTOR OF PHOTOGRAPHY: DORA SOMOSI
PHOTO EDITORS: KRISTA PRESTEK, JUSTIN O'NEILL,
JESSE LEE, EMILY ROSENBERG, JOLANTA BIELAT,
TOBY KAUFMANN
CREATIVE DIRECTOR, FASHION: JIM MOORE
EDITOR-IN-CHIEF: JIM NELSON
PUBLISHER: CONDÉ NAST PUBLICATIONS INC.
ISSUE: DECEMBER 2008
CATEGORY: DESIGN: ENTIRE ISSUE

10.12.08 Style

FOOD

Fighters

Young leaders who are changing the way we eat (and drink).

By CHRISTINE MUHLKE

Severine von Tscharner Fleming, 27
Filmmaker, advocate
Nevis, N.Y.

In college, Severine von Tscharner Fleming's "violent allergic reaction to L.A." drove her to help set up a guerrilla farming club, visit farmers on the West Coast in a vegetable-oil pickup truck and form the Society for Agriculture and Food Ecology at the University of California, Berkeley. Now von Tscharner Fleming, the child of urban planners from Cambridge, Mass., wants her peers to get dirty. "Farming is an attractive path for people who are getting out of school and feeling like there's kind of a toxic consumerism and not feeling too excited about working for the Man, especially seeing as he's been spoiling our politics and a lot of our ecology," she said. She started serveyourcountryfood.net, an interactive map charting farmers under 40, and is making "The Greenhorns," a documentary on "organic entrepreneurs." "I want to show how sweet and honest and brave and purposeful they are," she said of her subjects. With an office in the village of Red Hook and farmland she is renting in the Hudson River Valley, von Tscharner Fleming knows she needs to go beyond the field in order to effect real policy change: "They're making some kind of sausage in Washington, and I felt like some young farmer flavor would be appropriate."

Photographs by LARS TUNBJÖRK

79

SEASONAL FAST FOOD For decades, fast-food menus have remained stubbornly resistant to the whims of the seasons. But as some innovative fast-food restaurants have begun to source their food locally, they have given birth to something entirely new in the industry. At Burgerville, a family-owned chain with 39 restaurants in Oregon and Washington, the Walla Walla sweet-onion rings are available only during the summer. "You can't freeze or dry these onions, or they'll lose their texture and taste," says Burgerville's Jack Graves. Similarly, the blackberry milkshake — made from fresh berries picked at Leopold Farms in Boring, Ore. — is available only from July to September, followed in the fall by limited-time seasonal arugula and nutit-melon smoothies. And the trend is spreading: Larger chains like Panera Bread have introduced items like summer-corn chowder, and in Maine, McDonald's sometimes even offers a lobster roll. CHARLES WILSON

FARMER

In Chief

What the next president can
and should do to remake the way
we grow and eat our food.

By MICHAEL POLLAN

Dear Mr. President-Elect,
It may surprise you to learn that among the issues that will occupy much of your time in the coming years is one you barely mentioned during the campaign: food. Food policy is not something American presidents have had to give much thought to, at least since the Nixon administration — the last time high food prices presented a serious political peril. Since then, federal policies to promote maximum production of the commodity crops (corn, soybeans, wheat and rice) from which most of our supermarket foods are derived have succeeded impressively in keeping prices low and food more or less off the national political agenda. But with a suddenness that has taken us all by surprise, the era of cheap and abundant food appears to be drawing to a close. What this means is that you, like so many other leaders through history, will find yourself confronting the fact — so easy to overlook these past few

Photographs by ERWAN FROTIN

62

/105/ THE NEW YORK TIMES MAGAZINE
CREATIVE DIRECTOR: JANET FROELICH / ART DIRECTOR: AREM DUPLESSIS / DEPUTY ART DIRECTOR: GAIL BICHLER
DESIGNERS: CATHERINE GILMORE-BARNES, IAN ALLEN / DIRECTOR OF PHOTOGRAPHY: KATHY RYAN / PHOTO EDITOR: JOANNA MILTER
EDITOR-IN-CHIEF: GERRY MARZORATI / PUBLISHER: THE NEW YORK TIMES / ISSUE: OCTOBER 12, 2008 / CATEGORY: DESIGN: ENTIRE ISSUE

Crowded House

A firm based in Rotterdam
solves the problem of too many people on too small
a planet by tunneling down,
packing tight and making pigs fly.
By Darcy Frey

PHOTOGRAPH BY JULIAN FAULHABER

In the fall of 2002, a young Dutch architect named Winy Maas came to Yale to give a lecture on designing and building the 21st-century city, the challenges of which he illustrated by showing a 30-second video that could have been shot above any American metropolitan airport: a view of the tops of several buildings and then, as the camera rose, more and more buildings, more roads and bridges and asphalt lots, until an ugly concrete skin of low-rise development spread to all horizons. Maas was not the first architect to protest the unsightly sprawl that humans have left over much of the earth's surface, but he may have been the first to suggest that we preserve what's left of our finite planetary space by creating "vertical suburbia" — stacking all those quarter-acre plots into high-rise residential towers, each with its own hanging, cantilevered yard. "Imagine: It's Saturday afternoon, and all the barbecues are running," Maas said, unveiling his

Urban Flight. WoZoCos, a housing complex for Amsterdamers 55 and older.

54

The New, New City

Shenzhen and Dubai may
have outstripped Paris and New York as civic models.
But can an instant city ever feel
like the real thing?
By Nicolai Ouroussoff

PHOTOGRAPHS BY SZE TSUNG LEONG

"Don't tell anyone," Rem Koolhaas said to me several years ago as we headed down the F.D.R. Drive in New York, "but the 20th-century city is over. It has nothing new to teach us anymore. Our job is simply to maintain it." Koolhaas's viewpoint is widely shared by close observers of the evolution of cities. But not even Koolhaas, it seems, was completely prepared for what would come next.

In both China and the Persian Gulf, cities comparable in size to New York have sprouted up almost overnight. Only 30 years ago, Shenzhen was a small fishing village of a few thousand people, and Dubai had merely a quarter million people. Today Shenzhen has a population of eight million, and Dubai's glittering towers, rising out of the desert in disorderly rows, have become playgrounds for wealthy expatriates from Riyadh and Moscow. Long-established

New Shenzhen Encircles Old. In the center, one of the city's original urban villages, with its signature "handshake buildings" — so close together you could reach across to your neighbor.

70

/106/ **THE NEW YORK TIMES MAGAZINE**
CREATIVE DIRECTOR: JANET FROELICH / ART DIRECTOR: AREM DUPLESSIS / DEPUTY ART DIRECTOR: GAIL BICHLER
DESIGNERS: LEO JUNG, IAN ALLEN, JULIA MOBURG / DIRECTOR OF PHOTOGRAPHY: KATHY RYAN / PHOTO EDITOR: JOANNA MILTER
EDITOR-IN-CHIEF: GERRY MARZORATI / PUBLISHER: THE NEW YORK TIMES / ISSUE: JUNE 8, 2008 / CATEGORY: DESIGN: ENTIRE ISSUE

107

107

108

108

109

109

/107/ GLAMOUR
DESIGN DIRECTOR: GERALDINE HESSLER
ART DIRECTOR: THERESA GRIGGS
DIRECTOR OF PHOTOGRAPHY: SUZANNE DONALDSON
PUBLISHER: CONDÉ NAST PUBLICATIONS INC.
ISSUE: NOVEMBER 2008
CATEGORY: DESIGN: ENTIRE ISSUE

/108/ GLAMOUR
DESIGN DIRECTOR: GERALDINE HESSLER
ART DIRECTOR: THERESA GRIGGS
DIRECTOR OF PHOTOGRAPHY: SUZANNE DONALDSON
PUBLISHER: CONDÉ NAST PUBLICATIONS INC.
ISSUE: SEPTEMBER 2008
CATEGORY: DESIGN: ENTIRE ISSUE

/109/ W
DESIGN DIRECTOR: EDWARD LEIDA
ART DIRECTOR: NATHALIE KIRSHEH
DESIGNERS: LAURA KONRAD, GINA MANISCALCO
PHOTOGRAPHERS: BRAD PITT,
JUERGEN TELLER, JOEL STERNFELD
PUBLISHER: CONDÉ NAST PUBLICATIONS INC.
ISSUE: NOVEMBER 2008
CATEGORY: DESIGN: ENTIRE ISSUE

Vintage Spirits

110

110

111

111

112

112

/110/ **BON APPÉTIT**
DESIGN DIRECTOR: MATTHEW LENNING
ART DIRECTORS: ROBERT FESTINO,
TOM O'QUINN, CHRISTINE PARK
ILLUSTRATORS: JOEL HOLLAND, MASA,
CHRISTOPH NIEMANN, JASON LEE,
MONTSE BERNAL, BRIAN REA
PHOTO EDITORS: BAILEY FRANKLIN,
LIZ MATHEWS, ANGELICA MISTRO
PHOTOGRAPHER: TOM SCHIERLITZ
EDITOR-IN-CHIEF: BARBARA FAIRCHILD
PUBLISHER: CONDÉ NAST PUBLICATIONS, INC.
ISSUE: DECEMBER 2008
CATEGORY: DESIGN: ENTIRE ISSUE

/111/ **BLENDER**
CREATIVE DIRECTOR: DIRK BARNETT
ART DIRECTORS: ROBERT VARGAS,
CLAUDIA DE ALMEIDA
DESIGNERS: DIRK BARNETT, ROBERT VARGAS,
CLAUDIA DE ALMEIDA
ILLUSTRATORS: EDEL RODRIQUEZ, BOB LONDON,
ANDY FRIEDMAN, JAMESON SIMPSON,
AUTUMN WHITEHURST
DIRECTOR OF PHOTOGRAPHY: DAVID CARTHAS
PHOTO EDITORS: CHRIS EHRMANN, RORY WALSH
PHOTOGRAPHERS: MIKO LIM, BRENT HUMPHREYS,
STEVEN BRAHMS, BRYCE DUFFY,
TURE LILLEGRAVEN, DEAN CHALKLEY
EDITOR-IN-CHIEF: JOE LEVY
PUBLISHER: ALPHAMEDIA GROUP
ISSUE: JULY 2008
CATEGORY: DESIGN: ENTIRE ISSUE

/112/ **BLENDER**
CREATIVE DIRECTOR: DIRK BARNETT
ART DIRECTORS: ROBERT VARGAS,
CLAUDIA DE ALMEIDA
DESIGNERS: DIRK BARNETT, ROBERT VARGAS,
CLAUDIA DE ALMEIDA
ILLUSTRATORS: SERGE SIEDLITZ, JOHN RICE,
ANDY FRIEDMAN, AUTUMN WHITEHURST,
ADHEMAS BATISTA, JASON LEE
DIRECTOR OF PHOTOGRAPHY: AMY HOPPY
PHOTOGRAPHERS: GAVIN BOND, JAKE CHESSUM,
ANTONIN KRATOCHVIL, BRYAN SHEFFIELD,
RONY ALWIN
EDITOR-IN-CHIEF: JOE LEVY
PUBLISHER: ALPHAMEDIA GROUP
ISSUE: AUGUST 2008
CATEGORY: DESIGN: ENTIRE ISSUE

113

113

113

/113/ **MORE**
CREATIVE DIRECTOR: DEBRA BISHOP / ART DIRECTOR: JOSE FERNANDEZ / DESIGNERS: JENN MCMANUS, SUSANNE BAMBERGER, CYBELE GRANDJEAN
ILLUSTRATORS: CHRISTOPHER SILAS NEAL, NATASHA TIBBOTT, ZOHAR LAZAR, QUICKHONEY / DIRECTOR OF PHOTOGRAPHY: KAREN FRANK
PHOTO EDITORS: DAISY CAJAS, NATALIE GIALLUCA / PHOTOGRAPHERS: MATTHEW ROLSTON, ART STREIBER, ROBERT TRACHTENBERG, JESSICA ANTOLA,
FREDRIK BRODEN, CHARLES MASTERS / PUBLISHER: MEREDITH CORPORATION / ISSUE: NOVEMBER 2008 / CATEGORY: DESIGN: ENTIRE ISSUE

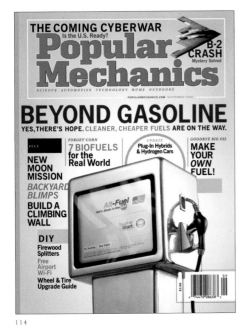

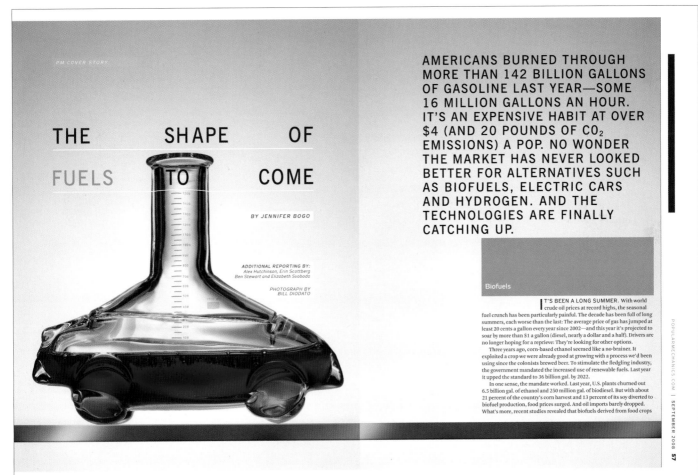

PM. COVER STORY.

THE SHAPE OF FUELS TO COME

BY JENNIFER BOGO

ADDITIONAL REPORTING BY:
Alex Hutchinson, Erin Scottberg
Ben Stewart and Elizabeth Svoboda

PHOTOGRAPH BY
BILL DIODATO

AMERICANS BURNED THROUGH MORE THAN 142 BILLION GALLONS OF GASOLINE LAST YEAR—SOME 16 MILLION GALLONS AN HOUR. IT'S AN EXPENSIVE HABIT AT OVER $4 (AND 20 POUNDS OF CO$_2$ EMISSIONS) A POP. NO WONDER THE MARKET HAS NEVER LOOKED BETTER FOR ALTERNATIVES SUCH AS BIOFUELS, ELECTRIC CARS AND HYDROGEN. AND THE TECHNOLOGIES ARE FINALLY CATCHING UP.

Biofuels

IT'S BEEN A LONG SUMMER. With world crude oil prices at record highs, the seasonal fuel crunch has been particularly painful. The decade has been full of long summers, each worse than the last: The average price of gas has jumped at least 20 cents a gallon every year since 2002—and this year it's projected to soar by more than $1 a gallon (diesel, nearly a dollar and a half). Drivers are no longer hoping for a reprieve: They're looking for other options.

Three years ago, corn-based ethanol seemed like a no-brainer. It exploited a crop we were already good at growing with a process we'd been using since the colonists brewed beer. To stimulate the fledgling industry, the government mandated the increased use of renewable fuels. Last year it upped the standard to 36 billion gal. by 2022.

In one sense, the mandate worked. Last year, U.S. plants churned out 6.5 billion gal. of ethanol and 250 million gal. of biodiesel. But with about 21 percent of the country's corn harvest and 13 percent of its soy diverted to biofuel production, food prices surged. And oil imports barely dropped. What's more, recent studies revealed that biofuels derived from food crops

POPULARMECHANICS.COM | SEPTEMBER 2008 57

/114/ **POPULAR MECHANICS**
DESIGN DIRECTOR: MICHAEL LAWTON / SENIOR ART DIRECTOR: PETER HERBERT / ASSOCIATE ART DIRECTOR: STRAVINSKI PIERRE
SENIOR DESIGNER: BRADLEY R. HUGHES / DIRECTOR OF PHOTOGRAPHY: ALLYSON TORRISI / PHOTO EDITOR: MICHELE ERVIN
DIGITAL IMAGING SPECIALIST: ANTHONY VERDUCCI / EDITOR-IN-CHIEF: JAMES B. MEIGS / PUBLISHER: THE HEARST CORPORATION-
MAGAZINES DIVISION / ISSUE: SEPTEMBER 2008 / CATEGORY: DESIGN: ENTIRE ISSUE

115

116

116

/115/ NEW YORK
DESIGN DIRECTOR: CHRIS DIXON
ART DIRECTOR: RANDY MINOR
DESIGNERS: CHRIS DIXON, RANDY MINOR,
HITOMI SATO, KATIE VAN SYCKLE, HILARY
FITZGIBBONS, CAROL HAYES, JEFF GLENDENNING
DIRECTOR OF PHOTOGRAPHY: JODY QUON
EDITOR-IN-CHIEF: ADAM MOSS
PUBLISHER: NEW YORK MAGAZINE HOLDINGS, LLC
ISSUE: OCTOBER 6, 2008
CATEGORY: DESIGN: ENTIRE ISSUE

/116/ NEW YORK
DESIGN DIRECTOR: CHRIS DIXON
ART DIRECTOR: RANDY MINOR
DESIGNERS: CHRIS DIXON, RANDY MINOR,
HITOMI SATO, KATIE VAN SYCKLE, CAROL HAYES,
CAROLINE JACKSON
DIRECTOR OF PHOTOGRAPHY: JODY QUON
EDITOR-IN-CHIEF: ADAM MOSS
PUBLISHER: NEW YORK MAGAZINE HOLDINGS, LLC
ISSUE: JUNE 23, 2008
CATEGORY: DESIGN: ENTIRE ISSUE

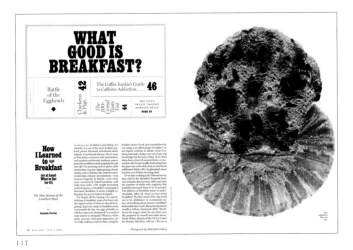

117

117

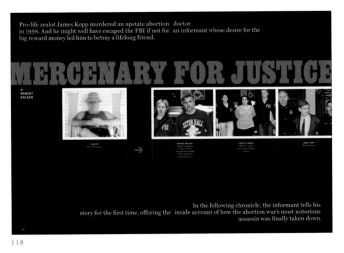

118

118

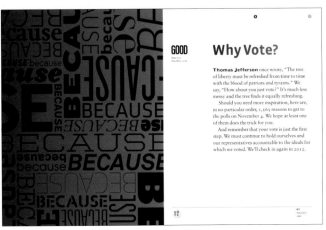

119

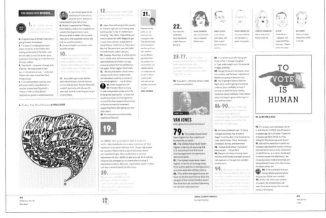

119

/117/ **NEW YORK**
DESIGN DIRECTOR: CHRIS DIXON
ART DIRECTOR: RANDY MINOR
DESIGNERS: CHRIS DIXON, RANDY MINOR,
HITOMI SATO, KATIE VAN SYCKLE, CAROL HAYES
DIRECTOR OF PHOTOGRAPHY: JODY QUON
EDITOR-IN-CHIEF: ADAM MOSS
PUBLISHER: NEW YORK MAGAZINE HOLDINGS, LLC
ISSUE: JUNE 9, 2008
CATEGORY: DESIGN: ENTIRE ISSUE

/118/ **NEW YORK**
DESIGN DIRECTOR: CHRIS DIXON
ART DIRECTOR: RANDY MINOR
DESIGNERS: CHRIS DIXON, RANDY MINOR, HITOMI
SATO, KATIE VAN SYCKLE, CAROL HAYES, HILARY
FITZGIBBONS
DIRECTOR OF PHOTOGRAPHY: JODY QUON
EDITOR-IN-CHIEF: ADAM MOSS
PUBLISHER: NEW YORK MAGAZINE HOLDINGS, LLC
ISSUE: NOVEMBER 10, 2008
CATEGORY: DESIGN: ENTIRE ISSUE

/119/ **GOOD**
DESIGN DIRECTOR: SCOTT STOWELL
DESIGNERS: ROB DILESO, SERIFCAN OZCAN,
RYAN THACKER
STUDIO: OPEN
PUBLISHER: GOOD WORLDWIDE, INC.
CLIENT: GOOD
ISSUE: NOVEMBER/DECEMBER 2008
CATEGORY: DESIGN: ENTIRE ISSUE

120

120

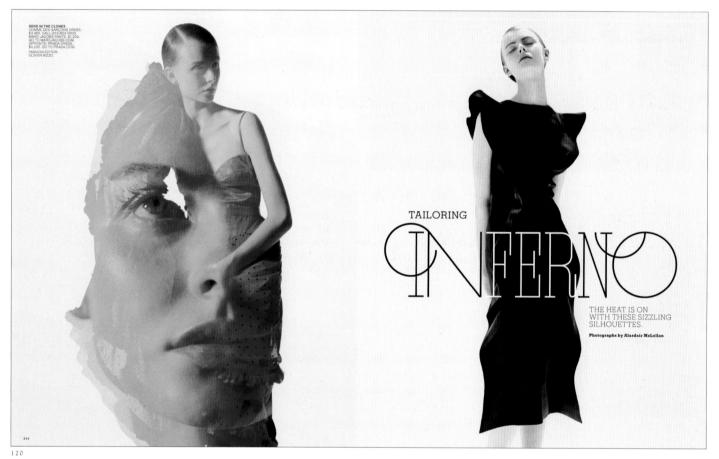

120

/120/ **T, THE NEW YORK TIMES STYLE MAGAZINE**
CREATIVE DIRECTOR: JANET FROELICH / SENIOR ART DIRECTOR: DAVID SEBBAH / ART DIRECTOR: CHRISTOPHER MARTINEZ / SENIOR DESIGNER: ELIZABETH SPIRIDAKIS
DIRECTOR OF PHOTOGRAPHY: KATHY RYAN / SENIOR PHOTO EDITOR: JUDITH PUCKETT-RINELLA / PHOTO EDITOR: SCOTT HALL / EDITOR-IN-CHIEF: STEFANO TONCHI
PUBLISHER: THE NEW YORK TIMES / ISSUE: AUGUST 17, 2008 / CATEGORY: DESIGN: ENTIRE ISSUE

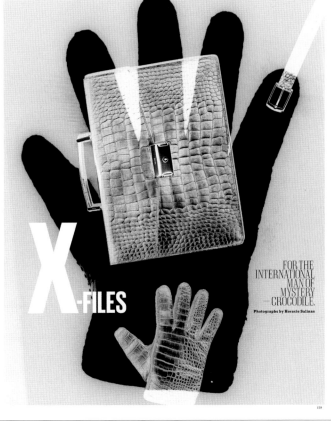

/121/ T, THE NEW YORK TIMES STYLE MAGAZINE
CREATIVE DIRECTOR: JANET FROELICH / SENIOR ART DIRECTOR: DAVID SEBBAH / ART DIRECTOR: CHRISTOPHER MARTINEZ / SENIOR DESIGNER: ELIZABETH SPIRIDAKIS
DIRECTOR OF PHOTOGRAPHY: KATHY RYAN / SENIOR PHOTO EDITOR: JUDITH PUCKETT-RINELLA / PHOTO EDITOR: SCOTT HALL / EDITOR-IN-CHIEF: STEFANO TONCHI
PUBLISHER: THE NEW YORK TIMES / ISSUE: SEPTEMBER 7, 2008 / CATEGORY: DESIGN: ENTIRE ISSUE

122

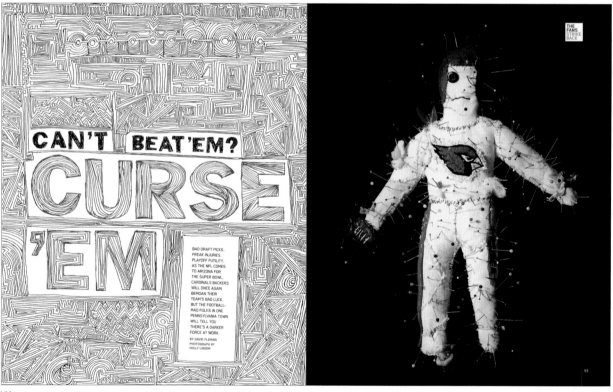

123

/122/ **GQ**
DESIGN DIRECTOR: FRED WOODWARD
DESIGNER: ANTON IOUKHNOVETS
DIRECTOR OF PHOTOGRAPHY: DORA SOMOSI
EDITOR-IN-CHIEF: JIM NELSON
PUBLISHER: CONDÉ NAST PUBLICATIONS INC.
ISSUE: JUNE 2008
CATEGORY: DESIGN: FEATURE: SERVICE
(SINGLE/SPREAD)

/123/ **ESPN THE MAGAZINE**
CREATIVE DIRECTOR: SIUNG TJIA
DESIGNER: JASON LANCASTER
DIRECTOR OF PHOTOGRAPHY: CATRIONA NI AOLAIN
PHOTO EDITOR: NANCY WEISMAN
PHOTOGRAPHER: HOLLY LINDEM
EDITOR-IN-CHIEF: GARY BELSKY
PUBLISHER: ESPN, INC.
ISSUE: FEBRUARY 11, 2008
CATEGORY: DESIGN: FEATURE: SERVICE
(SINGLE/SPREAD)

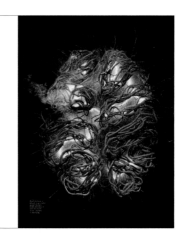

124

127

125

128

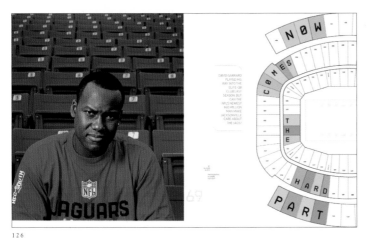

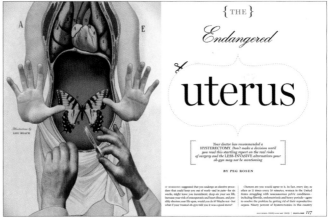

126

129

/124/ ESPN THE MAGAZINE
CREATIVE DIRECTOR: SIUNG TJIA
DESIGNER: JASON LANCASTER
DIRECTOR OF PHOTOGRAPHY: CATRIONA NI AOLAIN
PHOTO EDITOR: NANCY WEISMAN
PHOTOGRAPHER: GREG MILLER
EDITOR-IN-CHIEF: GARY BELSKY
PUBLISHER: ESPN, INC.
ISSUE: MAY 5, 2008
CATEGORY: DESIGN: FEATURE: SERVICE
(SINGLE/SPREAD)

/125/ ESPN THE MAGAZINE
CREATIVE DIRECTOR: SIUNG TJIA
DESIGNER: LOU VEGA
DIRECTOR OF PHOTOGRAPHY: CATRIONA NI AOLAIN
PHOTO EDITOR: MAISIE TODD
PHOTOGRAPHER: PEGGY SIROTA
EDITOR-IN-CHIEF: GARY BELSKY
PUBLISHER: ESPN, INC.
ISSUE: APRIL 21, 2008
CATEGORY: DESIGN: FEATURE: SERVICE
(SINGLE/SPREAD)

/126/ ESPN THE MAGAZINE
CREATIVE DIRECTOR: SIUNG TJIA
DESIGNER: JASON LANCASTER
DIRECTOR OF PHOTOGRAPHY: CATRIONA NI AOLAIN
PHOTO EDITOR: SHAWN VALE
PHOTOGRAPHER: MARK HEITHOFF
EDITOR-IN-CHIEF: GARY BELSKY
PUBLISHER: ESPN, INC.
ISSUE: MAY 19, 2008
CATEGORY: DESIGN: FEATURE: SERVICE
(SINGLE/SPREAD)

/127/ BEST LIFE
DESIGN DIRECTOR: BRANDON KAVULLA
DESIGNER: HEATHER JONES
DIRECTOR OF PHOTOGRAPHY: RYAN CADIZ
PHOTOGRAPHER: DAN FORBES
PUBLISHER: RODALE INC.
ISSUE: AUGUST 2008
CATEGORY: DESIGN: FEATURE: SERVICE
(SINGLE/SPREAD)

/128/ MEN'S HEALTH
DESIGN DIRECTOR: GEORGE KARABOTSOS
ART DIRECTORS: WILBERT GUTIÉRREZ, JOE HEROUN
DESIGNERS: WILBERT GUTIÉRREZ, JOE HEROUN
DIRECTOR OF PHOTOGRAPHY: BRENDA MILLIS
PHOTO EDITOR: BRENDA MILLIS
PHOTOGRAPHER: MICHAEL LEWIS
PUBLISHER: RODALE INC.
ISSUE: SEPTEMBER 2008
CATEGORY: DESIGN: FEATURE: SERVICE
(SINGLE/SPREAD)

/129/ MORE
CREATIVE DIRECTOR: DEBRA BISHOP
DESIGNER: DEBRA BISHOP
ILLUSTRATOR: LOU BEACH
DIRECTOR OF PHOTOGRAPHY: KAREN FRANK
PHOTO EDITORS: DAISY CAJAS, NATALIE GIALLUCA
PUBLISHER: MEREDITH CORPORATION
ISSUE: DECEMBER 2008/JANUARY 2009
CATEGORY: DESIGN: FEATURE: SERVICE
(SINGLE/SPREAD)

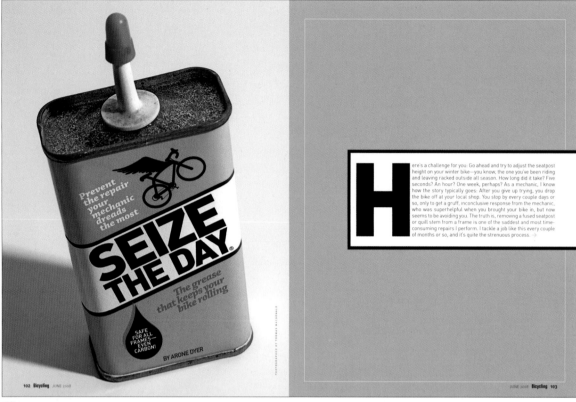

/130/ **BICYCLING**
DESIGN DIRECTOR: DAVID SPERANZA
ART DIRECTOR: ERIN BENNER
DESIGNER: ASHLEY FREEBY
DIRECTOR OF PHOTOGRAPHY: STACEY EMENECKER
PHOTO EDITOR: KATE MARRON
PHOTOGRAPHER: THOMAS MACDONALD
PUBLISHER: RODALE INC.
ISSUE: JUNE 2008
CATEGORY: DESIGN: FEATURE: SERVICE
(SINGLE/SPREAD)

/131/ **GLAMOUR**
DESIGN DIRECTOR: GERALDINE HESSLER
ART DIRECTOR: THERESA GRIGGS
DIRECTOR OF PHOTOGRAPHY: SUZANNE DONALDSON
PHOTOGRAPHER: JONATHON KANTOR
PUBLISHER: CONDÉ NAST PUBLICATIONS INC.
ISSUE: NOVEMBER 2008
CATEGORY: DESIGN: FEATURE: SERVICE
(SINGLE/SPREAD)

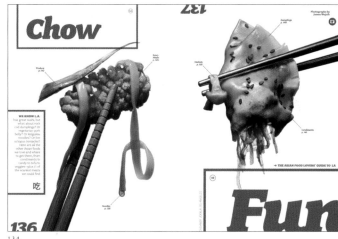

/132/ MARTHA STEWART LIVING
CREATIVE DIRECTOR: ERIC PIKE
DESIGN DIRECTOR: JAMES DUNLINSON
ART DIRECTOR: JAMES DUNLINSON
DESIGNER: LINSEY LAIDLAW
DIRECTOR OF PHOTOGRAPHY: HELOISE GOODMAN
PHOTO EDITOR: MARY CAHILL
PHOTOGRAPHER: HANS GISSINGER
EDITOR-IN-CHIEF: MICHAEL BOODRO
PUBLISHER: MARTHA STEWART LIVING OMNIMEDIA
ISSUE: APRIL 2008
CATEGORY: DESIGN: FEATURE: SERVICE
(SINGLE/SPREAD)

/133/ PSYCHOLOGY TODAY
CREATIVE DIRECTOR: EDWARD LEVINE
DIRECTOR OF PHOTOGRAPHY: CLAUDIA STEFEZIUS
PHOTOGRAPHER: KARJEAN LEVINE
STUDIO LEVINE DESIGN INC.
PUBLISHER: SUSSEX PUBLISHERS
ISSUE: MARCH/APRIL 2008
CATEGORY: DESIGN: FEATURE: SERVICE
(SINGLE/SPREAD)

/134/ LOS ANGELES
ART DIRECTOR: JOE KIMBERLING
PHOTO EDITOR: KATHLEEN CLARK
PHOTOGRAPHER: JAMES WOJCIK
EDITOR-IN-CHIEF: KIT RACHLIS
PUBLISHER: EMMIS COMMUNICATIONS CORP.
ISSUE: NOVEMBER 2008
CATEGORY: DESIGN: FEATURE: SERVICE
(SINGLE/SPREAD)

PIE *to the nth degree*

THE MOST INDULGENT OF DESSERTS, CREAM PIES MAY BE EVERY KID'S FAVORITE,
BUT THEY CAN ALSO ENTICE THE MOST SOPHISTICATED PALATE.

CHOCOLATE-CARAMEL

CREAM PIE Chocolate-covered caramels inspired
this rich, silken pudding and its whipped cream topping
that's suffused with caramel. A generous amount
of salt throughout balances the pie's sweetness
in an unexpected—yet welcome—way.

PHOTOGRAPHS BY CHRISTOPHER BAKER

TEXT BY GAIL MONAGHAN

LEMON-CHAMOMILE

CREAM PIE Soothing chamomile and cloudlike
meringue lend delicacy to this tart lemon classic.
A rustic cornmeal crust grounds the dessert.

MARTHASTEWART.COM 173

SUMMER FRUIT

CREAM PIE An explosion of the season: Farm-stand berries
are folded into a cinnamon-laced filling that's obscured not with
waves of whipped cream but with glistening glazed peaches.

SEE RECIPES SECTION | SEE GUIDE FOR SOURCES
CREATED BY SHIRA BOCAR, ABBEY KUSTER-PROKELL, AND AYESHA PATEL
ONLINE: CLASSIC CREAM-PIE RECIPES AT marthastewart.com/cream-pies

BUTTERSCOTCH-PRALINE

CREAM PIE Evoke memories of puddings, candies,
and other childhood comforts with this lush butterscotch
dessert, its grown-up look and taste derived from browned
butter and brown sugar in the filling and jewel-like
shards of hazelnut praline scattered on top.

MARTHASTEWART.COM 177

135

/135/ **MARTHA STEWART LIVING**
CREATIVE DIRECTOR: ERIC PIKE / DESIGN DIRECTOR: JAMES DUNLINSON / ART DIRECTOR: ABBEY KUSTER-PROKELL / DESIGNER: ABBEY KUSTER-PROKELL
DIRECTOR OF PHOTOGRAPHY: HELOISE GOODMAN / PHOTO EDITOR: MARY CAHILL / PHOTOGRAPHER: CHRISTOPHER BAKER / STYLISTS SHIRA BOCAR, AYESHA PATEL
EDITOR-IN-CHIEF: MICHAEL BOODRO / PUBLISHER: MARTHA STEWART LIVING OMNIMEDIA / ISSUE: JUNE 2008 / CATEGORY: DESIGN: FEATURE: SERVICE (STORY)

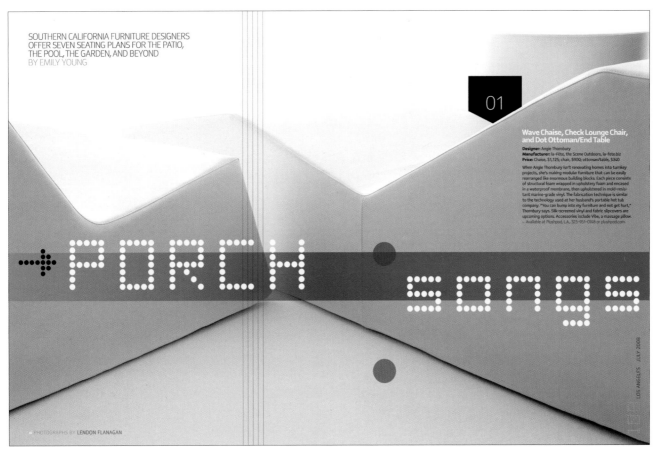

SOUTHERN CALIFORNIA FURNITURE DESIGNERS
OFFER SEVEN SEATING PLANS FOR THE PATIO,
THE POOL, THE GARDEN, AND BEYOND
BY EMILY YOUNG

+PORCH songs

01

Wave Chaise, Check Lounge Chair, and Dot Ottoman/End Table

Designer: Angie Thornbury
Manufacturer: la-fête, the Scene Outdoors, la-fete.biz
Price: Chaise, $1,125; chair, $900; ottoman/table, $340

When Angie Thornbury isn't renovating homes into turnkey projects, she's making modular furniture that can be easily rearranged like enormous building blocks. Each piece consists of structural foam wrapped in upholstery foam and encased in a waterproof membrane, then upholstered in mold-resistant marine-grade vinyl. The fabrication technique is similar to the technology used at her husband's portable hot tub company. "You can bump into my furniture and not get hurt," Thornbury says. Silk-screened vinyl and fabric slipcovers are upcoming options. Accessories include Vibe, a massage pillow.
~ Available at Plushpod, L.A., 323-951-0748 or plushpod.com.

PHOTOGRAPHS BY LENDON FLANAGAN

LOS ANGELES / JULY 2008

136

02

Frank Gehry
Furniture Collection Sofa

Designer: Frank Gehry
Manufacturer: Heller, helleronline.com
Price: $1,320

Architect Frank Gehry is no stranger to furniture design, having already explored the possibilities of corrugated cardboard and bent maple to dramatic effect. More recently, he's taken advantage of a process called rotational molding to produce outdoor furnishings that echo the torqued planes of his architectural landmarks. Made from a single piece of resin, each form is stout yet hollow. The sofa, for example, weighs a mere 86 pounds. Sunlight and shadows play across the sensuous curves the way they do at Walt Disney Concert Hall. Sit on this furniture, or just admire it as sculpture. » Available at Plushpod, L.A., 323-951-0748 or plushpod.com and Jules Seltzer Associates, L.A., 310-274-7243 or julesseltzer.com.

03

Scoop Chair

Designer: Craig Varterian
Manufacturer: Boom Design
Price: $200

There's something whimsical about a chair that looks like a ball of ice cream after you've eaten the first spoonful. If Craig Varterian's fiberglass form doesn't make you smile, the lively palette will. Molded and finished by hand (the way most surfboards are made) in Thailand, the chair comes in several colors, including fuchsia, white, mint green, and baby blue. A kid's version is available in black or white. Varterian, who studied briefly at Cranbrook Academy of Art in Michigan, shares Eero Saarinen's organic sensibility, "taking the hard edge and putting a soft touch on it." » Available at Boom Design, Culver City, 310-202-1697 or boomusa.com.

LOS ANGELES / JULY 2008

136

ART DIRECTOR: JOE KIMBERLING / PHOTO EDITOR: KATHLEEN CLARK / PHOTOGRAPHER: LENDON FLANAGAN
EDITOR-IN-CHIEF: KIT RACHLIS / PUBLISHER: EMMIS COMMUNICATIONS CORP. / ISSUE: JULY 2008
CATEGORY: DESIGN: FEATURE: SERVICE (STORY)

137

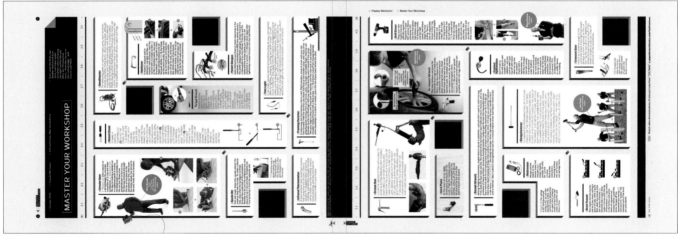

137

/137/ **POPULAR MECHANICS**
DESIGN DIRECTOR: MICHAEL LAWTON / SR. ART DIRECTOR: PETER HERBERT
DESIGNERS: MICHAEL LAWTON, STRAVINSKI PIERRE / ILLUSTRATOR: DOGO
DIRECTOR OF PHOTOGRAPHY: ALLYSON TORRISI / PHOTO EDITOR: MICHELE ERVIN
PHOTOGRAPHERS: MICHAEL LEWIS, CHAD HUNT / EDITOR-IN-CHIEF:
JAMES B. MEIGS / PUBLISHER: THE HEARST CORPORATION-MAGAZINES DIVISION
ISSUE: OCTOBER 2008 / CATEGORY: DESIGN: FEATURE: SERVICE (STORY)

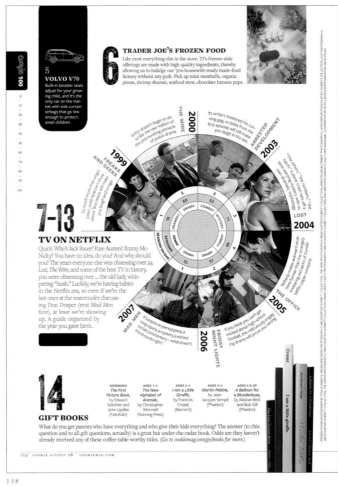

/138/ **COOKIE**
DESIGN DIRECTOR: KIRBY RODRIGUEZ / ART DIRECTOR: ALEX GROSSMAN
DESIGNERS: NICOLETTE BERTHELOT, SHANNA GREENBERG
PHOTO EDITOR: DARRICK HARRIS / ASSOCIATE PHOTO EDITOR: LINDA DENAHAN
ASSISTANT PHOTO EDITOR: AJA NUZZI / PHOTOGRAPHERS: TOM SCHIERLITZ,
FLOTO + WARNER, AYA BRACKETT, MARTIN SCHOELLER, DIANE FIELDS
PUBLISHER: CONDÉ NAST PUBLICATIONS INC. / ISSUE: OCTOBER 2008
CATEGORY: DESIGN: FEATURE: SERVICE (STORY)

/139/ **GREEN GUIDE**
ART DIRECTOR: CHALKLEY CALDERWOOD / DESIGNER: CHALKLEY CALDERWOOD
DIRECTOR OF PHOTOGRAPHY: NAOMI BEN-SHAHAR / PHOTOGRAPHER: SATOSHI
EDITOR-IN-CHIEF: SETH BAUER / PUBLISHER: NATIONAL GEOGRAPHIC
CLIENT NATHIONAL GEOGRAPHIC / ISSUE: FALL 2008 / CATEGORY: DESIGN:
FEATURE: SERVICE (STORY)

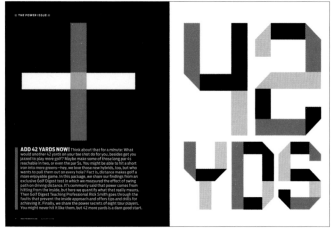

140

140

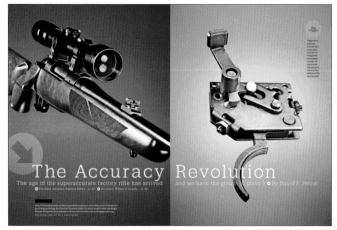

141

141

142

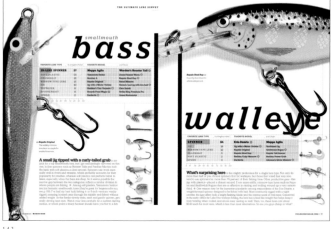

142

/140/ GOLF DIGEST
DESIGN DIRECTOR: KEN DELAGO
DESIGNER: TIM OLIVER
PHOTO EDITOR: CHRISTIAN IOOSS
PHOTOGRAPHER: J.D. CUBAN
PUBLISHER: CONDÉ NAST PUBLICATIONS INC.
ISSUE: AUGUST 2008
CATEGORY: DESIGN: FEATURE: SERVICE (STORY)

/141/ FIELD & STREAM
ART DIRECTOR: NEIL JAMIESON
DESIGNERS: MIKE LEY, IAN BROWN
ILLUSTRATOR: MIKE SUDAL
DIRECTOR OF PHOTOGRAPHY: AMY BERKLEY
PHOTOGRAPHER: DAN SAELINGER
ASSOCIATE PHOTO EDITOR: CAITLIN PETERS
PUBLISHER: BONNIER CORPORATION
ISSUE: JULY 2008
CATEGORY: DESIGN: FEATURE: SERVICE (STORY)

/142/ FIELD & STREAM
ART DIRECTOR: NEIL JAMIESON
DESIGNERS: MIKE LEY, IAN BROWN
DIRECTOR OF PHOTOGRAPHY: AMY BERKLEY
PHOTOGRAPHER: DAN SAELINGER
ASSOCIATE PHOTO EDITOR: CAITLIN PETERS
EDITOR-IN-CHIEF: ANTHONY LICATA
PUBLISHER: BONNIER CORPORATION
ISSUE: MARCH 2008
CATEGORY: DESIGN: FEATURE: SERVICE (STORY)

143

143

144

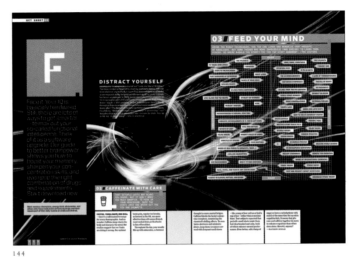

144

145

145

/143/ **GQ**
DESIGN DIRECTOR: FRED WOODWARD
DESIGNERS: ANTON IOUKHNOVETS, DRUE WAGNER
ILLUSTRATORS: ANDY FRIEDMAN, NICK DEWAR
DIRECTOR OF PHOTOGRAPHY: DORA SOMOSI
PHOTO EDITORS: KRISTA PRESTEK, JUSTIN O'NEILL
PHOTOGRAPHERS: MILES ALDRIDGE, NIGEL COX,
FRANÇOIS HALARD, ERIC RAY DAVIDSON,
SCOTT SCHUMAN, FRANCESCO CARROZZINI
CREATIVE DIRECTOR, FASHION: JIM MOORE
FASHION DIRECTOR: MADELINE WEEKS
EDITOR-IN-CHIEF: JIM NELSON
PUBLISHER: CONDÉ NAST PUBLICATIONS INC.
ISSUE: OCTOBER 2008
CATEGORY: DESIGN: FEATURE: SERVICE (STORY)

/144/ **WIRED**
CREATIVE DIRECTOR: SCOTT DADICH
DESIGN DIRECTOR: WYATT MITCHELL
ART DIRECTORS: CARL DETORRES, MAILI HOLIMAN
DESIGNER: CARL DETORRES
ILLUSTRATORS: CHRISTOPH NIEMANN, TOM
MUELLER, STEVEN WILSON
PHOTO EDITOR: CAROLYN RAUCH
PHOTOGRAPHER: BRENT HUMPHREYS
PUBLISHER: CONDÉ NAST PUBLICATIONS, INC.
ISSUE: MAY 2008
CATEGORY: DESIGN: FEATURE: SERVICE (STORY)

/145/ **SPIN**
DESIGN DIRECTOR: DEVIN PEDZWATER
ART DIRECTOR: IAN ROBINSON
DESIGNER: LIZ MACFARLANE
DIRECTOR OF PHOTOGRAPHY: MICHELLE EGIZIANO
PHOTO EDITORS: GAVIN STEVENS,
JENNIFER EDMONDSON
PHOTOGRAPHER: MICHAEL SCHMELLING
PUBLISHER: SPIN MEDIA LLC
ISSUE: APRIL 2008
CATEGORY: DESIGN: FEATURE: SERVICE (STORY)

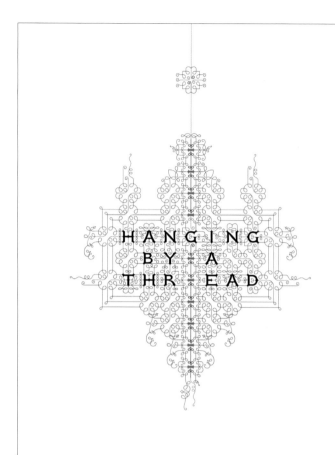

HANGING
BY A
THREAD

PHOTOGRAPH BY FRANK W. OCKENFELS 3

Runway acclaim and celebrity clients like Madonna made Louis Verdad
the most sought-after fashion designer from Los Angeles in years. Then he lost
everything: his business and the use of his own name **By Laurie Pike**

140 Los Angeles December 2008

December 2008 Los Angeles 141

146

HELLO, BEAUTIFUL!

MICHAEL LENEHAN

**BY RAISING HIS PIGS
THE NATURAL WAY,
AN INDIANA FARMER
has DEFIED the
INDUSTRIAL
STYLE OF ANIMAL PRODUCTION
and found
A HIGH-END MARKET
FOR HIS GORGEOUS
PORK
WITH SOME OF CHICAGO'S TOP CHEFS**

PHOTOGRAPHY BY KEVIN BANNA

147

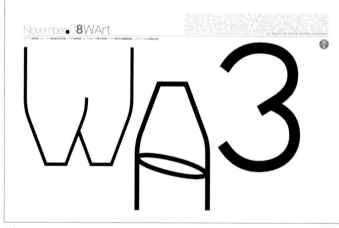

November 08 W Art

WA3

148

/146/ LOS ANGELES
ART DIRECTORS: JOE KIMBERLING, STEVEN E. BANKS
PHOTOGRAPHER: FRANK W. OCKENFELS 3
EDITOR-IN-CHIEF: KIT RACHLIS
PUBLISHER: EMMIS COMMUNICATIONS CORP.
ISSUE: DECEMBER 2008
CATEGORY: DESIGN: FEATURE: NON-CELEBRITY
PROFILE (SINGLE/SPREAD)

/147/ CHICAGO
ART DIRECTOR: JENNIFER MOORE
DESIGNER: JENNIFER MOORE
PHOTO EDITOR: BRITTNEY BLAIR
PHOTOGRAPHER: KEVIN BANNA
EDITOR-IN-CHIEF: RICHARD BABCOCK
PUBLISHER: CHICAGOLAND PUBLISHING
ISSUE: JUNE 2008
CATEGORY: DESIGN: FEATURE: NON-CELEBRITY
PROFILE (SINGLE/SPREAD)

/148/ W
DESIGN DIRECTOR: EDWARD LEIDA
ART DIRECTOR: NATHALIE KIRSHEH
DESIGNER: EDWARD LEIDA
PUBLISHER: CONDÉ NAST PUBLICATIONS INC.
ISSUE: NOVEMBER 2008
CATEGORY: DESIGN: FEATURE: NON-CELEBRITY
PROFILE (SINGLE/SPREAD)

Meet **Julia Allison.** She can't act. She can't sing. She's not rich. But thanks to a genius for self-promotion—plus Flickr, Twitter, and her blogs—she's become an internet celebrity. How she did it—and how you can, too.

HOW TO

● *Promote* YOURSELF P108

● *Boost* YOUR GEEK CRED P114

● *Be the* HERO P118

● *Fake It* TILL YOU MAKE IT P122

❋Almost Famous
by Jason Tanz
PHOTOGRAPHS BY PLATON

149

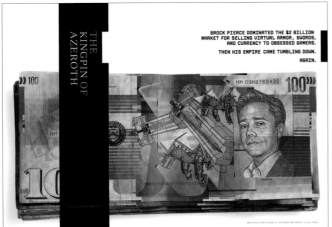

THE KINGPIN OF AZEROTH

BROCK PIERCE DOMINATED THE $2 BILLION MARKET FOR SELLING VIRTUAL ARMOR, SWORDS, AND CURRENCY TO OBSESSED GAMERS.

THEN HIS EMPIRE CAME TUMBLING DOWN.

AGAIN.

150

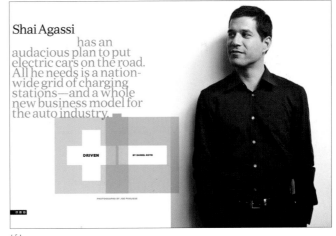

Shai Agassi has an audacious plan to put electric cars on the road. All he needs is a nationwide grid of charging stations—and a whole new business model for the auto industry.

DRIVEN BY DANIEL ROTH

PHOTOGRAPHED BY JOE PUGLIESE

151

/149/ **WIRED**
CREATIVE DIRECTOR: SCOTT DADICH
DESIGN DIRECTOR: WYATT MITCHELL
ART DIRECTOR: CARL DETORRES
DESIGNER: CARL DETORRES
PHOTO EDITOR: CAROLYN RAUCH
PHOTOGRAPHER: PLATON
PUBLISHER: CONDÉ NAST PUBLICATIONS, INC.
ISSUE: AUGUST 2008
CATEGORY: DESIGN: FEATURE: NON-CELEBRITY
PROFILE (SINGLE/SPREAD)

/150/ **WIRED**
CREATIVE DIRECTOR: SCOTT DADICH
DESIGN DIRECTOR: WYATT MITCHELL
DESIGNERS: VICTOR KRUMMENACHER, CARL
DETORRES
ILLUSTRATORS: MARTIN WOODTLI, NOLI NOVAK
PHOTO EDITOR: ANNA GOLDWATER ALEXANDER
PUBLISHER: CONDÉ NAST PUBLICATIONS, INC.
ISSUE: DECEMBER 2008
CATEGORY: DESIGN: FEATURE: NON-CELEBRITY
PROFILE (SINGLE/SPREAD)

/151/ **WIRED**
CREATIVE DIRECTOR: SCOTT DADICH
DESIGN DIRECTOR: WYATT MITCHELL
ART DIRECTOR: MAILI HOLIMAN
DESIGNER: MAILI HOLIMAN
PHOTO EDITOR: ZANA WOODS
PHOTOGRAPHER: JOE PUGLIESE
PUBLISHER: CONDÉ NAST PUBLICATIONS, INC.
ISSUE: SEPTEMBER 2008
CATEGORY: DESIGN: FEATURE: NON-CELEBRITY
PROFILE (SINGLE/SPREAD)

152

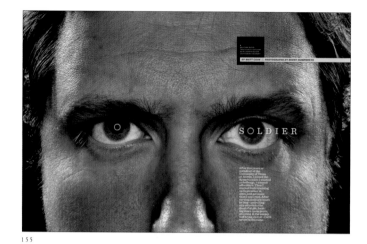

155

153

156

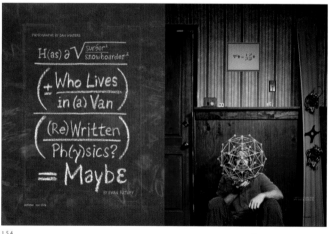

154

157

/152/ MINNESOTA MONTHLY
ART DIRECTOR: BRIAN JOHNSON
PHOTOGRAPHER: MIKE MCGREGOR
PUBLISHER: GREENSPRING MEDIA GROUP
ISSUE: AUGUST 2008
CATEGORY: DESIGN: FEATURE: NON-CELEBRITY
PROFILE (SINGLE/SPREAD)

/153/ OUTSIDE
CREATIVE DIRECTOR: HANNAH MCCAUGHEY
DEPUTY ART DIRECTORS: KATE ILTIS,
JOHN MCCAULEY
DESIGNERS: SUSANNE DUCKER,
MACE FLEEGER, KRISTIN MULZER
DIRECTOR OF PHOTOGRAPHY: LESLEY MEYER
PHOTO EDITORS: AMY FEITELBERG,
AMBER TERRANOVA
PHOTOGRAPHER: SIAN KENNEDY
PUBLISHER: MARIAH MEDIA, INC.
ISSUE: APRIL 2008
CATEGORY: DESIGN: FEATURE: NON-CELEBRITY
PROFILE (SINGLE/SPREAD)

/154/ OUTSIDE
CREATIVE DIRECTOR: HANNAH MCCAUGHEY
DEPUTY ART DIRECTORS: KATE ILTIS,
JOHN MCCAULEY
DESIGNERS: SUSANNE DUCKER, KRISTIN MULZER
DIRECTOR OF PHOTOGRAPHY: LESLEY MEYER
PHOTO EDITORS: AMY FEITELBERG,
AMBER TERRANOVA
PHOTOGRAPHER: DAN WINTERS
PUBLISHER: MARIAH MEDIA, INC.
ISSUE: MAY 2008
CATEGORY: DESIGN: FEATURE: NON-CELEBRITY
PROFILE (SINGLE/SPREAD)

/155/ TEXAS MONTHLY
ART DIRECTOR: T.J. TUCKER
DESIGNER: CALEB BENNETT
PHOTO EDITOR: LESLIE BALDWIN
PHOTOGRAPHER: BRENT HUMPHREYS
PUBLISHER: EMMIS COMMUNICATIONS CORP.
ISSUE: JULY 2008
CATEGORY: DESIGN: FEATURE: NON-CELEBRITY
PROFILE (SINGLE/SPREAD)

/156/ FOUNDATION, THE MIXTAPE MAGAZINE
ART DIRECTOR: SHAUN BARON
PHOTOGRAPHER: ROB HANEY
EDITOR-IN-CHIEF: CHRIS MALO
PUBLISHER: FOUNDATION MEDIA GROUP, LLC
ISSUE: SEPTEMBER 2008
CATEGORY: DESIGN: FEATURE: NON-CELEBRITY
PROFILE (SINGLE/SPREAD)

/157/ FIELD & STREAM
PUBLICATION: FIELD & STREAM
ART DIRECTOR: NEIL JAMIESON
DESIGNERS: MIKE LEY, IAN BROWN
DIRECTOR OF PHOTOGRAPHY: AMY BERKLEY
PHOTOGRAPHER: BRENT HUMPHREYS
ASSOCIATE PHOTO EDITOR: CAITLIN PETERS
PUBLISHER: BONNIER CORPORATION
ISSUE: AUGUST 2008
CATEGORY: DESIGN: FEATURE: NON-CELEBRITY
PROFILE (SINGLE/SPREAD)

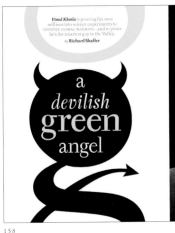
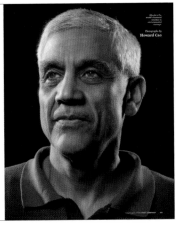

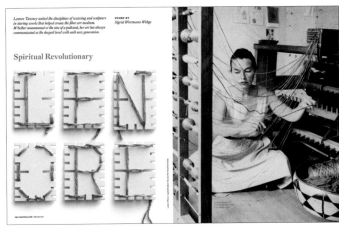

158

161

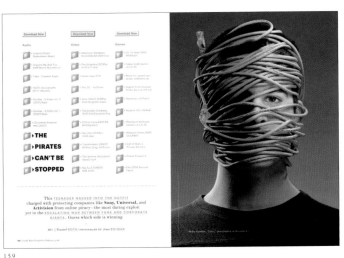

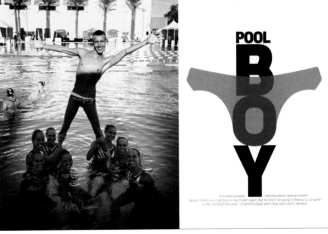

159

162

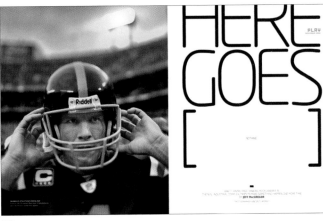

160

/158/ **FAST COMPANY**
ART DIRECTOR: DEAN MARKADAKIS
DESIGNER: JANA MEIER
DIRECTOR OF PHOTOGRAPHY: MEGHAN HURLEY
PHOTOGRAPHER: HOWARD CAO
PUBLISHER: MANSUETO VENTURES, LLC
ISSUE: JULY/AUGUST 2008
CATEGORY: DESIGN: FEATURE: NON-CELEBRITY
PROFILE (SINGLE/SPREAD)

/159/ **CONDÉ NAST PORTFOLIO**
DESIGN DIRECTOR: ROBERT PRIEST
ART DIRECTOR: GRACE LEE
DESIGNER: JANA MEIER
DIRECTOR OF PHOTOGRAPHY: LISA BERMAN
PHOTO EDITOR: SARAH WEISSMAN
PHOTOGRAPHER: JONO ROTMAN
EDITOR-IN-CHIEF: JOANNE LIPMAN
PUBLISHER: CONDÉ NAST PUBLICATIONS INC.
ISSUE: FEBRUARY 2008
CATEGORY: DESIGN: FEATURE: NON-CELEBRITY
PROFILE (SINGLE/SPREAD)

/160/ **PLAY, THE NEW YORK TIMES SPORT MAGAZINE**
CREATIVE DIRECTOR: JANET FROELICH
ART DIRECTOR: ROB HEWITT
DESIGNER: ROB HEWITT
DIRECTOR OF PHOTOGRAPHY: KATHY RYAN
PHOTO EDITOR: KIRA POLLACK
PHOTOGRAPHER: VINCENT LAFORET
EDITOR-IN-CHIEF: MARK BRYANT
PUBLISHER: THE NEW YORK TIMES
ISSUE: NOVEMBER 2008
CATEGORY: DESIGN: FEATURE: NON-CELEBRITY
PROFILE (SINGLE/SPREAD)

/161/ **AMERICAN CRAFT**
CREATIVE DIRECTOR: JEANETTE ABBINK
DESIGNER: EMILY CM ANDERSON
PHOTOGRAPHERS: LAURIE FRANKEL, DAVID ATTIE
STUDIO: RATIONAL BEAUTY
EDITOR-IN-CHIEF: ANDREW WAGNER
PUBLISHER: AMERICAN CRAFT COUNCIL
CLIENT: AMERICAN CRAFT COUNCIL
ISSUE: FEBRUARY/MARCH 2008
CATEGORY: DESIGN: FEATURE: NON-CELEBRITY
PROFILE (SINGLE/SPREAD)

/162/ **DETAILS**
CREATIVE DIRECTOR: ROCKWELL HARWOOD
ART DIRECTOR: ANDRE JOINTE
DESIGNER: ANDRE JOINTE
PHOTO EDITORS: ALEX GHEZ, CHANDRA GLICK
PHOTOGRAPHER: CHRIS MCPHERSON
SENIOR PHOTO EDITOR: HALI TARA FELDMAN
EDITOR-IN-CHIEF: DANIEL PERES
PUBLISHER: CONDÉ NAST PUBLICATIONS
ISSUE: AUGUST 2008
CATEGORY: DESIGN: FEATURE: NON-CELEBRITY
PROFILE (SINGLE/SPREAD)

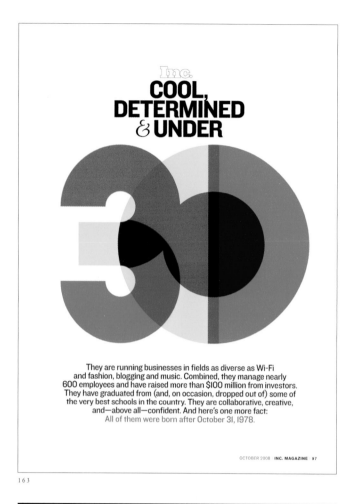

163

163

163

164

164

/163/ **INC.**
CREATIVE DIRECTOR: BLAKE TAYLOR
ART DIRECTOR: JASON MISCHKA
DIRECTOR OF PHOTOGRAPHY: TRAVIS RUSE
PHOTOGRAPHER: KAREEM BLACK
EDITOR-IN-CHIEF: JANE BERENTSON
PUBLISHER: MANSUETO VENTURES
ISSUE: OCTOBER 2008
CATEGORY: DESIGN: FEATURE:
NON-CELEBRITY PROFILE (STORY)

/164/ **OUT**
CREATIVE DIRECTOR: DAVID GRAY
ART DIRECTOR: NICK VOGELSON
DESIGNER: JASON SELDON
DIRECTOR OF PHOTOGRAPHY: JO-EY TANG
PHOTO EDITOR: ANNIA CHIA
PHOTOGRAPHER: MICHEL HADDI
EDITOR-IN-CHIEF: AARON HICKLIN
PUBLISHER: REGENT MEDIA
ISSUE: OCTOBER 2008
CATEGORY: DESIGN: FEATURE:
NON-CELEBRITY PROFILE (STORY)

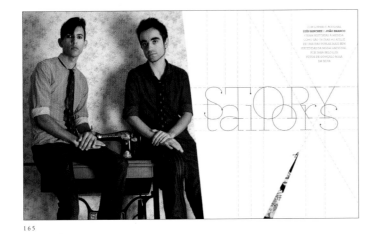

165

165

166

166

Karen Johnson Boyd and the Art of Stealth Philanthropy

This astounding but steadfast benefactor has promoted a broader perspective of art by assembling museum-quality examples of contemporary craft and exhibiting them in the larger context of painting and sculpture.

STORY BY
Mija Riedel

PHOTOGRAPHY BY
Cameron Wittig

167

167

/165/ **VISÃO**
CREATIVE DIRECTOR: VASCO FERREIRA
ART DIRECTOR: JONAS REKER
PHOTOGRAPHER: GONGALO ROSA DA SILVA
PUBLISHER: IMPREJA PUBLISHING
ISSUE: OCTOBER 9, 2008
CATEGORY: DESIGN: FEATURE: NON-CELEBRITY
PROFILE (STORY)

/166/ **THE NEW YORK TIMES MAGAZINE**
CREATIVE DIRECTOR: JANET FROELICH
ART DIRECTOR: AREM DUPLESSIS
DEPUTY ART DIRECTOR: GAIL BICHLER
DESIGNERS: IAN ALLEN, AREM DUPLESSIS
DIRECTOR OF PHOTOGRAPHY: KATHY RYAN
PHOTO EDITOR: KIRA POLLACK
PHOTOGRAPHER: ROBBIE COOPER
EDITOR-IN-CHIEF: GERRY MARZORATI
PUBLISHER: THE NEW YORK TIMES
ISSUE: NOVEMBER 23, 2008
CATEGORY: DESIGN: FEATURE: NON-CELEBRITY
PROFILE (STORY)

/167/ **AMERICAN CRAFT**
CREATIVE DIRECTOR: JEANETTE ABBINK
DESIGNER: NATASHA CHANDANI
PHOTOGRAPHER: CAMERON WITTIG
STUDIO: RATIONAL BEAUTY
EDITOR-IN-CHIEF: ANDREW WAGNER
PUBLISHER: AMERICAN CRAFT COUNCIL
CLIENT: AMERICAN CRAFT COUNCIL
ISSUE: DECEMBER 2007/JANUARY 2008
CATEGORY: DESIGN: FEATURE: NON-CELEBRITY
PROFILE (STORY)

BY ROB SHEFFIELD PHOTOGRAPHS BY BEN WATTS

168

169

/168/ BLENDER
CREATIVE DIRECTOR: DIRK BARNETT / DESIGNER: DIRK BARNETT
DIRECTOR OF PHOTOGRAPHY: DAVID CARTHAS / PHOTOGRAPHER:
BEN WATTS / EDITOR-IN-CHIEF: JOE LEVY / PUBLISHER: ALPHAMEDIA
GROUP / ISSUE: NOVEMBER 2008 / CATEGORY: DESIGN: FEATURE:
CELEBRITY/ENTERTAINMENT PROFILE (SINGLE/SPREAD)

/169/ BLENDER
CREATIVE DIRECTOR: DIRK BARNETT / DESIGNER: DIRK BARNETT
DIRECTOR OF PHOTOGRAPHY: DAVID CARTHAS / PHOTOGRAPHER: RENNIO
MAIFREDI / EDITOR-IN-CHIEF: JOE LEVY / PUBLISHER: ALPHAMEDIA GROUP
ISSUE: NOVEMBER 2008 / CATEGORY: DESIGN: FEATURE: CELEBRITY/
ENTERTAINMENT PROFILE (SINGLE/SPREAD)

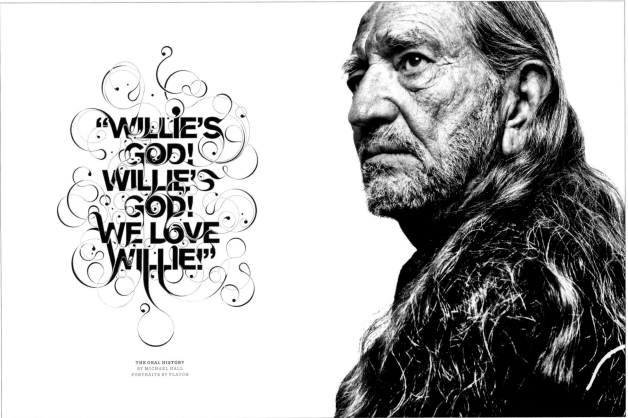

/170/ **MORE**
CREATIVE DIRECTOR: MAXINE DAVIDOWITZ / ART DIRECTOR: JOSE FERNANDEZ
DIRECTOR OF PHOTOGRAPHY: KAREN FRANK / PHOTO EDITORS: NATALIE
GIALLUCA, ALLISON CHIN / PHOTOGRAPHER: MARTIN SCHOELLER
PUBLISHER: MEREDITH CORPORATION / ISSUE: MAY 2008 / CATEGORY: DESIGN:
FEATURE: CELEBRITY/ENTERTAINMENT PROFILE (SINGLE/SPREAD)

/171/ **TEXAS MONTHLY**
ART DIRECTOR: T.J. TUCKER / DESIGNER: T.J. TUCKER / PHOTO EDITOR: LESLIE
BALDWIN / PHOTOGRAPHER: PLATON / LETTERING: SI SCOTT / PUBLISHER: EMMIS
COMMUNICATIONS CORP. / ISSUE: MAY 2008 / CATEGORY: DESIGN: FEATURE:
CELEBRITY/ENTERTAINMENT PROFILE (SINGLE/SPREAD)

A HIGHER CALLING

**HOW PHILIP
SEYMOUR HOFFMAN
HAS WORKED HIMSELF
INTO THE GREATEST
CHARACTER ACTOR
OF OUR TIME.**

BY LYNN HIRSCHBERG
PHOTOGRAPH BY BRIGITTE LACOMBE

172

173

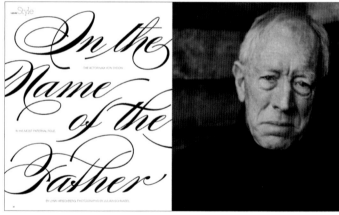

174

/172/ **THE NEW YORK TIMES MAGAZINE**
CREATIVE DIRECTOR: JANET FROELICH
ART DIRECTOR: AREM DUPLESSIS
DESIGNER: AREM DUPLESSIS
DIRECTOR OF PHOTOGRAPHY: KATHY RYAN
PHOTO EDITOR: KIRA POLLACK
PHOTOGRAPHER: BRIGITTE LACOMBE
DEPUTY ART DIRECTOR: GAIL BICHLER
EDITOR-IN-CHIEF: GERRY MARZORATI
PUBLISHER: THE NEW YORK TIMES
ISSUE: DECEMBER 21, 2008
CATEGORY: DESIGN: FEATURE: CELEBRITY/
ENTERTAINMENT PROFILE (SINGLE/SPREAD)

/173/ **THE NEW YORK TIMES MAGAZINE**
CREATIVE DIRECTOR: JANET FROELICH
ART DIRECTOR: AREM DUPLESSIS
DEPUTY ART DIRECTOR: GAIL BICHLER
DESIGNER: AREM DUPLESSIS
DIRECTOR OF PHOTOGRAPHY: KATHY RYAN
PHOTO EDITOR: DAVID CARTHAS
PHOTOGRAPHER: NADAV KANDER
EDITOR-IN-CHIEF: GERRY MARZORATI
PUBLISHER: THE NEW YORK TIMES
ISSUE: JULY 27, 2008
CATEGORY: DESIGN: FEATURE: CELEBRITY/
ENTERTAINMENT PROFILE (SINGLE/SPREAD)

/174/ **THE NEW YORK TIMES MAGAZINE**
CREATIVE DIRECTOR: JANET FROELICH
ART DIRECTOR: AREM DUPLESSIS
DEPUTY ART DIRECTOR: GAIL BICHLER
DESIGNER: NANCY HARRIS ROUEMY
DIRECTOR OF PHOTOGRAPHY: KATHY RYAN
PHOTOGRAPHER: JULIAN SCHNABEL
EDITOR-IN-CHIEF: GERRY MARZORATI
PUBLISHER: THE NEW YORK TIMES
ISSUE: JANUARY 27, 2008
CATEGORY: DESIGN: FEATURE: CELEBRITY/
ENTERTAINMENT PROFILE (SINGLE/SPREAD)

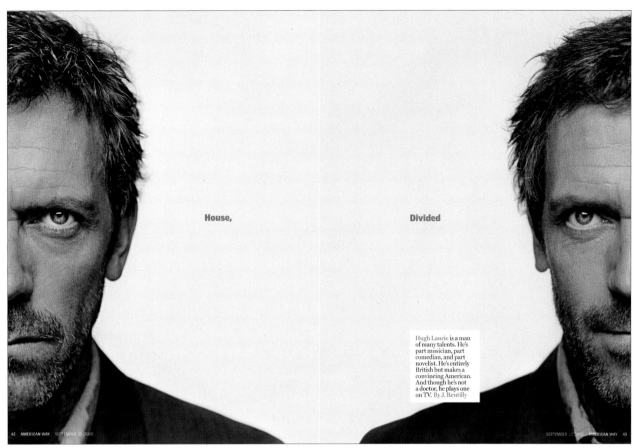

House,   Divided

Hugh Laurie is a man
of many talents. He's
part musician, part
comedian, and part
novelist. He's entirely
British but makes a
convincing American.
And though he's not
a doctor, he plays one
on TV. By J. Rentilly

42 AMERICAN WAY SEPTEMBER 15 2008

SEPTEMBER 15 2008 AMERICAN WAY 43

175

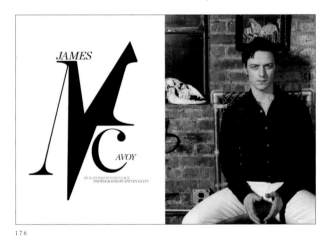

176

177

/175/ **AMERICAN WAY**
DESIGN DIRECTOR: J.R. AREBALO, JR.
ART DIRECTOR: SAMUEL SOLOMON
PHOTOGRAPHER: MITCH JENKINS
PUBLISHER: AMERICAN AIRLINES PUBLISHING
CLIENT: AMERICAN AIRLINES
ISSUE: SEPTEMBER 15, 2008
CATEGORY: DESIGN: FEATURE: CELEBRITY/
ENTERTAINMENT PROFILE (SINGLE/SPREAD)

/176/ **DETAILS**
CREATIVE DIRECTOR: ROCKWELL HARWOOD
ART DIRECTOR: ANDRE JOINTE
DESIGNER: ROCKWELL HARWOOD
SENIOR PHOTO EDITOR: HALI TARA FELDMAN
PHOTO EDITORS: ALEX GHEZ, CHANDRA GLICK
PHOTOGRAPHER: STEVEN KLEIN
EDITOR-IN-CHIEF: DANIEL PERES
PUBLISHER: CONDÉ NAST PUBLICATIONS
ISSUE: AUGUST 2008
CATEGORY: DESIGN: FEATURE: CELEBRITY/
ENTERTAINMENT PROFILE (SINGLE/SPREAD)

/177/ **DETAILS**
CREATIVE DIRECTOR: ROCKWELL HARWOOD
ART DIRECTOR: ANDRE JOINTE
DESIGNER: ROCKWELL HARWOOD
SENIOR PHOTO EDITOR: HALI TARA FELDMAN
PHOTOGRAPHER: MACIEK KOBIELSKI
EDITOR-IN-CHIEF: DANIEL PERES
PUBLISHER: CONDÉ NAST PUBLICATIONS
ISSUE: DECEMBER 2008
CATEGORY: DESIGN: FEATURE: CELEBRITY/
ENTERTAINMENT PROFILE (SINGLE/SPREAD)

178

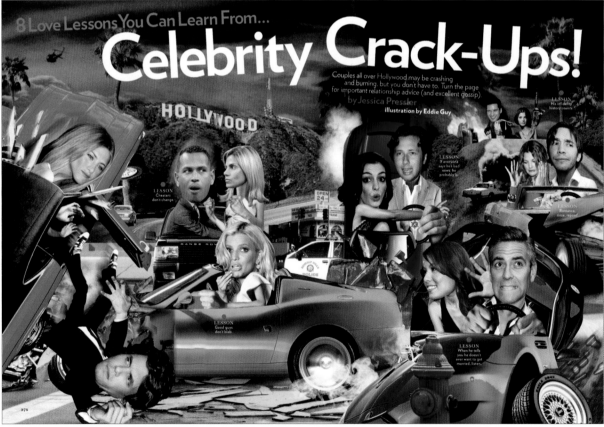

179

/178/ **GLAMOUR**
DESIGN DIRECTOR: GERALDINE HESSLER
ART DIRECTOR: THERESA GRIGGS
DIRECTOR OF PHOTOGRAPHY: SUZANNE DONALDSON
PUBLISHER: CONDÉ NAST PUBLICATIONS INC.
ISSUE: SEPTEMBER 2008
CATEGORY: DESIGN: FEATURE: CELEBRITY/
ENTERTAINMENT PROFILE (SINGLE/SPREAD)

/179/ **GLAMOUR**
DESIGN DIRECTOR: GERALDINE HESSLER
ART DIRECTOR: THERESA GRIGGS
DIRECTOR OF PHOTOGRAPHY: SUZANNE DONALDSON
PUBLISHER: CONDÉ NAST PUBLICATIONS INC.
ISSUE: NOVEMBER 2008
CATEGORY: DESIGN: FEATURE: CELEBRITY/
ENTERTAINMENT PROFILE (SINGLE/SPREAD)

180

183

181

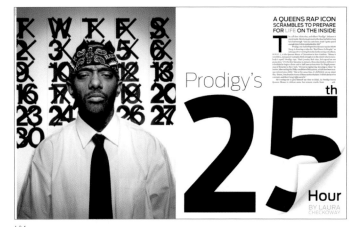

184

182

185

/180/ **BLENDER**
CREATIVE DIRECTOR: DIRK BARNETT
ART DIRECTOR: ROBERT VARGAS
DESIGNER: ROBERT VARGAS
PHOTO EDITORS: AMY HOPPY, RORY WALSH
PHOTOGRAPHERS: TURE LILLEGRAVEN, COOLIFE
EDITOR-IN-CHIEF: JOE LEVY
PUBLISHER: ALPHAMEDIA GROUP
ISSUE: NOVEMBER 2008
CATEGORY: DESIGN: FEATURE: CELEBRITY/
ENTERTAINMENT PROFILE (SINGLE/SPREAD)

/181/ **BLENDER**
CREATIVE DIRECTOR: DIRK BARNETT
ART DIRECTORS: ROB VARGAS,
CLAUDIA DE ALMEIDA
DESIGNERS: DIRK BARNETT, ROB VARGAS,
CLAUDIA DE ALMEIDA
DIRECTOR OF PHOTOGRAPHY: AMY HOPPY
PHOTOGRAPHER: ANDREW ECCLES
EDITOR-IN-CHIEF: JOE LEVY
PUBLISHER: ALPHAMEDIA GROUP
ISSUE: MAY 2008
CATEGORY: DESIGN: FEATURE: CELEBRITY/
ENTERTAINMENT PROFILE (SINGLE/SPREAD)

/182/ **BLENDER**
CREATIVE DIRECTOR: DIRK BARNETT
DESIGNER: DIRK BARNETT
DIRECTOR OF PHOTOGRAPHY: AMY HOPPY
PHOTOGRAPHER: GAVIN BOND
EDITOR-IN-CHIEF: JOE LEVY
PUBLISHER: ALPHAMEDIA GROUP
ISSUE: AUGUST 2008
CATEGORY: DESIGN: FEATURE: CELEBRITY/
ENTERTAINMENT PROFILE (SINGLE/SPREAD)

/183/ **ENTERTAINMENT WEEKLY**
DESIGN DIRECTOR: BRIAN ANSTEY
DESIGNER: MICHAEL SCHNAIDT
DIRECTOR OF PHOTOGRAPHY: LISA BERMAN
MANAGING EDITOR: RICK TETZELI
PUBLISHER: TIME INC.
ISSUE: AUGUST 15, 2008
CATEGORY: DESIGN: FEATURE: CELEBRITY/
ENTERTAINMENT PROFILE (SINGLE/SPREAD)

/184/ **THE VILLAGE VOICE**
ART DIRECTOR: IVYLISE SIMONES
PHOTOGRAPHER: CHAD GRIFFITH
PUBLISHER: VILLAGE VOICE MEDIA
ISSUE: FEBRUARY 13, 2008
CATEGORY: DESIGN: FEATURE: CELEBRITY/
ENTERTAINMENT PROFILE (SINGLE/SPREAD)

/185/ **GQ**
DESIGN DIRECTOR: FRED WOODWARD
DESIGNER: DELGIS CANAHUATE
DIRECTOR OF PHOTOGRAPHY: DORA SOMOSI
PHOTOGRAPHER: MARK SELIGER
EDITOR-IN-CHIEF: JIM NELSON
PUBLISHER: CONDÉ NAST PUBLICATIONS INC.
ISSUE: JANUARY 2008
CATEGORY: DESIGN: FEATURE: CELEBRITY/
ENTERTAINMENT PROFILE (SINGLE/SPREAD)

The

(Hot-Dog-Vending, Knife-Fighting,
Break-Dancing,
Spielberg-Wooing)

Adventures
Of Young
Shia
LaBeouf

By Kevin Conley
Photographs
By Peggy Sirota

PAGE
132
GQ.COM
JUNE 2008

186

187

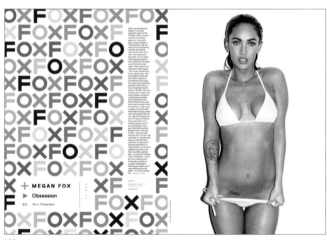

188

/186/ **GQ**
DESIGN DIRECTOR: FRED WOODWARD
DESIGNER: ROB HEWITT
DIRECTOR OF PHOTOGRAPHY: DORA SOMOSI
PHOTOGRAPHER: PEGGY SIROTA
CREATIVE DIRECTOR, FASHION: JIM MOORE
EDITOR-IN-CHIEF: JIM NELSON
PUBLISHER: CONDÉ NAST PUBLICATIONS INC.
ISSUE: JUNE 2008
CATEGORY: DESIGN: FEATURE: CELEBRITY/
ENTERTAINMENT PROFILE (SINGLE/SPREAD)

/187/ **GQ**
DESIGN DIRECTOR: FRED WOODWARD
DESIGNER: ANTON IOUKHNOVETS
DIRECTOR OF PHOTOGRAPHY: DORA SOMOSI
PHOTO EDITOR: KRISTA PRESTEK
PHOTOGRAPHER: TERRY RICHARDSON
CREATIVE DIRECTOR, FASHION: JIM MOORE
EDITOR-IN-CHIEF: JIM NELSON
PUBLISHER: CONDÉ NAST PUBLICATIONS INC.
ISSUE: OCTOBER 2008
CATEGORY: DESIGN: FEATURE: CELEBRITY/
ENTERTAINMENT PROFILE (SINGLE/SPREAD)

/188/ **GQ**
DESIGN DIRECTOR: FRED WOODWARD
DESIGNER: ANTON IOUKHNOVETS
DIRECTOR OF PHOTOGRAPHY: DORA SOMOSI
PHOTO EDITOR: KRISTA PRESTEK
PHOTOGRAPHER: TERRY RICHARDSON
CREATIVE DIRECTOR, FASHION: JIM MOORE
EDITOR-IN-CHIEF: JIM NELSON
PUBLISHER: CONDÉ NAST PUBLICATIONS INC.
ISSUE: DECEMBER 2008
CATEGORY: DESIGN: FEATURE: CELEBRITY/
ENTERTAINMENT PROFILE (SINGLE/SPREAD)

189

190

191

/189/ **W**
DESIGN DIRECTOR: EDWARD LEIDA
ART DIRECTOR: NATHALIE KIRSHEH
DESIGNER: NATHALIE KIRSHEH
PHOTOGRAPHERS: MERT ALAS, MARCUS PIGGOTT
PUBLISHER: CONDÉ NAST PUBLICATIONS INC.
ISSUE: SEPTEMBER 2008
CATEGORY: DESIGN: FEATURE: CELEBRITY/
ENTERTAINMENT PROFILE (SINGLE/SPREAD)

/190/ **W**
DESIGN DIRECTOR: EDWARD LEIDA
ART DIRECTOR: NATHALIE KIRSHEH
PHOTOGRAPHER: STEVEN KLEIN
PUBLISHER: CONDÉ NAST PUBLICATIONS INC.
ISSUE: MARCH 2008
CATEGORY: DESIGN: FEATURE: CELEBRITY/
ENTERTAINMENT PROFILE (SINGLE/SPREAD)

/191/ **W**
DESIGN DIRECTOR: EDWARD LEIDA
ART DIRECTOR: NATHALIE KIRSHEH
PHOTOGRAPHER: JACKIE NICKERSON
PUBLISHER: CONDÉ NAST PUBLICATIONS INC.
ISSUE: SEPTEMBER 2008
CATEGORY: DESIGN: FEATURE: CELEBRITY/
ENTERTAINMENT PROFILE (SINGLE/SPREAD)

"We're going to give the album away."
That's how Radiohead frontman
THOM YORKE explains the decision
to offer his band's new record as a
name-your-price digital download.
Is this the future of music? WIRED sent
DAVID BYRNE to Oxford to learn more.

THE RADIOHEAD REVOLUTION
PHOTOGRAPHS BY JAMES DAY

192

AND RISE OF MUSIC
PHOTOGRAPH BY JAMES DAY

THE FALL

The CD? It's dead. Good thing
the music industry is about more
than selling plastic discs.
Today's artists have surprising
new ways to reach fans
and make a living. A guided
tour of what's next.
BY DAVID BYRNE

192

/192/ **WIRED**
CREATIVE DIRECTOR: SCOTT DADICH / DESIGN DIRECTOR: WYATT MITCHELL / DESIGNERS: SCOTT DADICH, MARGARET SWART
PHOTO EDITOR: ZANA WOODS / PHOTOGRAPHER: JAMES DAY / PUBLISHER: CONDÉ NAST PUBLICATIONS, INC.
ISSUE: JANUARY 2008 / CATEGORY: DESIGN: FEATURE: CELEBRITY/ENTERTAINMENT PROFILE (STORY)

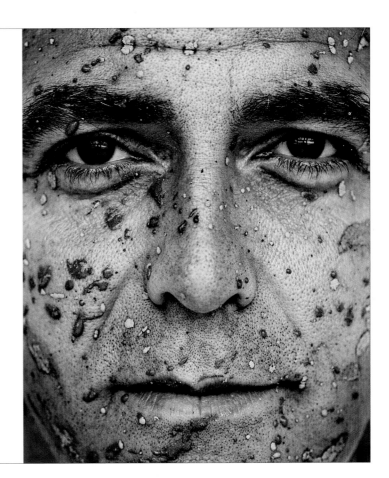

11

The Muckraker

FROM ROMANTIC COMEDY TO POLITICAL DIATRIBE, GEORGE CLOONEY
HAS GONE THE WHOLE NINE YARDS. BY LYNN HIRSCHBERG

Photographs by JEAN-BAPTISTE MONDINO

Your new film, "Leatherheads," which you directed and star in, is about the
early days of professional football. What attracted you to this project?
I like to direct. I consider myself more a director than an actor. And after "Good Night, and Good Luck" I realized that I
was really good at juggling a hundred things at once. In fact, I needed to: when the hundred things stop, I get into
trouble. After "Good Night," every offer I got to direct was for an issue film. And I don't want to be the "issues"
guy. I want to be a director with longevity, so I picked "Leatherheads." It was a complete departure — a romantic comedy with football.

Q: Did you watch a lot of romantic comedies to prepare?
A: I believe in stealing. I ripped off "His Girl Friday" and "The Philadelphia Story." I was ripping off everything — I'll
send apology letters to everyone. I've sent an apology to Sydney Pollack already — there's a scene I stole from

193

"Absence of Malice" that is so close we had to change it.

Q: Did you play football as a kid growing up in Kentucky?
A: No. My school, which was a public school, was too small. You need 11
guys, and I think there were just 11 guys in my entire senior class. I
played baseball — specifically, center field, which means that you are the
captain of the outfield, which I liked.

Q: The movie is, in many ways, a celebration of small-town America.
How important was it to you that you grew up in a small town?
A: It's informed almost everything I've done. It was a great place to
grow up because you could do anything you wanted to do. The town was
our baby sitter. My dad was gone until late at night doing the news
on local television, and my mom was working, too. I'd be at a friend's
house and I'd check in once in a while. It's the only time in your life
that you have intimate contact with how other people live. For instance,
my family would say grace before every meal in a particular rhythm.
At my buddy's house, they did it double time because there were 12 kids
and if you didn't say grace fast enough, you didn't eat.

Q: But you still wanted to leave Kentucky?
A: Badly. I was restless. My aunt Rosemary [the singer Rosemary
Clooney] and her five kids lived in Beverly Hills, and I would hear of
these exciting things they were doing. I remember that they went
skiing in Switzerland. We didn't live like that ever, and I was jealous.
We may have been in show business, but it was down-and-dirty local
TV. They were in Hollywood! I thought, That's the life.

Q: Did your parents encourage you?
A: Absolutely not. My father and his sister went through a difficult time
for many years when she was addicted to Percodan. My aunt's addiction
haunted me when I injured my back [during the making of "Syriana"].
The doctors gave me a tub of Vicodin, but I didn't take any. I thought,
This is a bad time to decide to be a drug addict. It's all timing: when
I'm 80, I'm all for being a drug addict, but not now. Anyway, when I
said I wanted to be an actor, my father told me: "This isn't going to turn
out well." I'm glad I didn't take his advice, but it was the right advice.
Adversity is not a bad thing. I worked two times as hard to show them.
And, even now, the feeling that this might not work out has not left me.

Q: Do you think doing lots and lots of television was helpful or hurtful
for your movie career?
A: Absolutely helpful. Especially doing sitcoms. At a comedy show,
everybody is involved in making the project better. You're not just
concerned with yourself. And then an audience comes in, and you learn
to make instant decisions. And I learned about love scenes. I've probably
played every romantic scene in television. I was on a show called "Sisters,"
and I remember telling the producers what women want. The producers
always wanted me to be the guy who said to the girl, "I'll be waiting for
you." I told them that while all women say they want that guy, no woman
wants that on the screen. I learned not to be the wuss. Mostly, TV gave
me a chance at variety. I was lucky that I never became famous until "ER."
I wasn't successful for years and years, and at the time, I hated that,
but thank God I wasn't a big hit on "The Facts of Life." If that happens,
no matter what your talent level, you never get out of that box.

Q: Did you try to get into movies?
A: Oh, yeah, but no one wanted to see me. I was making $40,000 an episode
on some hour show, and I couldn't get an audition for a two-line part in a
film called "Guarding Tess." During my first break from "ER," I knew I had

to do a movie. When "From Dusk Till Dawn" came around, I knew it
was a lucky shot. I knew if I didn't do it, the juggernaut would disappear.

Q: Did you always have it in the back of your mind to try and tackle more
political films?
A: Yes, but nobody encourages you to do "Syriana." They want you to
be the glamorous guy. It was very hard to get "Syriana" made in 2004. The
war in Iraq was popular when we were pitching the movie. People would
only whisper that they agreed with me. Let's be straightforward: there's
a huge part of the country that until 9/11 did not know the difference
between an Israeli and an Arab. They thought the Middle East was just
a bunch of guys with towels on their heads. "Syriana" was an attempt
to show a world that's still unclear to most Americans.

Q: You seem to like to make things hard on yourself.
A: If you're successful, you feel more responsible for other issues. You
think they're going to take it away from you.

Q: That sounds so Catholic. Were you raised religiously?
A: I was an altar boy. I don't consider myself Catholic anymore, but
that religion remains deep in your soul. The last time I went to
confession, I was 17. I'm 46 now, so I have some sins to confess [laughs].
Living in a small town, I knew the priest and the priest knew me.
My friend Pete told me that he read in the Bible about a saint who put a
pebble in his shoe for penance. So, I'd confess what I thought was
important for the priest to hear, and then I'd fill my shoes with gravel
and jump off the top of my bunk bed. I thought that covered it.

Q: Why don't you run for elected office?
A: That would be a terrible idea. I would be the worst candidate. I'm
supporting Barack Obama, and I don't even think it's a good idea
for me to stump for him. They can pull out some old video of me
saying something crazy, and then it suddenly becomes about defending
something that I've said that has nothing to do with the campaign. I
think Huckabee has been incredibly effective, but the least smart thing
I've seen him do is stand there with Chuck Norris. It's like, What —
can't you get your own fans?
I've met Hillary several times, and I like her very much. I think the
problem is sort of like this: I'm having a good year with "Michael
Clayton," but this is Daniel Day-Lewis's year. He's the actor that all
actors are jealous of. I don't have any understanding of that kind of acting.
For me, it's like a foreign object. And that's Hillary and Obama.

Q: Hasn't politics become more like Hollywood? So far, this election seems
particularly camera-ready.
A: Since the Kennedy and Nixon debate, presidential campaigns have
been Hollywood. You're never going to vote for a candidate who
has a high, squeaky voice. They consult on everything now: part your
hair on the left because it's more soothing; wear blue because it
inspires confidence. Rather than win over the masses, they are trying
to pick off demographics. That happens everywhere — in news,
in movies and with candidates. It's all the same. ■

POLO BY RALPH LAUREN THREE-PIECE COTTON-AND-LINEN SUIT, MADE TO MEASURE.
COTTON SHIRT, $145, AND COTTON TIE, $115. GO TO RALPHLAUREN.COM.
FASHION ASSISTANTS: SHANDI ALEXANDER AND RACHAEL WANG. GROOMING BY ITSUKI
AT THE WALL GROUP. PROP STYLING BY MEGAN CAPONETTO AT APOSTROPHE.
FASHION EDITOR: BILL MULLEN.

SCREEN TEST TO VIEW ORIGINAL SHORT FILMS ABOUT GEORGE CLOONEY AND OTHER
COVER SUBJECTS, GO TO NYTIMES.COM/TMAGAZINE.

193

/193/ **T, THE NEW YORK TIMES STYLE MAGAZINE**
CREATIVE DIRECTOR: JANET FROELICH / SENIOR ART DIRECTOR: DAVID SEBBAH / ART DIRECTOR: CHRISTOPHER MARTINEZ
DESIGNER: CHRISTOPHER MARTINEZ / DIRECTOR OF PHOTOGRAPHY: KATHY RYAN / SENIOR PHOTO EDITOR: JUDITH PUCKETT-RINELLA
PHOTOGRAPHER: JEAN-BAPTISTE MONDINO / EDITOR-IN-CHIEF: STEFANO TONCHI / PUBLISHER: THE NEW YORK TIMES
ISSUE: MARCH 9, 2008 / CATEGORY: DESIGN: FEATURE: CELEBRITY/ENTERTAINMENT PROFILE (STORY)

194

194

/194/ **GQ**
DESIGN DIRECTOR: FRED WOODWARD / DESIGNER: ROB HEWITT / ILLUSTRATOR: ZOHAR LAZAR / DIRECTOR OF PHOTOGRAPHY: DORA SOMOSI
PHOTOGRAPHERS: CHRIS BUCK, MARTIN SCHOELLER, PEGGY SIROTA / CREATIVE DIRECTOR, FASHION: JIM MOORE / EDITOR-IN-CHIEF: JIM NELSON
PUBLISHER: CONDÉ NAST PUBLICATIONS INC. / ISSUE: AUGUST 2008 / CATEGORY: DESIGN: FEATURE: CELEBRITY/ENTERTAINMENT PROFILE (STORY)

195

195

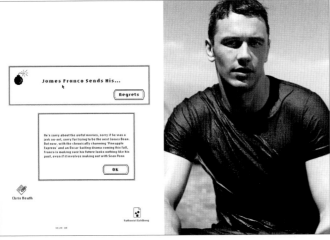

196

196

197

197

/195/ **GQ**
DESIGN DIRECTOR: FRED WOODWARD
DESIGNER: ROB HEWITT
ILLUSTRATOR: ZOHAR LAZAR
DIRECTOR OF PHOTOGRAPHY: DORA SOMOSI
PHOTOGRAPHER: PEGGY SIROTA
EDITOR-IN-CHIEF: JIM NELSON
PUBLISHER: CONDÉ NAST PUBLICATIONS INC.
ISSUE: AUGUST 2008
CATEGORY: DESIGN: FEATURE: CELEBRITY/
ENTERTAINMENT PROFILE (STORY)

/196/ **GQ**
DESIGN DIRECTOR: FRED WOODWARD
DESIGNER: ANTON IOUKHNOVETS
DIRECTOR OF PHOTOGRAPHY: DORA SOMOSI
PHOTOGRAPHER: NATHANIEL GOLDBERG
CREATIVE DIRECTOR, FASHION: JIM MOORE
EDITOR-IN-CHIEF: JIM NELSON
PUBLISHER: CONDÉ NAST PUBLICATIONS INC.
ISSUE: SEPTEMBER 2008
CATEGORY: DESIGN: FEATURE: CELEBRITY/
ENTERTAINMENT PROFILE (STORY)

/197/ **W**
DESIGN DIRECTOR: EDWARD LEIDA
ART DIRECTOR: NATHALIE KIRSHEH
DESIGNER: NATHALIE KIRSHEH
PHOTOGRAPHER: STEVEN KLEIN
PUBLISHER: CONDÉ NAST PUBLICATIONS INC.
ISSUE: FEBRUARY 2008
CATEGORY: DESIGN: FEATURE: CELEBRITY/
ENTERTAINMENT PROFILE (STORY)

PART FOUR

NATURE'S REVENGE

Inside Chernobyl's Zone of Alienation, one of the largest wildlife preserves in Europe teaches us a lesson about the durability of nature   and the fragility of man

By Donovan Webster

Photographs by Christopher Sturman

URBAN RENEWAL
The top-floor viewing area of a luxury hotel in Pripyat, Ukraine, overlooks a city that once teemed with life.

198

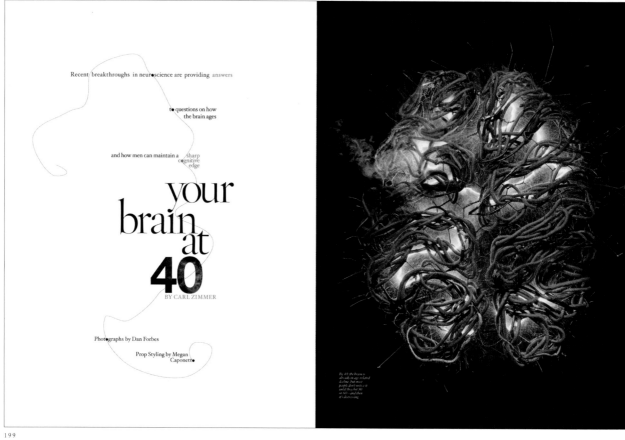

Recent breakthroughs in neuroscience are providing answers

to questions on how the brain ages

and how men can maintain a sharp cognitive edge

your brain at 40
BY CARL ZIMMER

Photographs by Dan Forbes

Prop Styling by Megan Caponetto

199

/198/ **BEST LIFE**
DESIGN DIRECTOR: BRANDON KAVULLA / DESIGNER: BRANDON KAVULLA
DIRECTOR OF PHOTOGRAPHY: RYAN CADIZ / PHOTOGRAPHER:
CHRISTOPHER STURMAN / PUBLISHER: RODALE INC. / ISSUE: NOVEMBER
2008CATEGORY: DESIGN: FEATURE: NEWS/REPORTAGE (SINGLE/SPREAD)

/199/ **BEST LIFE**
DESIGN DIRECTOR: BRANDON KAVULLA / DESIGNER: HEATHER JONES
DIRECTOR OF PHOTOGRAPHY: RYAN CADIZ / PHOTOGRAPHER: DAN FORBES
PUBLISHER: RODALE INC. / ISSUE: DECEMBER 2008 / CATEGORY: DESIGN:
FEATURE: NEWS/REPORTAGE (SINGLE/SPREAD)

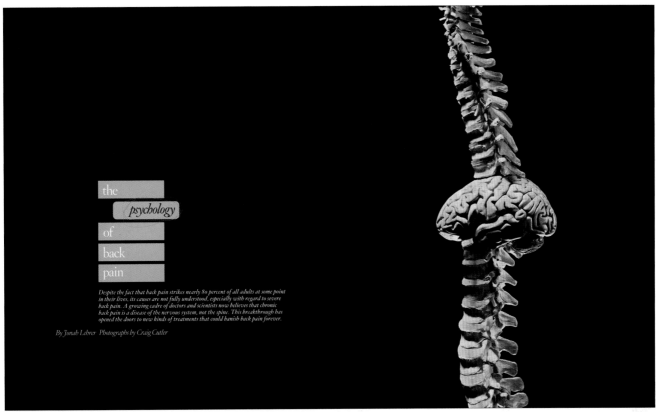

the
psychology
of
back
pain

Despite the fact that back pain strikes nearly 80 percent of all adults at some point in their lives, its causes are not fully understood, especially with regard to severe back pain. A growing cadre of doctors and scientists now believes that chronic back pain is a disease of the nervous system, not the spine. This breakthrough has opened the doors to new kinds of treatments that could banish back pain forever.

By Jonah Lehrer Photographs by Craig Cutler

200

To Die For

Our chief
restaurant
critic travels
to Tokyo
to eat the
world's most
dangerous
meal. So what
does fugu
taste like?
And what's
that funny
tingling
in his throat?

By **Adam Platt**
Photograph by James Wojcik

39

201

/200/ **BEST LIFE**
DESIGN DIRECTOR: BRANDON KAVULLA / DESIGNERS: BRANDON KAVULLA, HEATHER JONES / DIRECTOR OF PHOTOGRAPHY: RYAN CADIZ
PHOTO EDITOR: JEANNE GRAVES / PHOTOGRAPHER: CRAIG CUTLER
PUBLISHER: RODALE INC. / ISSUE: FEBRUARY 2008 / CATEGORY: DESIGN: FEATURE: NEWS/REPORTAGE (SINGLE/SPREAD)

/201/ **NEW YORK**
DESIGN DIRECTOR: CHRIS DIXON / ART DIRECTOR: RANDY MINOR
DESIGNER: HITOMI SATO / DIRECTOR OF PHOTOGRAPHY: JODY QUON
PHOTOGRAPHER: JAMES WOJCIK / EDITOR-IN-CHIEF: ADAM MOSS
PUBLISHER: NEW YORK MAGAZINE HOLDINGS, LLC / ISSUE: MAY 5, 2008
CATEGORY: DESIGN: FEATURE: NEWS/REPORTAGE (SINGLE/SPREAD)

202

205

203

206

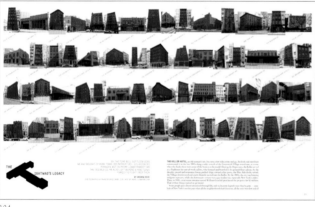

204

207

/202/ **BEST LIFE**
DESIGN DIRECTOR: BRANDON KAVULLA
DESIGNER: BRANDON KAVULLA
DIRECTOR OF PHOTOGRAPHY: RYAN CADIZ
PHOTOGRAPHER: JAMIE CHUNG
PUBLISHER: RODALE INC.
ISSUE: SEPTEMBER 2008
CATEGORY: DESIGN: FEATURE:
NEWS/REPORTAGE (SINGLE/SPREAD)

/203/ **BEST LIFE**
DESIGN DIRECTOR: BRANDON KAVULLA
DESIGNER: BRANDON KAVULLA
DIRECTOR OF PHOTOGRAPHY: RYAN CADIZ
PHOTOGRAPHER: TITOUAN LAMAZOU
PUBLISHER: RODALE INC.
ISSUE: NOVEMBER 2008
CATEGORY: DESIGN: FEATURE:
NEWS/REPORTAGE (SINGLE/SPREAD)

/204/ **KEY, THE NEW YORK TIMES
REAL ESTATE MAGAZINE**
CREATIVE DIRECTOR: JANET FROELICH
ART DIRECTOR: JEFF GLENDENNING
DESIGNER: JEFF GLENDENNING
DIRECTOR OF PHOTOGRAPHY: KATHY RYAN
PHOTO EDITORS: JOANNA MILTER, DAVID CARTHAS
PHOTOGRAPHER: MARVIN ORELLANA
COLLAGE BY ABBY CLAWSON LOW
EDITOR-IN-CHIEF: GERRY MARZORATI
PUBLISHER: THE NEW YORK TIMES
ISSUE: SPRING 2008
CATEGORY: DESIGN: FEATURE:
NEWS/REPORTAGE (SINGLE/SPREAD)

/205/ **FORTUNE**
DESIGN DIRECTOR: ROBERT PERINO
ART DIRECTOR: DEANNA LOWE
DESIGNER: DEANNA LOWE
DIRECTOR OF PHOTOGRAPHY: GREG POND
PHOTO EDITOR: LAUREN WINFIELD
PHOTOGRAPHER: ANTONIN KRATOCHVIL
PUBLISHER: TIME INC.
ISSUE: JUNE 9, 2008
CATEGORY: DESIGN: FEATURE:
NEWS/REPORTAGE (SINGLE/SPREAD)

/206/ **NEW YORK**
DESIGN DIRECTOR: CHRIS DIXON
ART DIRECTOR: RANDY MINOR
DESIGNER: HITOMI SATO
DIRECTOR OF PHOTOGRAPHY: JODY QUON
PHOTOGRAPHER: CARA BARER
EDITOR-IN-CHIEF: ADAM MOSS
PUBLISHER: NEW YORK MAGAZINE HOLDINGS, LLC
ISSUE: SEPTEMBER 22, 2008
CATEGORY: DESIGN: FEATURE:
NEWS/REPORTAGE (SINGLE/SPREAD)

/207/ **THE NEW YORK TIMES MAGAZINE**
CREATIVE DIRECTOR: JANET FROELICH
ART DIRECTOR: AREM DUPLESSIS
DEPUTY ART DIRECTOR: GAIL BICHLER
DESIGNER: GAIL BICHLER
DIRECTOR OF PHOTOGRAPHY: KATHY RYAN
PHOTO EDITOR: CLINTON CARGILL
PHOTOGRAPHER: JEFF RIEDEL
EDITOR-IN-CHIEF: GERRY MARZORATI
PUBLISHER: THE NEW YORK TIMES
ISSUE: MAY 18, 2008
CATEGORY: DESIGN: FEATURE:
NEWS/REPORTAGE (SINGLE/SPREAD)

208

211

209

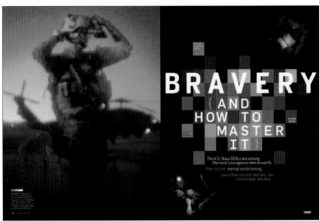

212

210

213

/208/ TWIN CITIES METRO
ART DIRECTOR: BRYAN NANISTA
DESIGNER: BRYAN NANISTA
EDITOR-IN-CHIEF: BARBARA KNOX
PUBLISHER: TIGER OAK
ISSUE: AUGUST 2008
CATEGORY: DESIGN: FEATURE:
NEWS/REPORTAGE (SINGLE/SPREAD)

/209/ GOOD
DESIGN DIRECTOR: SCOTT STOWELL
DESIGNER: RYAN THACKER
ILLUSTRATOR: LUKE BEST
PHOTOGRAPHER: LOLA LONDON
STUDIO: OPEN
PUBLISHER: GOOD WORLDWIDE, INC.
CLIENT: GOOD
ISSUE: SEPTEMBER/OCTOBER 2008
CATEGORY: DESIGN: FEATURE:
NEWS/REPORTAGE (SINGLE/SPREAD)

/210/ MEN'S HEALTH
DESIGN DIRECTOR: GEORGE KARABOTSOS
ART DIRECTOR: JOHN DIXON
DESIGNER: JOHN DIXON
DIRECTOR OF PHOTOGRAPHY: BRENDA MILLIS
PHOTO EDITOR: BRENDA MILLIS
PHOTOGRAPHER: MAX BECHERER
PUBLISHER: RODALE INC.
ISSUE: APRIL 2008
CATEGORY: DESIGN: FEATURE:
NEWS/REPORTAGE (SINGLE/SPREAD)

/211/ UD & SE
DESIGN DIRECTOR: TORSTEN HOGH RASMUSSEN
PHOTOGRAPHER: ANDERS BIRCH
PUBLISHER: DSB
CATEGORY: DESIGN: FEATURE:
NEWS/REPORTAGE (SINGLE/SPREAD)

/212/ GOLF DIGEST
DESIGN DIRECTOR: KEN DELAGO
DESIGNER: KEN DELAGO
ILLUSTRATOR: BRYAN CHRISTIE
PUBLISHER: CONDÉ NAST PUBLICATIONS INC.
ISSUE: SEPTEMBER 2008
CATEGORY: DESIGN: FEATURE:
NEWS/REPORTAGE (SINGLE/SPREAD)

/213/ TEXAS MONTHLY
ART DIRECTOR: T.J. TUCKER
DESIGNER: ANDI BEIERMAN
PHOTO EDITOR: LESLIE BALDWIN
PHOTOGRAPHERS: O. RUFUS LOVETT, RANDAL FORD
PUBLISHER: EMMIS COMMUNICATIONS CORP.
ISSUE: SEPTEMBER 2008
CATEGORY: DESIGN: FEATURE:
NEWS/REPORTAGE (SINGLE/SPREAD)

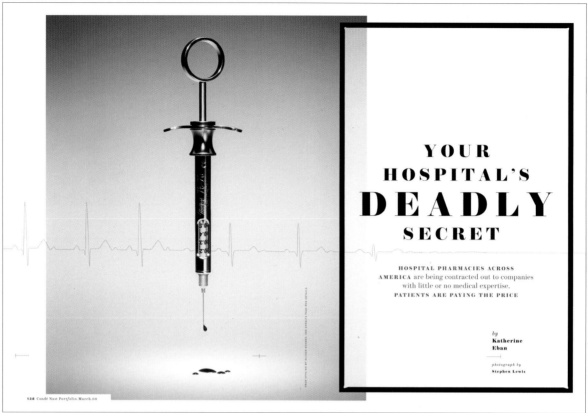

214

215

/214/ **CONDÉ NAST PORTFOLIO**
DESIGN DIRECTOR: ROBERT PRIEST
ART DIRECTOR: GRACE LEE
DESIGNER: COLIN TUNSTALL
DIRECTOR OF PHOTOGRAPHY: LISA BERMAN
PHOTO EDITOR: JOHN TOOLAN
PHOTOGRAPHER: STEPHEN LEWIS
EDITOR-IN-CHIEF: JOANNE LIPMAN
PUBLISHER: CONDÉ NAST PUBLICATIONS INC.
ISSUE: MARCH 2008
CATEGORY: DESIGN: FEATURE:
NEWS/REPORTAGE (SINGLE/SPREAD)

/215/ **CONDÉ NAST PORTFOLIO**
DESIGN DIRECTOR: ROBERT PRIEST
ART DIRECTOR: GRACE LEE
DESIGNER: GRACE LEE
ILLUSTRATOR: SAM WEBER
EDITOR-IN-CHIEF: JOANNE LIPMAN
PUBLISHER: CONDÉ NAST PUBLICATIONS INC.
ISSUE: JULY 2008
CATEGORY: DESIGN: FEATURE:
NEWS/REPORTAGE (SINGLE/SPREAD)

216

219

217

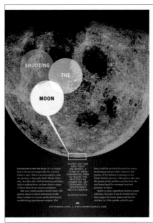

220

218

221

/216/ CONDÉ NAST PORTFOLIO
ART DIRECTOR: GRACE LEE
DESIGNER: GRACE LEE
DIRECTOR OF PHOTOGRAPHY: LISA BERMAN
PHOTO EDITOR: SARAH WEISSMAN
PHOTOGRAPHER: CHRISTOPHER GRIFFITH
EDITOR-IN-CHIEF: JOANNE LIPMAN
PUBLISHER: CONDÉ NAST PUBLICATIONS INC.
ISSUE: MARCH 2008
CATEGORY: DESIGN: FEATURE:
NEWS/REPORTAGE (SINGLE/SPREAD)

/217/ GQ
DESIGN DIRECTOR: FRED WOODWARD
DESIGNER: ROB HEWITT
DIRECTOR OF PHOTOGRAPHY: DORA SOMOSI
PHOTO EDITOR: JUSTIN O'NEILL
PHOTOGRAPHER: EDWARD BURTYNSKY
EDITOR-IN-CHIEF: JIM NELSON
PUBLISHER: CONDÉ NAST PUBLICATIONS INC.
ISSUE: MARCH 2008
CATEGORY: DESIGN: FEATURE:
NEWS/REPORTAGE (SINGLE/SPREAD)

/218/ GQ
DESIGN DIRECTOR: FRED WOODWARD
DESIGNER: MICHAEL PANGILINAN
DIRECTOR OF PHOTOGRAPHY: DORA SOMOSI
PHOTO EDITOR: JUSTIN O'NEILL
PHOTOGRAPHER: DAN WINTERS
EDITOR-IN-CHIEF: JIM NELSON
PUBLISHER: CONDÉ NAST PUBLICATIONS INC.
ISSUE: JANUARY 2008
CATEGORY: DESIGN: FEATURE:
NEWS/REPORTAGE (SINGLE/SPREAD)

/219/ GQ
DESIGN DIRECTOR: FRED WOODWARD
DESIGNER: DRUE WAGNER
DIRECTOR OF PHOTOGRAPHY: DORA SOMOSI
PHOTO EDITOR: JOLANTA BIELAT
PHOTOGRAPHER: DAN WINTERS
EDITOR-IN-CHIEF: JIM NELSON
PUBLISHER: CONDÉ NAST PUBLICATIONS INC.
ISSUE: SEPTEMBER 2008
CATEGORY: DESIGN: FEATURE:
NEWS/REPORTAGE (SINGLE/SPREAD)

/220/ DETAILS
CREATIVE DIRECTOR: ROCKWELL HARWOOD
ART DIRECTOR: ANDRE JOINTE
DESIGNER: ANDRE JOINTE
PHOTO EDITORS: CHANDRA GLICK, ALEX GHEZ
PHOTOGRAPHER: CHRISTOPHER GRIFFITH
SENIOR PHOTO EDITOR: HALI TARA FELDMAN
EDITOR-IN-CHIEF: DANIEL PERES
PUBLISHER: CONDÉ NAST PUBLICATIONS
ISSUE: MARCH 2008
CATEGORY: DESIGN: FEATURE:
NEWS/REPORTAGE (SINGLE/SPREAD)

/221/ POPULAR MECHANICS
DESIGN DIRECTOR: MICHAEL LAWTON
DIRECTOR OF PHOTOGRAPHY: ALLYSON TORRISI
EDITOR-IN-CHIEF: JAMES B. MEIGS
PUBLISHER: THE HEARST CORPORATION-
MAGAZINES DIVISION
ISSUE: SEPTEMBER 2008
CATEGORY: DESIGN: FEATURE:
NEWS/REPORTAGE (SINGLE/SPREAD)

The New York Times Magazine / SEPTEMBER 21, 2008

Does teaching make you a bad writer? Could it make you a good president?
How would you teach on YouTube? How would you teach in Dubai? How can you teach with … style? From Alaska
to Alabama to the Persian Gulf, we look at the mysteries of teaching in all its variety. Words aside,
however, the look of this issue is all-student: headline type, photographs and illustrations are all the work of undergraduate
and graduate students from across the country, and a few from overseas as well.

PHILOSOPHY   START-UP   READ/WRITE   STUDYING   LAW SCHOOL   NEGOTIATE   LECTURE   PERFORM

LETTERING BY **ERIC KU** **School of Visual Arts**
ILLUSTRATIONS BY **EMILY DWYER** **Ringling College of Art and Design**

53

/222/ **THE NEW YORK TIMES MAGAZINE**
CREATIVE DIRECTOR: JANET FROELICH / ART DIRECTOR: AREM DUPLESSIS / DEPUTY ART DIRECTOR: GAIL BICHLER / DESIGNERS: HILARY GREENBAUM, LEO JUNG,
SARA MCKAY / ILLUSTRATORS: LORIN BROWN, ERIK DE GRAAFF, KYLE BEAN, ABI HUYNH, STEVE HASLIP, STEVEN SMITH, ERIC KU, EMILY DWYER, SIMON CORRY,
JENNA BROUSE, HYE JIN LEE, GUDMUNDUR INGI ULFASRRON, MADS FREUND BRUNSE, ROSIE GAINSBOROUGH, ELISHEA NICHOLSON, TILL WIEDECK, BRYAN ISCHE,
CHRISTOPHER MORABITO, TOM VAN DE VELDE, SARAH CWYNAR, MITCH BLUNT, LUKE WILLIAMS / DIRECTOR OF PHOTOGRAPHY: KATHY RYAN / PHOTO EDITOR: CLINTON
CARGILL / PHOTOGRAPHERS: DAVID LA SPINA, MATT SARTAIN, ALEC HOLST, ANNICK ROSENFIELD, SAM RICHARDS, CHRISTOPHER KIM, DRU DONOVAN, JESSICA NELSON,
VICTORIA HELY-HUTCHINSON, JONATHAN BRUCE WILLIAMS, GEORGE AWDE / EDITOR-IN-CHIEF: GERRY MARZORATI / PUBLISHER: THE NEW YORK TIMES
ISSUE: SEPTEMBER 21, 2008 / CATEGORY: DESIGN: FEATURE: NEWS/REPORTAGE (STORY)

223

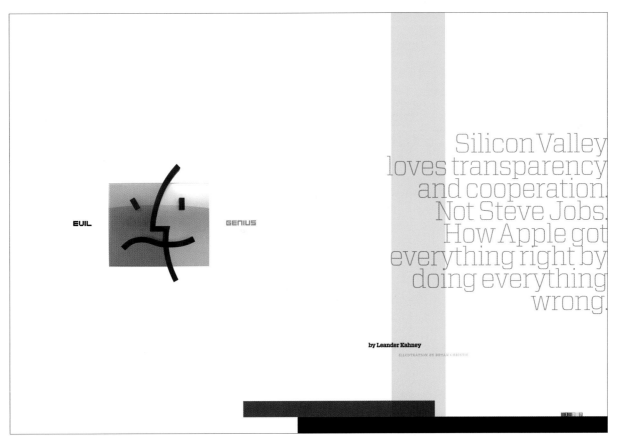

EUIL **GENIUS**

Silicon Valley
loves transparency
and cooperation.
Not Steve Jobs.
How Apple got
everything right by
doing everything
wrong.

by Leander Kahney

ILLUSTRATION BY BRYAN CHRISTIE

223

/223/ **WIRED**
CREATIVE DIRECTOR: SCOTT DADICH / DESIGN DIRECTOR: WYATT MITCHELL / ART DIRECTORS: MAILI HOLIMAN, CHRISTY SHEPPARD / DESIGNER: MAILI HOLIMAN
ILLUSTRATORS: RONALD J. CALA, NICK DEWAR, CHRISTOPH NIEMANN, RICCARDO VECCHIO, SI SCOTT, NATE WILLIAMS, BRIAN REA, JAMES VICTORE, BRYAN CHRISTIE,
TETSUYA NAGATO / PHOTO EDITOR: CAROLYN RAUCH / PHOTOGRAPHER: MAURICIO ALEJO / PUBLISHER: CONDÉ NAST PUBLICATIONS, INC. / ISSUE: APRIL 2008
CATEGORY: DESIGN: FEATURE: NEWS/REPORTAGE (STORY)

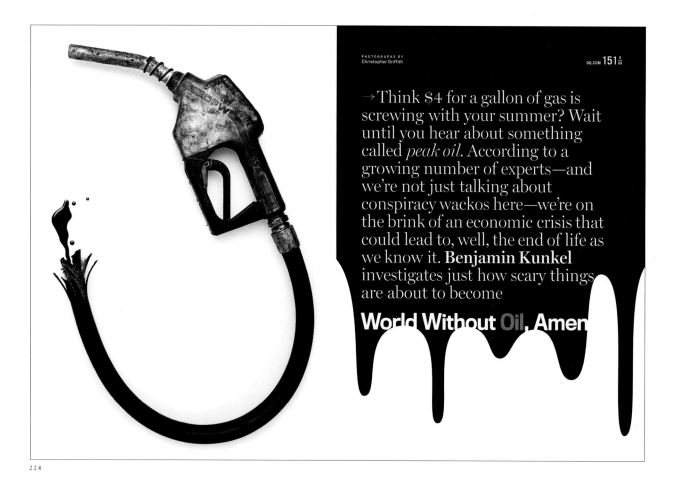

PHOTOGRAPHS BY
Christopher Griffith

GQ.COM 151 ₈/₀₈

→Think $4 for a gallon of gas is screwing with your summer? Wait until you hear about something called *peak oil*. According to a growing number of experts—and we're not just talking about conspiracy wackos here—we're on the brink of an economic crisis that could lead to, well, the end of life as we know it. **Benjamin Kunkel** investigates just how scary things are about to become

World Without Oil, Amen

224

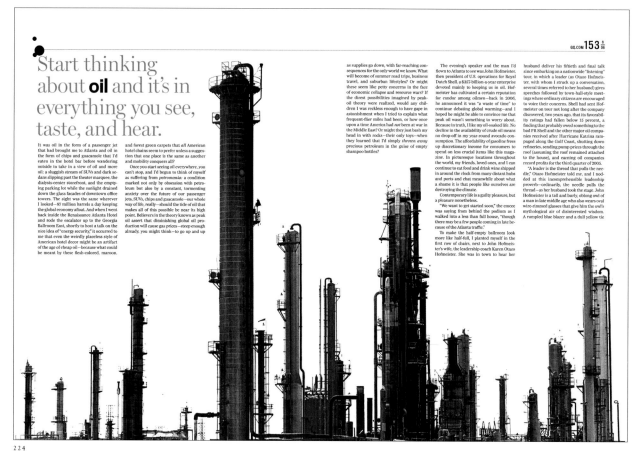

GQ.COM 153 ₈/₀₈

Start thinking about **oil** and it's in everything you see, taste, and hear.

It was oil in the form of a passenger jet that had brought me to Atlanta and oil in the form of chips and guacamole that I'd eaten in the hotel bar before wandering outside to take in a view of oil and more oil: a sluggish stream of SUVs and dark sedans slipping past the theater marquee, the dialysis-center storefront, and the emptying parking lot while the sunlight drained down the glass facades of downtown office towers. The sight was the same wherever I looked—87 million barrels a day keeping the global economy afloat. And when I went back inside the Renaissance Atlanta Hotel and rode the escalator up to the Georgia Ballroom East, shortly to host a talk on the nice idea of "energy security," it occurred to me that even the weirdly placeless style of American hotel decor might be an artifact of the age of cheap oil—because what could be meant by these flesh-colored, maroon,

and forest green carpets that *all* American hotel chains seem to prefer unless a suggestion that one place is the same as another and mobility conquers all?

Once you start seeing oil everywhere, you can't stop, and I'd begun to think of myself as suffering from *petromania*: a condition marked not only by obsession with petroleum but also by a constant, tormenting anxiety over the future of our passenger jets, SUVs, chips and guacamole—our whole way of life, really—should the tide of oil that makes all of this possible be near its high point. Believers in the theory known as peak oil assert that diminishing global oil production will cause gas prices—steep enough already, you might think—to go up and up

as supplies go down, with far-reaching consequences for the only world we know. What will become of summer road trips, business travel, and suburban lifestyles? Or might these seem like petty concerns in the face of economic collapse and resource wars? If the direst possibilities imagined by peak-oil theory were realized, would any children I was reckless enough to have gape in astonishment when I tried to explain what frequent-flier miles had been, or how once upon a time America had *not* been at war in the Middle East? Or might they just bash my head in with rocks—their only toys—when they learned that I'd simply *thrown away* precious petroleum in the guise of empty shampoo bottles?

The evening's speaker and the man I'd flown to Atlanta to see was John Hofmeister, then president of U.S. operations for Royal Dutch Shell, a $357-billion-a-year enterprise devoted mainly to keeping us in oil. Hofmeister has cultivated a certain reputation for candor among oilmen—back in 2006, he announced it was "a waste of time" to continue debating global warming—and I hoped he might be able to convince me that peak oil wasn't something to worry about. Because in truth, I like my oil-soaked life. No decline in the availability of crude oil means no drop-off in my year-round avocado consumption. The affordability of gasoline frees up discretionary income for consumers to spend on less crucial items like this magazine. In picturesque locations throughout the world, my friends, loved ones, and I can continue to eat food and drink wine shipped in around the clock from many distant hubs and ports and chat meanwhile about what a shame it is that people like ourselves are destroying the climate. Contemporary life is a guilty pleasure, but a pleasure nonetheless.

"We want to get started soon," the emcee was saying from behind the podium as I walked into a less than full house, "though there may be a few people coming in late because of the Atlanta traffic."

To make the half-empty ballroom look more like half-full, I planted myself in the first row of chairs, next to John Hofmeister's wife, the leadership coach Karen Otazo Hofmeister. She was in town to hear her

husband deliver his fiftieth and final talk since embarking on a nationwide "listening" tour, in which a leader (as Otazo Hofmeister, with whom I struck up a conversation, several times referred to her husband) gives speeches followed by town-hall-style meetings where ordinary citizens are encouraged to voice their concerns. Shell had sent Hofmeister on tour not long after the company discovered, two years ago, that its favorability ratings had fallen below 15 percent, a finding that probably owed something to the bad PR Shell and the other major oil companies received after Hurricane Katrina rampaged along the Gulf Coast, shutting down refineries, sending pump prices through the roof (assuming the roof remained attached to the house), and earning oil companies record profits for the third quarter of 2005.

"A leader is the thread that pulls the needle," Otazo Hofmeister told me, and I nodded at this incomprehensible leadership proverb—ordinarily, the needle pulls the thread—as her husband took the stage. John Hofmeister is a tall and burly, oblong owl of a man in late middle age who also wears oval wire-rimmed glasses that give him the owl's mythological air of disinterested wisdom. A rumpled blue blazer and a dull yellow tie

224

/224/ **GQ**
DESIGN DIRECTOR: FRED WOODWARD / DESIGNER: THOMAS ALBERTY / DIRECTOR OF PHOTOGRAPHY: DORA SOMOSI
PHOTO EDITOR: JUSTIN O'NEILL / PHOTOGRAPHER: CHRISTOPHER GRIFFITH / EDITOR-IN-CHIEF: JIM NELSON
PUBLISHER: CONDÉ NAST PUBLICATIONS INC. / ISSUE: AUGUST 2008 / CATEGORY: DESIGN: FEATURE: NEWS/REPORTAGE (STORY)

Forty years ago, the nation staggered through twelve cataclysmic months. We know them well. We were there.

THE MEMORIES ARE HARD-WIRED IN OUR HEADS. No other time was as turbulent or tragic—or, for many of us—as life changing. When marked the pivotal turning point of an era—when every established norm seemed under siege. When idealism clashed with fear. When our national psyche went from hopeful to despairing in such a freefall that some began to wonder whether the America they knew could endure. / So extraordinary were the dramas that we relive them now in shorthand: Vietnam and Tet. Assassinations. Chicago. Mexico City. Nixon. Riots. Student rebellion. Black Power. Sisterhood. Prague. Paris. Poland. All coursed through our lives against a backdrop of music-making and cultural expression that was as riveting as it was groundbreaking. Here were the Beatles, Jimi Hendrix, Aretha Franklin, the Rolling Stones, setting new artistic standards. Here was television, brazenly changing the political landscape with raw images of war and repression.

Here were men orbiting the moon, LSD, free love, Broadway nudity, and Yippies, outrageously testing the limits of countercultural freedom. / It was a heady time. And we were there—fighting, grieving, demanding change, experiencing the ecstasy and the agony of our new morality, or new attitude. Or not. Some of us were proud and vigilant protectors of the world as it was. Others watched from the sidelines, stoically putting one foot in front of the other, making a life as best we could. / Whoever we were and were becoming, one thing was certain: we could not totally shut out the world around us. And so here, on the following pages, are our stories—stories from you, the readers; stories from the famous; stories from those whose public acts 40 years ago are now etched in history. Together they paint a picture of how that momentous year informed who we would become as individuals and, ultimately, as a nation.   INTERVIEWS BY ED DWYER, VERN SMITH, AND LARKIN WARREN

48 www.aarpmagazine.org/1968

"There must be some way out of here / Said the joker to the thief / There's too much confusion / I can't get no relief"   —Bob Dylan, "All Along the Watchtower," sung by Jimi Hendrix

1968
Trauma

ON JANUARY 1, we were out in the bush on the Cambodian border, in these big foxholes, what they call a two-company perimeter, with artillery. We'd set up a kind of a quick LZ [landing zone], and for some reason all the packages for Christmas arrived on the 1st. I was opening all these beautiful things that were sent from home, from Mom, from my friends. Then the night came—and that was some night. We got hit with a two-battalion human-wave attack by the NVA [North Vietnamese Army]. That was a hell of a way to start the year. It was hard. But I became a better soldier that year. I learned a lot about life and the realities of dealing with other men. I saved lives. I didn't kill people unnecessarily. I kept my soul, while a lot of people came out dead. Still, I knew I would never be the same again.
—**OLIVER STONE,** 61, film-maker and screenwriter, who received a Bronze Star and a Purple Heart for his service in Vietnam; his upcoming film, Pinkville, explores the investigation that followed the My Lai massacre

▲ Oliver Stone, Bravo Company

ON MARCH 16, 1968, the men of Charlie Company opened fire on some 500 un-armed Vietnamese civilians during what would become known, darkly, as the My Lai massacre. Much later, the world would dis-cover that it was pilot Hugh Thompson, 24, who landed his helicopter at the scene and ordered his gunners—Lawrence Colburn, 19, and Glenn Andreotta, 20—to fire on the U.S. soldiers if need be. Meantime, Thompson rescued a dozen civilians inside a bunker and airlifted them to safety with the help of two nearby helicopter gunships. Colburn, now 58, says the nightmares still come. / When we'd gotten the people out of the bunker and were ready to leave, Glenn saw movement in the ditch, went in, and, among all the mutilated bodies, found this little boy. He handed him up to me, and I grabbed him by the back of his little silk shirt, and I remember thinking, "I hope these buttons are sewn on tight." I just had him in my left hand, my weapon in my right, and I couldn't even feel any weight—so much adrenaline pumping. We took him to a hospital, and I prayed that he was so young and so traumatized that he wouldn't remember. The whole experience has made me less trustful and less happy in my life, but it's what it is. I don't stand in judgment of anyone.

VOICE OF THE READER
While waiting at the airport for my plane to go back to the United States, men were loading body bags. One of the bags fell open, and a head rolled out. As the plane took off, every one of us wept. I had wanted to be a career soldier, but the war changed all that. All I wanted to do was go home.
—RAYMOND DAY, 61, Bushkill, Pennsylvania

► American troops on the road to Khe Sanh, during the Tet Offensive

66 **I have traveled and I have listened to the young people of our nation and felt their anger about the war that they are sent to fight and about the world they are about to inherit.**
—SENATOR ROBERT F. KENNEDY, DECLARING HIS PRESIDENTIAL CANDIDACY

◄ Coretta Scott King and daughter Yolanda at Dr. King's funeral

"I'M NOT WORRIED ABOUT ANYTHING. I'M NOT FEARING ANY MAN."
—THE REVEREND MARTIN LUTHER KING JR., THE NIGHT BEFORE HIS ASSASSINATION

WHEN I HEARD DR. KING had been murdered, I was 18, a Negro girl from Charlotte, North Carolina, trying des-perately to make sense of my place on the campus of a tiny, white Wisconsin college. I cried so hard as I staggered to my dorm room that I don't even remember how I got there. I waited in wailing. My white roommate was at her desk studying, and I asked her to come with me to the candlelight vigil. She said no, she had to study for exams. Then she bent back over her books. I stood there, stunned and disbelieving. I never spoke to her again.
—BERNESTINE SINGLEY, 59, lawyer, writer, editor of When Race Becomes Real: Black and White Writers Confront Their Personal Histories (Southern Illinois University Press, 2008)

THE NIGHT BOBBY WAS SHOT—and I was standing next to him—it was like "I must not fail!" There was the memory of Dallas and how it wasn't recorded properly. I was saying to myself, "This is for history; don't mess up now." I watched someone I genuinely liked dying in front of me, and five other people were shot all around me, but I couldn't hang back. It's a strange thing, though, with violence—you either fall to pieces or else you come out stronger than how you went in. That's the way I've always felt about America—it had its nervous breakdown in 1968, but that was a bump in the road. I mean, we're still here.—HARRY BENSON, 78, photographer who has chronicled more than 50 years of history, for publications from Life to Vanity Fair

▼ Harry Benson

VOICE OF THE READER
I got married the day Bobby Kennedy died. I was 18. I was devastated. It was a day of loss—a loss of inno-cence. I married to have family, because that was the only way out for so many girls at that time. So I felt the direction of my life and the direction of the country were irretrievably altered and amazingly intertwined that day.—GLORIA ESTES, 58, Aurora, Colorado

JANUARY 5	15		16	FEBRUARY 1	8		10	12	15	16	24	27

► TIMELINE
1968
A HISTORY OF POLITICS, CULTURE, INNOVATION, AND UNREST

Pediatrician Benjamin Spock, M.D., and four others are indicted for aiding and abetting draft dodgers.

"Sisterhood Is Powerful"
5,000 women march on Washington to demand an end to the Vietnam War.

Activists Jerry Rubin and Abbie Hoffman, below, establish the Youth International Party—the Yippies.

Photojournalist Eddie Adams takes his famous photo of South Vietnamese police chief Nguyen Ngoc Loan executing a Vietcong prisoner.

Three student protesters are killed and dozens are injured at a South Carolina State University rally against the segregation of a local bowling alley.

Figure skater Peggy Fleming wins the only U.S. gold medal at the Winter Olympics in France.

ELDRIDGE CLEAVER PUBLISHES SOUL ON ICE

The International Olympic Commit-tee votes to readmit South Africa to partici-pate in the Sum-mer Games, but withdraws the invitation months later, after dozens of countries threaten to boycott.

9 1 1
A police station in Haleyville, Alaba-ma, is the first to officially use 911, the nation's uni-versal emergency number.

Janis Joplin makes the cover of Rolling Stone.

CBS news anchor Wal-ter Cronkite famously questions the poten-tial for American success in Vietnam.

51

/225/ **AARP THE MAGAZINE**
DESIGN DIRECTOR: ANDRZEJ JANERKA / ART DIRECTOR: TODD ALBERTSON / DESIGNERS: TODD ALBERTSON, DIAN HOLTON
DIRECTOR OF PHOTOGRAPHY: QUENTIN NARDI / PHOTO EDITORS: TISH KING, SARI HENRY
PHOTOGRAPHERS: ERIKA LARSEN, GREGG SEGAL, BEN BAKER / EDITOR-IN-CHIEF: STEVEN SLON
PUBLISHER: AARP PUBLICATIONS / ISSUE: MAY/JUNE 2008 / CATEGORY: DESIGN: FEATURE: NEWS/REPORTAGE (STORY)

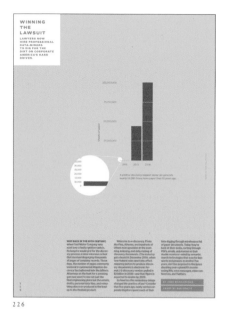

226

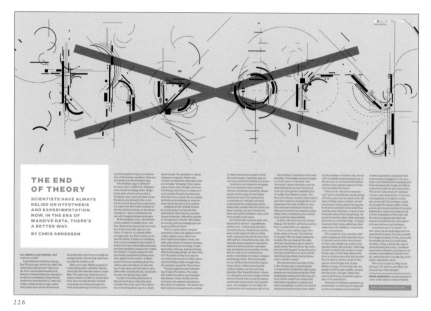

226

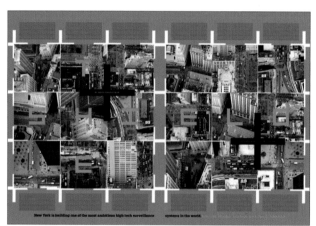

227

227

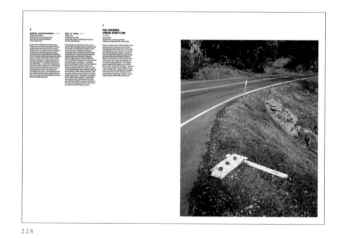

228

228

/226/ **WIRED**
CREATIVE DIRECTOR: SCOTT DADICH
DESIGN DIRECTOR: WYATT MITCHELL
ART DIRECTOR: MAILI HOLIMAN
DESIGNERS: MAILI HOLIMAN, VICTOR
KRUMMENACHER, CARL DETORRES
ILLUSTRATORS: MARIAN BANTJES, FIRSTBORN,
BOB DINETZ, STUDIO TONNE, OFFICE, BUILD,
BRYAN CHRISTIE, FERNANDA VIÉGAS, MARTIN
WATTENBERG, KATE HOLLENBACK
PHOTO EDITOR: ZANA WOODS
PUBLISHER: CONDÉ NAST PUBLICATIONS, INC.
ISSUE: JULY 2008
CATEGORY: DESIGN: FEATURE:
NEWS/REPORTAGE (STORY)

/227/ **WIRED**
CREATIVE DIRECTOR: SCOTT DADICH
DESIGN DIRECTOR: WYATT MITCHELL
ART DIRECTOR: WYATT MITCHELL
DESIGNER: WYATT MITCHELL
PHOTO EDITOR: CAROLYN RAUCH
PHOTOGRAPHER: VINCENT LAFORET
PUBLISHER: CONDÉ NAST PUBLICATIONS, INC.
ISSUE: MAY 2008
CATEGORY: DESIGN: FEATURE:
NEWS/REPORTAGE (STORY)

/228/ **WIRED**
CREATIVE DIRECTOR: SCOTT DADICH
DESIGN DIRECTOR: WYATT MITCHELL
DESIGNERS: SCOTT DADICH, CHRISTY SHEPPARD
PHOTO EDITOR: ZANA WOODS
PHOTOGRAPHER: NICK WAPLINGTON
PUBLISHER: CONDÉ NAST PUBLICATIONS, INC.
ISSUE: APRIL 2008
CATEGORY: DESIGN: FEATURE:
NEWS/REPORTAGE (STORY)

229

The next president
will inherit an America with
a great deal less economic and
strategic influence
than it had eight years ago.
And China isn't the half of it.
By Parag Khanna

Who Shrank
The Superpower?

The New York Times Magazine

Waving Goodbye to Hegemony

Just a few
years ago, America's
hold on global power
seemed unshakable. But
a lot has changed while we've
been in Iraq — and the
next president is going to be
dealing with not only
a triumphant China and a
retooled Europe but
also the quiet rise of a
second world.

By Parag Khanna

PHOTO ILLUSTRATIONS BY KEVIN VAN AELST

229

The
New,
New
City

230

Guerrilla
Gardening

230

(Out of Sight)

231

For the 140 students lucky enough
to attend the Texas School for the
Blind, life is about team sports, class
plays, *American Idol* parties, and prom
night. In fact, it's the one place where
they can see themselves for who they
really are: typical teenagers.
by Pamela Colloff
photographs by Sarah Wilson

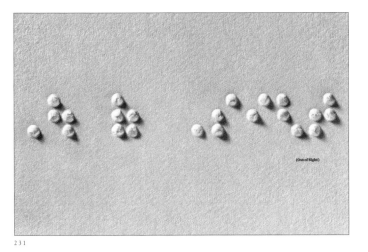

231

/229/ THE NEW YORK TIMES MAGAZINE
CREATIVE DIRECTOR: JANET FROELICH
ART DIRECTOR: AREM DUPLESSIS
DEPUTY ART DIRECTOR: GAIL BICHLER
DESIGNER: LEO JUNG
DIRECTOR OF PHOTOGRAPHY: KATHY RYAN
PHOTO EDITOR: CLINTON CARGILL
PHOTOGRAPHER: KEVIN VAN AELST
EDITOR-IN-CHIEF: GERRY MARZORATI
PUBLISHER: THE NEW YORK TIMES
ISSUE: JANUARY 27, 2008
CATEGORY: DESIGN: FEATURE:
NEWS/REPORTAGE (STORY)

/230/ THE NEW YORK TIMES MAGAZINE
CREATIVE DIRECTOR: JANET FROELICH
ART DIRECTOR: AREM DUPLESSIS
DEPUTY ART DIRECTOR: GAIL BICHLER
DESIGNERS: LEO JUNG, IAN ALLEN, JULIA MOBURG
DIRECTOR OF PHOTOGRAPHY: KATHY RYAN
PHOTO EDITOR: JOANNA MILTER
EDITOR-IN-CHIEF: GERRY MARZORATI
PUBLISHER: THE NEW YORK TIMES
ISSUE: JUNE 8, 2008
CATEGORY: DESIGN: FEATURE:
NEWS/REPORTAGE (STORY)

/231/ TEXAS MONTHLY
ART DIRECTOR: T.J. TUCKER
DESIGNER: T.J. TUCKER
PHOTO EDITOR: LESLIE BALDWIN
PHOTOGRAPHERS: SARAH WILSON, RANDAL FORD
PUBLISHER: EMMIS COMMUNICATIONS CORP.
ISSUE: AUGUST 2008
CATEGORY: DESIGN: FEATURE:
NEWS/REPORTAGE (STORY)

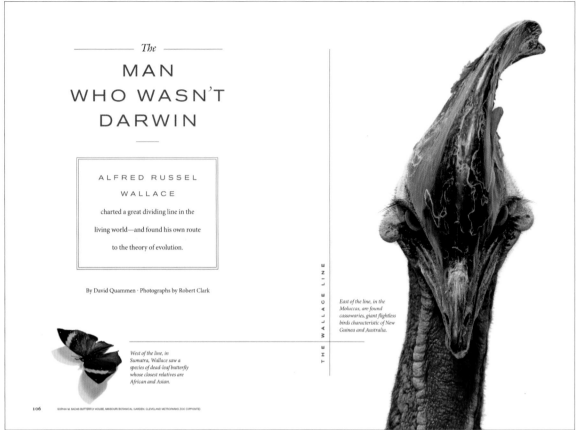

ALFRED RUSSEL

WALLACE

charted a great dividing line in the

living world—and found his own route

to the theory of evolution.

By David Quammen · Photographs by Robert Clark

East of the line, in the Moluccas, are found cassowaries, giant flightless birds characteristic of New Guinea and Australia.

THE WALLACE LINE

West of the line, in Sumatra, Wallace saw a species of dead-leaf butterfly whose closest relatives are African and Asian.

106   SOPHIA M. SACHS BUTTERFLY HOUSE, MISSOURI BOTANICAL GARDEN, CLEVELAND METROPARKS ZOO (OPPOSITE)

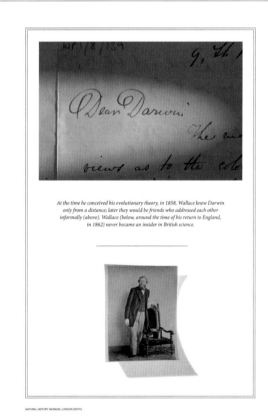

At the time he conceived his evolutionary theory, in 1858, Wallace knew Darwin only from a distance; later they would be friends who addressed each other informally (above). Wallace (below, around the time of his return to England, in 1862) never became an insider in British science.

NATURAL HISTORY MUSEUM, LONDON (BOTH)

W

THE ISLAND OF TERNATE is a small, graceful volcanic cone rising leafy green from the sea in northeastern Indonesia, 600 miles east of Borneo. Although it's an out-of-the-way place, tucked between much larger islands, Ternate was once an entrepôt of the Dutch empire, from which spices and other precious tropical commodities traveled westward by ship. Today its busy dock area, its fruit and fish markets, its mosques, its old forts, its sultan's palace, and its tidy concrete houses are strung like carousel lights along a single ring road that traces the coastline. Its upland slopes are mostly forested and unpopulated, and in those woods, if you're lucky, you might still spot a certain resplendent bird, emerald-breasted, with two long white plumes dangling capelike from each shoulder, whose scientific name—*Semioptera wallacii*—honors the man who first brought it to scientific attention. That man was Alfred Russel Wallace, a young English naturalist who did fieldwork throughout the Malay Archipelago in the late 1850s and early '60s. What you won't see on Ternate is any grand plaque or statue commemorating Wallace's place in scientific history or the fact that, from this little island, on March 9, 1858, he sent off a highly consequential letter, aboard a Dutch mail steamer headed westward.

The letter was addressed to Mr. Charles Darwin. Along with it Wallace enclosed a brief paper titled "On the Tendency of Varieties to depart indefinitely from the Original Type." It was the product of two nights' hasty scribbling, which followed a moment's epiphany during a fever, which in turn followed more than ten years of speculation and careful research. What the paper described was a theory of evolution (though not under that name) by natural selection (not using that phrase) remarkably similar to the theory that Darwin himself, then an eminent naturalist of rather conventional reputation, had developed but hadn't yet published.

This is a classic episode in the history of science, a story of a coincidence and its aftermath, told and retold in books about how evolutionary biology came to be: the near simultaneous formulation of what we now think of as Darwin's theory by Darwin himself and a young upstart, Alfred Russel Wallace. Classic or not, many people nowadays are unaware of it. Wallace, famed during his life as Darwin's junior partner and for his other contributions to science and social thought, fell into obscurity after his death, in 1913. In recent decades his renown has been revivified, both by scholars who mine every aspect of Darwin's life—Wallace was a crucial part—and by a few popular writers. His grave marker, in the village of Broadstone, no longer stands crumbling and overgrown by tree limbs. His portrait now hangs, along with an older one of Darwin, in the meeting room of the Linnean Society in London, the same scientific society to which the Darwin-Wallace co-discovery was announced 150 years ago, on the evening of July 1, 1858. His writings, on subjects from evolutionary theory and social justice to life on Mars, are coming back into print or turning up on the Web. He is recognized among science historians as a founder of evolutionary biogeography (the study of which species live where, and why), as a pioneer of island biogeography in particular (from which the science of conservation biology grew), as an early theorist on adaptive mimicry, and as a prescient voice on behalf of what we now call biodiversity. That is, he's a towering figure in the transition from old-fashioned natural history to modern biology. During his years afield Wallace was also a prolific collector, a ruthless harvester of natural wonders; his insect and bird specimens added richly to museum holdings and the discipline of taxonomy. Still, most people who know of Alfred Russel Wallace know him only as Charles Darwin's secret sharer, the man who co-discovered the theory of evolution by natural selection but failed to get an equal share of the credit.

ALFRED RUSSEL WALLACE 113

/232/ **NATIONAL GEOGRAPHIC**
DESIGN DIRECTOR: DAVID WHITMORE / DESIGNER: DAVID WHITMORE / DIRECTOR OF PHOTOGRAPHY: DAVID GRIFFIN / PHOTO EDITOR: KATHY MORAN
PHOTOGRAPHER: ROBERT CLARK / EDITOR-IN-CHIEF: CHRIS JOHNS / PUBLISHER: NATIONAL GEOGRAPHIC SOCIETY / ISSUE: DECEMBER 2008
CATEGORY: DESIGN: FEATURE: NEWS/REPORTAGE (STORY)

233

233

234

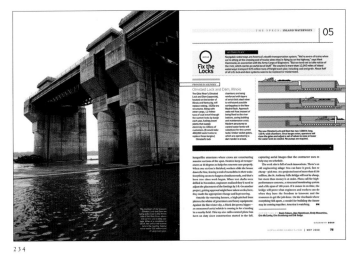

234

235

/233/ **NATIONAL GEOGRAPHIC**
DESIGN DIRECTOR: DAVID WHITMORE
DESIGNER: DAVID WHITMORE
DIRECTOR OF PHOTOGRAPHY: DAVID GRIFFIN
PHOTO EDITOR: SARAH LEEN
PHOTOGRAPHERS: FRITZ HOFFMANN,
GEORGE STEINMETZ
EDITOR-IN-CHIEF: CHRIS JOHNS
PUBLISHER: NATIONAL GEOGRAPHIC SOCIETY
ISSUE: MAY 2008
CATEGORY: DESIGN: FEATURE:
NEWS/REPORTAGE (STORY)

/234/ **POPULAR MECHANICS**
DESIGN DIRECTOR: MICHAEL LAWTON
ILLUSTRATOR: DOGO
DIRECTOR OF PHOTOGRAPHY: ALLYSON TORRISI
PHOTOGRAPHER: CHRISTOPHER GRIFFITH
EDITOR-IN-CHIEF: JAMES B. MEIGS
PUBLISHER: THE HEARST CORPORATION-
MAGAZINES DIVISION
ISSUE: MAY 2008
CATEGORY: DESIGN: FEATURE:
NEWS/REPORTAGE (STORY)

/235/ **POPULAR MECHANICS**
DESIGN DIRECTOR: MICHAEL LAWTON
DIRECTOR OF PHOTOGRAPHY: ALLYSON TORRISI
PHOTOGRAPHER: HENRY LEUTWYLER
PUBLISHER: THE HEARST CORPORATION-
MAGAZINES DIVISION
ISSUE: JULY 2008
CATEGORY: DESIGN: FEATURE:
NEWS/REPORTAGE (STORY)

236

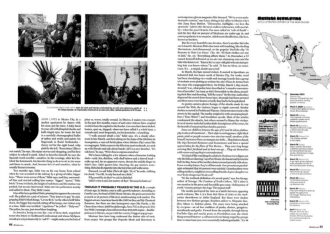

236

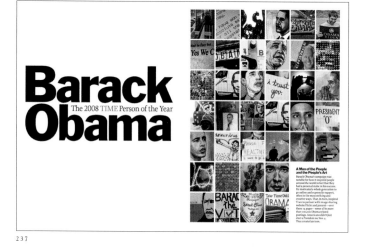

237

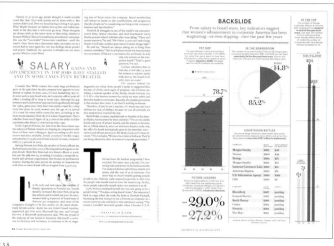

237

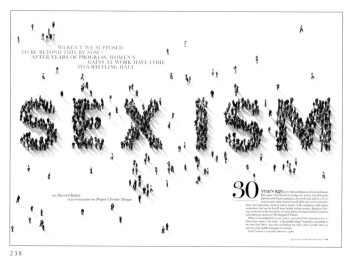

238

238

/236/ **BLENDER**
CREATIVE DIRECTOR: DIRK BARNETT
ART DIRECTOR: ROBERT VARGAS
DESIGNER: ROBERT VARGAS
ILLUSTRATOR: JASON LEE
DIRECTOR OF PHOTOGRAPHY: AMY HOPPY
PHOTOGRAPHER: TONI FRANÇOIS
EDITOR-IN-CHIEF: JOE LEVY
PUBLISHER: ALPHAMEDIA GROUP
ISSUE: JUNE 2008
CATEGORY: DESIGN: FEATURE:
NEWS/REPORTAGE (STORY)

/237/ **TIME**
ART DIRECTOR: ARTHUR HOCHSTEIN
DESIGNER: D.W. PINE
CHIEF PICTURE EDITOR: ALICE GABRINER
EDITOR-IN-CHIEF: JOHN HUEY
PUBLISHER: TIME INC.
ISSUE: DECEMBER 29, 2008
CATEGORY: DESIGN: FEATURE:
NEWS/REPORTAGE (STORY)

/238/ **CONDÉ NAST PORTFOLIO**
DESIGN DIRECTOR: ROBERT PRIEST
ART DIRECTOR: GRACE LEE
DESIGNER: GRACE LEE
ILLUSTRATOR: BRYAN CHRISTIE DESIGN
DIRECTOR OF PHOTOGRAPHY: LISA BERMAN
PHOTO EDITOR: JANE YEOMANS
DIRECTOR OF INFORMATION GRAPHICS:
JOHN GRIMWADE
GRAPHICS COORDINATOR: DANIELLE JETT
EDITOR-IN-CHIEF: JOANNE LIPMAN
PUBLISHER: CONDÉ NAST PUBLICATIONS INC.
ISSUE: APRIL 2008
CATEGORY: DESIGN: FEATURE:
NEWS/REPORTAGE (STORY)

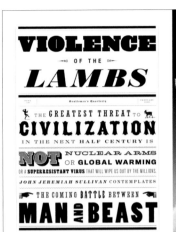

239

239

240

240

241

241

/239/ **GQ**
DESIGN DIRECTOR: FRED WOODWARD
DESIGNER: THOMAS ALBERTY
DIRECTOR OF PHOTOGRAPHY: DORA SOMOSI
PHOTO EDITOR: JUSTIN O'NEILL
PHOTOGRAPHER: JILL GREENBERG
EDITOR-IN-CHIEF: JIM NELSON
PUBLISHER: CONDÉ NAST PUBLICATIONS INC.
ISSUE: FEBRUARY 2008
CATEGORY: DESIGN: FEATURE:
NEWS/REPORTAGE (STORY)

/240/ **GQ**
DESIGN DIRECTOR: FRED WOODWARD
DESIGNER: ROB HEWITT
DIRECTOR OF PHOTOGRAPHY: DORA SOMOSI
PHOTO EDITOR: JUSTIN O'NEILL
PHOTOGRAPHER: EDWARD BURTYNSKY
EDITOR-IN-CHIEF: JIM NELSON
PUBLISHER: CONDÉ NAST PUBLICATIONS INC.
ISSUE: MARCH 2008
CATEGORY: DESIGN: FEATURE:
NEWS/REPORTAGE (STORY)

/241/ **NEW YORK**
DESIGN DIRECTOR: CHRIS DIXON
ART DIRECTOR: RANDY MINOR
DESIGNER: HITOMI SATO
DIRECTOR OF PHOTOGRAPHY: JODY QUON
PHOTOGRAPHER: TOM SCHIERLITZ
MAKEUP BY JOHN MAUVAD, JENAI CHIN
EDITOR-IN-CHIEF: ADAM MOSS
PUBLISHER: NEW YORK MAGAZINE HOLDINGS, LLC
ISSUE: APRIL 28, 2008
CATEGORY: DESIGN: FEATURE:
NEWS/REPORTAGE (STORY)

260

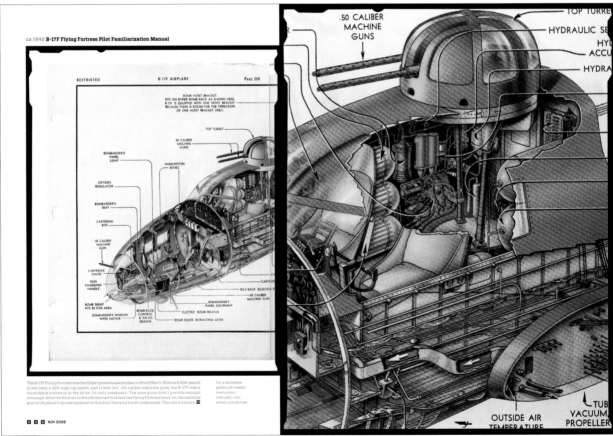

260

/260/ **WIRED**
CREATIVE DIRECTOR: SCOTT DADICH / DESIGN DIRECTOR: WYATT MITCHELL / DESIGNERS: SCOTT DADICH, CHRISTY SHEPPARD
PHOTO EDITOR: ANNA ALEXANDER GOLDWATER / PHOTOGRAPHER: DAN WINTERS / PUBLISHER: CONDÉ NAST PUBLICATIONS, INC.
ISSUE: NOVEMBER 2008 / CATEGORY: DESIGN: FEATURE: TRAVEL/FOOD/STILL LIFE (STORY)

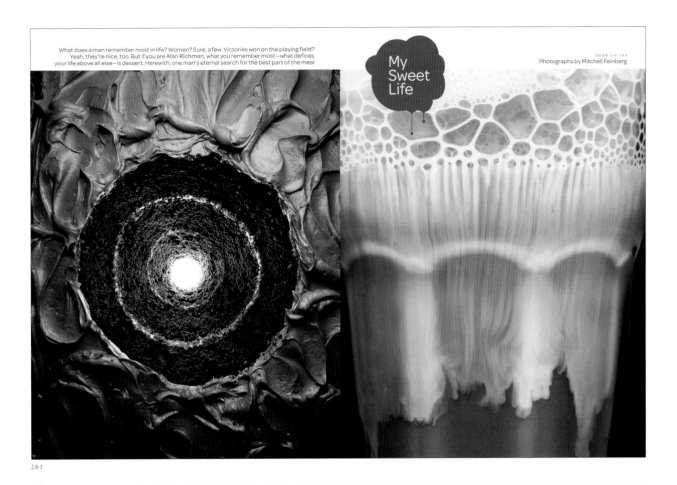

What does a man remember most in life? Women? Sure, a few. Victories won on the playing field? Yeah, they're nice, too. But if you are Alan Richman, what you remember most—what defines your life above all else—is dessert. Herewith, one man's eternal search for the best part of the meal

My Sweet Life

2008.GQ.153

Photographs by Mitchell Feinberg

261

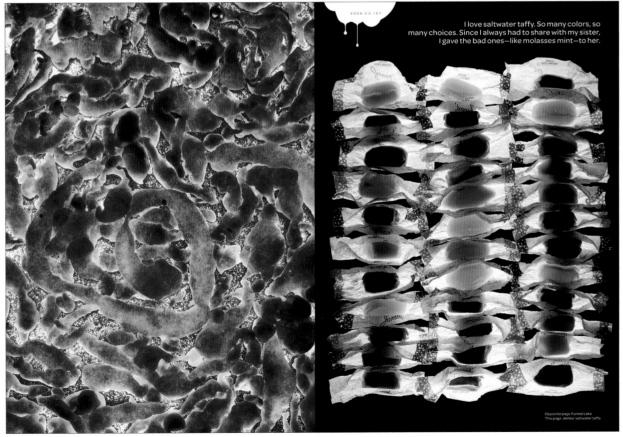

2008.GQ.157

I love saltwater taffy. So many colors, so many choices. Since I always had to share with my sister, I gave the bad ones—like molasses mint—to her.

Opposite page Funnel cake
This page James' saltwater taffy

261

/261/ **GQ**
DESIGN DIRECTOR: FRED WOODWARD / DESIGNER: DELGIS CANAHUATE / DIRECTOR OF PHOTOGRAPHY: DORA SOMOSI / PHOTO EDITOR: JUSTIN O'NEILL / PHOTOGRAPHER: MITCHELL FEINBERG / EDITOR-IN-CHIEF: JIM NELSON / PUBLISHER: CONDÉ NAST PUBLICATIONS INC.
ISSUE: JULY 2008 / CATEGORY: DESIGN: FEATURE: TRAVEL/FOOD/STILL LIFE (STORY)

Fired Up
● **The Complete**
GQ Guide to Grilling

Nothing should be simpler—and tastier—than putting food to flame. Then how come we always end up with overcharred chicken, underdone sirloin, and ribs that never, ever fall off the bone? Follow these ten tips and you'll forever be king of the grill Photographs by **Tom Schierlitz**

JUNE 2008 GQ.COM 139

262

8.
The Skewer
Hunks of protein threaded on a spear and seared over an open flame—is that manly enough for you? But instead of reaching for chunks of lamb or chicken, try shrimp. It absorbs marinade extremely well, and it cooks quickly, making for an excellent grab-and-chomp dish that requires nothing in the way of girlie utensils.

(1) Buy relatively large shrimp, heads on or off, shelled or unshelled.
(2) Marinate them for an hour in 1 cup of soy sauce, 3 cups of rice-wine vinegar, 4 tablespoons of brown sugar, 2 tablespoons of regular or hot sesame oil, and lots of fresh ginger and garlic.
(3) Skewer the shrimp. **If you're using wood skewers, soak the skewers in water for 30 minutes first,** so they don't burn.
(4) Cook for 1 to 2 minutes per side over medium heat **till orange and firm.**
(5) Unskewer the shrimp onto a large plate, **place in the center of your table, and chomp away.**

9.
The Tools
You will not need an arsenal of tools that come twelve to a set and live in a Halliburton briefcase. In fact, the less your grilling gear resembles ordnance, the better, as turning food over heat is not about aggressive poking and stabbing but rather about precision gripping and control. That said, stock two utensils: restaurant-grade spring-loaded tongs (sans char-prone wooden handles) and a stainless-steel dogleg spatula (yes, like the shape of a long par-5). Both implements should have some length in order to keep your hands away from the heat, but they also need to be sturdy. Your tongs should never bow when flipping a rack of ribs. Use that spatula for more delicate dishes—like fish and loose-packed burgers—to ensure that they reach the plate instead of the bottom of the grill. www .bowerykitchens.com/tongs

10.
The Dessert
Tell your buddies that you're grilling peaches for dessert and you'll get a look that says, "You may inhabit the body of a man, you may display certain familiar male traits, but you are not, in fact, a man." The insinuation is that you—how to put it?—are somehow lacking in the sack department. These friends of yours, though, are fools. A grilled peach is pretty much, without fail, the most memorable thing at any given Sunday barbecue. Sweet and salty, hot and cold, not without nutritional value. What's not to like?

(1) Look for good peaches. In season. If you have a farmers' market nearby: that kind of peach. **Get them on the firm side, as the fire will soften them up.**

(2) Halve the peaches and remove the pits. Leave skin on. Set the peach halves on a platter, flesh-side up. In a saucepan, heat a couple of tablespoons of salted butter. Remove from heat. Add 1 half-teaspoon of good vanilla and a pinch of brown sugar. (Note: Overdo the sugar and you will burn the peaches.) Mix. **Brush mixture over flesh side of the peaches, and be generous with it.**
(3) You're grilling these after dinner, so the fire should be fairly mellow by now. Place the peaches on the grill, flat-side (flesh-side) down. After about 5 minutes, turn. Cook on skin side for 2 to 3 minutes. You don't want the skin to char or blister. They're ready when the flesh is easily penetrated by a fork—soft but not mushy. They should be golden in color.
(4) Serve immediately. **Each person gets 2 halves and, on top, a pat of butter or a scoop of vanilla ice cream,** which should be melting when eaten. A spoon might be called for. Who's the man now?

MORE ↓
FOOD-AND-WINE WISDOM ON "FORKED," ALAN RICHMAN'S BLOG, AT.

GQ ● COM

144 GQ.COM JUNE 2008

JUNE 2008 GQ.COM 145

262

/262/ **GQ**
DESIGN DIRECTOR: FRED WOODWARD
DESIGNER: DRUE WAGNER
DIRECTOR OF PHOTOGRAPHY: DORA SOMOSI
PHOTO EDITOR: JUSTIN O'NEILL
PHOTOGRAPHER: TOM SCHIERLITZ
EDITOR-IN-CHIEF: JIM NELSON
PUBLISHER: CONDÉ NAST PUBLICATIONS INC.
ISSUE: JUNE 2008 / CATEGORY: DESIGN: FEATURE:
TRAVEL/FOOD/STILL LIFE (STORY)

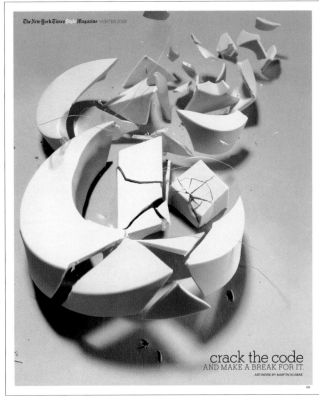

263

265

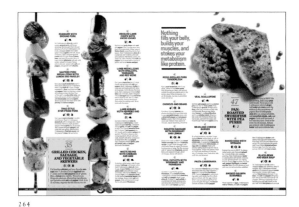

264

265

/263/ T, THE NEW YORK TIMES STYLE MAGAZINE
CREATIVE DIRECTOR: JANET FROELICH
SENIOR ART DIRECTOR: DAVID SEBBAH
ART DIRECTOR: CHRISTOPHER MARTINEZ
SENIOR DESIGNER: ELIZABETH SPIRIDAKIS
ARTWORK BY SEAN CAPONE, MARTIN KLIMAS
EDITOR-IN-CHIEF: STEFANO TONCHI
PUBLISHER: THE NEW YORK TIMES
ISSUES: FEBRUARY 24, 2008, APRIL 13, 2008, AUGUST
17, 2008, SEPTEMBER 7, 2008, NOVEMBER 16, 2008
CATEGORY: DESIGN: FEATURE:
TRAVEL/FOOD/STILL LIFE (STORY)

/264/ MEN'S HEALTH
DESIGN DIRECTOR: GEORGE KARABOTSOS
ART DIRECTOR: JOHN DIXON
DESIGNER: JOHN DIXON
DIRECTOR OF PHOTOGRAPHY: BRENDA MILLIS
PHOTO EDITOR: BRENDA MILLIS
PHOTOGRAPHER: JEFF HARRIS
PUBLISHER: RODALE INC.
ISSUE: APRIL 2008
CATEGORY: DESIGN: FEATURE:
TRAVEL/FOOD/STILL LIFE (STORY)

/265/ MORE
CREATIVE DIRECTOR: DEBRA BISHOP
DESIGNERS: JENN MCMANUS, SUSANNE BAMBERGER,
CYBELE GRANDJEAN
DIRECTOR OF PHOTOGRAPHY: KAREN FRANK
PHOTO EDITORS: DAISY CAJAS, NATALIE GIALLUCA
PHOTOGRAPHER: CHARLES MASTERS
PUBLISHER: MEREDITH CORPORATION
ISSUE: NOVEMBER 2008
CATEGORY: DESIGN: FEATURE:
TRAVEL/FOOD/STILL LIFE (STORY)

266

266

267

267

268

268

/266/ **BON APPÉTIT**
DESIGN DIRECTOR: MATTHEW LENNING
ART DIRECTOR: ROBERT FESTINO
DESIGNER: ROBERT FESTINO
PHOTO EDITOR: LIZ MATHEWS
PHOTOGRAPHER: JAMES WOJCIK
EDITOR-IN-CHIEF: BARBARA FAIRCHILD
PUBLISHER: CONDÉ NAST PUBLICATIONS, INC.
ISSUE: JULY 2008
CATEGORY: DESIGN: FEATURE:
TRAVEL/FOOD/STILL LIFE (STORY)

/267/ **COOKIE**
DESIGN DIRECTOR: KIRBY RODRIGUEZ
ART DIRECTOR: ALEX GROSSMAN
DESIGNERS: NICOLETTE BERTHELOT,
SHANNA GREENBERG
PHOTO EDITOR: DARRICK HARRIS
ASSOCIATE PHOTO EDITOR: LINDA DENAHAN
ASSISTANT PHOTO EDITOR: AJA NUZZI
PHOTOGRAPHER: BROWN CANNON III
PUBLISHER: CONDÉ NAST PUBLICATIONS INC.
ISSUE: AUGUST 2008
CATEGORY: DESIGN: FEATURE:
TRAVEL/FOOD/STILL LIFE (STORY)

/268/ **CONDÉ NAST PORTFOLIO**
DESIGN DIRECTOR: ROBERT PRIEST
ART DIRECTOR: GRACE LEE
DESIGNER: GRACE LEE
DIRECTOR OF PHOTOGRAPHY: LISA BERMAN
PHOTO EDITOR: JOHN TOOLAN
PHOTOGRAPHERS: SUE TALLON, JEFF MINTON
EDITOR-IN-CHIEF: JOANNE LIPMAN
PUBLISHER: CONDÉ NAST PUBLICATIONS INC.
ISSUE: FEBRUARY 2008
CATEGORY: DESIGN: FEATURE:
TRAVEL/FOOD/STILL LIFE (STORY)

270

270

269

269

/269/ EVERYDAY WITH RACHAEL RAY
CREATIVE DIRECTOR: TRACY EVERDING
ART DIRECTORS: EMILY FURLANI,
JACLYN STEINBERG
DESIGNER: JACLYN STEINBERG
ILLUSTRATOR: BRIAN REA
DIRECTOR OF PHOTOGRAPHY: KIM GOUGENHEIM
PHOTO EDITOR: LISA DALSIMER
PHOTOGRAPHER: KANG KIM
PUBLISHER: READER'S DIGEST ASSOCIATION
ISSUE: NOVEMBER 2008
CATEGORY: DESIGN: FEATURE:
TRAVEL/FOOD/STILL LIFE (STORY)

/270/ ELLE DÉCOR
ART DIRECTOR: FLORENTINO PAMINTUAN
PUBLISHER: HACHETTE FILIPACCHI MEDIA U.S.
ISSUE: JANUARY/FEBRUARY 2008
CATEGORY: DESIGN: FEATURE:
TRAVEL/FOOD/STILL LIFE (STORY)

/271/ **THE NEW YORK TIMES MAGAZINE**
CREATIVE DIRECTOR: JANET FROELICH / ART DIRECTOR: AREM DUPLESSIS
DEPUTY ART DIRECTORS: GAIL BICHLER, MELISSA VENTOSA MARTIN
DESIGNER: NANCY HARRIS ROUEMY / PHOTOGRAPHER: CHAD PITMAN
FASHION EDITOR: MELISSA VENTOSA MARTIN / EDITOR-IN-CHIEF: GERRY
MARZORATI / PUBLISHER: THE NEW YORK TIMES / ISSUE: AUGUST 3, 2008
CATEGORY: DESIGN: FEATURE: FASHION/BEAUTY (SINGLE/SPREAD)

/272/ **THE NEW YORK TIMES MAGAZINE**
CREATIVE DIRECTOR: JANET FROELICH / ART DIRECTOR: AREM DUPLESSIS
DEPUTY ART DIRECTOR: GAIL BICHLER / DESIGNER: NANCY HARRIS ROUEMY
PHOTOGRAPHER: MACIEK KOBIELSKI / FASHION EDITOR: ANNE CHRISTENSEN
EDITOR-IN-CHIEF: GERRY MARZORATI / PUBLISHER: THE NEW YORK TIMES
ISSUE: SEPTEMBER 7, 2008 / CATEGORY: DESIGN: FEATURE: FASHION/BEAUTY
(SINGLE/SPREAD)

273

274

/273/ DETAILS

CREATIVE DIRECTOR: ROCKWELL HARWOOD / ART DIRECTOR: ANDRE JOINTE
DESIGNER: ROCKWELL HARWOOD / SENIOR PHOTO EDITOR: HALI TARA FELDMAN
PHOTOGRAPHER: MARIANO VIVANCO / EDITOR-IN-CHIEF: DANIEL PERES
PUBLISHER: CONDÉ NAST PUBLICATIONS / ISSUE: SEPTEMBER 2008
CATEGORY: DESIGN: FEATURE: FASHION/BEAUTY (SINGLE/SPREAD)

/274/ VIBE

ART DIRECTOR: MARK SHAW / PHOTO EDITOR: ROBYN FOREST
PHOTOGRAPHER: CLIFF WATTS / PUBLISHER: VIBE MEDIA GROUP LLC
ISSUE: APRIL 2008 / CATEGORY: DESIGN: FEATURE: FASHION/BEAUTY
(SINGLE/SPREAD)

275

278

276

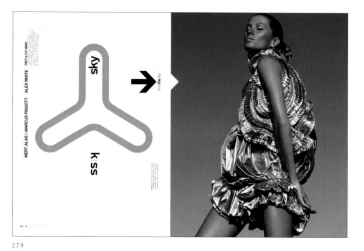

279

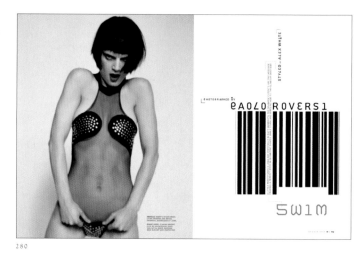

277

280

/275/ **W**
DESIGN DIRECTOR: EDWARD LEIDA
ART DIRECTOR: NATHALIE KIRSHEH
DESIGNER: EDWARD LEIDA
PHOTOGRAPHER: STEVEN KLEIN
PUBLISHER: CONDÉ NAST PUBLICATIONS INC.
ISSUE: OCTOBER 2008
CATEGORY: DESIGN: FEATURE:
FASHION/BEAUTY (SINGLE/SPREAD)

/276/ **W**
DESIGN DIRECTOR: EDWARD LEIDA
ART DIRECTOR: NATHALIE KIRSHEH
DESIGNER: EDWARD LEIDA
PHOTOGRAPHER: CRAIG MCDEAN
PUBLISHER: CONDÉ NAST PUBLICATIONS INC.
ISSUE: OCTOBER 2008
CATEGORY: DESIGN: FEATURE:
FASHION/BEAUTY (SINGLE/SPREAD)

/277/ **W**
DESIGN DIRECTOR: EDWARD LEIDA
ART DIRECTOR: NATHALIE KIRSHEH
DESIGNER: EDWARD LEIDA
PHOTOGRAPHERS: MERT ALAS, MARCUS PIGGOTT
PUBLISHER: CONDÉ NAST PUBLICATIONS INC.
ISSUE: SEPTEMBER 2008
CATEGORY: DESIGN: FEATURE:
FASHION/BEAUTY (SINGLE/SPREAD)

/278/ **W**
DESIGN DIRECTOR: EDWARD LEIDA
ART DIRECTOR: NATHALIE KIRSHEH
DESIGNER: EDWARD LEIDA
PHOTOGRAPHERS: MERT ALAS, MARCUS PIGGOTT
PUBLISHER: CONDÉ NAST PUBLICATIONS INC.
ISSUE: MARCH 2008
CATEGORY: DESIGN: FEATURE:
FASHION/BEAUTY (SINGLE/SPREAD)

/279/ **W**
DESIGN DIRECTOR: EDWARD LEIDA
ART DIRECTOR: NATHALIE KIRSHEH
DESIGNER: EDWARD LEIDA
PHOTOGRAPHERS: MERT ALAS, MARCUS PIGGOTT
PUBLISHER: CONDÉ NAST PUBLICATIONS INC.
ISSUE: AUGUST 2008
CATEGORY: DESIGN: FEATURE:
FASHION/BEAUTY (SINGLE/SPREAD)

/280/ **W**
DESIGN DIRECTOR: EDWARD LEIDA
ART DIRECTOR: NATHALIE KIRSHEH
DESIGNER: EDWARD LEIDA
PHOTOGRAPHER: PAOLO ROVERSI
PUBLISHER: CONDÉ NAST PUBLICATIONS INC.
ISSUE: AUGUST 2008
CATEGORY: DESIGN: FEATURE:
FASHION/BEAUTY (SINGLE/SPREAD)

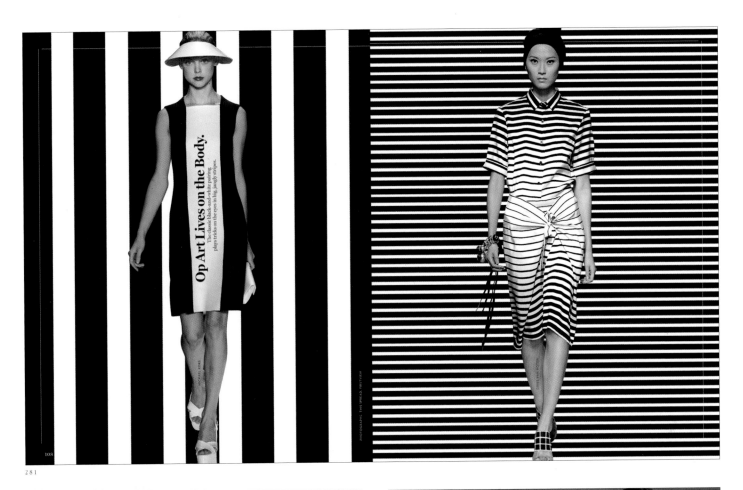

281

282

283

/281/ LOOK NEW YORK
DESIGN DIRECTOR: CHRIS DIXON
ART DIRECTOR: RANDY MINOR
DESIGNER: RANDY MINOR
DIRECTOR OF PHOTOGRAPHY: JODY QUON
PHOTOGRAPHER: FIRSTVIEW
EDITOR-IN-CHIEF: ADAM MOSS
PUBLISHER: NEW YORK MAGAZINE HOLDINGS, LLC
ISSUE: SPRING FASHION 2009
CATEGORY: DESIGN: FEATURE:
FASHION/BEAUTY (SINGLE/SPREAD)

/282/ BEST LIFE
DESIGN DIRECTOR: BRANDON KAVULLA
DESIGNER: BRANDON KAVULLA
DIRECTOR OF PHOTOGRAPHY: RYAN CADIZ
PHOTOGRAPHER: RICHARD PHIBBS
PUBLISHER: RODALE INC.
ISSUE: DECEMBER 2008
CATEGORY: DESIGN: FEATURE:
FASHION/BEAUTY (SINGLE/SPREAD)

/283/ BEST LIFE
DESIGN DIRECTOR: BRANDON KAVULLA
DESIGNER: BRANDON KAVULLA
DIRECTOR OF PHOTOGRAPHY: RYAN CADIZ
PHOTOGRAPHER: ANDREW MCPHERSON
PUBLISHER: RODALE INC.
ISSUE: OCTOBER 2008
CATEGORY: DESIGN: FEATURE:
FASHION/BEAUTY (SINGLE/SPREAD)

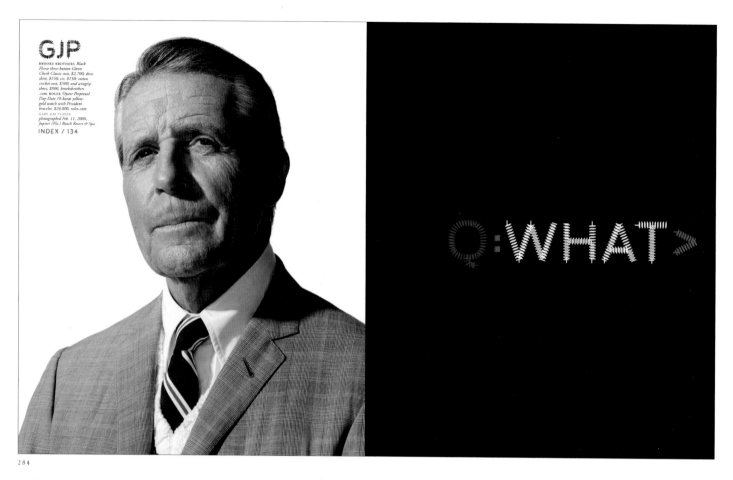

/284/ **GOLF DIGEST INDEX**
DESIGN DIRECTOR: KEN DELAGO / DESIGNER: MARNE MAYER / PHOTO EDITOR: RYAN CLINE / PHOTOGRAPHER: ART STREIBER
PUBLISHER: CONDÉ NAST PUBLICATIONS INC. / ISSUE: SPRING 2008 / CATEGORY: DESIGN: FEATURE: FASHION/BEAUTY (STORY)

/285/ **GQ**
DESIGN DIRECTOR: FRED WOODWARD / DESIGNER: ROB HEWITT / ILLUSTRATOR: ZOHAR LAZAR / DIRECTOR OF PHOTOGRAPHY: DORA SOMOSI
PHOTOGRAPHER: PEGGY SIROTA / CREATIVE DIRECTOR, FASHION JIM MOORE / FASHION DIRECTOR MICHAEL NASH / EDITOR-IN-CHIEF: JIM NELSON
PUBLISHER: CONDÉ NAST PUBLICATIONS INC. / ISSUE: AUGUST 2008 / CATEGORY: DESIGN: FEATURE: FASHION/BEAUTY (STORY)

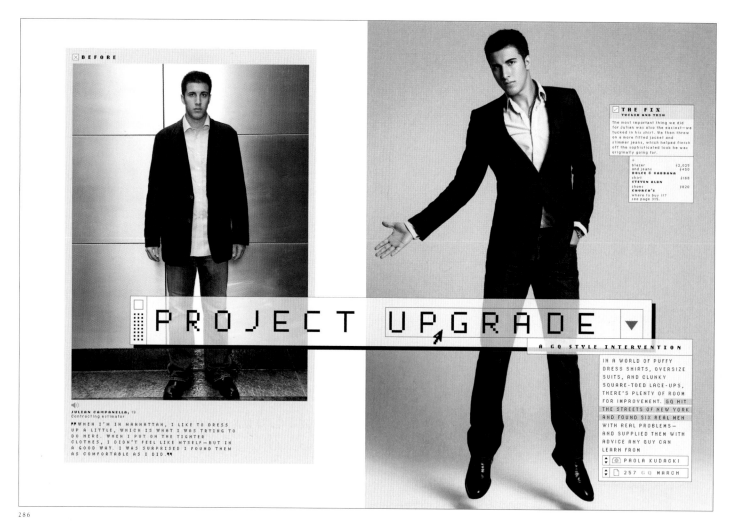

/286/ **GQ**
DESIGN DIRECTOR: FRED WOODWARD
DESIGNER: ANTON IOUKHNOVETS
DIRECTOR OF PHOTOGRAPHY: DORA SOMOSI
PHOTO EDITOR: JUSTIN O'NEILL
PHOTOGRAPHER: PAOLA KUDACKI
CREATIVE DIRECTOR, FASHION: JIM MOORE
FASHION DIRECTOR: BRIAN COATS
EDITOR-IN-CHIEF: JIM NELSON
PUBLISHER: CONDÉ NAST PUBLICATIONS INC.
ISSUE: MARCH 2008
CATEGORY: DESIGN: FEATURE:
FASHION/BEAUTY (STORY)

/287/ **GQ**
DESIGN DIRECTOR: FRED WOODWARD
DESIGNER: ANTON IOUKHNOVETS
DIRECTOR OF PHOTOGRAPHY: DORA SOMOSI
PHOTOGRAPHER: PEGGY SIROTA
CREATIVE DIRECTOR, FASHION: JIM MOORE
EDITOR-IN-CHIEF: JIM NELSON
PUBLISHER: CONDÉ NAST PUBLICATIONS INC.
ISSUE: JANUARY 2008
CATEGORY: DESIGN: FEATURE:
FASHION/BEAUTY (STORY)

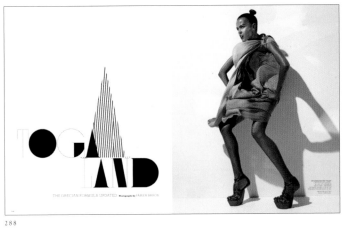

288

288

Risk

*Playing it safe is not an option. Find your cliff
and jump! The flight will be terrifying and
exhilarating, but if you keep your head up,
you'll leave regret in the dust.*

JUNE/JULY 2008 ● WWW.LATINA.COM **129**

290

289

290

/288/ T, THE NEW YORK TIMES STYLE MAGAZINE
CREATIVE DIRECTOR: JANET FROELICH
SENIOR ART DIRECTOR: DAVID SEBBAH
ART DIRECTOR: CHRISTOPHER MARTINEZ
SENIOR DESIGNER: ELIZABETH SPIRIDAKIS
DIRECTOR OF PHOTOGRAPHY: KATHY RYAN
SENIOR PHOTO EDITOR: JUDITH PUCKETT-RINELLA
PHOTOGRAPHER: FABIEN BARON
EDITOR-IN-CHIEF: STEFANO TONCHI
PUBLISHER: THE NEW YORK TIMES
ISSUE: FEBRUARY 24, 2008
CATEGORY: DESIGN: FEATURE:
FASHION/BEAUTY (STORY)

/289/ LATINA
CREATIVE DIRECTOR: FLORIAN BACHLEDA
DESIGN DIRECTOR: DENISE SEE
DESIGNERS: PHOEBE FLYNN RICH, LAURA STROM
DIRECTOR OF PHOTOGRAPHY: GEORGE PITTS
PHOTO EDITOR: JENNIFER SARGENT
PHOTOGRAPHER: ELIZABETH YOUNG
STUDIO: FB DESIGN
EDITOR-IN-CHIEF: MIMI VALDÉS RYAN
PUBLISHER: LATINA MEDIA VENTURES
CATEGORY: DESIGN: FEATURE:
FASHION/BEAUTY (STORY)

/290/ T, THE NEW YORK TIMES STYLE MAGAZINE
CREATIVE DIRECTOR: JANET FROELICH
SENIOR ART DIRECTOR: DAVID SEBBAH
ART DIRECTOR: CHRISTOPHER MARTINEZ
SENIOR DESIGNER: ELIZABETH SPIRIDAKIS
DIRECTOR OF PHOTOGRAPHY: KATHY RYAN
PHOTO EDITOR: SCOTT HALL
PHOTOGRAPHER: PAOLO ROVERSI
EDITOR-IN-CHIEF: STEFANO TONCHI
PUBLISHER: THE NEW YORK TIMES
ISSUE: AUGUST 17, 2008
CATEGORY: DESIGN: FEATURE:
FASHION/BEAUTY (STORY)

291

291

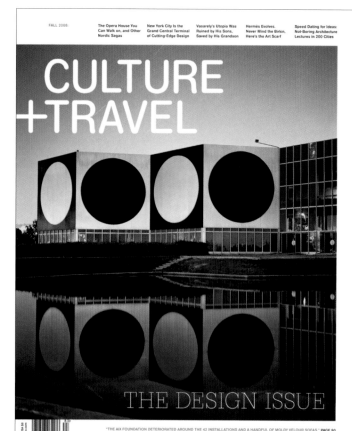

292

292

292

/291/ FIELD & STREAM
ART DIRECTOR: NEIL JAMIESON
DESIGNERS: MIKE LEY, IAN BROWN
DIRECTOR OF PHOTOGRAPHY: AMY BERKLEY
PHOTOGRAPHERS: TRAVIS RATHBONE, BRENT
HUMPHREYS, DAN SAELINGER
ASSOCIATE PHOTO EDITOR: CAITLIN PETERS
EDITOR-IN-CHIEF: ANTHONY LICATA
PUBLISHER: BONNIER CORPORATION
ISSUE: DECEMBER 2008
CATEGORY: REDESIGN: AFTER ISSUE

/292/ CULTURE + TRAVEL
CREATIVE DIRECTOR: EMILY CRAWFORD
DESIGNER: EMILY CRAWFORD
DIRECTOR OF PHOTOGRAPHY: CORY JACOBS
PHOTO EDITORS: LISA CORSON, SABINE ROGERS
PUBLISHER: LOUISE BLOUIN MEDIA
ISSUE: FALL 2008
CATEGORY: REDESIGN: AFTER ISSUE

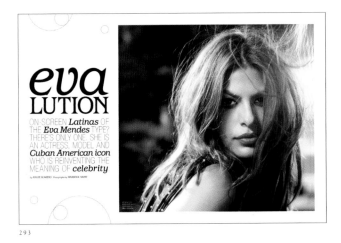

293

296

294

297

295

298

/293/ **LATINA**
CREATIVE DIRECTOR: FLORIAN BACHLEDA
DESIGN DIRECTOR: DENISE SEE
DESIGNERS: ALICÉ ALVES,
GRACE MARTINEZ, LAURA STROM
DIRECTOR OF PHOTOGRAPHY: GEORGE PITTS
PHOTO EDITORS: JENNIFER SARGENT,
CHRISTIE DEL NERO
DESIGN CONSULTANT: ROBERT NEWMAN
STUDIO: FB DESIGN
EDITOR-IN-CHIEF: MIMI VALDÉS RYAN
PUBLISHER: LATINA MEDIA VENTURES
CLIENT: LATINA
ISSUE: DECEMBER 2008/JANUARY 2009
CATEGORY: REDESIGN: AFTER ISSUE

/294/ **GLAMOUR**
DESIGN DIRECTOR: GERALDINE HESSLER
ART DIRECTOR: THERESA GRIGGS
DIRECTOR OF PHOTOGRAPHY: SUZANNE DONALDSON
PUBLISHER: CONDÉ NAST PUBLICATIONS INC.
ISSUE: SEPTEMBER 2008
CATEGORY: REDESIGN: AFTER ISSUE

/295/ **THE ATLANTIC**
ART DIRECTORS: MICHAEL BIERUT/PENTAGRAM,
LUKE HAYMAN/PENTAGRAM, JASON TREAT
DESIGNERS: JOE MARIANEK, BEN KING/PENTAGRAM
STUDIO: PENTAGRAM DESIGN, INC.
EDITOR-IN-CHIEF: JAMES BENNET
PUBLISHER: ATLANTIC MEDIA COMPANY
CLIENT: THE ATLANTIC
ISSUE: NOVEMBER 2008
CATEGORY: REDESIGN: AFTER ISSUE

/296/ **VIBE**
CREATIVE DIRECTOR: LUKE HAYMAN
ART DIRECTOR: MARK SHAW
DESIGNERS: MICHAEL DIGIACOMO,
TOM LOWE, RAMI MOGHADAM
PHOTO EDITORS: ROBYN FOREST,
DIONNA KING
STUDIO: PENTAGRAM
PUBLISHER: VIBE MEDIA GROUP LLC
ISSUE: OCTOBER 2008
CATEGORY: REDESIGN: AFTER ISSUE

/297/ **BON**
CREATIVE DIRECTOR: MICHAEL ELMENBECK
ART DIRECTOR: JOHAN AVEDAL / DESIGNERS: JOHAN
AVEDAL, JACOB HUURINAINEN / ILLUSTRATORS:
GUN LARSON, MILENA SILVANO / PHOTO EDITOR:
JOHAN AVEDAL / PHOTOGRAPHERS: PIERRE BJÖRK,
CHRISTIAN COINBERGH, MIKAEL DAHL, SANDRA
FREIJ, HENRIK HALVARSSON, TONY KIM, LISA ROZE,
MARK SANDERS, MARTIN VALLIN, ANDRÉ WOLFF,
STEFAN ZSCHERNITZ / EDITOR-IN-CHIEF:
MADELAINE LEVY / PUBLISHER: LETTERHEAD AB
ISSUE: SEPTEMBER 15, 2008 / CATEGORY: REDESIGN:
AFTER ISSUE

/298/ **PLATINO**
ART DIRECTOR: RODRIGO CASTILLO BONNER
DESIGNERS: MARIANA SASSO ROJAS, GABRIEL
BOBADILLA, MÓNICA MANZANO, MARÍA DEL
CARMEN MERCADO, JANINE ARROYO FONSECA
PHOTO EDITOR: SOFÍA ZAMBRANO DE LE FUENTE
EDITOR-IN-CHIEF: MICHAEL ROWE / PUBLISHER:
GRUPO EDITORIAL IMPRESIONES AÉREAS
CLIENT AEROMÉXICO / ISSUE: DICIEMBRE 2008
CATEGORY: REDESIGN: AFTER ISSUE

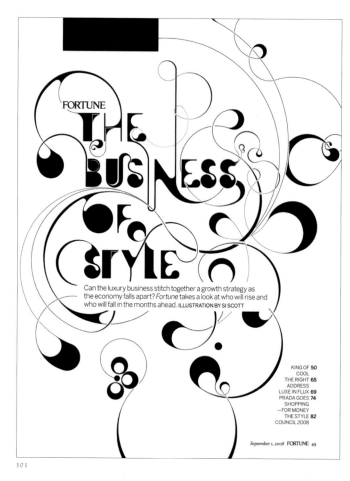

299

301

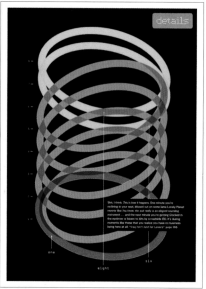

300

302

303

/299/ **GQ**
DESIGN DIRECTOR: FRED WOODWARD
DESIGNERS: ANTON IOUKHNOVETS, DRUE WAGNER
DIRECTOR OF PHOTOGRAPHY: DORA SOMOSI
EDITOR-IN-CHIEF: JIM NELSON
PUBLISHER: CONDÉ NAST PUBLICATIONS INC.
ISSUE: SEPTEMBER 2008
CATEGORY: DESIGN: SECTION (SINGLE/SPREAD)

/300/ **DETAILS**
CREATIVE DIRECTOR: ROCKWELL HARWOOD
ART DIRECTOR: ANDRE JOINTE
DESIGNER: CHRIS SEGEDY
EDITOR-IN-CHIEF: DANIEL PERES
PUBLISHER: CONDÉ NAST PUBLICATIONS
ISSUE: DECEMBER 2008
CATEGORY: DESIGN: SECTION (SINGLE/SPREAD)

/301/ **FORTUNE**
DESIGN DIRECTOR: ROBERT PERINO
ART DIRECTOR: DEANNA LOWE / DESIGNER: ALICE
ALVES / ILLUSTRATOR: SCOTT SI / PUBLISHER: TIME
INC. / ISSUE: SEPTEMBER 1, 2008 / CATEGORY:
DESIGN: SECTION (SINGLE/SPREAD)

/302/ **WIRED**
CREATIVE DIRECTOR: SCOTT DADICH
DESIGN DIRECTOR: WYATT MITCHELL
ART DIRECTOR: MARGARET SWART
DESIGNER: MARGARET SWART
PHOTO EDITORS: ZANA WOODS, SARAH FILIPPI
PHOTOGRAPHER: COOLIFE
PUBLISHER: CONDÉ NAST PUBLICATIONS, INC.
ISSUE: SEPTEMBER 2008
CATEGORY: DESIGN: SECTION (SINGLE/SPREAD)

/303/ **LOS ANGELES**
ART DIRECTOR: JOE KIMBERLING
DESIGNER: DEBBIE KIM
PHOTO EDITOR: KATHLEEN CLARK
PHOTOGRAPHER: DAN WINTERS
EDITOR-IN-CHIEF: KIT RACHLIS
PUBLISHER: EMMIS COMMUNICATIONS CORP.
ISSUE: AUGUST 2008
CATEGORY: DESIGN: SECTION (SINGLE/SPREAD)

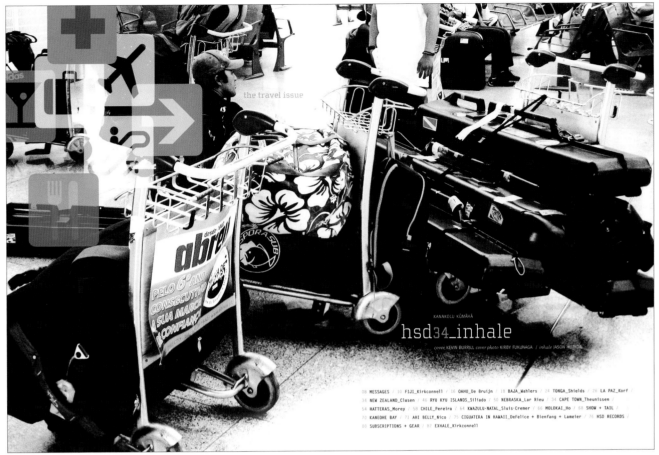

304

305

306

/304/ **HAWAII SKIN DIVER**
DESIGN DIRECTOR: CLIFFORD CHENG
DESIGNER: CLIFFORD CHENG
PHOTOGRAPHER: JASON HIJIRIDA
STUDIO: VOICE DESIGN
PUBLISHER: HAWAII SKIN DIVER PUBLISHING
CLIENT: HAWAII SKIN DIVER
ISSUE: SPRING 2008
CATEGORY: DESIGN: SECTION (SINGLE/SPREAD)

/305/ **T, THE NEW YORK TIMES STYLE MAGAZINE**
CREATIVE DIRECTOR: JANET FROELICH
SENIOR ART DIRECTOR: DAVID SEBBAH
ART DIRECTOR: CHRISTOPHER MARTINEZ
SENIOR DESIGNER: ELIZABETH SPIRIDAKIS
DESIGNER: JAMIE BARTOLACCI
DIRECTOR OF PHOTOGRAPHY: KATHY RYAN
PHOTO EDITOR: SCOTT HALL
COLLAGE BY DEANNE CHEUK
EDITOR-IN-CHIEF: STEFANO TONCHI
PUBLISHER: THE NEW YORK TIMES
ISSUE: DECEMBER 7, 2008
CATEGORY: DESIGN: SECTION (SINGLE/SPREAD)

/306/ **CONDÉ NAST PORTFOLIO**
DESIGN DIRECTOR: ROBERT PRIEST
ART DIRECTOR: GRACE LEE
DESIGNER: SARAH VIÑAS
ILLUSTRATOR: BRYAN CHRISTIE DESIGN
EDITOR-IN-CHIEF: JOANNE LIPMAN
PUBLISHER: CONDÉ NAST PUBLICATIONS INC.
ISSUE: FEBRUARY 2008
CATEGORY: DESIGN: SECTION (SINGLE/SPREAD)

307

307

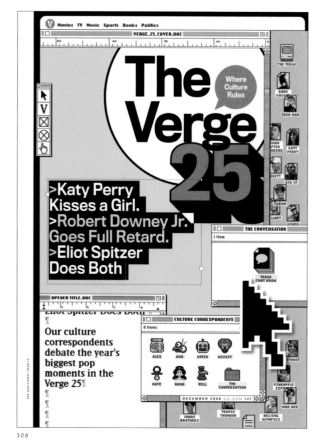

308

308

/307/ **GQ**
DESIGN DIRECTOR: FRED WOODWARD / ART DIRECTOR: ANTON IOUKHNOVETS
DESIGNER: DELGIS CANAHUATE / DIRECTOR OF PHOTOGRAPHY: DORA SOMOSI
PHOTO EDITOR: JESSE LEE / PHOTOGRAPHER: CEDRIC ANGELES
EDITOR-IN-CHIEF: JIM NELSON / PUBLISHER: CONDÉ NAST PUBLICATIONS INC.
ISSUE: MARCH 2008 / CATEGORY: DESIGN: SECTION (SERIES OF PAGES)

/308/ **GQ**
DESIGN DIRECTOR: FRED WOODWARD / DESIGNER: THOMAS ALBERTY
DIRECTOR OF PHOTOGRAPHY: DORA SOMOSI / EDITOR-IN-CHIEF: JIM NELSON
PUBLISHER: CONDÉ NAST PUBLICATIONS INC. / ISSUE: DECEMBER 2008
CATEGORY: DESIGN: SECTION (SERIES OF PAGES)

309

309

310

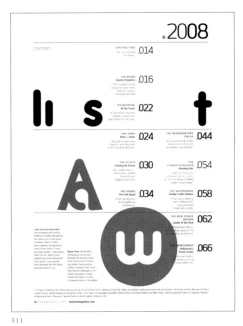

311

311

/309/ **W**
DESIGN DIRECTOR: EDWARD LEIDA
ART DIRECTOR: NATHALIE KIRSHEH
DESIGNERS: LAURA KONRAD, GINA MANISCALCO
PHOTO EDITOR: NADIA VELLAM
PHOTOGRAPHERS: NIGEL COX, ANTHONY COTSIFAS,
PATRICIA HEAL, STEPHEN LEWIS
PUBLISHER: CONDÉ NAST PUBLICATIONS INC.
ISSUES: FEBRUARY 2008, MAY 2008, AUGUST 2008,
SEPTEMBER 2008, OCTOBER 2008, NOVEMBER 2008
CATEGORY: DESIGN: SECTION (SERIES OF PAGES)

/310/ **W**
DESIGN DIRECTOR: EDWARD LEIDA
ART DIRECTOR: NATHALIE KIRSHEH
DESIGNERS: GINA MANISCALCO, LAURA KONRAD
PUBLISHER: CONDÉ NAST PUBLICATIONS INC.
ISSUES: FEBRUARY 2008, JULY 2008, DECEMBER 2008
CATEGORY: DESIGN: SECTION (SERIES OF PAGES)

/311/ **W**
DESIGN DIRECTOR: EDWARD LEIDA
ART DIRECTOR: NATHALIE KIRSHEH
DESIGNERS: GINA MANISCALCO, LAURA KONRAD
PHOTOGRAPHER: ARI MARCOPOULOS
PUBLISHER: CONDÉ NAST PUBLICATIONS INC.
ISSUE: FEBRUARY 2008
CATEGORY: DESIGN: SECTION (SERIES OF PAGES)

312

313

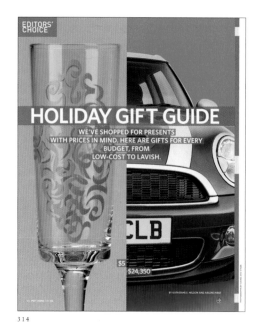

314

312

313

314

/312/ WIRED
CREATIVE DIRECTOR: SCOTT DADICH
DESIGN DIRECTOR: WYATT MITCHELL
ART DIRECTOR: MAILI HOLIMAN
DESIGNERS: MAILI HOLIMAN, SHANNON SAWTELLE,
MARGARET SWART
PUBLISHER: CONDÉ NAST PUBLICATIONS, INC.
ISSUE: OCTOBER & NOVEMBER 2008
CATEGORY: DESIGN: SECTION (SERIES OF PAGES)

/313/ BLENDER
CREATIVE DIRECTOR: DIRK BARNETT
ART DIRECTOR: ROBERT VARGAS
DESIGNER: ROBERT VARGAS
ILLUSTRATORS: EAMO, JAMESON SIMPSON
DIRECTOR OF PHOTOGRAPHY: AMY HOPPY
PHOTO EDITORS: RORY WALSH, CHRIS EHRMAN
PHOTOGRAPHERS: DARIN LEDFORD, ASGER CARLSEN
EDITOR-IN-CHIEF: JOE LEVY
PUBLISHER: ALPHAMEDIA GROUP
ISSUE: SEPTEMBER 2008
CATEGORY: DESIGN: SECTION (SERIES OF PAGES)

/314/ METROPOLITAN HOME
DESIGN DIRECTOR: KEITH D'MELLO
ART DIRECTOR: JEFFREY FELMUS
PHOTO EDITOR: CATHRYNE CZUBEK
PHOTOGRAPHER: DAVIES AND STARR
PUBLISHER: HACHETTE FILIPACCHI MEDIA U.S.
ISSUE: DECEMBER 2008
CATEGORY: DESIGN: SECTION (SERIES OF PAGES)

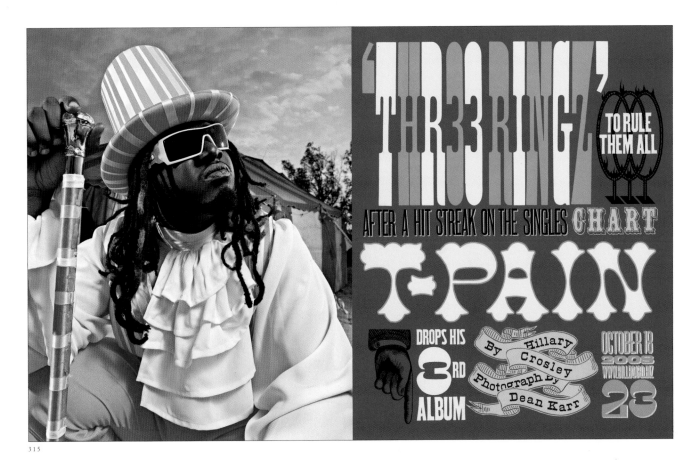

315

316

/315/ BILLBOARD
ART DIRECTOR: CHRISTINE BOWER-WRIGHT / SENIOR DESIGNER: GREG GRABOWY
PHOTO EDITOR: AMELIA HALVERSON / PHOTOGRAPHER: DEAN KARR
PUBLISHER: NIELSEN BUSINESS MEDIA / ISSUE: OCTOBER 18, 2008
CATEGORY: DESIGN: SINGLE/SPREAD/STORY

/316/ MOVIEMAKER
ART DIRECTOR: ROB HEWITT, CURIOUS OUTSIDER / DESIGNER: ROB HEWITT
STUDIO: CURIOUS OUTSIDER / EDITOR-IN-CHIEF: TIMOTHY E. RHYS
PUBLISHER: MOVIEMAKER LLC / CLIENT: MOVIEMAKER / ISSUE: SEPTEMBER 2008
CATEGORY: DESIGN: SINGLE/SPREAD/STORY

317

318

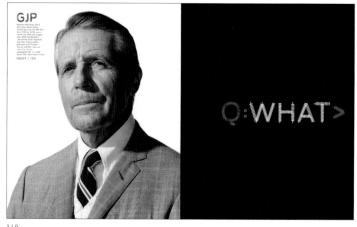

319

/317/ **GOLF DIGEST INDEX**
DESIGN DIRECTOR: KEN DELAGO
DESIGNER: KEN DELAGO
ILLUSTRATOR: JAMESON SIMPSON
PUBLISHER: CONDÉ NAST PUBLICATIONS INC.
ISSUE: FALL 2008
CATEGORY: DESIGN: SINGLE/SPREAD/STORY

/318/ **CONTRIBUTE**
DESIGN DIRECTOR: MITCH SHOSTAK
ART DIRECTOR: SUSANA SOARES
PHOTOGRAPHERS: ERIC SHAMBROOM, WALTER
CALAHAN, JASON GROW, RICK FRIEDMAN
STUDIO: SHOSTAK STUDIOS
EDITOR-IN-CHIEF: MARCIA STEPANEK
PUBLISHER: CONTRIBUTE MEDIA
CLIENT: CONTRIBUTE
ISSUE: JANUARY/FEBRUARY 2008
CATEGORY: DESIGN: SINGLE/SPREAD/STORY

/319/ **GOLF DIGEST INDEX**
DESIGN DIRECTOR: KEN DELAGO
DESIGNER: MARNE MAYER
PHOTO EDITOR: RYAN CLINE
PHOTOGRAPHER: ART STREIBER
PUBLISHER: CONDÉ NAST PUBLICATIONS INC.
ISSUE: SPRING 2008
CATEGORY: DESIGN: SINGLE/SPREAD/STORY

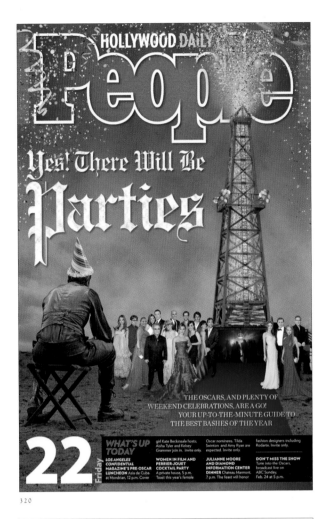

320

322

323

321

324

/320/ **PEOPLE**
DESIGN DIRECTOR: SARA WILLIAMS
ART DIRECTOR: GREG MONFRIES
DESIGNER: KEIR NOVESKY
DIRECTOR OF PHOTOGRAPHY: CHRIS DOUGHERTY
PHOTO EDITOR: LINDSAY TYLER
DIGITAL IMAGING: HUBIE LAU
PUBLISHER: TIME INC.
ISSUE: FEBRUARY 22, 2008
CATEGORY: DESIGN: SINGLE/SPREAD/STORY

/321/ **GREEN SOURCE**
CREATIVE DIRECTOR: FRANCESCA MESSINA
ART DIRECTORS: MITCH SHOSTAK, COREY KUEPFER
ILLUSTRATOR: I-NI CHEN
PHOTOGRAPHERS: VIVAN SUNDARAM,
CHRIS JORDAN
STUDIO: SHOSTAK STUDIOS
PUBLISHER: MCGRAW-HILL CONSTRUCTION
CLIENT: GREEN SOURCE
ISSUE: NOVEMBER/DECEMBER 2008
CATEGORY: DESIGN: SINGLE/SPREAD/STORY

/322/ **GO**
ART DIRECTOR: SHANE LUITJENS
PHOTOGRAPHER: BEN WATTS
STUDIO: INK PUBLISHING
EDITOR-IN-CHIEF: ORION RAY-JONES
PUBLISHER: INK PUBLISHING
CLIENT: AIRTRAN AIRWAYS
ISSUE: MAY 2008
CATEGORY: DESIGN: SINGLE/SPREAD/STORY

/323/ **GO**
ART DIRECTOR: SHANE LUITJENS
DESIGNER: KEVIN MAZUR
PHOTOGRAPHER: KEVIN MAZUR
STUDIO: INK PUBLISHING
EDITOR-IN-CHIEF: ORION RAY-JONES
PUBLISHER: INK PUBLISHING
CLIENT: AIRTRAN AIRWAYS
ISSUE: JANUARY 2008
CATEGORY: DESIGN: SINGLE/SPREAD/STORY

/324/ **GO**
ART DIRECTOR: SHANE LUITJENS
PHOTOGRAPHER: JUSTIN STEPHENS
STUDIO: INK PUBLISHING
EDITOR-IN-CHIEF: ORION RAY-JONES
PUBLISHER: INK PUBLISHING
CLIENT: AIRTRAN AIRWAYS
ISSUE: SEPTEMBER 2008
CATEGORY: DESIGN: SINGLE/SPREAD/STORY

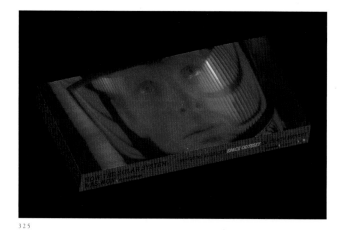

325

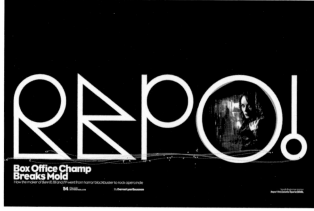

328

326

329

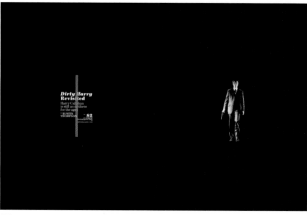

327

330

/325/ **MOVIEMAKER**
ART DIRECTOR: ROB HEWITT, CURIOUS OUTSIDER
DESIGNER: ROB HEWITT
STUDIO: CURIOUS OUTSIDER
EDITOR-IN-CHIEF: TIMOTHY E. RHYS
PUBLISHER: MOVIEMAKER LLC
CLIENT: MOVIEMAKER
ISSUE: SUMMER 2008
CATEGORY: DESIGN: SINGLE/SPREAD/STORY

/326/ **MOVIEMAKER**
ART DIRECTOR: ROB HEWITT, CURIOUS OUTSIDER
DESIGNER: ROB HEWITT
PHOTOGRAPHER: DEVRILL WEEKES
STUDIO: CURIOUS OUTSIDER
EDITOR-IN-CHIEF: TIMOTHY E. RHYS
PUBLISHER: MOVIEMAKER LLC
CLIENT: MOVIEMAKER
ISSUE: SEPTEMBER 2008
CATEGORY: DESIGN: SINGLE/SPREAD/STOR

/327/ **MOVIEMAKER**
ART DIRECTOR: ROB HEWITT, CURIOUS OUTSIDER
DESIGNER: ROB HEWITT
STUDIO: CURIOUS OUTSIDER
EDITOR-IN-CHIEF: TIMOTHY E. RHYS
PUBLISHER: MOVIEMAKER LLC
CLIENT: MOVIEMAKER
ISSUE: SEPTEMBER 2008
CATEGORY: DESIGN: SINGLE/SPREAD/STORY

/328/ **MOVIEMAKER**
ART DIRECTOR: ROB HEWITT, CURIOUS OUTSIDER
DESIGNER: ROB HEWITT
STUDIO: CURIOUS OUTSIDER
EDITOR-IN-CHIEF: TIMOTHY E. RHYS
PUBLISHER: MOVIEMAKER LLC
CLIENT: MOVIEMAKER
ISSUE: FALL 2008
CATEGORY: DESIGN: SINGLE/SPREAD/STORY

/329/ **EARNSHAW'S**
CREATIVE DIRECTOR: NANCY CAMPBELL
ART DIRECTOR: TREVETT MCCANDLISS
DESIGNER: TREVETT MCCANDLISS
PHOTOGRAPHERS: ANETA BARTOS,
ALISON CARTWRIGHT
EDITOR-IN-CHIEF: CALETHA CRAWFORD
PUBLISHER: SYMPHONY PUBLISHING
ISSUE: JULY 2008
CATEGORY: DESIGN: SINGLE/SPREAD/STORY

/330/ **FOOTWEAR PLUS**
CREATIVE DIRECTOR: NANCY CAMPBELL
ART DIRECTOR: TREVETT MCCANDLISS
DESIGNER: TREVETT MCCANDLISS
PHOTOGRAPHER: ALEXANDRA CARR
EDITOR-IN-CHIEF: GREG DUTTER
PUBLISHER: SYMPHONY PUBLISHING
ISSUE: FEBRUARY 2008
CATEGORY: DESIGN: SINGLE/SPREAD/STORY

331

333

332

334

/331/ ONEARTH
ART DIRECTOR: GAIL GHEZZI
PHOTO EDITORS: MONICA BRADLEY, GAIL HENRY
PHOTOGRAPHER: VERN EVANS
EDITOR-IN-CHIEF: DOUGLAS S. BARASCH
PUBLISHER: NRDC
ISSUE: SUMMER 2008
CATEGORY: DESIGN: SINGLE/SPREAD/STORY

/332/ ILLUMINATION
ART DIRECTOR: BLAKE DINSDALE
DESIGNER: BLAKE DINSDALE
ILLUSTRATOR: JUSTIN WOOD
EDITOR-IN-CHIEF: CHARLES REINEKE
PUBLISHER: UNIVERSITY OF MISSOURI
ISSUE: SPRING 2008
CATEGORY: DESIGN: SINGLE/SPREAD/STORY

/333/ 2008 HRC ANNUAL REPORT
CREATIVE DIRECTORS: PUM LEFEBURE,
JAKE LEFEBURE
ART DIRECTOR: PUM LEFEBURE
DESIGNER: SUCHA BECKY
STUDIO: DESIGN ARMY
CLIENT: HUMAN RIGHTS CAMPAIGN
ISSUE: OCTOBER 2008
CATEGORY: DESIGN: ENTIRE ISSUE

/334/ U OF T MAGAZINE
CREATIVE DIRECTORS: CLAIRE DAWSON,
FIDEL PEÑA / DESIGNER: CLAIRE DAWSON
PHOTOGRAPHER: PAUL WEEKS
STUDIO: UNDERLINE STUDIO
EDITOR-IN-CHIEF: SCOTT ANDERSON
PUBLISHER: UNIVERSITY OF TORONTO
CLIENT: UNIVERSITY OF TORONTO
ISSUE: SEPTEMBER 2008
CATEGORY: DESIGN: SINGLE/SPREAD/STORY

RICHARD FERRETTI
RICHARD PIERCE
RICHARD SANDLER
RICHIE SWANN
RINA STONE
RITA SALGUEIRO
ROB HEWITT
ROB HOWARD
ROB IRINGALI
ROBBIE COOPER
ROBERT FESTINO
ROBERT MAXWELL
ROBERT PERINO
ROBERT POLIDORI
ROBERT PRIEST
ROBERT TRACHTENBERG
ROCKWELL HARWOOD
RODRIGO SAIAS
ROMAN-LUBA
ROMULO YANES
RON HAVIV
RON PLYMAN
RONY ALWIN
RORY WALSH
RUSSELL ESTES
RUVEN AFANADOR
RYAN CADIZ
RYAN MCGINLEY
SAM JONES
SANDRA FREJ
SANDRA GARCIA
SARA WILLIAMS
SARAH GARCIA
SASHA CUTTER
SCOTT HALL
SCOTT DADICH
SCOTT PHILLIPS
SEAN JOHNSTON
SEAN KENNEDY-SANTOS
SEBASTIÃO SALGADO
SERGIO GOES
SETH WENIG
SHANNA GREENBERG
SIAN KENNEDY
STEFAN YAYAMADA
SIUNG TJIA
SOLVE SUNDSBØ
SONIA KHATRI
SONIA BILBAO

LOUIS-CHARLES TIAR

MAILI HOLIMAN

MAISIE TODD
MANUELLO PAGANELLI
MARA LILIANA GONZÁLEZ

MARC ASNIN

MARC KAUFMAN
MARC STEINMETZ
MARCUS BROOKS
MARCUS PIGGOTT

MARGARET SWART

MARILYN MINTER

MARINO ZULLICH
MARIO SORRENTI

MARK HEITHOFF

MARK MICHAELSON
MARK SANDERS
MARK SELIGER

MARLA KAPLAN
MARNE MAYER
MARSHALL MCKINNEY

MARTIN KLIMAS
MARTIN KUENSTING
MARTIN SCHOELLER
MARTIN VALLIN

MARY-ELLEN MARK

MASSIMO GAMMACURTA

MATTHEW FROST
MATTHEW LENNING
MATTHEW MILLMAN

MATTHEW SPORZYNSKI
MAURICIO ALEJO
MAX AGUILERA-HELLWEG

MELANIE ACEVEDO

MELISSA HOM

MERT ALAS

MICHAEL BRIAN

MICHAEL ELMENBECK
MICHAEL LAWTON

MICHAEL MULLER
MICHAEL NORSENG

MICHAEL SCHMELLING
MICHAEL SCHNAIDT

MICHELE OUTLAND
MICHELLE LITVIN

MIKAEL DAHL
MIKE LEY
MIKE POWELL

HORACIO SALINAS

HUGH KRETSCHMER

IAN ALLEN
IAN ROBINSON
IAN BROWN
ILAN RUBIN
INGO ARNDT

IXEL OSARIO

JACKIE DASHEVSKY

JACOB HUURIMAINEN

JAIMEY EASTER
JAKE CHESSUM
JAKOB CARLSEN
JAMES DAY
JAMES DUNLINSON
JAMES NACHTWEY
JAMES WELLING
JAMES WOJCIK
JAMIE CHUNG
JAN STROMME

JANET FROELICH

JASON MAKOWSKI

JASON NOCITO

JASON SEIDON

JAY MAISEL
JEAN-BAPTISTE MONDINO
JEAN-LUC BÉNARD

JEFF BEAMER

JEFF GLENDENNING

JEFF RIEDEL
JEFF SCIORTINO

JEFFREY FELLMUS

JEFFREY SALTER
JENIFER WALSH
JENN MCMANUS

JENNIFER BIANCELLA

JEPPE CARLSEN
JERI HEIDEN

JEURGEN TELLER
HIL GREENBERG

JOANNA MILLER
JODY QUON
JOE KIMBERLING

JODY PECKMAN

JOHN BENNETT FITTS
JOHN DIXON
JOHN TOLL

CRAIG CUTLER

CRYSTAL PHILLIPS

CYNTHIA A. HOFFMAN
CYNTHIA SEARIGHT
D.W. PINE
DAKOTA KECK

DAN FORBES
DAN REVITTE
DAN SAELINGER
DAN WINTERS

DANIEL MÜLLER-GROTE
DANNY CLINCH

DANNY WILCOX-FRAZIER

DAVID BOWMAN

DAVID CLUGSTON

DAVID GRIFFIN
DAVID GRAY
DAVID HARRIS
DAVID HILTON

DAVID ROEMER
DAVID SCHLOW
DAVID SEBBAH

DAVID WHITMORE

DAVIES+STARR

DELGIS CANAHUATE
DENA VERDESCA
DENISE SEE
DENNIS FREEDMAN

DEVIN PEDZWATER

DIANA KLEIN

DIRK BARNETT

DONNA FERRATO
DORA SOMOSI
DRAGOS LEMNEI
BRUE WAGNER

EDWARD BURTYNSKY
EDWARD KEATING
EDWARD LEIDA
EDWARD LEVINE
ELAINE AHN
ELEANOR WILLIAMSON

ELIZABETH SPIRIDAKIS
ELIZABETH YOUNG

EUENE WUNDROK

EMILY CRAWFORD

/CONTRIBUTORS/
AARON GOODMAN

ABRIL Y DE LA CARRERA
ADAM BILLYEALD
ADAM BOOKBINDER
ADAM LOGAN FULRATH

AGNÈS DHERBEYS
ALAN MAHON
ALBERTO GARCÍA-ALIX

ALEX GHEZ
ALEX GROSSMAN
ALEX MARTINEZ

ALLISON CHIN

AMID CAPECI
AMY KLOBENZER
AMY BERKLEY

AMY HOPPY

AMY SHROADS

ANDRE JOINTE
ANDRE WOLFF
ANDREA CHU

ANDREA MODICA

ANDREAS SERRANO
ANDREAS SJODIN

ANDREW ECCLES
ANDREW HORTON

ANDY ANDERSON

ANNA WILLIAMS
ANNA WOLF
ANNE BRUN

ANNE LEIBOVITZ

ANTON IOUKHNOVETS
ANTONIN KRATOCHVIL

ART STREIBER

ASHLEY FREBY
AYA SALATOVA

AYA BRACKETT

BEN BAYNER

BENJAMIN LOWY
BERNARD SCHARF
BERT STERN
BERTO MARTINEZ

photo/

W
WIRED
VANITY FAIR
TIME
TIME INTERNATIONAL
TIME OUT NEW YORK
TV GUIDE MAGAZINE
THE NEW YORKER
THE NEW YORK TIMES MAGAZINE
THE FADER
TEXAS MONTHLY
T
SPORTS ILLUSTRATED
STANFORD MAGAZINE
SPIN
SHOPSMART)
SHUTTI
SELF
SAMVIRKE
RUNNER'S WORLD
ROOM
ROLLING STONE
REAL SIMPLE
PROTO
PSYCHOLOGY TODAY
POPULAR MECHANICS
PLAY
PEOPLE
OUT
NYLON
NOX
NEWSWEEK
NEW YORK
NATIONAL GEOGRAPHIC
MORE
METROPOLITAN HOME
MINNESOTA MONTHLY
MEN'S JOURNAL
MEN'S HEALTH
MEDICINE AT MICHIGAN
MAXIM
MARTHA STEWART LIVING
MADRIZ

STEVE DUENES
STEVE HOFFMAN
STEVEN KLEIN
STEVEN MEISEL
STRAVINSKI PIERRE
SUE TALLON
SUSANNE BAMBERGER
SUZANNE DONALDSON
T.J. TUCKER
TAMMY MORTON FERNANDEZ
THERESA GRIGGS
THOMAS ALBERTY
THOMAS KELLNER
TIM BALDWIN
TIM LAPALME
TIM OLIVER
TIM WALKER
TINA TYRELL
TOBY MCFARLAN POND
TODD WEINBERGER
TOM O'QUINN
TOM SCHIERLITZ
TONY KIM
TONY MARRO
TREVETT MCCANDLISS
TURE LILLEGRAVEN
UTA MAXIN
VALERIE DOWNES
VIBRACGBRADESIGN
VICENS CASTELLTORT
WALTER C. BAUMANN
WENDELL WEBBER
WENDY REINGOLD
WILLIAM ABRANOWICZ
WILLIAM HOOKS
WILLIAMS + HIRAKAWA
WYATT MITCHELL
YURI KOZYREV
ZANA WOODS

MONICA BUCK
NADAV KANDER
NANCY CAMPBELL
NANCY HARRIS ROUEMY
NATE VAN DYKE
NATHALIE KIRSHEH
NATHAN SINCLAIR
NEIL JAMIESON
NICK VOGELSON
NICK WAPLINGTON
NICOLETTE BERTHELOT
NIGEL COX
NIGEL PARRY
NOBUYOSHI ARAKI
NORMAN JEAN ROY
OLAF BLECKER
OLAF OTTO BECKER
ORIE ICHIHASHI
OSCAR ARAGON
PABLO BERNASCONI
PAOLO PELLEGRIN
PATRICIA REIS
PATRICIA SANCHEZ
PATRICK DEMARCHELIER
PATRIK GIARDINO
PATTY ALVAREZ
PAUL GRAHAM
PAUL LEPREUX
PAUL MARTINEZ
PAUL MCDONOUGH
PEGGY SIROTA
PETER VAN AG
PETER YANG
PETRA KOBAYASHI
PHIL BICKER
PHIL MORRISON
PHILIP BLENKINSOP
PHILIP-LORCA DICORCIA
PHILLIP TOLEDANO
PHOEBE FLYNN RICH
PIERRE BJORK
PLAMEN PETKOV
PLATON
QUIQUE CIRIA
PETER FRANK EDWARDS
RANDY MINOR
RAYMOND MEIER
REBECCA LOUTSCH
RICARDO TERICHE

ERIKA OLIVEIRA
AVGOUSTA (JUNG) JONATHAN GROES [JUNG]
EVAN CAMPISI
EVELYN HOCKSTEIN
FABIEN BARON
JOSE-MANUEL FERRATER
JOSEPH HUTCHINSON
FERNANDO MASELLI
FILIPA GREGORIO
JOSHUA JORDAN
JUAN MANUEL CASTRO PRIETO
JUDITH PUCKETRINSELA
FIRSTVIEW
FLORIAN BACHLEDA
JULIA MOBURG
JULIANA SOHN
JULIE WEISS
JULIO CONTRERAS
JUTTA KRUEGER
KANG KIM
KANTI ISHII
KAREEM ILIYA
KARLA LIMA
KATHY RYAN
KEITH D'MELLO
KEITH LADZINSKI
KEN DELAGO
KENJI TOMA
KIRA POLLACK
KIRBY RODRIGUEZ
KORY KENNEDY
KRISANNE JOHNSON
KUNIO HAYASHI
KURT ISWARIENKO
KYLE BLUE
LAMSWEERDE & MATADIN
LAURA KONRAD
LAURA LETINSKY
LAUREN FLEISHMAN
LEE WILLIAMS
LEE WILSON
LEO JUNG
LINSEY LAIDLAW
LISA HUBBARD
LISA BERMAN
LISA LIMER
LISA ROZE
LIVIA CORONA
LIZ MACFARLANE
LOU CORREDOR

BRANDON & WOLF
BRANDON CALLAHAN
BRENNAN MILLIAS
BRIAN ANSTEY
BRIAN SCOTT
BRIGITTE LACOMBE
BROOK KRAFT
BROWN CANNON III
BRUCE WEBER
BURKHARD SCHITTNY
CALLIE SHELL
CARL DE TORRES
CARLOS SERRAO
CAROLYN RAUCH
CARTER SMITH
CASEY TIERNEY
CASS BIRD
CATHERINE GILMORE-BARNES
CATHERINE HAWTHORN
CATRIONA NICOLAIN
CECELIA WONG
CEDRIC ANGELES
CELINE ROBERT
CHANDRA GLICK
CHARLENE BENSON
CHARLES MASTERS
CHELSEA CARDINAL
CHRIS DIXON
CHRIS HERCIK
CHRIS SEGEDY
CHRIS MUELLER
CHRISTEL FRYDKJAER
CHRISTIAN COINBERGH
CHRISTIAN WITKIN
CHRISTINE PARK
CHRISTOPHER ANDERSON
CHRISTOPHER GRIFFITH
CHRISTOPHER MARTINEZ
CHRISTOPHER MCLALLEN
CHRISTOPHER MORRIS
CHRISTOPHER WIELICZKO
CHRISTY SHEPPARD
CINDY ALLEN
CLARE CHONG
CLINTON CARGILL
COPPI BARBIERI
CORY JACOBS
COURTNEY WADDELL ECKERSLEY

FRANK W. OCKENFELS 3
FRED WOODWARD
FRITZ HOFFMANN
GAIL ALBERT HALABAN
GAIL BICHLER
GAVIN BOND
GEOFF HALBER
GEORGE ARTHUR
GEORGE KARABOTSOS
GEORGE PITTS
GERALDINE HESSLER
GERARD RANCINAN
GIANNINA MACIAS
GINA MANISCALCO
GLENN MATSUMURA
GRACE LEE
GRACE MARTINEZ
GRACIELA ARTIGA
GREG KADEL
GREG KESSLER
GREGG SEGAL
GREG POND
GREGOR HALENDA
GREGORY DERKENNE
GUIDO VITTI
GUILLERMO CABALLERO
GUN LARSON
GUY AROCH
HANNAH WHITAKER
HANS GISSINGER
HARF ZIMMERMAN
HARRY BENSON
HEATH BROCKWELL
HEATHER JONES
HECTOR SANCHEZ
HEIDI SITMANE
HEINZ KLUETMEIER
HENDRIK KERSTENS
HENRIK HALVARSSON
HENRIQUE CAYATTE
HANG HUANG
HILLARY WALSH

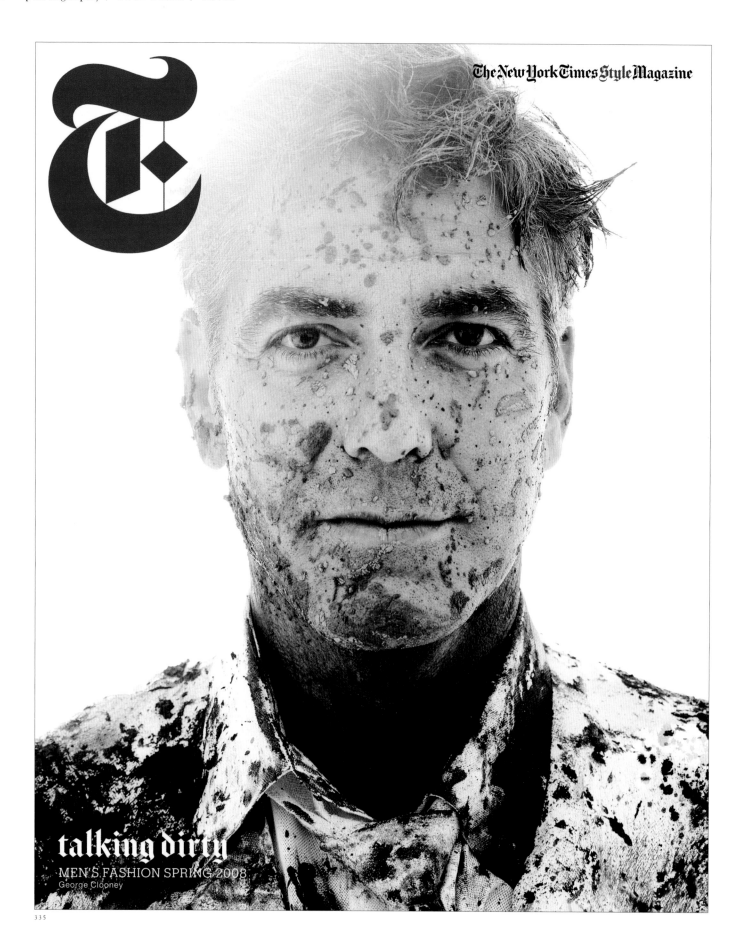

The New York Times Style Magazine

talking dirty
MEN'S FASHION SPRING 2008
George Clooney

335

/335/ **T, THE NEW YORK TIMES STYLE MAGAZINE**
CREATIVE DIRECTOR: JANET FROELICH / SENIOR ART DIRECTOR: DAVID SEBBAH / ART DIRECTOR: CHRISTOPHER MARTINEZ / SENIOR DESIGNER: ELIZABETH SPIRIDAKIS
SENIOR PHOTO EDITOR: JUDITH PUCKETT-RINELLA / PHOTOGRAPHER: JEAN-BAPTISTE MONDINO / EDITOR-IN-CHIEF: STEFANO TONCHI / PUBLISHER: THE NEW YORK TIMES
ISSUE: MARCH 9, 2008 / CATEGORY PHOTO: COVER

Fred Kaplan: What the Defense Secretary Really Thinks About Iraq (and Iran) **Annie Murphy Paul:** When Does a Fetus Feel Pain?

The New York Times Magazine

FEBRUARY 10, 2008

Some came out
of nowhere. Others came across as never
before. This year's ...

Breakthrough
Performances in Film

Ellen Page
of "Juno," so pregnant
with possibility.

Twenty-eight pages of portraits by Ryan McGinley, with an essay by Lynn Hirschberg

336

/336/ **THE NEW YORK TIMES MAGAZINE**
CREATIVE DIRECTOR: JANET FROELICH / ART DIRECTOR: AREM DUPLESSIS / DEPUTY ART DIRECTOR: GAIL BICHLER / DESIGNERS: AREM DUPLESSIS, GAIL BICHLER
DIRECTOR OF PHOTOGRAPHY: KATHY RYAN PHOTO EDITOR: KIRA POLLACK / PHOTOGRAPHER: RYAN MCGINLEY / EDITOR-IN-CHIEF: GERRY MARZORATI
PUBLISHER: THE NEW YORK TIMES / ISSUE: FEBRUARY 10, 2008 / CATEGORY PHOTO: ENTIRE ISSUE

Paul Dano
"THERE WILL BE BLOOD"

Dano first
appears like
a ghost
in "There
Will Be Blood" — his
ambitious
evangelist grows
in strength
as oil is found
on his family's land.
In the movie,
Dano seemed
to be touched by
the holy
spirit — his
manipulations,
in the name
of God,
are sneaky,
persuasive
and thrilling
to watch.

Photographed
in East
Stroudsburg, Pa.

74

Jennifer Jason Leigh
"MARGOT AT THE WEDDING"

As the
younger sister of
an egomaniacal
writer, Leigh
created a
richly layered
portrait
of a
conflicted,
needy
personality.

Photographed at
the Glynwood Center,
Cold Spring, N.Y.

71

/337/ **THE NEW YORK TIMES MAGAZINE**
CREATIVE DIRECTOR: JANET FROELICH / ART DIRECTOR: AREM DUPLESSIS / DESIGNERS: AREM DUPLESSIS, GAIL BICHLER / DIRECTOR OF PHOTOGRAPHY: KATHY RYAN
PHOTO EDITOR: KIRA POLLACK / PHOTOGRAPHER: RYAN MCGINLEY / DEPUTY ART DIRECTOR: GAIL BICHLER / EDITOR-IN-CHIEF: GERRY MARZORATI
PUBLISHER: THE NEW YORK TIMES / ISSUE: FEBRUARY 10, 2008 / CATEGORY PHOTO: ENTIRE ISSUE

Sienna Miller
"INTERVIEW"

Based on the Dutch
movie by the late
Theo van Gogh, "Interview"
is a battle of
wills between a
well-known actress
and the journalist
who is profiling
her. Miller amplified the role of the actress,
who is cannier
about the power
of beauty and celebrity
than the audience
(and the journalist) suspects.
Miller's experience
as a tabloid staple
may have informed her
performance, but this is
not a copycat
version of real life.
Instead, Miller neatly defies
expectation — her
portrayal of the complicated actress
is smart, assured and,
finally, transformative.

Photographed
at Hertfordshire House,
Coleshill, Buckinghamshire,
England.

338

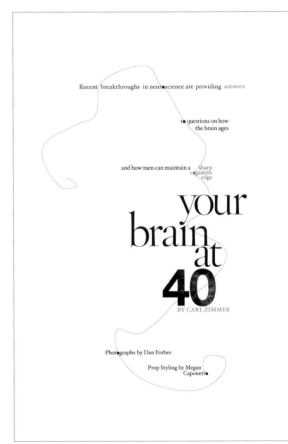

Recent breakthroughs in neuroscience are providing answers

to questions on how
the brain ages

and how men can maintain a   sharp
cognitive
edge

your
brain
at
40
BY CARL ZIMMER

Photographs by Dan Forbes

*Prop Styling by Megan
Caponetto*

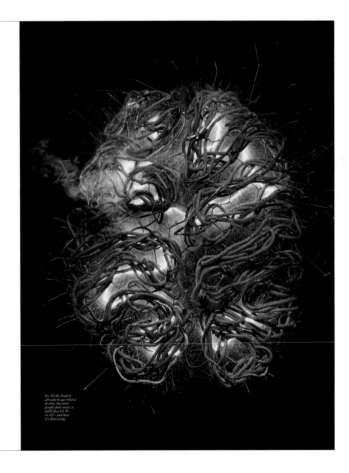

By 40, the brain is
already in age-related
decline, but most
people don't notice it
until they hit 50
or 60—and then
it's distressing.

338

/338/ **BEST LIFE**
DESIGN DIRECTOR: BRANDON KAVULLA / DESIGNER: HEATHER JONES / DIRECTOR OF PHOTOGRAPHY: RYAN CADIZ / PHOTOGRAPHER: DAN FORBES
PUBLISHER: RODALE INC. / ISSUE: AUGUST 2008 / CATEGORY PHOTO: FEATURE: SERVICE (SINGLE/SPREAD)

KUSAMA DOT COM
IS SHE MAD OR MERELY CUNNING? WHILE THE ART WORLD DEBATES, YAYOI KUSAMA CLIMBS BACK ON TOP. BY ALEXI WORTH

"We hope you will understand." With typically fervent Japanese politeness, Yayoi Kusama's staff warned me that the resurgent queen of the Japanese art world, now approaching 80, no longer permits herself to be photographed. But when she learned that the photographer in question was Nobuyoshi Araki, the celebrated master of nude bondage pictures, it turned out that Kusama was only too happy to oblige. And so, on a quiet Thursday afternoon, after an hour or so of failed efforts to interview Kusama, I waited with the artist and her staff around a conference table for Araki's arrival. Wearing a bright red wig, matching lipstick and her signature polka-dot motif — a red kimono-like dress adorned with circles of black and white felt — Kusama looked like a small grave clown, in the lull before a birthday party begins.

When the elevator doors finally opened, a potbellied man with a fringe of gray hair bounded into the room, followed by a crew of gear-laden assistants. Araki, the most famous Japanese photographer, was an ebullient self-caricature. Grunting, laughing, shouting orders and dirty jokes, he seemed a mischievous antidote to the notion of Japanese reserve. The assistants scrambled to set up a tripod and a pair of giant lights, and to seat Kusama in front of one of her radiant new paintings, so that Araki's performance could begin: squatting, swiveling, lunging back and forth between Kusama and his equipment, he moved through the small, crowded space with an enchanting unpredictability. After 10 minutes, he was sweating profusely. The rest of us watched him, more or less transfixed. But Kusama sat motionless, silent, never smiling, showing no response to Araki's virtuosic patter. For most of an hour, she stared unblinkingly into the

PHOTOGRAPH BY NOBUYOSHI ARAKI

267

339

New York

YOU WALK WRONG

It took 4 million years of evolution
to perfect the human foot.
But we're wrecking it with every
step we take.

By ADAM STERNBERGH

WALKING IS EASY. It's so easy that no one ever has to teach you how to do it. It's so easy, in fact, that we often pair it with other easy activities—talking, chewing gum—and suggest that if you can't do both simultaneously, you're some sort of insensate clod. So you probably think you've got this walking thing pretty much nailed. As you stroll around the city, worrying about the economy, or the environment, or your next month's rent, you might assume that the one thing you don't need to worry about is the way in which you're strolling around the city.

Well, I'm afraid I have some bad news for you: You walk wrong.

Look, it's not your fault. It's your shoes. Shoes are bad. I don't just mean stiletto heels, or cowboy boots, or tottering espa-

drilles, or any of the other fairly obvious foot-torture devices into which we wincingly jam our feet. I mean all shoes. Shoes hurt your feet. They change how you walk. In fact, your feet—your poor, tender, abused, ignored, maligned, misunderstood feet—are getting trounced in a war that's been raging for roughly a thousand years: the battle of shoes versus feet.

Last year, researchers at the University of the Witwatersrand in Johannesburg, South Africa, published a study titled "Shod Versus Unshod: The Emergence of Forefoot Pathology in Modern Humans?" in the podiatry journal *The Foot*. The study examined 180 modern humans from three different population groups (Sotho, Zulu, and European), comparing their feet to one another's, as well as to

the feet of 2,000-year-old skeletons. The researchers concluded that, prior to the invention of shoes, people had healthier feet. Among the modern subjects, the Zulu population, which often goes barefoot, had the healthiest feet while the Europeans—i.e., the habitual shoe-wearers—had the unhealthiest. One of the lead researchers, Dr. Bernhard Zipfel, when commenting on his findings, lamented that the American Podiatric Medical Association does not "actively encourage outdoor barefoot walking for healthy individuals. This flies in the face

This shoe and the stilettos and Adidas sneakers on the subsequent pages are trompe-l'oeil paintings applied directly to the feet. Nice as they look, you can't buy them.

24 *Photographs by Tom Schierlitz. Makeup by John Maurad and Jenai Chin.*

340

/339/ T, THE NEW YORK TIMES STYLE MAGAZINE
CREATIVE DIRECTOR: JANET FROELICH
SENIOR ART DIRECTOR: DAVID SEBBAH
ART DIRECTOR: CHRISTOPHER MARTINEZ
SENIOR DESIGNER: ELIZABETH SPIRIDAKIS
DIRECTOR OF PHOTOGRAPHY: KATHY RYAN
PHOTO EDITOR: JENNIFER PASTORE
PHOTOGRAPHER: NOBUYOSHI ARAKI
EDITOR-IN-CHIEF: STEFANO TONCHI
PUBLISHER: THE NEW YORK TIMES
ISSUE: FEBRUARY 24, 2008
CATEGORY PHOTO: FEATURE:
NON-CELEBRITY PROFILE (SINGLE/SPREAD)

/340/ NEW YORK
DESIGN DIRECTOR: CHRIS DIXON
DIRECTOR OF PHOTOGRAPHY: JODY QUON
PHOTO EDITOR: LEANA ALAGIA
PHOTOGRAPHER: TOM SCHIERLITZ
EDITOR-IN-CHIEF: ADAM MOSS
PUBLISHER: NEW YORK MAGAZINE HOLDINGS, LLC
ISSUE: APRIL 28, 2008
CATEGORY PHOTO: FEATURE: SERVICE (STORY)

MYTHOLOGY

Swifter, Higher and all that

Beijing Olympians,
Doing What They Do

PHOTOGRAPHS BY
Paolo Pellegrin

DAVID BOUDIA,
THOMAS FINCHUM
SYNCHRONIZED
PLATFORM DIVING
UNITED STATES
2007 PAN AMERICAN GAMES
GOLD MEDALISTS

10

341

YELENA ISINBAYEVA
POLE VAULT
RUSSIA
2004 OLYMPIC GOLD MEDALIST

ATHLETES IN EXCELSIS
A slide show of
Paolo Pellegrin's images
of Olympians at
work nytimes.com/play

PHOTOGRAPHS BY
PAOLO PELLEGRIN/MAGNUM
FOR THE NEW YORK TIMES

10

341

/341/ **PLAY, THE NEW YORK TIMES SPORT MAGAZINE**
CREATIVE DIRECTOR: JANET FROELICH
ART DIRECTOR: ROB HEWITT / DESIGNERS: ROB HEWITT,
DRAGOS LEMNEI / DIRECTOR OF PHOTOGRAPHY: KATHY RYAN
PHOTO EDITOR: KIRA POLLACK / PHOTOGRAPHER: PAOLO
PELLEGRIN / EDITOR-IN-CHIEF: MARK BRYANT
PUBLISHER: THE NEW YORK TIMES / ISSUE: AUGUST 2008
CATEGORY PHOTO: FEATURE: NON-CELEBRITY PROFILE (STORY)

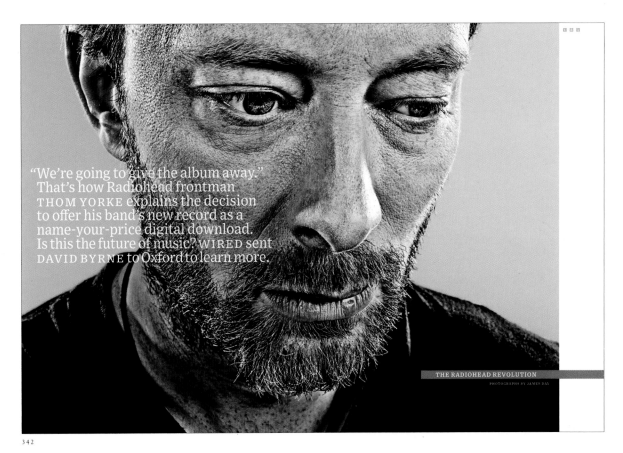

342

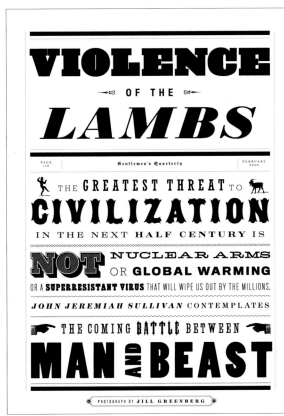

343

/342/ **WIRED**
CREATIVE DIRECTOR: SCOTT DADICH
DESIGN DIRECTOR: WYATT MITCHELL
DESIGNERS: SCOTT DADICH, MARGARET SWART
PHOTO EDITOR: ZANA WOODS
PHOTOGRAPHER: JAMES DAY
PUBLISHER: CONDÉ NAST PUBLICATIONS, INC.
ISSUE: NOVEMBER 2008
CATEGORY PHOTO: FEATURE:
CELEBRITY/ENTERTAINMENT PROFILE (SINGLE/SPREAD)

/343/ **GQ**
DESIGN DIRECTOR: FRED WOODWARD
ART DIRECTOR: ANTON IOUKHNOVETS
DIRECTOR OF PHOTOGRAPHY: DORA SOMOSI
PHOTO EDITOR: JUSTIN O'NEILL
PHOTOGRAPHER: JILL GREENBERG
EDITOR-IN-CHIEF: JIM NELSON
PUBLISHER: CONDÉ NAST PUBLICATIONS INC.
ISSUE: FEBRUARY 2008
CATEGORY PHOTO: FEATURE:
NEWS/REPORTAGE (SINGLE/SPREAD)

Marion Cotillard
"LA VIE EN ROSE"

Cotillard played
the great
singer Edith
Piaf, from her youth
to her early death.
The beauty of the performance is its intimacy:
Cotillard, as Piaf,
is both big
and small,
a diva
with an
undertow
of great sadness.

Photographed in
Montauk, N.Y.

62

344

Josh Brolin
"NO COUNTRY FOR OLD MEN"

In this
reworking
of the western, Brolin has the grace,
instincts and skills
of a modern-day cowboy.
When his
character meets
his inevitable
end, the
movie seems
to hold
its breath:
Brolin is so vivid,
you can't
believe
he's gone.

Photographed
in Pismo
Beach, Calif.

76

77

344

/344/ THE NEW YORK TIMES MAGAZINE
CREATIVE DIRECTOR: JANET FROELICH / ART DIRECTOR: AREM DUPLESSIS / DEPUTY ART DIRECTOR: GAIL BICHLER / DESIGNERS: AREM DUPLESSIS, GAIL BICHLER
DIRECTOR OF PHOTOGRAPHY: KATHY RYAN / PHOTO EDITOR: KIRA POLLACK / PHOTOGRAPHER: RYAN MCGINLEY / EDITOR-IN-CHIEF: GERRY MARZORATI
PUBLISHER: THE NEW YORK TIMES / ISSUE: FEBRUARY 10, 2008 / CATEGORY PHOTO: FEATURE: CELEBRITY/ENTERTAINMENT PROFILE (STORY)

181

Children of

God

*The young women —
willing wives? abuse victims? —
of the polygamist
Fundamentalist Church of Jesus Christ
of Latter-day Saints.*

PHOTOGRAPHS BY
STEPHANIE SINCLAIR

ESSAY BY
SARA CORBETT

On a humid Wednesday in late June, as she waited to be summoned by a grand jury, 16-year-old Teresa Jeffs hitched up her navy blue prairie dress and hoisted herself into the crooked arms of a live oak tree that sits in front of the Schleicher County Courthouse in Eldorado, Tex. For a few minutes, she was not — as has been speculated about many of the young women of the Fundamentalist Church of Jesus Christ of Latter-day Saints, or F.L.D.S. — a possible child bride, or a sexual-abuse victim, or a member of an out-of-touch, polygamous religious sect. She was just a kid in a tree, perched serenely above the heads of all the lawyers, reporters and sheriff's deputies — a moon-faced girl with an auburn coxcomb of hair and a mischievous grin.

We understand so little about the view from that tree, about what the world known simply as "outside" looks like

LeAnn Jeffs, 17 (center), and her 1-year-old daughter were removed from the Yearning for Zion Ranch after it was raided by Texas law-enforcement officers in April. She now lives in a rented home in a San Antonio subdivision with her mother, Sally, 52 (right), and some of her 14 siblings. A friend, Joy Darger, 25, is at left.

26

LEFT A trampoline provides entertainment for the 13 children living at the house in New Braunfels. Pictured here, jumping, is Teresa Jeffs, 16, Lenora's sister and a daughter of Warren S. Jeffs.
TOP Veda Keate, 19, and her 2-year-old daughter at their rented home in Converse, Tex.
MIDDLE Josephine Jeffs, 15, a sister of Teresa, Lenora and Hannah, in New Braunfels.
BOTTOM An investigator from the Texas attorney general's office collects DNA from the 2-year-old daughter of Janet Jeffs, 19, in San Antonio.

are common F.L.D.S. surnames.) Both women claim to have escaped abusive, arranged marriages and have since written best-selling memoirs detailing a world in which women are forced into unconditional obedience and rapid-fire childbearing as a ticket to eternal salvation.

We may never know much about the individual circumstances of the young women in these pages or, most important, whether the relationships that carried some of them into motherhood were forced upon them. The women Sinclair met offered no information about the nature of their marriages or who the fathers of their children are.

For at least some F.L.D.S. mothers, these are uneasy times. It would stand to reason that simply by giving their ages and the ages of their children to a grand jury, coupled with court-ordered paternity tests, some of these mothers may — willingly or not — contribute to the indictments of their children's fathers. (Because plural marriages are often considered "spiritual unions" and not legally

40 PHOTOGRAPHS BY STEPHANIE SINCLAIR/VII NETWORK, FOR THE NEW YORK TIMES.

/345/ **THE NEW YORK TIMES MAGAZINE**
CREATIVE DIRECTOR: JANET FROELICH / ART DIRECTOR: AREM DUPLESSIS / DEPUTY ART DIRECTOR: GAIL BICHLER / DESIGNER: LEO JUNG
DIRECTOR OF PHOTOGRAPHY: KATHY RYAN / PHOTO EDITOR: STACEY BAKER / PHOTOGRAPHER: STEPHANIE SINCLAIR / EDITOR-IN-CHIEF: GERRY MARZORATI
PUBLISHER: THE NEW YORK TIMES / ISSUE: JULY 27, 2008 / CATEGORY PHOTO: FEATURE: NEWS/REPORTAGE (STORY)

STRATEGIST

THE BEST BET Along with last week's record-breaking heat and humidity came that other unavoidable scourge of summer: bugs. (You could almost hear the city collectively swatting itself.) Fend off the intruders—including mosquitoes, gnats, black flies, and ants—with a DEET-free insect spray that actually works. **Herbal Armor** uses ingredients like cedar, peppermint, and citronella in lieu of foul-smelling chemicals ($8.99 for four ounces at Eastern Mountain Sports, 591 Broadway, nr. Houston St.; 212-966-8730). And because it's sweat- and water-resistant, you won't have to carry it around all day for frequent re-ups. For more bug-inspired products, turn the page.

Photograph by Tom Schierlitz

43

346

/346/ **NEW YORK**
DESIGN DIRECTOR: CHRIS DIXON / DIRECTOR OF PHOTOGRAPHY: JODY QUON / PHOTO EDITOR: CAROLINE SMITH / PHOTOGRAPHER: TOM SCHIERLITZ / EDITOR-IN-CHIEF: ADAM MOSS / PUBLISHER: NEW YORK MAGAZINE HOLDINGS, LLC / ISSUE: JUNE 23, 2008 / CATEGORY PHOTO: FEATURE: TRAVEL/FOOD/STILL LIFE (SINGLE/SPREAD)

CAIRO

WITH ITS TIMELESS MINARETS AND OLD QUARTER NOT FAR FROM THE DESERT
SANDS, THE EGYPTIAN CAPITAL HAS A CAPTIVATING BEAUTY. IT'S ALSO AN
IDEAL SETTING FOR UNDERSTATED LITTLE BLACK DRESSES AND EVENING NUMBERS.

PHOTOGRAPHED BY **PHILIP-LORCA** DI**CORCIA**
STYLED BY **CAMILLA NICKERSON**

347

347

/347/ **W**
CREATIVE DIRECTOR: DENNIS FREEDMAN / DESIGN DIRECTOR: EDWARD LEIDA / ART DIRECTOR: NATHALIE KIRSHEH / PHOTOGRAPHER: PHILIP-LORCA DICORCIA /
PUBLISHER: CONDÉ NAST PUBLICATIONS INC. / ISSUE: MAY 2008 / CATEGORY PHOTO: FEATURE: TRAVEL/FOOD/STILL LIFE (STORY)

Facing page: Laundry dress, $285, Saks Fifth Avenue. Christian Louboutin heels, $650, Jeffrey Atlanta.

CREATIVE DIRECTOR: HECTOR SANCHEZ / ART DIRECTOR: MARLA KAPLAN / DESIGNER: MARLA KAPLAN / PHOTOGRAPHER: ALEX MARTINEZ
PUBLISHER: EMMIS COMMUNICATIONS CORP. / ISSUE: JUNE 2008 / CATEGORY PHOTO: FEATURE: FASHION/BEAUTY (SINGLE/SPREAD)

A quiet moment during hair and makeup at DKNY, New York, February 3.

DOCUMENTARY

SIDESHOWS

Photographs by
*CHRISTOPHER
ANDERSON*

2

76 NEW YORK LOOK | FALL 2008

349

A male model gets prepped with body bronzer before John Galliano, Paris, March 1.

90 NEW YORK LOOK | FALL 2008

349

/349/ **LOOK NEW YORK**
DESIGN DIRECTOR: CHRIS DIXON / ART DIRECTOR: RANDY MINOR / DIRECTOR OF PHOTOGRAPHY: JODY QUON / PHOTO EDITOR: NADIA LACHANCE
PHOTOGRAPHER: CHRISTOPHER ANDERSON / EDITOR-IN-CHIEF: ADAM MOSS / PUBLISHER: NEW YORK MAGAZINE HOLDINGS, LLC / ISSUE: SPRING 2008
CATEGORY PHOTO: FEATURE: FASHION/BEAUTY (STORY)

at the market
cucumbers
....

TEXT BY AMY ALBERT
RECIPES BY
AMELIA SALTSMAN

*one
ingredient
at its seasonal
peak and
delicious
things to do
with it*

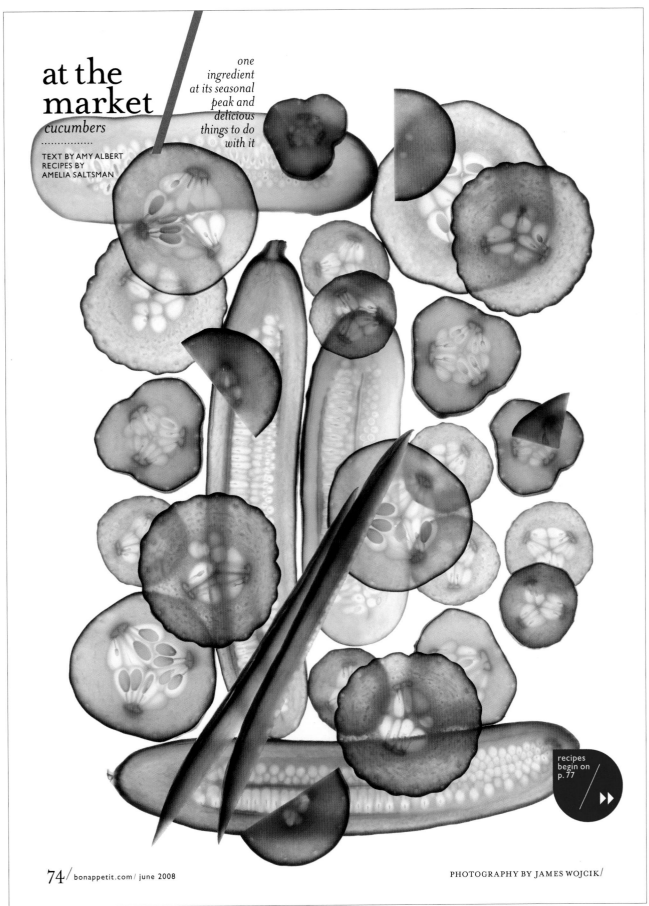

recipes
begin on
p. 77
▶▶

74/ bonappetit.com/ june 2008

PHOTOGRAPHY BY JAMES WOJCIK/

350

/350/ **BON APPÉTIT**
DESIGN DIRECTOR: MATTHEW LENNING / ART DIRECTOR: ROBERT FESTINO / DESIGNER: REBECCA LOUTSCH / PHOTO EDITORS: LIZ MATHEWS, SHARON SUH
PHOTOGRAPHER: JAMES WOJCIK / EDITOR-IN-CHIEF: BARBARA FAIRCHILD / PUBLISHER: CONDÉ NAST PUBLICATIONS, INC. / ISSUE: JUNE 2008
CATEGORY PHOTO: SECTION (SINGLE/SPREAD)

Edward Burtynsky
Quarries

PERSPECTIVE

"Rock of Ages #4"
Abandoned Section
Adam-Pirie Quarry
Barre, Vermont, 1991

158 November 2008

Dwell

Dwell

November 2008 159

/351/ **DWELL**
DESIGN DIRECTOR: KYLE BLUE / DESIGNERS: BRENDAN CALLAHAN, DAKOTA KECK, BRIAN SCOTT / DIRECTOR OF PHOTOGRAPHY: KATE STONE FOSS
PHOTO EDITORS: AMY SILBERMAN, ANDREA LAWSON, ALEXIS TJIAN / PHOTOGRAPHER: EDWARD BURTYNSKY / DESIGN PRODUCTION MANAGER: KATHRYN HANSON
PUBLISHER: DWELL LLC / ISSUE: NOVEMBER 2008 / CATEGORY PHOTO: SECTION (SERIES OF PAGES)

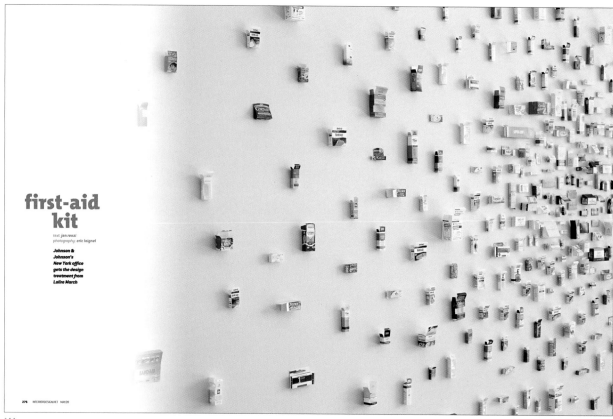

/352/ **INTERIOR DESIGN**
CREATIVE DIRECTOR: CINDY ALLEN
ART DIRECTOR: MARINO ZULLICH
DESIGNERS: ZIGENG LI KARLA LIMA,
GIANNINA MACIAS
PHOTO EDITOR: HELENE OBERMAN
PHOTOGRAPHER: ERIC LAIGNEL
PUBLISHER: REED BUSINESS INFORMATION
ISSUE: MAY 2008
CATEGORY: PHOTO: SINGLE/SPREAD/STORY

/353/ **VANITY FAIR**
DESIGN DIRECTOR: DAVID HARRIS
ART DIRECTORS: JULIE WEISS, CHRIS MUELLER
ILLUSTRATORS: ANDREW NIMMO, BETH BARTHOLOMEW
EDITOR-IN-CHIEF: GRAYDON CARTER
PUBLISHER: CONDÉ NAST PUBLICATIONS INC.
ISSUE: MAY 2008
CATEGORY: PHOTO-ILLUSTRATION: SINGLE/SPREAD/STORY

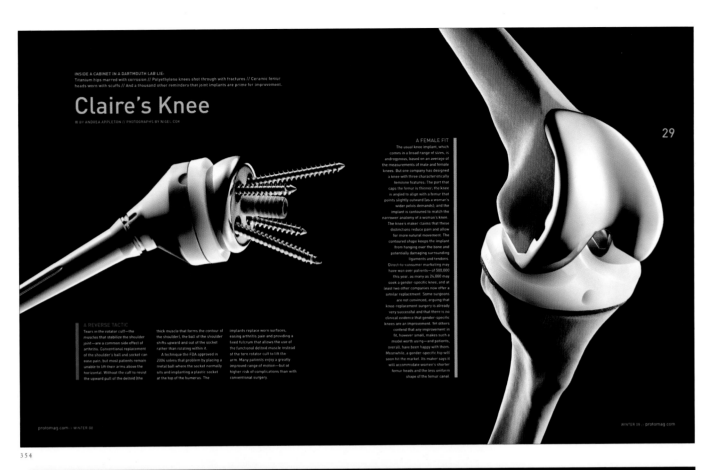

INSIDE A CABINET IN A DARTMOUTH LAB LIE:
Titanium hips marred with corrosion // Polyethylene knees shot through with fractures // Ceramic femur
heads worn with scuffs // And a thousand other reminders that joint implants are prime for improvement.

Claire's Knee

BY ANDREA APPLETON // PHOTOGRAPHS BY NIGEL COX

A FEMALE FIT

The usual knee implant, which comes in a broad range of sizes, is androgynous, based on an average of the measurements of male and female knees. But one company has designed a knee with three characteristically feminine features: The part that caps the femur is thinner; the knee is angled to align with a femur that points slightly outward (as a woman's wider pelvis demands); and the implant is contoured to match the narrower anatomy of a woman's knee. The knee's maker claims that these distinctions reduce pain and allow for more natural movement. The contoured shape keeps the implant from hanging over the bone and potentially damaging surrounding ligaments and tendons. Direct-to-consumer marketing may have won over patients—of 500,000 this year, as many as 24,000 may seek a gender-specific knee, and at least two other companies now offer a similar replacement. Some surgeons are not convinced, arguing that knee-replacement surgery is already very successful and that there is no clinical evidence that gender-specific knees are an improvement. Yet others contend that any improvement in fit, however small, makes such a model worth using—and patients, overall, have been happy with them. Meanwhile, a gender-specific hip will soon hit the market. Its maker says it will accommodate women's shorter femur heads and the less uniform shape of the femur canal.

29

A REVERSE TACTIC

Tears in the rotator cuff—the muscles that stabilize the shoulder joint—are a common side effect of arthritis. Conventional replacement of the shoulder's ball and socket can ease pain, but most patients remain unable to lift their arms above the horizontal. Without the cuff to resist the upward pull of the deltoid [the thick muscle that forms the contour of the shoulder], the ball of the shoulder shifts upward and out of the socket rather than rotating within it.

A technique the FDA approved in 2004 solves that problem by placing a metal ball where the socket normally sits and implanting a plastic socket at the top of the humerus. The implants replace worn surfaces, easing arthritis pain and providing a fixed fulcrum that allows the use of the functional deltoid muscle instead of the torn rotator cuff to lift the arm. Many patients enjoy a greatly improved range of motion—but at higher risk of complications than with conventional surgery.

30

A NIMBLER KNUCKLE

These pieces, when paired, form a sleek facsimile of the main knuckle [the metacarpophalangeal joint], which is often gnarled by arthritis. Made of pyrolytic carbon, the same ultra-durable material used in heart valves and nuclear reactor fuel, the prosthesis has an elasticity similar to bone. This is an important feature: If the prosthesis is too soft, like polyethylene, bone might deform it; if it's too hard, like zircon titanium, it might wear down the bone.

This knuckle is just one example of more than 30 models that have emerged since the metallic hinge—the first finger joint replacement—which was so simple that it was supposedly designed on a cocktail napkin. The best surgical candidate has only one or two severely arthritic digits. (Too much surgery on one hand can lead to exponential complications.) Yet even one fewer painful joint can provide immeasurable relief—and so be it if, as some patients have reported, the new one squeaks.

A CLOSER SHAVE

31

It used to be that the only surgical option for hip repair was to fuse the femur and pelvis, which impaired the patient's gait. When total hip replacement came along in the early 1960s, it was lauded as the century's greatest achievement in orthopedic surgery. The procedure now restores mobility to more than 200,000 patients each year.

But even this advance has had serious limitations: During surgery, the entire head and neck of the femur are replaced, and because the life expectancy of an implant rarely surpasses 20 years, younger patients may eventually need to endure replacement of the replacement. This is both complicated and risky, because little bone remains within which to anchor a new implant.

Now there's hip resurfacing: Surgeons shift the patient's femur out of the socket, shave six to eight millimeters off the top and a few off the sides, and apply a smooth cobalt chrome cap. Though the procedure requires a larger incision and the detachment of more soft tissue than does traditional hip replacement, it has the key advantage of preserving more bone. So in the event that an implant wears out, revision surgery will be much easier, at least in theory.

/354/ **PROTO**
CREATIVE DIRECTOR: CHARLENE BENSON
DESIGN DIRECTOR: ROMAN LUBA / DESIGNER: LEE WILLIAMS
DIRECTOR OF PHOTOGRAPHY: ANN DE SAUSSURE DAVIDSON
PHOTO EDITOR: DENISE BOSCO / PHOTOGRAPHER: NIGEL COX
PUBLISHER: TIME INC. CONTENT SOLUTIONS /
ISSUE: WINTER 2008 / CATEGORY /PHOTO: SINGLE/SPREAD/STORY

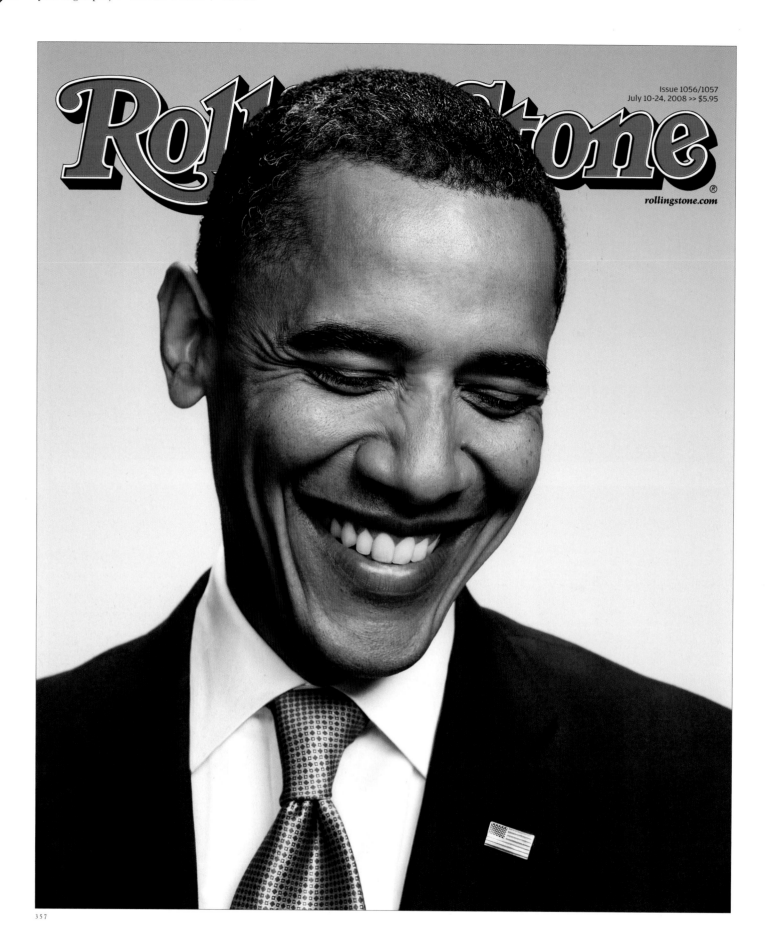

Issue 1056/1057
July 10-24, 2008 >> $5.95

rollingstone.com

357

/357/ **ROLLING STONE**
ART DIRECTOR: JOSEPH HUTCHINSON / DESIGNER: JOSEPH HUTCHINSON / DIRECTOR OF PHOTOGRAPHY: JODI PECKMAN / PHOTOGRAPHER: PETER YANG
PUBLISHER: WENNER MEDIA / ISSUE: JULY 10-24, 2008 / CATEGORY: PHOTO: COVER

N.Y:40

HEAD-LINERS

What became
of ten
memorable
newsmakers

**Photographs by
DAN WINTERS**

Joel Steinberg's abused girlfriend, her testimony helped convict him of killing their adopted daughter **HEDDA NUSSBAUM**

In 1988, Nussbaum testified that her live-in boyfriend, Joel Steinberg, had beaten their 6-year-old adopted daughter, Lisa, to death. (The adoption was never formally recognized by the state.) Nussbaum, a children's-book editor at Random House, had suffered severe beatings at Steinberg's hands; police discovered the couple living in squalor in a West Village townhouse. Prosecutors dropped murder charges against Nussbaum in exchange for her testimony, triggering criticism from those who believed she was complicit in the crime. Steinberg was convicted of first-degree manslaughter; after the trial, Nussbaum had extensive reconstructive surgery and found work at a battered-women's shelter. (She's now retired.) Today she speaks publicly about domestic violence, but lives in hiding from Steinberg, who was released from prison in 2004. She's had her name legally changed. "Sometimes I think maybe after all these years it's overly cautious," she says, "but then I just don't know."

70 NEW YORK | OCTOBER 6, 2008

358

Mia Farrow

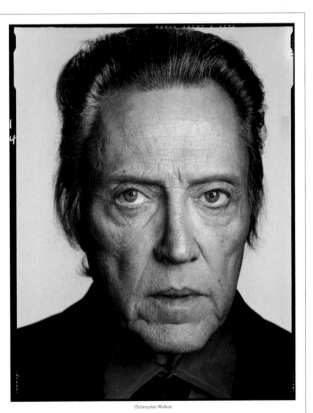

Christopher Walken

162

358

/358/ **NEW YORK**
DESIGN DIRECTOR: CHRIS DIXON / DIRECTOR OF PHOTOGRAPHY: JODY QUON / PHOTO EDITORS: LEANA ALAGIA, ALEX POLLACK, LEA GOLIS, CAROLINE SMITH, NADIA LACHANCE / PHOTOGRAPHERS: DAN WINTERS, EDWARD KEATING, DONNA FERRATO, PAUL MCDONOUGH, JAY MAISEL, ROB HOWARD, HARRY BENSON, RICHARD SANDLER, HANNAH WHITAKER / EDITOR-IN-CHIEF: ADAM MOSS / PUBLISHER: NEW YORK MAGAZINE HOLDINGS, LLC / ISSUE: OCTOBER 6, 2008
CATEGORY: PHOTO: ENTIRE ISSUE

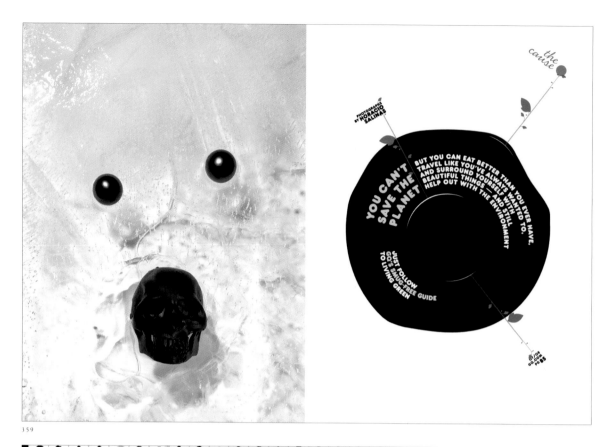

359

360

/359/ **GQ**
DESIGN DIRECTOR: FRED WOODWARD
ART DIRECTOR: ANTON IOUKHNOVETS
DIRECTOR OF PHOTOGRAPHY: DORA SOMOSI
PHOTOGRAPHER: HORACIO SALINAS
EDITOR-IN-CHIEF: JIM NELSON
PUBLISHER: CONDÉ NAST PUBLICATIONS INC.
ISSUE: JULY 2008
CATEGORY PHOTO: FEATURE: SERVICE (SINGLE/SPREAD)

/360/ **SPORTS ILLUSTRATED**
CREATIVE DIRECTOR: STEVE HOFFMAN
ART DIRECTOR: CHRIS HERCIK
PHOTOGRAPHER: GERARD RANCINAN
PUBLISHER: TIME INC.
ISSUE: JULY 28, 2008
CATEGORY PHOTO: FEATURE:
NON-CELEBRITY PROFILE (SINGLE/SPREAD)

classic egg custard pie

WITH LOTS OF NUTMEG *Old-fashioned yet quietly innovative, this custard pie juxtaposes two ordinarily opposing forces—satisfyingly creamy and ethereally light—within a single filling. It's also unsparing with the spice and all the better as a result.*

SEE RECIPES SECTION | SEE GUIDE FOR SOURCES | CREATED BY CHRISTINE ALBANO, JAMES DUNLINSON, AND PAMELA MORRIS

miniature grapefruit soufflés

WITH GINGER *Airy and elegant, just as one would expect, these individual desserts surprise with the pleasantly bitter tang of red grapefruit and fresh ginger. Rest assured, there's plenty of rich egg to round out any sharp edges.*

MARTHASTEWART.COM | 151

361

exemplary eggs

Nature's most perfect form may contain nature's most perfect food. Adaptable and versatile, the egg is delicious in every one of its many guises.

egg glossary CHICKEN (1–6, 10, 11, 13, 14, 16) *The standard by which all others are judged. Color variations in the shell (whether white, mottled brown, palest blue) reflect the breed of hen and make little difference, if any, in flavor. Araucana eggs (14), a relative rarity and Martha's favorite, are available at some farmers' markets.* EMU (7) *Its emerald-green shell makes this variety more coveted for crafts than cooking.* QUAIL (8, 9) *Often served soft-cooked, which shows off its speckled surface and diminutive stature to great effect.* DUCK (12) *Richer and more robust in flavor and color—both outside and within—than the average egg.* GOOSE (15) *Exceptionally mild.* OSTRICH (17) *The largest egg of all but virtually indistinguishable in flavor from a chicken's.*

PHOTOGRAPHS BY HANS GISSINGER TEXT BY JONATHAN GOLD

simple soft-cooked egg

AND TOAST *With its yolk barely set at the edges and defiantly runny throughout, this three-minute egg is, indeed, perfect—but not quite complete without a slice of chewy, thick-cut country-style bread, toasted as you please and served on the side for dipping.*

MARTHASTEWART.COM | 445

361

/361/ **MARTHA STEWART LIVING**
CREATIVE DIRECTOR: ERIC PIKE
DESIGN DIRECTOR: JAMES DUNLINSON
ART DIRECTOR: JAMES DUNLINSON
DESIGNER: LINSEY LAIDLAW
DIRECTOR OF PHOTOGRAPHY: HELOISE GOODMAN
PHOTO EDITOR: MARY CAHILL
PHOTOGRAPHER: HANS GISSINGER
STYLISTS: CHRISTINE ALBANO, PAMELA MORRIS
EDITOR-IN-CHIEF: MICHAEL BOODRO
PUBLISHER: MARTHA STEWART LIVING OMNIMEDIA
ISSUE: APRIL 2008
CATEGORY PHOTO: FEATURE: SERVICE (STORY)

362

362

/362/ ROLLING STONE
ART DIRECTOR: JOSEPH HUTCHINSON
DESIGNER: JOSEPH HUTCHINSON
DIRECTOR OF PHOTOGRAPHY: JODI PECKMAN
PHOTOGRAPHER: SEBASTIÃO SALGADO
PUBLISHER: WENNER MEDIA
ISSUE: OCTOBER 30, 2008
CATEGORY: PHOTO: FEATURE:
NON-CELEBRITY PROFILE (STORY)

The New York Times Magazine / NOVEMBER 30, 2008

HIS FISTS ARE UP
AND
HIS GUARD IS DOWN

Mickey Rourke gets his career off the mat with 'The Wrestler.'
But there is plenty that he's still battling. By Pat Jordan

YOU MEET MICKEY, you can't help liking him. He rescues abused dogs! He cries a lot: over his stepfather's supposed abuse; the loss of his brother to cancer and his dogs to old age; the failure of his marriage to the actress Carré Otis. He admits he destroyed his own career, because, as he puts it: "I was arrogant. ... I wasn't smart enough or educated enough" to deal with stardom. He is candid about the people he has crossed paths with: Nicole Kidman is "an ice cube"; Michael Cimino, the director of "Heaven's Gate," "is crazy" and "nuts"; and the producer Samuel Goldwyn Jr. is "a liar."

So what if he cries at the same moment in the same story in every interview? So what if his candor sometimes sounds like the bad dialogue from one of his many bad movies ("I have no one to go to to fix the broken pieces in myself") or that his self-deprecation seems culled from the stock stories of so many fading actors ("I was

Photograph by Inez van Lamsweerde and Vinoodh Matadin

16

363

Deep Down In Iowa

THE 1993 DELUGE THAT swamped Iowa and much of the Upper Midwest was supposed to be a 500-year flood. Fifteen years later, Iowans are rethinking that judgment. In a spring of calamitous weather, the state's can-do stoicism was tested by two tornadoes; one tore through a Boy Scout camp and killed four teenagers. Rains then swelled the rivers and strained the levees, which burst indiscriminately. Iowa's second largest city, Cedar Rapids (pop. 124,000), and one of its smallest towns, Chelsea (pop. 276), were inundated. On Friday the 13th, downtown Des Moines was under voluntary evacuation. The surge was both overwhelming and fickle. Neighbors on high ground saw friends next door lose cars to a furious downpour. The massive tide is sweeping through Illinois, Missouri and points downstream, raising questions about the adequacy of the levee system designed to guard against flooding. In Iowa the cost mounts: 20% of the corn crop has drowned, 38,000 people have been displaced, and Cedar Rapids alone may need $1 billion to recover.
—BY BETSY RUBINER/DES MOINES

Raging Rivers
For more pictures of the Iowa floods,
go to time.com/iowafloods

Inundated *The Iowa River broke through a levee near Oakville (pop. 428) on June 14, swamping the town and thousands of acres of surrounding farmland*
Photograph for TIME by Danny Wilcox Frazier—Redux

364

/363/ **THE NEW YORK TIMES MAGAZINE**
CREATIVE DIRECTOR: JANET FROELICH
ART DIRECTOR: AREM DUPLESSIS
DEPUTY ART DIRECTOR: GAIL BICHLER
DESIGNER: AREM DUPLESSIS
DIRECTOR OF PHOTOGRAPHY: KATHY RYAN
PHOTO EDITOR: JOANNA MILTER
PHOTOGRAPHERS: INEZ VAN LAMSWEERDE, VINOODH MATADIN
EDITOR-IN-CHIEF: GERRY MARZORATI
PUBLISHER: THE NEW YORK TIMES
ISSUE: NOVEMBER 30, 2008
CATEGORY PHOTO: FEATURE:
CELEBRITY/ENTERTAINMENT PROFILE (SINGLE/SPREAD)

/364/ **TIME**
ART DIRECTOR: ARTHUR HOCHSTEIN
DEPUTY ART DIRECTOR: D. W. PINE
CHIEF PICTURE EDITOR: ALICE GABRINER
ASSOCIATE PICTURE EDITOR: LESLIE DELA VEGA
PHOTOGRAPHER: DANNY WILCOX-FRAZIER — REDUX
EDITOR-IN-CHIEF: JOHN HUEY
PUBLISHER: TIME INC.
ISSUE: JUNE 30, 2008
CATEGORY PHOTO: FEATURE: NEWS/REPORTAGE (SINGLE/SPREAD)

KATIE HOLMES BEEFS UP HER
RESUME OF MOVIES AND
MARRIAGE WITH A LITTLE HELP
FROM BROADWAY

INTERVIEW BY
LYNN HIRSCHBERG

PHOTOGRAPHS BY
SOLVE SUNDSBO

BEST
SUPPORTING
ACTRESS

365

INTERVIEW BY
LYNN HIRSCHBERG

PHOTOGRAPHS BY
SOLVE SUNDSBO

LIFETIME
ACHIEVER

COMEDY,
ACTION, DRAMA,
FATHERHOOD —
TOM CRUISE
EMBRACES THE
WILD RIDE

365

/365/ **T, THE NEW YORK TIMES STYLE MAGAZINE**
CREATIVE DIRECTOR: JANET FROELICH / SENIOR ART DIRECTOR: DAVID SEBBAH / ART DIRECTOR: CHRISTOPHER MARTINEZ / SENIOR DESIGNER: ELIZABETH SPIRIDAKIS
DIRECTOR OF PHOTOGRAPHY: KATHY RYAN / SENIOR PHOTO EDITOR: JUDITH PUCKETT-RINELLA / PHOTOGRAPHER: SOLVE SUNDSBO / EDITOR-IN-CHIEF: STEFANO TONCHI
PUBLISHER: THE NEW YORK TIMES / ISSUE: DECEMBER 7, 2008 / CATEGORY PHOTO: FEATURE: CELEBRITY/ENTERTAINMENT PROFILE (STORY)

A Cutting Tradition

Inside a female-circumcision ceremony for young Muslim girls.

Photographs by
Stephanie Sinclair

TEXT BY SARA CORBETT

When a girl is taken — usually by her mother — to a free circumcision event held each spring in Bandung, Indonesia, she is handed over to a small group of women who, swiftly and yet with apparent affection, cut off a small piece of her genitals. Sponsored by the Assalaam Foundation, an Islamic educational and social-services organization, circumcisions take place in a prayer center or an emptied-out elementary-school classroom where desks are pushed together and covered with sheets and a pillow to serve as makeshift beds. The procedure takes several minutes. There is little blood involved. Afterward, the girl's genital area is swabbed with the antiseptic Betadine. She is then helped back into her underwear and returned to a waiting area, where she's given a small, celebratory gift — some fruit or a donated piece of clothing — and offered a cup of milk for refreshment. She has now joined

—

Female circumcisers and their attendants waiting in an elementary-school classroom, where they do their work.

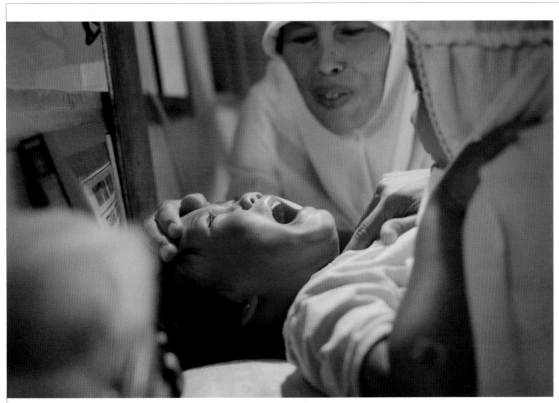

A girl cries as she is circumcised.

forbidding medical personnel to practice it, but the decree — which has yet to be backed by legislation — does not affect traditional circumcisers and birth attendants, who are thought to do most female circumcisions. Many agree that a full ban is unlikely without strong support from the country's religious leaders. According to the Population Council study, many Indonesians view circumcision for boys and girls as a religious duty.

Female circumcision in Indonesia is reported to be less extreme than the kind practiced in other parts of the globe — Africa, particularly. Worldwide, female genital cutting affects up to 140 million women and girls in varying degrees of severity, according to estimates from the World Health Organization. The most common form of female genital cutting, representing about 82 percent of cases around the world, includes the excision of the clitoris and the labia minora. A more extreme version of the practice, known as Pharaonic circumcision or infibulation, accounts for 15 percent of cases globally and involves the removal of all external genitalia and a stitching up of the vaginal opening.

Studies have shown that in some parts of Indonesia, female circumcision is more ritualistic — a rite of passage meant to purify the genitals and bestow gender identity on a female child — with a practitioner rubbing turmeric on the genitals or pricking the clitoris once with a needle to draw a symbolic drop of blood. In other instances, the procedure is more invasive, involving what WHO classifies as "Type I" female genital mutilation, defined as excision of the clitoral hood, called the prepuce, with or without incision of the clitoris itself. The Population Council's 2003 study said that 82 percent of Indonesian mothers who witnessed their daughters' circumcision reported that it involved "cutting." The women most often

PHOTOGRAPH BY STEPHANIE SINCLAIR 49

/366/ **THE NEW YORK TIMES MAGAZINE**
CREATIVE DIRECTOR: JANET FROELICH / ART DIRECTOR: AREM DUPLESSIS / DEPUTY ART DIRECTOR: GAIL BICHLER / DESIGNER: LEO JUNG
DIRECTOR OF PHOTOGRAPHY: KATHY RYAN / PHOTO EDITOR: CLINTON CARGILL / PHOTOGRAPHER: STEPHANIE SINCLAIR / EDITOR-IN-CHIEF: GERRY MARZORATI
PUBLISHER: THE NEW YORK TIMES / ISSUE: JANUARY 20, 2008 / CATEGORY PHOTO: FEATURE: NEWS/REPORTAGE (STORY)

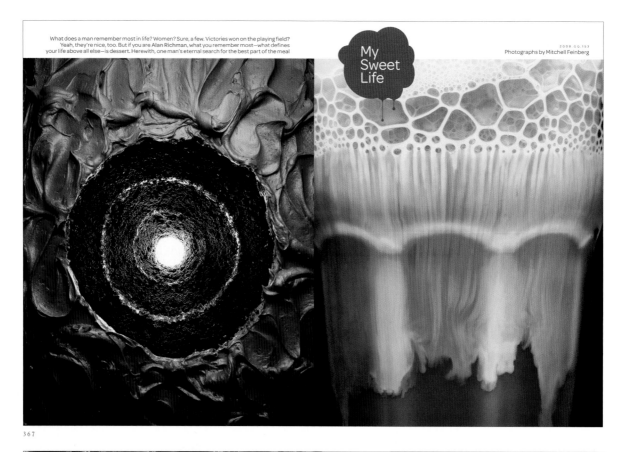

What does a man remember most in life? Women? Sure, a few. Victories won on the playing field? Yeah, they're nice, too. But if you are Alan Richman, what you remember most—what defines your life above all else—is dessert. Herewith, one man's eternal search for the best part of the meal

My Sweet Life

2008.GQ.153
Photographs by Mitchell Feinberg

367

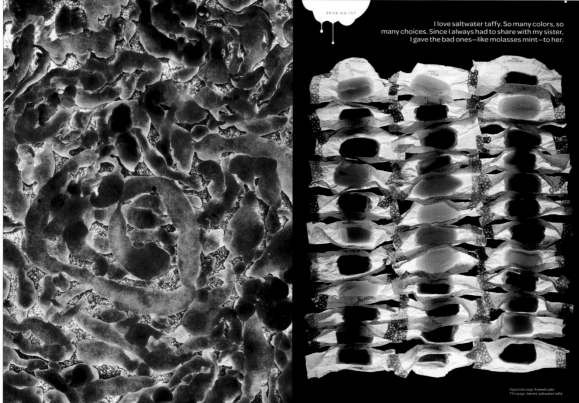

2008.GQ.157

I love saltwater taffy. So many colors, so many choices. Since I always had to share with my sister, I gave the bad ones—like molasses mint—to her.

Opposite page: Funnel cake
This page: James' saltwater taffy

367

/367/ **GQ**
DESIGN DIRECTOR: FRED WOODWARD / ART DIRECTOR: ANTON IOUKHNOVETS / DESIGNER: DELGIS CANAHUATE / DIRECTOR OF PHOTOGRAPHY: DORA SOMOSI
PHOTO EDITOR: JUSTIN O'NEILL / PHOTOGRAPHER: MITCHELL FEINBERG / EDITOR-IN-CHIEF: JIM NELSON / PUBLISHER: CONDÉ NAST PUBLICATIONS INC.
ISSUE: JULY 2008 / CATEGORY PHOTO: FEATURE: TRAVEL/FOOD/STILL LIFE (STORY)

pasta in a new light

Super-fresh summer sauces paired with the perfect noodle

BY SARA FOSTER/
PHOTOGRAPH BY MITCHELL FEINBERG

368

369

/368/ BON APPÉTIT
DESIGN DIRECTOR: MATTHEW LENNING
ART DIRECTOR: ROBERT FESTINO
DESIGNER: ROBERT FESTINO
PHOTO EDITORS: LIZ MATHEWS, SHARON SUH
PHOTOGRAPHER: MITCHELL FEINBERG
EDITOR-IN-CHIEF: BARBARA FAIRCHILD
PUBLISHER: CONDÉ NAST PUBLICATIONS, INC.
ISSUE: JUNE 2008
CATEGORY PHOTO: FEATURE:
TRAVEL/FOOD/STILL LIFE (SINGLE/SPREAD)

/369/ SHUFTI
CREATIVE DIRECTOR: SEAN KENNEDY SANTOS
ART DIRECTOR: SEAN KENNEDY SANTOS
DESIGNERS: PHIL MORRISON, SI BILLAM, JON BANKS
PHOTOGRAPHER: SEAN KENNEDY SANTOS
EDITOR-IN-CHIEF: MATT AUSTIN
PUBLISHER: VAST AGENCY UK
ISSUE: OCTOBER 2008
CATEGORY PHOTO: FEATURE:
FASHION/BEAUTY (SINGLE/SPREAD)

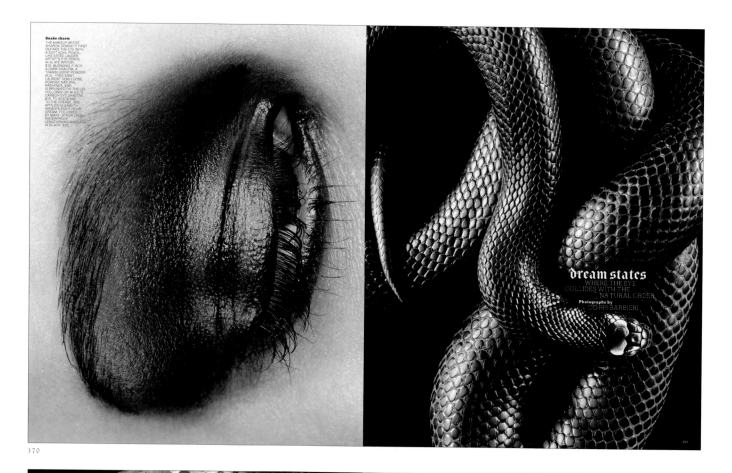

Snake charm
THE MAKEUP ARTIST
SHARON DOWSETT FIRST
DEFINES THE EYE WITH
A SOFT KOHL PENCIL,
LIKE ESTÉE LAUDER
ARTIST'S EYE PENCIL
IN SLATE WRITER,
$19, BLENDING IT INTO
A DARK SHADOW. A
TRANSLUCENT POWDER
(E.G., YVES SAINT
LAURENT SEMI-LOOSE
POWDER NATURAL
RADIANCE, $58)
IS BRUSHED ON THE LID,
FOLLOWED BY M.A.C.
CARBON EYE SHADOW,
$15, TO ADD SHINE
TO THE CREASE. SHE
APPLIES ELIZABETH
ARDEN'S EIGHT HOUR
CREAM, FOLLOWED
BY MAKE UP FOR EVER
WATERPROOF
LENGTHENING MASCARA
IN BLACK, $20.

dream states
WHERE THE EYE
COLLIDES WITH THE
NATURAL ORDER
Photographs by
COPPI BARBIERI

370

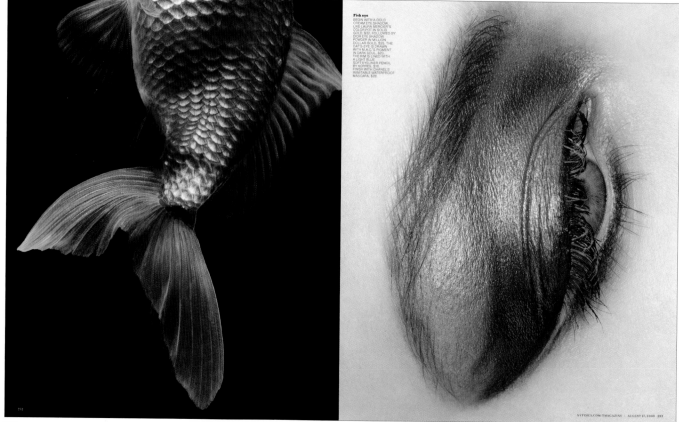

Fish eye
BEGIN WITH A GOLD
CREAM EYE SHADOW,
LIKE LAURA MERCIER'S
COLOR POT IN SOLID
GOLD, $30, FOLLOWED BY
DIOR EYE SHADOW
POWDER IN MILLION
DOLLAR GOLD, $29. THE
CAT-EYE IS DRAWN
WITH M.A.C.'S PIGMENT
IN DARK GOLD, $20.
THE RIM IS LINED WITH
A LIGHT BLUE
SOFT EYELINER PENCIL
BY KORRES, $16.
FINISH WITH CHANEL'S
INIMITABLE WATERPROOF
MASCARA, $26.

NYTIMES.COM/TMAGAZINE | AUGUST 17, 2008 233

/370/ **T, THE NEW YORK TIMES STYLE MAGAZINE**
CREATIVE DIRECTOR: JANET FROELICH / SENIOR ART DIRECTOR: DAVID SEBBAH / ART DIRECTOR: CHRISTOPHER MARTINEZ
SENIOR DESIGNER: ELIZABETH SPIRIDAKIS / DIRECTOR OF PHOTOGRAPHY: KATHY RYAN / PHOTO EDITOR: SCOTT HALL / PHOTOGRAPHER: COPPI BARBIERI
EDITOR-IN-CHIEF: STEFANO TONCHI / PUBLISHER: THE NEW YORK TIMES / ISSUE: AUGUST 17, 2008 / CATEGORY PHOTO: FEATURE: FASHION/BEAUTY (STORY)

iconoclast ●

WE'VE WITNESSED HIS TOTAL PHYSICAL TRANSFORMATION, READ HIS INCREASINGLY OUTSPOKEN COMMENTS, AND WONDERED: WHAT MAKES A HIGHLY SUCCESSFUL MAN WHO'S THE CREATIVE VISION BEHIND A $5 BILLION BUSINESS RESOLVE TO CHANGE HIS BODY, DYE HIS HAIR BLUE, DATE A FORMER ESCORT, AND START SPEAKING HIS MIND? WELL, ASK THE MAN HIMSELF

| LUCY KAYLIN | MARTIN SCHOELLER

Marc Jacobs Doesn't Give a F***

CHANCES ARE THAT over the past few weeks, Marc Jacobs has done something outrageous. Maybe he's at the center of a Spitzer-sized sex scandal or tapped Flavor Flav to be the new face of Louis Vuitton. There's no evidence, as yet, of either, but the way the perfectly zany Jacobs narrative is hurtling along, anything seems possible. Consider the highlights of the past year: a porn star crowing online about threesomes with Jacobs and Jacobs's former-escort boyfriend; a tune-up in rehab; allegations that his line paid bribes for use of New York's 26th Street Armory for his shows; then starting those shows at least two hours late, turning the normally adoring fashion press into a pitchfork-wielding mob.

And yet nothing has created a greater stir than his startling new look. Where he once had long greasy locks and the pallor of a shut-in, he now, at 45, has an iridescent blue crop, honking

Harry Winston diamond studs, a gallery of tattoos, and a painstakingly ripped bod. After years of hiding in baggy sweatshirts while contemplating the beauty of others—of pondering any human facade but his own—Jacobs has discovered the consuming joy of narcissism. It's his new addiction. Some would say, his midlife crisis.

"I don't feel like I'm in crisis, and I don't know that it's the middle of my life," Jacobs says, looking a little like Jeff Goldblum circa *The Fly*—large, dark, worried eyes weirdly belied by a do-me physique. It's a measure of how closely he is watched and the stir he has caused that even a self-described attention whore like Jacobs is starting to weary of the scrutiny. "Why is there this division all of a sudden between people in support of me and people against me? How did this happen? I haven't done anything to

anybody? I look at Karl Lagerfeld and John Galliano—everybody has their shtick. And just because this wasn't my shtick two years ago, it's a problem."

As Jacobs tells it, before now he simply had no budget in his psyche for self-maintenance: "I didn't care what I looked like, because I knew I'd be on the floor picking up pins or drawing all day." It's a Friday afternoon in his cluttered, loftlike office in SoHo where boxes of Wheat Thins are stashed next to packs of Marlboro Lights and cheapo lighters. His hair juts like a Mohawk—the effect is thrusting, roosterish, in contrast to the Pre-Raphaelite languor of the long-haired Marc Jacobs in the photo on the wall behind him. "I thought, *Who cares about my appearance? They only care about what I'm making.*"

Then he got the existential bitch-slap of ulcerative colitis, the disease that led to his father's death when Jacobs was only 7. A nutritionist, Lindsey Duncan, recommended a monastic diet—no flour, dairy,

MAY 2008 GQ.COM 119

371

372

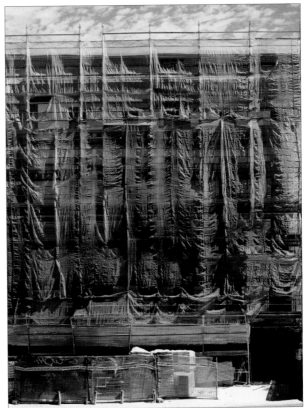

372

/371/ **GQ**
DESIGN DIRECTOR: FRED WOODWARD
ART DIRECTOR: ANTON IOUKHNOVETS
DIRECTOR OF PHOTOGRAPHY: DORA SOMOSI
PHOTO EDITOR: KRISTA PRESTEK
PHOTOGRAPHER: MARTIN SCHOELLER
EDITOR-IN-CHIEF: JIM NELSON
PUBLISHER: CONDÉ NAST PUBLICATIONS INC.
ISSUE: MAY 2008
CATEGORY PHOTO: SECTION (SINGLE/SPREAD)

/372/ **MADRIZ**
CREATIVE DIRECTOR: LOUIS-CHARLES TIAR
ART DIRECTOR: SONIA BILBAO
PHOTOGRAPHER: FERNANDO MASELLI
PUBLISHER: REVISTAS EXCLUSIVAS S.L.
ISSUE: FALL 2008 / WINTER 2009
CATEGORY PHOTO: SECTION (SERIES OF PAGES)

373

373

/373/ **EARNSHAW'S**
CREATIVE DIRECTOR: NANCY CAMPBELL
ART DIRECTOR: TREVETT MCCANDLISS
DESIGNER: TREVETT MCCANDLISS
PHOTOGRAPHER: MICHAEL BRIAN
EDITOR-IN-CHIEF: CALETHA CRAWFORD
PUBLISHER: SYMPHONY PUBLISHING
ISSUE: APRIL 2008
CATEGORY PHOTO: SINGLE/SPREAD/STORY

'Ready For War'
The black supremacist wing of the Hebrew Israelite movement is spreading and its leaders are growing increasingly militant

374

Innovation > The Outer Limits

THE FUTURE OF GAMING

MASTERS OF REALITY

THE BIG IDEA

You and your pal have almost made it the two blocks from the parking lot to your office when two zombies pop out of a doorway. No time to draw a gun, but that's all right—just thinking really nasty thoughts is enough to vaporize the ghouls. You trade grins with your friend, who's actually 1,700 miles away, unplug your mind-reading headset and virtual reality glasses from your cell phone, and make your way up to your office. Gaming is about to break down the barriers between the real world and fantasy, thanks to devices that will read your thoughts, gestures, and expressions; project gaming action onto the streets around you; and populate these quasi-real worlds not only with your distant gaming buddies but with characters that seem as real and wily as Ben from *Lost*.

duit Labs, a start-up in Cambridge, Massachusetts, is working on a hybrid social-networking and gaming environment—think Facebook meets World of Warcraft.

A WORD FROM THE NAYSAYERS

It's no sure thing that artificial intelligence has progressed far enough to endow characters with the smarts needed to make them appear truly real and interesting. And some insist accurate brain-wave measurement is an iffy prospect in an affordable device, so the technique could be glitch ridden for all but the most basic interactions.

COMPANY CLOSE-UP

Emotiv Systems, a start-up in San Francisco, plans to introduce its brain-wave-reading headset at the end of this year. The $299 device measures brain electrical activity via 16 scalp sensors, which the company claims allow recognition of basic emotions and up to 30 specific thoughts, such as "lift this object," "fire death ray," or "fly forward." The idea, says Tan Le, the company's president and co-founder, is to create games that adapt the action to the changing moods and thoughts of the players. "Games have never had a feedback loop for understanding how the user experiences content," she says. "When you have that feedback, you can vary the music, the lighting, and the story to help take the player through an emotional journey." The company has raised $13.4 million and has a team of 40 researchers, half of whom have Ph.D.s.

TIME TO MARKET

Brain-wave-reading headsets are about to hit the market. Devices that project virtual worlds onto the real world around you are less than five years out.

START-UPS TO WATCH

3DV Systems, a start-up in Yokneam, Israel, has devel-

oped a camera that observes a player's motions and translates them into commands in a video game so that the game responds to gestures and body language. Several start-ups, including EmSense in San Francisco and NeuroSky in San Jose, California, are working on head-mounted devices that detect brain waves. Con-

Several start-ups are working on head-mounted devices that detect **brain waves and relay them to video games.**

JUNE 2008 INC. MAGAZINE 107

Photograph by **PHILLIP TOLEDANO**

375

/374/ **INTELLIGENCE REPORT**
CREATIVE DIRECTOR: RUSSELL ESTES
ART DIRECTOR: RUSSELL ESTES
DESIGNERS: VALERIE DOWNES,
CRYSTAL PHILLIPS, SCOTT PHILLIPS
PHOTOGRAPHER: JOHN HEALEY
EDITOR-IN-CHIEF: MARK POTOK
PUBLISHER: SOUTHERN POVERTY LAW CENTER
ISSUE: FALL 2008
CATEGORY PHOTO: SINGLE/SPREAD/STORY

/375/ **INC.**
CREATIVE DIRECTOR: BLAKE TAYLOR
ART DIRECTOR: SARAH GARCEA
DIRECTOR OF PHOTOGRAPHY: TRAVIS RUSE
PHOTOGRAPHER: PHILLIP TOLEDANO
EDITOR-IN-CHIEF: JANE BERENTSON
PUBLISHER: MANSUETO VENTURES
ISSUE: JUNE 2008
CATEGORY PHOTO-ILLUSTRATION: SINGLE/SPREAD/STORY

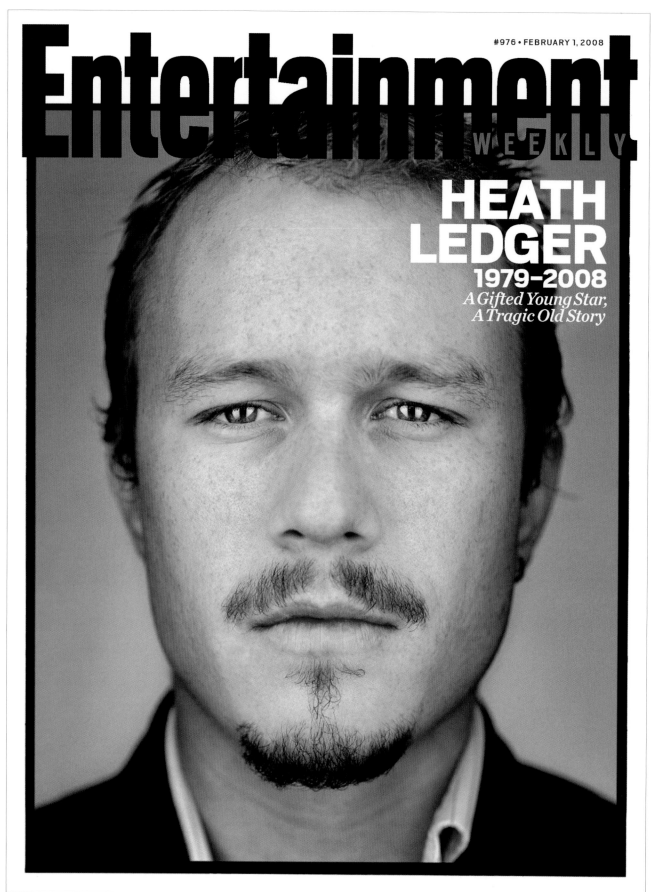

Entertainment WEEKLY

#976 • FEBRUARY 1, 2008

HEATH LEDGER
1979–2008
A Gifted Young Star,
A Tragic Old Story

376

DESIGN DIRECTOR: GERALDINE HESSLER / DIRECTOR OF PHOTOGRAPHY: FIONA MCDONAGH / PHOTOGRAPHER: MARTIN SCHOELLER / PUBLISHER: TIME INC.
ISSUE: FEBRUARY 1, 2008 / CATEGORY: PHOTO: COVER

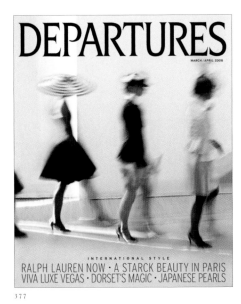

377

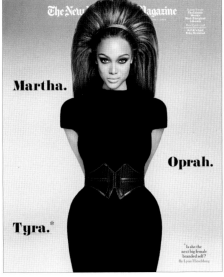

379

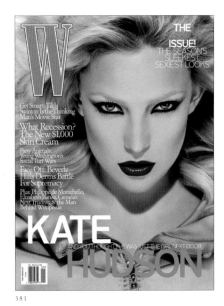

381

378

380

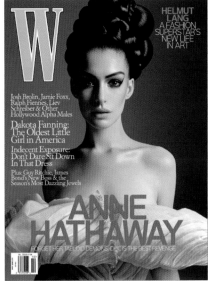

382

/377/ **DEPARTURES**
CREATIVE DIRECTOR: BERNARD SCHARF
ART DIRECTOR: ADAM BOOKBINDER
DESIGNER: LOU CORREDOR
PHOTO EDITOR: JESSICA DIMSON
PHOTOGRAPHER: BERNARD SCHARF
PUBLISHER: AMERICAN EXPRESS PUBLISHING CO.
ISSUE: APRIL 2008
CATEGORY: PHOTO: COVER

/378/ **T, THE NEW YORK TIMES STYLE MAGAZINE**
CREATIVE DIRECTOR: JANET FROELICH
SENIOR ART DIRECTOR: DAVID SEBBAH
ART DIRECTOR: CHRISTOPHER MARTINEZ
SENIOR DESIGNER: ELIZABETH SPIRIDAKIS
DIRECTOR OF PHOTOGRAPHY: KATHY RYAN
SENIOR PHOTO EDITOR: JUDITH PUCKETT-RINELLA
PHOTOGRAPHER: RAYMOND MEIER
EDITOR-IN-CHIEF: STEFANO TONCHI
PUBLISHER: THE NEW YORK TIMES
ISSUE: NOVEMBER 16, 2008
CATEGORY: PHOTO: COVER

/379/ **THE NEW YORK TIMES MAGAZINE**
CREATIVE DIRECTOR: JANET FROELICH
ART DIRECTOR: AREM DUPLESSIS
DEPUTY ART DIRECTOR: GAIL BICHLER
DESIGNER: AREM DUPLESSIS
DIRECTOR OF PHOTOGRAPHY: KATHY RYAN
PHOTO EDITOR: KIRA POLLACK
PHOTOGRAPHER: RUVEN AFANADOR
EDITOR-IN-CHIEF: GERRY MARZORATI
PUBLISHER: THE NEW YORK TIMES
ISSUE: JUNE 1, 2008
CATEGORY: PHOTO: COVER

/380/ **T, THE NEW YORK TIMES STYLE MAGAZINE**
CREATIVE DIRECTOR: JANET FROELICH
SENIOR ART DIRECTOR: DAVID SEBBAH
ART DIRECTOR: CHRISTOPHER MARTINEZ
SENIOR DESIGNER: ELIZABETH SPIRIDAKIS
DIRECTOR OF PHOTOGRAPHY: KATHY RYAN
SENIOR PHOTO EDITOR: JUDITH PUCKETT-RINELLA
PHOTOGRAPHER: SOLVE SUNDSBO
EDITOR-IN-CHIEF: STEFANO TONCHI
PUBLISHER: THE NEW YORK TIMES
ISSUE: DECEMBER 7, 2008
CATEGORY: PHOTO: COVER

/381/ **W**
CREATIVE DIRECTOR: DENNIS FREEDMAN
DESIGN DIRECTOR: EDWARD LEIDA
ART DIRECTOR: NATHALIE KIRSHEH
DESIGNER: NATHALIE KIRSHEH
PHOTOGRAPHERS: MERT ALAS, MARCUS PIGGOTT
PUBLISHER: CONDÉ NAST PUBLICATIONS INC.
ISSUE: SEPTEMBER 2008
CATEGORY: PHOTO: COVER

/382/ **W**
CREATIVE DIRECTOR: DENNIS FREEDMAN
DESIGN DIRECTOR: EDWARD LEIDA
ART DIRECTOR: NATHALIE KIRSHEH
DESIGNER: NATHALIE KIRSHEH
PHOTOGRAPHER: MARIO SORRONTI
PUBLISHER: CONDÉ NAST PUBLICATIONS INC.
ISSUE: OCTOBER 2008
CATEGORY: PHOTO: COVER

383

385

384

386

/383/ **INTERIOR DESIGN**
CREATIVE DIRECTOR: CINDY ALLEN
ART DIRECTOR: MARINO ZULLICH
DESIGNERS: ZIGENG LI, KARLA LIMA,
GIANNINA MACIAS / PHOTO EDITOR: HELENE OBERMAN
PHOTOGRAPHERS: SIERYO YAMADA, SIERYO STUDIO
PUBLISHER: REED BUSINESS INFORMATION
ISSUE: JULY 2008
CATEGORY: PHOTO: COVER

/384/ **THE NEW YORK TIMES MAGAZINE**
CREATIVE DIRECTOR: JANET FROELICH
ART DIRECTOR: AREM DUPLESSIS
DEPUTY ART DIRECTOR: GAIL BICHLER
DESIGNERS: CATHERINE GILMORE-BARNES,
AREM DUPLESSIS / DIRECTOR OF PHOTOGRAPHY:
KATHY RYAN / PHOTO EDITOR: JOANNA MILTER
PHOTOGRAPHER: MARTIN KILMAS
EDITOR-IN-CHIEF: GERRY MARZORATI
PUBLISHER: THE NEW YORK TIMES
ISSUE: OCTOBER 2008
CATEGORY: PHOTO: COVERCATEGORY::
DESIGN, FEATURE STORY

/385/ **T, THE NEW YORK TIMES STYLE MAGAZINE**
CREATIVE DIRECTOR: JANET FROELICH
SENIOR ART DIRECTOR: DAVID SEBBAH
ART DIRECTOR: CHRISTOPHER MARTINEZ
SENIOR DESIGNER: ELIZABETH SPIRIDAKIS
SENIOR PHOTO EDITOR: JUDITH PUCKETT-RINELLA
PHOTOGRAPHER: RAYMOND MEIER
EDITOR-IN-CHIEF: STEFANO TONCHI
PUBLISHER: THE NEW YORK TIMES
ISSUE: SEPTEMBER 21, 2008
CATEGORY: PHOTO: COVER

/386/ **THE NEW YORK TIMES MAGAZINE**
CREATIVE DIRECTOR: JANET FROELICH
ART DIRECTOR: AREM DUPLESSIS
DEPUTY ART DIRECTOR: GAIL BICHLER
DESIGNER: AREM DUPLESSIS
DIRECTOR OF PHOTOGRAPHY: KATHY RYAN
PHOTO EDITOR: KIRA POLLACK
PHOTOGRAPHER: HENDRIK KERSTENS
EDITOR-IN-CHIEF: GERRY MARZORATI
PUBLISHER: THE NEW YORK TIMES
ISSUE: DECEMBER 21, 2008
CATEGORY: PHOTO: COVER

387

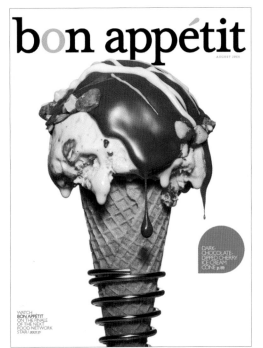

389

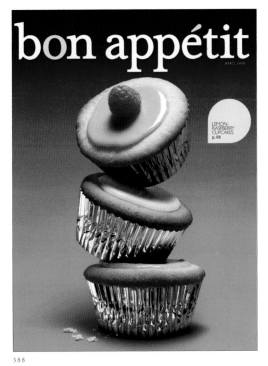

388

390

/387/ **GOURMET**
CREATIVE DIRECTOR: RICHARD FERRETTI
ART DIRECTOR: ERIKA OLIVEIRA
PHOTO EDITOR: AMY KOBLENZER
PHOTOGRAPHER: ROMULO YANES
EDITOR-IN-CHIEF: RUTH REICHL
PUBLISHER: CONDÉ NAST PUBLICATIONS, INC.
ISSUE: DECEMBER 2008
CATEGORY: PHOTO: COVER

/388/ **BON APPÉTIT**
DESIGN DIRECTOR: MATTHEW LENNING
PHOTO EDITOR: LIZ MATHEWS
PHOTOGRAPHER: JAMES WOJCIK
EDITOR-IN-CHIEF: BARBARA FAIRCHILD
PUBLISHER: CONDÉ NAST PUBLICATIONS, INC.
ISSUE: APRIL 2008
CATEGORY: PHOTO: COVER

/389/ **BON APPÉTIT**
DESIGN DIRECTOR: MATTHEW LENNING
ART DIRECTOR: ROBERT FESTINO
PHOTO EDITORS: LIZ MATHEWS, SHARON SUH, BAILEY FRANKLIN
PHOTOGRAPHER: KENJI TOMA
EDITOR-IN-CHIEF: BARBARA FAIRCHILD
PUBLISHER: CONDÉ NAST PUBLICATIONS, INC.
ISSUE: AUGUST 2008
CATEGORY: PHOTO: COVER

/390/ **BON APPÉTIT**
DESIGN DIRECTOR: MATTHEW LENNING
DESIGNER: ROBERT FESTINO
PHOTO EDITORS: LIZ MATHEWS, BAILEY FRANKLIN
PHOTOGRAPHER: NIGEL COX
EDITOR-IN-CHIEF: BARBARA FAIRCHILD
PUBLISHER: CONDÉ NAST PUBLICATIONS, INC.
ISSUE: JULY 2008
CATEGORY: PHOTO: COVER

391

393

395

392

394

396

/391/ **W**
CREATIVE DIRECTOR: DENNIS FREEDMAN
DESIGN DIRECTOR: EDWARD LEIDA
ART DIRECTOR: NATHALIE KIRSHEH
DESIGNER: NATHALIE KIRSHEH
PHOTOGRAPHER: STEVEN KLEIN
PUBLISHER: CONDÉ NAST PUBLICATIONS INC.
ISSUE: MARCH 2008
CATEGORY: PHOTO: COVER

/392/ **BLENDER**
CREATIVE DIRECTOR: DIRK BARNETT
DESIGNER: DIRK BARNETT
DIRECTOR OF PHOTOGRAPHY: AMY HOPPY
PHOTOGRAPHER: GAVIN BOND
EDITOR-IN-CHIEF: JOE LEVY
PUBLISHER: ALPHAMEDIA GROUP
ISSUE: AUGUST 2008
CATEGORY: PHOTO: COVER

/393/ **NEW YORK**
DESIGN DIRECTOR: CHRIS DIXON
DIRECTOR OF PHOTOGRAPHY: JODY QUON
PHOTO EDITOR: LEANA ALAGIA
PHOTOGRAPHER: NIGEL PARRY
EDITOR-IN-CHIEF: ADAM MOSS
PUBLISHER: NEW YORK MAGAZINE HOLDINGS, LLC
ISSUE: AUGUST 25, 2008
CATEGORY: PHOTO: COVER

/394/ **NEW YORK**
DESIGN DIRECTOR: CHRIS DIXON
DIRECTOR OF PHOTOGRAPHY: JODY QUON
PHOTOGRAPHER: BRIGITTE LACOMBE
EDITOR-IN-CHIEF: ADAM MOSS
PUBLISHER: NEW YORK MAGAZINE HOLDINGS, LLC
ISSUE: JUNE 23, 2008
CATEGORY: PHOTO: COVER

/395/ **SPORTS ILLUSTRATED**
DESIGN DIRECTOR: CHRIS HERCIK
PHOTO EDITOR: JIMMY COLTON
PUBLISHER: TIME INC.
ISSUE: DECEMBER 12, 2008
CATEGORY: PHOTO: COVER

/396/ **VANITY FAIR**
DESIGN DIRECTOR: DAVID HARRIS
ART DIRECTORS: JULIE WEISS, CHRIS MUELLER
DIRECTOR OF PHOTOGRAPHY: SUSAN WHITE
PHOTOGRAPHER: STEVEN MEISEL
EDITOR-IN-CHIEF: GRAYDON CARTER
PUBLISHER: CONDÉ NAST PUBLICATIONS INC.
ISSUE: MAY 2008
CATEGORY: PHOTO: COVER

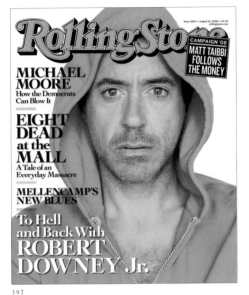

397

398

399

400

/397/ **ROLLING STONE**
ART DIRECTOR: JOSEPH HUTCHINSON
DESIGNER: JOSEPH HUTCHINSON
DIRECTOR OF PHOTOGRAPHY: JODI PECKMAN
PHOTOGRAPHER: SAM JONES
PUBLISHER: WENNER MEDIA
ISSUE: AUGUST 21, 2008
CATEGORY: PHOTO: COVER

/398/ **SPIN**
DESIGN DIRECTOR: DEVIN PEDZWATER
ART DIRECTOR: IAN ROBINSON
DESIGNER: LIZ MACFARLANE
DIRECTOR OF PHOTOGRAPHY: MICHELLE EGIZIANO
PHOTO EDITORS: GAVIN STEVENS,
JENNIFER EDMONDSON
PHOTOGRAPHER: HEDI SLIMANE
PUBLISHER: SPIN MEDIA LLC
ISSUE: FEBRUARY 2008
CATEGORY: PHOTO: COVER

/399/ **TIME OUT NEW YORK**
DESIGN DIRECTOR: ADAM LOGAN FULRATH
DIRECTOR OF PHOTOGRAPHY: COURTENAY KENDALL
PHOTOGRAPHER: MARILYN MINTER
PUBLISHER: TIME OUT NEW YORK PARTNERS, L.P.
ISSUE: JULY 24-30, 2008
CATEGORY: PHOTO: COVER

/400/ **TV GUIDE MAGAZINE**
CREATIVE DIRECTOR: JOHN WALKER
DIRECTOR OF PHOTOGRAPHY: DONNA BENDER
PHOTO EDITORS: ALYSSA ADAMS, GERALDINE AGONCILLO
PHOTOGRAPHER: ANDREW ECCLES
EDITOR-IN-CHIEF: DEBRA BIRNBAUM
PUBLISHER: TV GUIDE MAGAZINE LLC
ISSUE: SEPTEMBER 29, 2008
CATEGORY: PHOTO: COVER

401

401

401

401

402

402

/401/ BON APPÉTIT
DESIGN DIRECTOR: MATTHEW LENNING
ART DIRECTORS: ROBERT FESTINO, TOM O'QUINN
DESIGNERS: REBECCA LOUTSCH, CHRISTINE PARK
PHOTO EDITORS: BAILEY FRANKLIN, LIZ MATHEWS
PHOTOGRAPHERS: CRAIG CUTLER, OLAF BLECKER,
SIAN KENNEDY, NIGEL COX, MISHA GRAVENOR,
JAMIE CHUNG, LAURA LETINSKY, STEPHEN LEWIS,
ANDREA CHU, HANS GISSINGER
EDITOR-IN-CHIEF: BARBARA FAIRCHILD
PUBLISHER: CONDÉ NAST PUBLICATIONS, INC.
ISSUE: OCTOBER 2008
CATEGORY: PHOTO: ENTIRE ISSUE

/402/ COOKIE
DESIGN DIRECTOR: KIRBY RODRIGUEZ
ART DIRECTOR: ALEX GROSSMAN
DESIGNERS: NICOLETTE BERTHELOT, SHANNA GREENBERG
PHOTO EDITOR: DARRICK HARRIS
ASSOCIATE PHOTO EDITOR: LINDA DENAHAN
ASSISTANT PHOTO EDITOR: AJA NUZZI
PUBLISHER: CONDÉ NAST PUBLICATIONS INC.
ISSUE: AUGUST 2008
CATEGORY: PHOTO: ENTIRE ISSUE

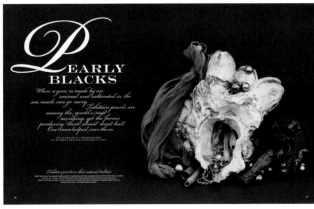

CULTURE
+TRAVEL

Japan:
A Voyage to Art

"THERE IS NO TRASH ON THE STREET IN JAPAN. ANYWHERE. NOR ARE THERE TRASH CANS, SO FIGURE THAT ONE OUT." PAGE 98

403

PEARLY
BLACKS

403

BREAD
OF HEAVEN

403

THE
ITALIAN

JOB

193

THE
NEW
PARIS
BISTRO

155

404

404

/403/ **CULTURE + TRAVEL**
CREATIVE DIRECTOR: EMILY CRAWFORD
DIRECTOR OF PHOTOGRAPHY: CORY JACOBS
PHOTO EDITOR: NATALIE MATUTSCHOVSKY
PUBLISHER: LOUISE BLOUIN MEDIA
ISSUE: MARCH/APRIL 2008
CATEGORY: PHOTO: ENTIRE ISSUE

/404/ **BON APPÉTIT**
DESIGN DIRECTOR: MATTHEW LENNING
ART DIRECTOR: ROBERT FESTINO
DESIGNERS: REBECCA LOUTSCH, HANK HUANG
PHOTO EDITORS: LIZ MATHEWS, SHARON SUH
PHOTOGRAPHERS: CRAIG CUTLER, TOM SCHIERLITZ,
PLAMEN PETKOV, LISA HUBBARD, ANNA WOLF, CEDRIC ANGELES,
LISA LIMER, JEAN-LUC BÉNARD, TURE LILLEGRAVEN
EDITOR-IN-CHIEF: BARBARA FAIRCHILD
PUBLISHER: CONDÉ NAST PUBLICATIONS, INC.
ISSUE: MAY 2008
CATEGORY: PHOTO: ENTIRE ISSUE

MOTY

JON HAMM

Breakout

How does a man this handsome—and this talented—hide in Hollywood for a decade? Jon Hamm's long, tortured journey into the (klieg) light

Brett Martin

405

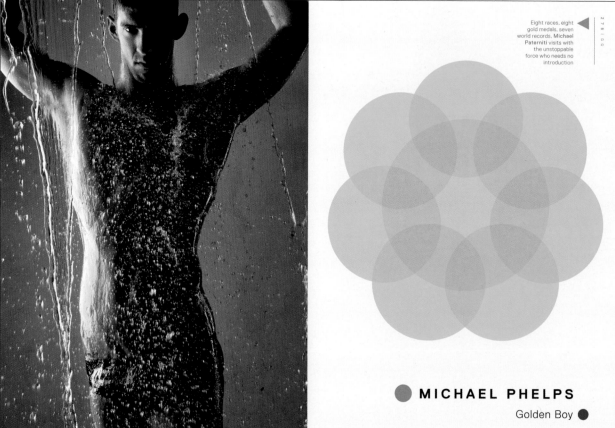

Eight races, eight gold medals, seven world records. Michael Paterniti visits with the unstoppable force who needs no introduction

MICHAEL PHELPS

Golden Boy

405

/405/ **GQ**

DESIGN DIRECTOR: FRED WOODWARD / ART DIRECTOR: ANTON IOUKHNOVETS / DESIGNERS: THOMAS ALBERTY, DRUE WAGNER, CHELSEA CARDINAL, DELGIS CANAHUATE
DIRECTOR OF PHOTOGRAPHY: DORA SOMOSI / PHOTO EDITORS: KRISTA PRESTEK, JUSTIN O'NEILL, JESSE LEE, EMILY ROSENBERG, JOLANTA BIELAT, TOBY KAUFMANN
PHOTOGRAPHER: MARK SELIGER / CREATIVE DIRECTOR, FASHION: JIM MOORE / EDITOR-IN-CHIEF: JIM NELSON / PUBLISHER: CONDÉ NAST PUBLICATIONS INC.
ISSUE: DECEMBER 2008 / CATEGORY: PHOTO: ENTIRE ISSUE

406

406

407

407

408

408

/406/ **NEW YORK**
DESIGN DIRECTOR: CHRIS DIXON
DIRECTOR OF PHOTOGRAPHY: JODY QUON
PHOTO EDITORS: LEANA ALAGIA, ALEX POLLACK,
LEA GOLIS, CAROLINE SMITH, NADIA LACHANCE
PHOTOGRAPHERS: BERT STERN, JEFF RIEDEL,
HEDI SLIMANE, ANDREAS SJÖDIN, TINA TYRELL,
ANDREAS SERRANO, BURKHARD SCHITTNY,
MARTINE FOUGERON, JERI HEIDEN, NADAV KANDER,
CHRISTIAN WITKIN, JAKE CHESSUM, KANG KIM,
ANDREW ECCLES, PLATON, STÉPHANE COUTELLE
EDITOR-IN-CHIEF: ADAM MOSS
PUBLISHER: NEW YORK MAGAZINE HOLDINGS, LLC
ISSUE: FEBRUARY 25, 2008
CATEGORY: PHOTO: ENTIRE ISSUE

/407/ **ENTERTAINMENT WEEKLY**
DESIGN DIRECTOR: BRIAN ANSTEY
DEPUTY ART DIRECTOR: ERIC PAUL
ASSISTANT ART DIRECTOR: THERESA GRIGGS
DESIGNERS: JACKIE DASHEVSKY, EVAN CAMPISI,
MICHAEL SCHNAIDT, THERESA GRIGGS,
WILLIAM HOOKS, JENNIFER BIANCELLA
ILLUSTRATORS: ZOHAR LAZAR, OMNIVORE,
JODY HEWGIL, DAVID M. BRITNLEY, ROBERTO PARADO,
ALISON BECHDEL, JOHN UELAND
DIRECTOR OF PHOTOGRAPHY: LISA BERMAN
PHOTO EDITORS: RICHARD MALTZ, MICHELE ROMERO,
SUZANNE REGAN, FREYDA TAVIN, KRISTINE CHIN,
SAMANTHA XU, RACHAEL LIEBERMAN, MELISSA ROGUE
PHOTOGRAPHERS: MICHAEL MULLER, KURT
ISWARIENKO, BRIGITTE LACOMBE, GUY AROCH,
ROBERT MAXWELL, JAKE CHESSUM, ART STREIBER,
WILLIAMS + HIRAKAWA, TURE LILLEGRAVEN,
DANNY CLINCH, CHRISTOPHER MCLALLEN
MANAGING EDITOR: RICK TETZELI
PUBLISHER: TIME INC.
ISSUE: JUNE 27 - JULY 4, 2008
CATEGORY: PHOTO: ENTIRE ISSUE

/408/ **COOKIE**
DESIGN DIRECTOR: KIRBY RODRIGUEZ
ART DIRECTOR: ALEX GROSSMAN
DESIGNERS: NICOLETTE BERTHELOT,
SHANNA GREENBERG
PHOTO EDITOR: DARRICK HARRIS
ASSOCIATE PHOTO EDITOR: LINDA DENAHAN
ASSISTANT PHOTO EDITOR: AJA NUZZI
PUBLISHER: CONDÉ NAST PUBLICATIONS INC.
ISSUE: OCTOBER 2008
CATEGORY: PHOTO: ENTIRE ISSUE

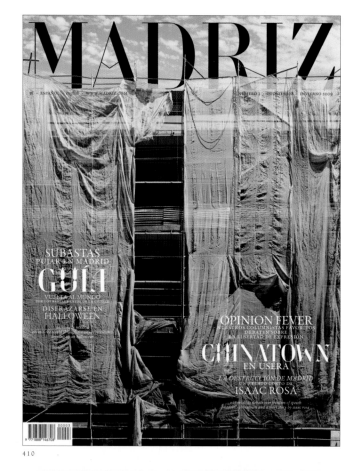

410

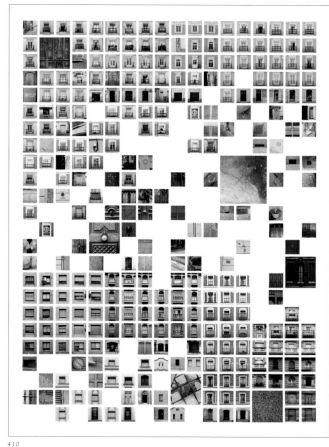

410

411

411

/410/ **MADRIZ**
CREATIVE DIRECTOR: LOUIS-CHARLES TIAR
ART DIRECTORY: SONIA BILBAO
ILLUSTRATORS: KAREEM ILIYA,
PABLO BERNASCONI, BERTO MARTINEZ
PHOTOGRAPHERS: FERNANDO MASELLI,
KANJI ISHII, PAUL LEPREUX,
GRÉGOIRE ALEXANDRE, GRÉGORY DERKENNE
EDITOR-IN-CHIEF: MARIO CANAL
PUBLISHER: REVISTAS EXCLUSIVAS S.L.
ISSUE: FALL 2008 / WINTER 2009
CATEGORY: PHOTO: ENTIRE ISSUE

/411/ **BON APPÉTIT**
DESIGN DIRECTOR: MATTHEW LENNING
ART DIRECTOR: ROBERT FESTINO
DESIGNERS: REBECCA LOUTSCH, ELAINE AHN
PHOTO EDITORS: LIZ MATHEWS, SHARON SUH, BAILEY FRANKLIN
PHOTOGRAPHERS: KENJI TOMA, NIGEL COX, GAIL ALBERT HALABAN,
AYA BRACKETT, CRAIG CUTLER
EDITOR-IN-CHIEF: BARBARA FAIRCHILD
PUBLISHER: CONDÉ NAST PUBLICATIONS, INC.
ISSUE: AUGUST 2008
CATEGORY: PHOTO: ENTIRE ISSUE

412

412

413

413

414

414

/412/ LOOK NEW YORK
DESIGN DIRECTOR: CHRIS DIXON
ART DIRECTOR: RANDY MINOR
DIRECTOR OF PHOTOGRAPHY: JODY QUON
PHOTO EDITOR: NADIA LACHANCE
PHOTOGRAPHERS: CHRISTOPHER ANDERSON,
JAMES WELLING, DAVIES+STARR, FIRSTVIEW.COM
FASHION EDITOR: HARRIET MAYS POWELL
EDITOR-IN-CHIEF: ADAM MOSS
PUBLISHER: NEW YORK MAGAZINE HOLDINGS, LLC
ISSUE: FALL FASHION 2008
CATEGORY: PHOTO: ENTIRE ISSUE

/413/ GEO
ART DIRECTOR: JUTTA KRUEGER
DESIGNERS: DANIEL MÜLLER-GROTE,
UTA MAXIN, MARTIN KUENSTING
DIRECTOR OF PHOTOGRAPHY: RUTH EICHHORN
PHOTO EDITORS: TINA AHRENS, JULIANE
BERENSMANN-NAGEL, DERND DINKEL, BAERBEL EDSE,
VENITA KALEPS, NADJA MASRI, MARKUS SEEWALD,
ELISABETH TRAUTNITZ, SABINE WUENSCH
PHOTOGRAPHERS: INGO ARNDT, JONAS BENDIUSEN,
ANNIE LEIBOWITZ, MARC STEINMETZ
EDITOR-IN-CHIEF: PETER-MATTHIAS GAEDE
PUBLISHER: GRUNER & JAHR
ISSUE: MARCH 2008
CATEGORY: PHOTO: ENTIRE ISSUE

/414/ LOOK NEW YORK
DESIGN DIRECTOR: CHRIS DIXON
ART DIRECTOR: RANDY MINOR
DIRECTOR OF PHOTOGRAPHY: JODY QUON
PHOTO EDITOR: NADIA LACHANCE
PHOTOGRAPHERS: BENJAMIN LOWY,
HANNAH WHITAKER, MELISSA HOM,
FIRSTVIEW.COM, GREG KESSLER
FASHION EDITOR: HARRIET MAYS POWELL
EDITOR-IN-CHIEF: ADAM MOSS
PUBLISHER: NEW YORK MAGAZINE HOLDINGS, LLC
ISSUE: FALL 2008
CATEGORY: PHOTO: ENTIRE ISSUE

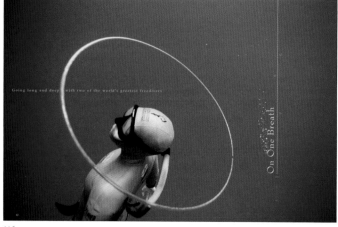

415

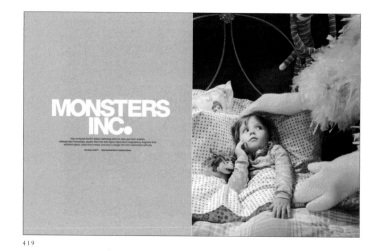

419

416

420

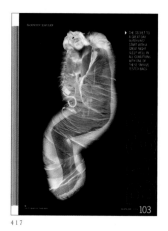

417

418

/415/ **HANA HOU!**
DESIGN DIRECTOR: KUNIO HAYASHI
PHOTO EDITOR: LEIGH MORRISON
PHOTOGRAPHER: SERGIO GOES
PUBLISHER: PACIFIC TRAVELOGUE
ISSUE: AUGUST/SEPTEMBER 2008
CATEGORY: PHOTO: FEATURE:
SERVICE (SINGLE/SPREAD)

/416/ **MARTHA STEWART LIVING**
CREATIVE DIRECTOR: ERIC PIKE
DESIGN DIRECTOR: JAMES DUNLINSON
ART DIRECTORS: JAMES DUNLINSON,
STEPHEN JOHNSON
DESIGNER: STEPHEN JOHNSON
DIRECTOR OF PHOTOGRAPHY: HELOISE GOODMAN
PHOTO EDITOR: MARY CAHILL
PHOTOGRAPHER: SANG AN
STYLISTS: LINDSEY TAYLOR, AYESHA PATEL
EDITOR-IN-CHIEF: MICHAEL BOODRO
PUBLISHER: MARTHA STEWART LIVING OMNIMEDIA
ISSUE: JUNE 2008
CATEGORY: PHOTO: FEATURE:
SERVICE (SINGLE/SPREAD)

/417/ **BACKPACKER**
DESIGN DIRECTOR: MATTHEW BATES
PHOTO EDITOR: JULIA VANDENOEVER
PHOTOGRAPHER: DAVID ARKY
PUBLISHER: ACTIVE INTEREST MEDIA
ISSUE: MARCH 2008
CATEGORY: PHOTO: FEATURE:
SERVICE (SINGLE/SPREAD)

/418/ **MARTHA STEWART LIVING**
CREATIVE DIRECTOR: ERIC PIKE
DESIGN DIRECTOR: JAMES DUNLINSON
ART DIRECTOR: ERIC PIKE
DESIGNER: JEFFREY KURTZ
DIRECTOR OF PHOTOGRAPHY: HELOISE GOODMAN
PHOTO EDITOR: MARY CAHILL
PHOTOGRAPHER: SANG AN
STYLISTS: MARCIE MCGOLDRICK,
NICHOLAS ANDERSEN, TANYA GRAFF, JULIE HO
EDITOR-IN-CHIEF: MICHAEL BOODRO
PUBLISHER: MARTHA STEWART LIVING OMNIMEDIA
ISSUE: OCTOBER 2008
CATEGORY: PHOTO: FEATURE:
SERVICE (SINGLE/SPREAD)

/419/ **BEST LIFE**
DESIGN DIRECTOR: BRANDON KAVULLA
DESIGNERS: BRANDON KAVULLA, DENA VERDESCA
DIRECTOR OF PHOTOGRAPHY: RYAN CADIZ
PHOTO EDITOR: SARAH ADAMS
PHOTOGRAPHER: GREGG SEGAL
PUBLISHER: RODALE INC.
ISSUE: DECEMBER 2008
CATEGORY: PHOTO: FEATURE:
SERVICE (SINGLE/SPREAD)

/420/ **INSTYLE**
CREATIVE DIRECTOR: RINA STONE
DESIGNER: RINA STONE
DIRECTOR OF PHOTOGRAPHY: ALIX B. CAMPBELL
PHOTO EDITOR: NICOLE HYATT
PHOTOGRAPHER: CHARLES MASTERS
MANAGING EDITOR: CHARLA LAWHON
PUBLISHER: TIME INC.
ISSUE: APRIL 2008
CATEGORY: PHOTO: FEATURE:
SERVICE (SINGLE/SPREAD)

421

423

422

424

425

/421/ **MEN'S HEALTH**
DESIGN DIRECTOR: GEORGE KARABOTSOS
ART DIRECTOR: MARK MICHAELSON
DESIGNER: MARK MICHAELSON
DIRECTOR OF PHOTOGRAPHY: BRENDA MILLIS
PHOTO EDITOR: BRENDA MILLIS
PHOTOGRAPHER: MIKE POWELL
PUBLISHER: RODALE INC.
ISSUE: MAY 2008
CATEGORY: PHOTO: FEATURE:
SERVICE (SINGLE/SPREAD)

/422/ **GARDEN & GUN**
ART DIRECTOR: MARSHALL MCKINNEY
DESIGNER: RICHIE SWANN
DIRECTOR OF PHOTOGRAPHY:
MAGGIE BRETT KENNEDY
PHOTOGRAPHER: ANDY ANDERSON
ISSUE: DECEMBER 2008/JANUARY 2009
CATEGORY: PHOTO: FEATURE:
SERVICE (SINGLE/SPREAD)

/423/ **PSYCHOLOGY TODAY**
CREATIVE DIRECTOR: EDWARD LEVINE
DIRECTOR OF PHOTOGRAPHY: CLAUDIA STEFEZIUS
PHOTOGRAPHER: FREDRIK BRODEN
STUDIO: LEVINE DESIGN INC.
PUBLISHER: SUSSEX PUBLISHERS
CLIENT: PSYCHOLOGY TODAY
ISSUE: MARCH/APRIL 2008
CATEGORY: PHOTO: FEATURE:
SERVICE (SINGLE/SPREAD)

/424/ **POPULAR MECHANICS**
DESIGN DIRECTOR: MICHAEL LAWTON
DESIGNER: STRAVINSKI PIERRE
DIRECTOR OF PHOTOGRAPHY: ALLYSON TORRISI
PHOTOGRAPHER: GREGOR HALENDA
EDITOR-IN-CHIEF: JAMES B. MEIGS
PUBLISHER: THE HEARST CORPORATION-
MAGAZINES DIVISION
ISSUE: DECEMBER 2008
CATEGORY: PHOTO: FEATURE: SERVICE
(SINGLE/SPREAD)

/425/ **ESPN THE MAGAZINE**
CREATIVE DIRECTOR: SIUNG TJIA
DIRECTOR OF PHOTOGRAPHY: CATRIONA NI AOLAIN
PHOTO EDITOR: SHAWN VALE
PHOTOGRAPHER: DAN WINTERS
EDITOR-IN-CHIEF: GARY BELSKY
PUBLISHER: ESPN, INC.
CATEGORY: PHOTO: FEATURE:
SERVICE (SINGLE/SPREAD)

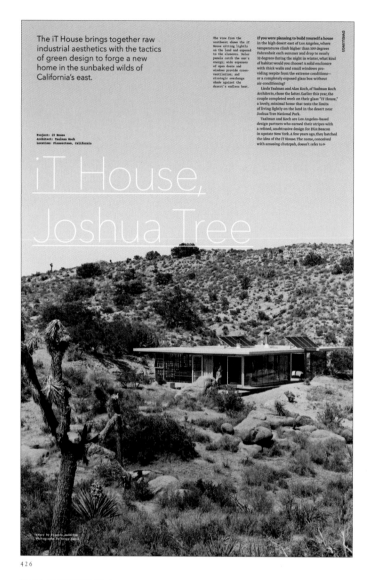

The iT House brings together raw industrial aesthetics with the tactics of green design to forge a new home in the sunbaked wilds of California's east.

Project: iT House
Architect: Taalman Koch
Location: Pioneertown, California

iT House, Joshua Tree

The view from the southwest shows the iT House sitting lightly on the land and exposed to the elements. Solar panels catch the sun's energy; wide expanses of open doors and windows provide cross-ventilation; and strategic overhangs shade against the desert's endless heat.

If you were planning to build yourself a house in the high desert east of Los Angeles, where temperatures climb higher than 100 degrees Fahrenheit each summer and drop to nearly 32 degrees during the night in winter, what kind of habitat would one choose? A solid enclosure with thick walls and small windows providing respite from the extreme conditions—or a completely exposed glass box without air-conditioning?

Linda Taalman and Alan Koch, of Taalman Koch Architects, chose the latter. Earlier this year, the couple completed work on their glass "iT House," a lovely, minimal home that tests the limits of living lightly on the land in the desert near Joshua Tree National Park.

Taalman and Koch are Los Angeles–based design partners who earned their stripes with a refined, unobtrusive design for DIA:Beacon in upstate New York. A few years ago, they hatched the idea of the iT House. The name, conceived with amusing chutzpah, doesn't refer to ▶

in a space like that was important to me until we built this house."

To make such naked shelter possible they employed passive heating and cooling strategies—the windows and sliding doors are made of Solar Ban 60 glass, coated with a low-e coating for long-wave radiation—and the roof is configured so that it blocks the summer sun. In winter, when the sun is lower and temperatures drop, sunlight can penetrate through the windows. Solar power generates hot water and electricity. Despite these efforts, however, the couple admits that the house gets very hot in summer and very cold in winter.

But exposure is what they like about it. "It can be really windy sometimes and I wonder if it's going to blow away," says Taalman. "But I'm leery of spaces that are over-controlled. I like to know if it's day or night—and when it's hot, it's totally different than when it's cold. And when it snows it's magical. You can see the moon rise and you can wake up with the sun. We don't use any clocks out here." ∎

A view out from the entrance lobby (below left) shows Koch leaving the house by way of the stairs, seen below right of his room. (Note below: Taalman [right] bathes flowers with Koch opened onto the courtyard. The bath and basin are by Duravit; the orange wall by Plüm Firm. The iT House (below) is an exploration of the couple's architectural ideas, built with the help of friends over many weekends away from Los Angeles. It brings the precise and the cool together with the wild and untamed. ∎

LIQUID Assets

FROM ROCHESTER to ROSEAU, THERE are MORE THAN 10,000 REASONS to LOVE SUMMER in MINNESOTA. And WHETHER YOU WANT to SAIL, SWIM, FISH, SCUBA, or SUNBATHE in the NUDE (REALLY), WE'VE FOUND the BEST PLACES for YOU to EXPERIENCE the BEST TIME OF YEAR.

/426/ **DWELL**
DESIGN DIRECTOR: KYLE BLUE
DESIGNERS: BRENDAN CALLAHAN,
DAKOTA KECK, BRIAN SCOTT
DIRECTOR OF PHOTOGRAPHY: KATE STONE FOSS
PHOTO EDITORS: AMY SILBERMAN,
ANDREA LAWSON, ALEXIS TJIAN
PHOTOGRAPHER: GREGG SEGAL
DESIGN PRODUCTION MANAGER: KATHRYN HANSEN
PUBLISHER: DWELL LLC
ISSUE: NOVEMBER 2008
CATEGORY: PHOTO: FEATURE: SERVICE (STORY)

/427/ **MINNESOTA MONTHLY**
ART DIRECTOR: BRIAN JOHNSON
PHOTOGRAPHER: DAVID BOWMAN
PUBLISHER: GREENSPRING MEDIA GROUP
ISSUE: JUNE 2008
CATEGORY: PHOTO: FEATURE: SERVICE (STORY)

In San Francisco, modernist architect Anne Fougeron transformed a South of Market warehouse into a transparent, dramatic loft home for a city-loving young family.

Urban Eco-tecture

The main living floor of Jason Shelton and Amy Shimer's loft building is organized around a central light-filled courtyard that's open to the sky. "Imagine having a balcony inside," says Shimer. Furnishings include an Arco sofa from Flexform and Paul Kjaerholm wicker chairs from Design Within Reach; the coffee table is a George Nelson classic. Top right: A Mira Cooper dries up to the ground floor office space.

MET HOME APRIL08 131

Rather than being seen as a hindrance, issues of sustainability were integral to the development of Fougeron's design, including her provisions for the home's ample daytime light. Despite the tall ceilings and north-facing windows, the existing loft was dark and disconnected from the outside. Fougeron, who received her degree in architecture from UC Berkeley, solved the problem through a series of straightforward and innovative gestures that are typical of her work, which often explores light and transparency.

Additional skylights were an easy fix. Less obvious and in fact quite transforming was her creation of the internal 16-foot-square courtyard that pulls unfiltered light into the center of the building and divides the floor plan into its distinct areas of use. The size of the courtyard was no accident: It maximizes light from above within the confines of structural logistics, and it is placed in the path of the most light as the sun arcs overhead. The courtyard's sliders also allow for cross-ventilation, at no energy cost at all. All the new glazing in the building is insulated and has a low-E coating; artificial light is provided by high-efficiency, dimmable T-5 fluorescent tubes.

Even though it was an extravagance given the project budget, the clients insisted on a glassed-in master-suite penthouse, the addition of which required seismic retrofitting of the entire building—complex, unglamorous and expensive (although not a bad thing to have done in a masonry building in earthquake country). Even with the added cost and construction, "The penthouse wasn't a tough decision," says Shimer. "It makes the entire project for us."

This page: The kitchen is nestled within one of the original column bays and against the courtyard. All the custom-made cabinets are below the counters for maximum views; a bank of doors along the back wall hides the refrigerator and pantry. Opposite: Shelton plays with his daughter in the courtyard, with its dramatic black riverstone and patch of moss. "You can go outside and never leave the house," he says.

MET HOME APRIL08 137

/428/ **METROPOLITAN HOME**
DESIGN DIRECTOR: KEITH D'MELLO
ART DIRECTOR: JEFFREY FELMUS
PHOTO EDITOR: CATHRYNE CZUBEK
PHOTOGRAPHER: MATTHEW MILLMAN
PUBLISHER: HACHETTE FILIPACCHI MEDIA U.S.
ISSUE: APRIL 2008
CATEGORY: PHOTO: FEATURE: SERVICE (STORY)

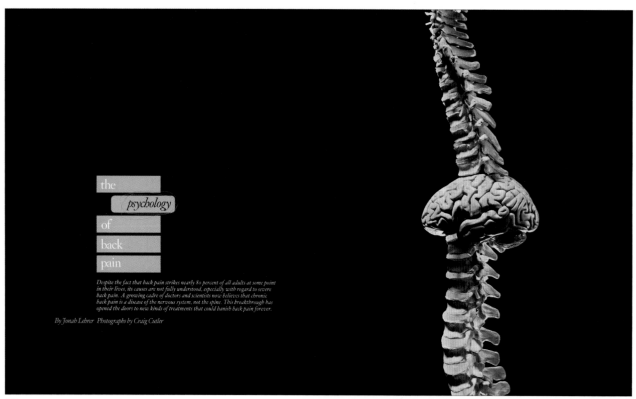

the
psychology
of
back
pain

Despite the fact that back pain strikes nearly 80 percent of all adults at some point in their lives, its causes are not fully understood, especially with regard to severe back pain. A growing cadre of doctors and scientists now believes that chronic back pain is a disease of the nervous system, not the spine. This breakthrough has opened the doors to new kinds of treatments that could banish back pain forever.

By Jonah Lehrer Photographs by Craig Cutler

429

---

the psychology of back pain

In its darkest moods, the demon lurking in Marc Sopher's back made it almost impossible for the family doctor to carry on with his daily routine. It would pound his lower back, sending dull throbs of pain up his spine, and then fire sharp bolts of pain down one leg and then the other. At first, Dr. Sopher tried to ignore the pain. He assumed that he'd strained something in his spine, perhaps herniated a disk or pinched a nerve. "I'm a traditionally trained physician," he says. "I started taking some anti-inflammatories and I waited for my back to heal." But the demon wouldn't go away. When holding meetings, he'd have to stand up and stretch his back. When driving, he'd have to stop and get out of the car to ease the tension in his spine. When reading bedtime stories to his kids, he'd have to lie on his stomach. There was no anatomical explanation for the extremity of his pain. "I tried to soldier on the best I could," he says. "I honestly believed I'd be living with pain for the rest of my life."

The majority of people with back pain (estimates run as high as 90 percent) will get better within seven weeks with little or no medical treatment. The body heals itself, the inflammation subsides, and the nerve relaxes. These people go back to work, pledging to avoid the sort of physical triggers that caused the pain in the first place. About 10 percent of patients don't get better. Their pain gets worse and worse. It is chronic. One day, these people find themselves lying supine on the floor, wondering what they did to deserve such agony.

Today, Dr. Sopher, who lives in Exeter, New Hampshire, no longer has back pain. He has slain his demon. When I meet him, he's drenched in

sweat, having just run eight miles and played a game of tennis. Later, he'll ride his bike. His short hair is salted with white—Dr. Sopher is 46—and he still has the taut body of a young athlete. But Dr. Sopher wasn't healed by conventional medicine. He didn't undergo surgery or get epidural injections or take painkillers. Instead, Dr. Sopher is one of the thousands of patients suffering from chronic back pain who got better by treating his mind.

He learned to think differently about his pain, and that's when his pain went away. This narrative might sound suspicious—there's no shortage of phony treatments for chronic back pain—but a growing body of scientific evidence supports it. Chronic back pain is now predominantly seen as a disease of the nervous system, not the spine. It's a problem suited for psychologists and neuroscientists, not surgeons. The best treatments are often the least invasive.

America is in the midst of a back-pain epidemic. The numbers are staggering: There's an 80 percent chance that, at some point in your life, you'll suffer from severe back pain. Treating back pain costs about $26 billion annually and it currently accounts for 2.5 percent of our country's total health-care spending. If worker compensation and disability payments were taken into account, the cost would be even higher.

The conventional medical treatment for back pain follows a predictable script. After the patient is interviewed and given a physical exam, he or she undergoes a series of diagnostic tests. This normally includes x-rays, CT scans, and MRIs. The end result is an astonishing array of detailed anatomical pictures. Doctors no longer need to imagine the layers of tissue underneath the skin. Now they can see everything.

Unfortunately, all this seeing has limited results. After undergoing the full range of diagnostic tests, 85 percent of patients suffering from lower-back pain still don't receive a precise diagnosis. The pain can't be pinpointed; there are just too many moving parts. Instead, their suffering is parceled into a vague category, such as lumbar strain or spinal instability. But even when a patient is given a specific structural diagnosis, it's not clear how meaningful the diagnosis actually is. Look, for example, at herniated disks, one of the most common "causes" of back pain. A 1994 study published in *The New England Journal of Medicine* imaged the spinal regions of 98 people with no back pain or back-related problems. The pictures were then sent to doctors who didn't know that the patients were not in pain. The end result was disturbing: Eighty percent of the pain-free patients exhibited "serious problems" such as bulging, protruding, or herniated

disks. In 38 percent of patients, the MRIs revealed multiple damaged disks. The disconnect between "disk degeneration" and back pain increases with age: More than 80 percent of people over the age of 60 who don't have any back pain still demonstrate significant disk degeneration. These structural spinal abnormalities are often used to justify expensive treatments like surgery, and yet nobody would advocate surgery for people without pain. In the latest clinical guidelines issued by the American College of Physicians and the American Pain Society, doctors were strongly recommended not to "obtain imaging or other diagnostic tests in patients with nonspecific low back pain." In too many cases, the expensive tests proved worse than useless.

THE MIND-BODY PROPHET

Dr. Sopher banished his demon by reading a book. It was *Healing Back Pain*, by John Sarno, MD, a physician at New York University. "Once I started reading," says Dr. Sopher, "I couldn't stop. It was like a revelation. As the hours went by, I became aware that I'd been sitting for a long time without any pain." While nothing had changed in Dr. Sopher's back, he was learning how to think about his pain in a new way. "That's when I reminded myself that I'm a serious doctor, and just reading a book isn't supposed to cure pain. That's when I decided to contact Dr. Sarno. I needed to learn how this was done."

The Rusk Institute of Rehabilitation Medicine lies on the eastern edge of Manhattan. It's a squat brick building overlooking a highway. Watching patients enter the institute is a sobering experience. The full variety of human limps and gimps is on display. People hobble through the doors wearing cervical collars and shoulder slings and elaborate knee braces. They lean on canes and crutches. It's a slow-moving parade of pain.

Dr. Sarno is 84 years old—he has been practicing medicine since 1950—but he still sees new patients three days a week. He talks slowly, with the pedantic patience of someone used to explaining his ideas. "When I first started treating patients with back pain," says Dr. Sarno, "I practiced conventional medicine. I relied on all the usual tools, like injections and strengthening exercises. As the years passed, I grew very frustrated because I realized that all the conventional treatments were utterly useless. My patients weren't getting better."

Dr. Sarno's failure caused him to question a fundamental assumption of modern medicine. In general, doctors assume that bodily pain is a

BEST LIFE ONLINE For behind-the-scenes info on how photographer Craig Cutler brought these images to the page and to see additional shots, visit BestLifeOnline.com/backpain.

94 BEST LIFE FEBRUARY 2008

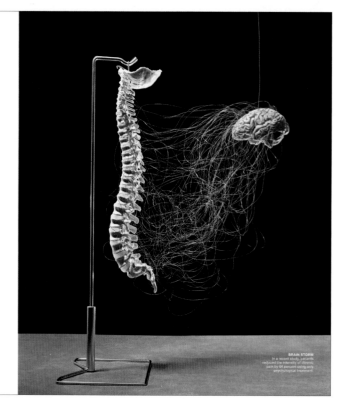

BRAIN STORM
In a recent study, patients reduced the intensity of chronic pain by 64 percent using only psychological treatment.

429

/429/ **BEST LIFE**
DESIGN DIRECTOR: BRANDON KAVULLA
DESIGNERS: BRANDON KAVULLA, HEATHER JONES
DIRECTOR OF PHOTOGRAPHY: RYAN CADIZ
PHOTO EDITOR: JEANNE GRAVES
PHOTOGRAPHER: CRAIG CUTLER
PUBLISHER: RODALE INC.
ISSUE: FEBRUARY 2008
CATEGORY: PHOTO: FEATURE: SERVICE (STORY)

/430/ **BODY + SOUL**
CREATIVE DIRECTOR: ERIC PIKE
ART DIRECTOR: ASYA PALATOVA
DESIGNER: ASYA PALATOVA
DIRECTOR OF PHOTOGRAPHY: HELOISE GOODMAN
PHOTO EDITOR: ERIKA PREUSS
PHOTOGRAPHER: RICHARD PIERCE
PUBLISHER: MARTHA STEWART LIVING OMNIMEDIA
ISSUE: JULY/AUGUST 2008
CATEGORY: PHOTO: FEATURE: SERVICE (STORY)

water & HEALTH

BY JESSICA CERRETANI
PHOTOGRAPHY BY RICHARD PIERCE

Are you drinking enough? Too much? In honor of the thirstiest season, we explore the most burning questions about the world's most popular beverage

If all those water bottles are any indication, we're the hydration generation. At work, at the gym, and on the road, it seems like everyone's toting a container of the clear stuff. Unlike a pair of pointy-toed heels, however, this trend is good for you, at least on the face of it. After all, water is our most effective health elixir: It makes up some 60 percent of our bodies, and all our systems—cardiovascular, respiratory, digestive—depend on it. It ferries nutrients to cells, keeps membranes moist, and flushes out toxins and waste via urine and sweat. "Water is the medium for everything that goes on in our bodies," explains Molly Morgan, a New York-based dietitian.

Sounds simple. But there's still no shortage of questions and controversy, on everything from the validity of the "eight glasses a day" rule to the healthfulness of those pink and orange "vitamin waters" to the scary news that our water supply might contain not only lead and pesticides (as if that weren't bad enough) but traces of pharmaceuticals, too. Here, Morgan and other hydration experts give us the lowdown on H_2O.

come with your bill); watch out for "detections" and "violations" in your supply. Common contaminants include lead, pesticides, industrial chemicals like benzene, and chlorine byproducts called trihalomethanes, which have been linked in animal studies to an increased risk of bladder cancer and miscarriages. If you're concerned about lead in your water from your home's pipes (which wouldn't show up on an annual report), find out with an at-home test kit.

"If you live in a community with an unsafe water supply, use a good water filter," Solomon says. Choose one that's certified to remove the specific contaminants in your tap water. Inexpensive activated-carbon filters like those by Brita reduce or eliminate many contaminants, including lead, says Solomon. But if your water contains perchlorate, a rocket-fuel chemical found in some water supplies, it's a good idea to invest in either an ion exchange filter or a reverse-osmosis filter. The latter, which Solomon calls "the Cadillac of water filters," costs anywhere from $160 to $450, plus installation fees.

Keep in mind that taste is not a reliable indicator of safety, but rather of the water's carbon dioxide and mineral contents. Many harmful substances in water are tasteless.

When taking your water to go, remember that Nalgene and other reusable plastic bottles have their problems. Many plastic bottles have a tendency to accumulate bacteria, and Nalgene bottles have been shown to leach the toxic chemical bisphenol A. (As of press time, Nalgene had announced plans to eliminate this chemical from its bottles.) Tote your H_2O in safe reusable bottles made from stainless steel, aluminum, or glass, and keep up on the safety issues surrounding plastic bottles.

Should I be worried about the reports of pharmaceuticals in drinking water?

Solomon and other experts are concerned about the recent reports of trace amounts of drugs like antibiotics, antidepressants, and birth-control pills in our water supply. "The EPA doesn't require water utilities to test for these chemicals, let alone remove them," says Solomon.

Unfortunately, affordable carbon filters do nothing to remove pharmaceuticals from drinking water. While reverse-osmosis filters are effective, Solomon advises a wait-and-see approach. "We don't know that the levels are high enough to be harmful," she explains, "so it's premature to go out and buy an expensive reverse-osmosis system to filter pharmaceuticals." A number of health and environ-

mental watchdog groups, including the NRDC, are calling on the EPA to quickly develop testing requirements and standards for pharmaceuticals and other chemicals.

What should I drink when exercising?

We're bombarded with ads showing sweaty-but-svelte models drinking Gatorade after a workout. But do sports drinks help the average exerciser? "If your workout lasts longer than an hour, sports drinks make a good option," says Morgan. These drinks contain a specific blend of carbohydrates, electrolytes, and water that replaces those you lose through sweat. That helps fuel your body fast.

But some sports drinks have a downside, so it's important to read labels carefully. "A lot of these products contain high-fructose corn syrup and artificial coloring," explains Hyman. "I do recommend electrolyte replacement for people who engage in heavy exercise or tend to sweat a lot, but I prefer simple products such as Pedialyte or similar unsweetened electrolyte drinks."

Do I need special water with vitamins or herbs?

In a word, no. These products may come in a kaleidoscope of colors, but their contents aren't so fun. One such bottle of nutrient-infused water, for example, contains 32.5 grams of sugar and 125 calories. What's more, there's no guarantee your body will absorb the vitamins, some of which need to be consumed with fat. "Like sports drinks, flavored waters tend to be full of sugar, artificial sweeteners, and other additives," says Hyman. "Plain water is better, ideally filtered and not in a plastic bottle." If you're taking herbs for a specific condition, do so in capsule or tincture form, not in the uncertain amounts found in special bottled water.

I've heard that carbonated water is unhealthy. Is this true?

Although some research suggests that the phosphorus in soft drinks may leach calcium from bones, evidence is mixed, and the effects from phosphorus in carbonated drinks are negligible, according to a report from the Tufts University Friedman School of Nutrition Science.

Mineral water, some of which is naturally carbonated, may actually offer health benefits, says some research. It contains small amounts of calcium and magnesium, and may reduce blood pressure slightly. "Just think of it as an added bonus," says Morgan. ◆

ESSENTIAL ELIXIR
Water's importance can't be underestimated; we can survive for only a few days without it.

PROP STYLING BY DAWN SINKOWSKI

431

432

433

/431/ **THE NEW YORKER**
DIRECTOR OF PHOTOGRAPHY: ELISABETH BIONDI
PHOTO EDITOR: WHITNEY JOHNSON
PHOTOGRAPHER: MARTIN SCHOELLER
STUDIO: MARTIN SCHOELLER STUDIO
PUBLISHER: CONDÉ NAST PUBLICATIONS INC.
CLIENT: THE NEW YORKER
ISSUE: AUGUST 11 & 18, 2008
CATEGORY: PHOTO: FEATURE:
NON-CELEBRITY PROFILE (SINGLE/SPREAD)

/432/ **FORTUNE**
DESIGN DIRECTOR: ROBERT PERINO
DIRECTOR OF PHOTOGRAPHY: GREG POND
PHOTO EDITOR: NANCY JO JOHNSON
PHOTOGRAPHER: NIGEL PARRY
PUBLISHER: TIME INC.
ISSUE: SEPTEMBER 29, 2008
CATEGORY: PHOTO: FEATURE:
NON-CELEBRITY PROFILE (SINGLE/SPREAD)

/433/ **MADRIZ**
CREATIVE DIRECTOR: LOUIS-CHARLES TIAR
DESIGNERS: ABRIL Y DE LA CARRERA,
GRACIELA ARTIGA
PHOTOGRAPHER: ALBERTO GARCÍA-ALIX
EDITOR-IN-CHIEF: MARIO CANAL
PUBLISHER: REVISTAS EXCLUSIVAS S.L.
ISSUE: FALL 2007 / WINTER 2008
CATEGORY: PHOTO: FEATURE:
NON-CELEBRITY PROFILE (SINGLE/SPREAD)

MEET TEAM USA

SWIMMING

America's new set of Olympians, nearly 600 strong, hails from 47 of the 50 states and includes identical twins, soldiers, teenagers, a cancer patient, a 58-year-old CEO and the daughter of a Super Bowl champion

by Brian Cazeneuve | *Portfolio by* Michael O'Neill

When **DARA TORRES** *(third from left)* won her first Olympic gold medal—in Los Angeles in 1984—26 of the 42 members of this year's swim team hadn't been born. No wonder 23-year-old **MICHAEL PHELPS** *(page 68)* calls Torres his "sort-of mom."

On a team full of prodigies Torres, 41, who came out of retirement after having a daughter two years ago and undergoing shoulder and knee surgeries in the last year, could be the story of the Games; in her fifth Olympics she'll likely add to her career haul of nine medals. **NATALIE COUGHLIN** *(far right)*, who broke the 100-meter world backstroke record at the trials in Omaha, tied a record at the 2004 Games with five medals (two of them gold)—a total that could be eclipsed by **KATIE HOFF** *(fourth from right)*, who will swim six events in Beijing. Another backstroke ace is **MARGARET HOELZER** *(third from right)*, the reigning 200-meter world champ and world-record holder. Beyond Phelps, the men's team is deep and experienced. In Athens, **AARON PIERSOL** *(fourth from left)* won three gold medals, while **RYAN LOCHTE** *(second from left)* took a relay gold and an individual silver. Then there are newcomers **GARRETT WEBER-GALE** *(far left)*, 22, a surprise winner of the 50- and 100-meter freestyles at the trials, and **CULLEN JONES** *(second from right)*, a Bronx native who set a U.S. 50-meter free record in Omaha. Jones is just the second African-American swimmer to qualify for an Olympic individual event.

434

JUST YOUR AVERAGE

FRIDGE-LIFTING, TRUCK-PULLING, TIRE-FLIPPING BARTENDER

EVER CHANNEL-SURFED LATE ONE NIGHT AND STUMBLED UPON BIG, BURLY GUYS LIFTING BIG, HEAVY THINGS? TURNS OUT, THERE ARE DOZENS OF THOSE STRONGMEN ROAMING AMERICA'S STREETS. AND ONE MAY HAVE JUST POURED YOU A DRINK.

BY GARE JOYCE

PHOTOGRAPHS BY MARTIN SCHOELLER

Steve MacDonald is a professional strongman and co-owner of Doubladay's in downtown Pittsburgh.

435

/434/ **SPORTS ILLUSTRATED**
CREATIVE DIRECTOR: STEVE HOFFMAN
ART DIRECTOR: CHRIS HERCIK
PHOTO EDITOR: JIMMY COLTON
PUBLISHER: TIME INC.
ISSUE: JULY 28, 2008
CATEGORY: PHOTO: FEATURE:
NON-CELEBRITY PROFILE (SINGLE/SPREAD)

/435/ **ESPN THE MAGAZINE**
CREATIVE DIRECTOR: SIUNG TJIA
DIRECTOR OF PHOTOGRAPHY: CATRIONA NI AOLAIN
PHOTO EDITOR: JULIE CLAIRE
PHOTOGRAPHER: MARTIN SCHOELLER
EDITOR-IN-CHIEF: GARY BELSKY
PUBLISHER: ESPN, INC.
CATEGORY: PHOTO: FEATURE:
NON-CELEBRITY PROFILE (SINGLE/SPREAD)

436

436

/436/ **THE NEW YORK TIMES MAGAZINE**
CREATIVE DIRECTOR: JANET FROELICH
DEPUTY ART DIRECTOR: GAIL BICHLER
ART DIRECTOR: AREM DUPLESSIS
DESIGNERS: IAN ALLEN, AREM DUPLESSIS
DIRECTOR OF PHOTOGRAPHY: KATHY RYAN
PHOTO EDITOR: KIRA POLLACK
PHOTOGRAPHER: ROBBIE COOPER
EDITOR-IN-CHIEF: GERRY MARZORATI
PUBLISHER: THE NEW YORK TIMES
ISSUE: NOVEMBER 23, 2008
CATEGORY: PHOTO: FEATURE:
NON-CELEBRITY PROFILE

Obama's Journey
Time photographer Callie Shell covered his campaign for two years. An intimate look back at the long path to victory

437

437

Barack Obama
The 2008 TIME Person of the Year

438

438

The Great Divide

After a dizzying, down-to-the-wire Super Tuesday, the Democratic Party is split between Hillary Clinton and Barack Obama, with a long and grueling battle ahead. TIME takes an intimate look at the Democrats' dueling candidates as they prepare for the next chapter in an already historic campaign

Photographs for TIME by Diana Walker and Callie Shell

439

439

/437/ **TIME**
ART DIRECTOR: ARTHUR HOCHSTEIN
DEPUTY ART DIRECTOR: D.W. PINE
CHIEF PICTURE EDITOR: ALICE GABRINER
ASSOCIATE PICTURE EDITOR: CRARY PULLEN
PHOTOGRAPHER: CALLIE SHELL — AURORA
EDITOR-IN-CHIEF: JOHN HUEY
PUBLISHER: TIME INC.
ISSUE: NOVEMBER 17, 2008
CATEGORY: PHOTO: FEATURE:
NON-CELEBRITY PROFILE (STORY)

/438/ **TIME**
ART DIRECTOR: ARTHUR HOCHSTEIN
DESIGNER: D.W. PINE
CHIEF PICTURE EDITOR: ALICE GABRINER
EDITOR-IN-CHIEF: JOHN HUEY
PUBLISHER: TIME INC.
ISSUE: DECEMBER 29, 2008
CATEGORY: DESIGN: FEATURE:
NEWS/REPORTAGE (STORY)

/439/ **TIME**
ART DIRECTOR: ARTHUR HOCHSTEIN
DEPUTY ART DIRECTOR: D.W. PINE
DIRECTOR OF PHOTOGRAPHY: MARYANNE GOLON
CHIEF PICTURE EDITOR: ALICE GABRINER
ASSOCIATE PICTURE EDITOR: LESLIE DELA VEGA
PHOTOGRAPHER: CALLIE SHELL — AURORA
EDITOR-IN-CHIEF: JOHN HUEY
PUBLISHER: TIME INC.
ISSUE: FEBRUARY 18, 2008
CATEGORY: PHOTO: FEATURE:
NON-CELEBRITY PROFILE

440

440

441

441

442

442

/440/ TEXAS MONTHLY
ART DIRECTOR: T.J. TUCKER
DESIGNER: T.J. TUCKER
PHOTO EDITOR: LESLIE BALDWIN
PHOTOGRAPHER: PETER YANG
PUBLISHER: EMMIS COMMUNICATIONS CORP.
ISSUE: JULY 2008
CATEGORY: PHOTO: FEATURE:
NON-CELEBRITY PROFILE (STORY)

/441/ TIME
ART DIRECTOR: ARTHUR HOCHSTEIN
DEPUTY ART DIRECTOR: D.W. PINE
CHIEF PICTURE EDITOR: ALICE GABRINER
ASSOCIATE PICTURE EDITOR: LESLIE DELA VEGA
PHOTOGRAPHER: CALLIE SHELL — AURORA
EDITOR-IN-CHIEF: JOHN HUEY
PUBLISHER: TIME INC.
ISSUE: SEPTEMBER 1, 2008
CATEGORY: PHOTO: FEATURE:
NON-CELEBRITY PROFILE (STORY)

/442/ ESPN THE MAGAZINE
CREATIVE DIRECTOR: SIUNG TJIA
DIRECTOR OF PHOTOGRAPHY: CATRIONA NI AOLAIN
PHOTO EDITOR: MAISIE TODD
PHOTOGRAPHER: CARLOS SERRAO
EDITOR-IN-CHIEF: GARY BELSKY
PUBLISHER: ESPN, INC.
CATEGORY: PHOTO: FEATURE:
NON-CELEBRITY PROFILE (STORY)

443

443

444

444

445

445

/443/ NEW YORK
DESIGN DIRECTOR: CHRIS DIXON
DIRECTOR OF PHOTOGRAPHY: JODY QUON
PHOTO EDITOR: CAROLINE SMITH
PHOTOGRAPHER: DAN WINTERS
EDITOR-IN-CHIEF: ADAM MOSS
PUBLISHER: NEW YORK MAGAZINE HOLDINGS, LLC
ISSUE: OCTOBER 6, 2008
CATEGORY: PHOTO: FEATURE:
NON-CELEBRITY PROFILE (STORY)

/444/ TIME
ART DIRECTOR: ARTHUR HOCHSTEIN
DEPUTY ART DIRECTOR: D.W. PINE
CHIEF PICTURE EDITOR: ALICE GABRINER
DEPUTY PICTURE EDITOR: DIETMAR LIZ-LEPIORZ
PHOTOGRAPHER: LISA JACK
EDITOR-IN-CHIEF: JOHN HUEY
PUBLISHER: TIME INC.
ISSUE: DECEMBER 29, 2008
CATEGORY: PHOTO: FEATURE:
NON-CELEBRITY PROFILE (STORY)

/445/ GARDEN & GUN
ART DIRECTOR: ROB HEWITT
DESIGNER: RICHIE SWANN
DIRECTOR OF PHOTOGRAPHY: MAGGIE BRETT KENNEDY
PHOTOGRAPHER: ANDY ANDERSON
ISSUE: JANUARY/FEBRUARY 2008
CATEGORY: PHOTO: FEATURE:
NON-CELEBRITY PROFILE (STORY)

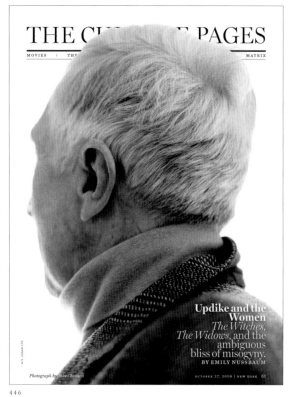

446

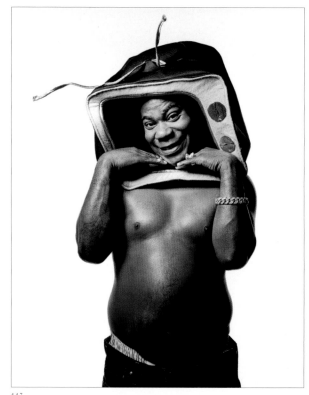

447

Her Highness Still Rules

How Queen Latifah Inc. keeps on keepin' on.

By Alex Witchel

The back seat of a stretch limo making a tight turn is no place to stick a pencil in your eye, but Queen Latifah didn't flinch. En route to a meeting at Cover Girl, where she is the face — and the name — of its Queen Collection (makeup for women of color), she did a quick touch-up. Peering into the mirror she had pulled down from the car's ceiling, she stretched her lower lid and, as the car swerved to the left, drew a perfect line inside it. I squinted at the pencil.

"Is that Cover Girl?" I asked.

"Yup," she said, without moving her eye from the mirror. "As far as you're concerned." I laughed as she dropped it quickly into her bag and pulled out a thick orange tube of Lash Blast mascara instead. "This is Cover Girl," she said.

With or without makeup, Latifah's face is at the center of her fortune. With her almond-shaped eyes and sweeping cheekbones, she could have been painted by Gauguin, though her beauty is recognizably her own, animated by a warmth, humor and innate self-confidence most women would kill for. Her stardom, in movies and television, has come from her gifts at playing the underdog or the outsider, the thick girl in body only, whose heart and brain

Photograph by Robert Maxwell

448

/446/ **NEW YORK**
DESIGN DIRECTOR: CHRIS DIXON
DIRECTOR OF PHOTOGRAPHY: JODY QUON
PHOTO EDITOR: LEANA ALAGIA
PHOTOGRAPHER: JAKE CHESSUM
EDITOR-IN-CHIEF: ADAM MOSS
PUBLISHER: NEW YORK MAGAZINE HOLDINGS, LLC
ISSUE: OCTOBER 27, 2008
CATEGORY: PHOTO: FEATURE: CELEBRITY/
ENTERTAINMENT PROFILE (SINGLE/SPREAD)

/447/ **INKED**
CREATIVE DIRECTOR: TODD WEINBERGER
DIRECTOR OF PHOTOGRAPHY: MARYA GULLO
PHOTO EDITOR: JOSH CLUTTER
PHOTOGRAPHER: MARK MANN
EDITOR-IN-CHIEF: JASON BUHRMESTER
PUBLISHER: PINCHAZO PUBLISHING
ISSUE: NOVEMBER 2008
CATEGORY: PHOTO: FEATURE: CELEBRITY/
ENTERTAINMENT PROFILE (SINGLE/SPREAD)

/448/ **THE NEW YORK TIMES MAGAZINE**
CREATIVE DIRECTOR: JANET FROELICH
ART DIRECTOR: AREM DUPLESSIS
DEPUTY ART DIRECTOR: GAIL BICHLER
DESIGNER: IAN ALLEN
DIRECTOR OF PHOTOGRAPHY: KATHY RYAN
PHOTO EDITOR: JOANNA MILTER
PHOTOGRAPHER: ROBERT MAXWELL
EDITOR-IN-CHIEF: GERRY MARZORATI
PUBLISHER: THE NEW YORK TIMES
ISSUE: OCTOBER 5, 2008
CATEGORY: PHOTO: FEATURE: CELEBRITY/
ENTERTAINMENT PROFILE (SINGLE/SPREAD)

Malkovich really does talk like Malkovich—that's his actual speaking voice. Wafty and fey, like that of some nineteenth-century consumptive in the throes of an ague, but with a touch of something murderous thrown in. That John Malkovich could be as Malkovichian as the "Malkovich" Malkovich played, and played off of, in *Being John Malkovich*—is too good to be true, right? Yet it is so. Malkovich breezily dismisses any concerns about "Malkovich"—that is, about whether his own cultish celebrity complicates his efforts to disappear into a character when he's acting on screen or stage.

"I don't find myself interested in that," Malkovich says. (Waftily, feyly.) "Of course, people have perceptions about me that may or not please me, because they may or may not be accurate. But I really never think about that."

The curious thing about John Malkovich is not that he's great; he's always great, whether the film's a classic like *Dangerous Liaisons* or a turkey like *Con Air*. It's that Malkovich's great performances almost always provoke a fetishistic response—a love of, and a thirst for, more "Malkovich." All those odd details, those choices he makes as an actor that are often as psychotic as they are brilliant. And indelible. In the *Line of Fire* came out fifteen years ago, but you've vividly retained the image of Malkovich performing that deranged hobo dance, right? As you have, say, the sight and sound of his bizarre Oreo mastications and hyperreal Russian accent ("Meeeester son of a beeeetch!

Let's PAH-lay zoom cardsss!") in 1998's *Rounders*, right? I like rehearsals, but I also like to just see what comes out," he says. "These gestures are almost always spontaneous. And when I do movies, I tend to do very different things in different takes. It's always interesting to me to see which take gets used." Thankfully, we've gotten to see a lot more Malkovich takes this year than we have in a while: 2008 boasts seven films featuring or starring John Malkovich, most notably the Coen brothers' *Burn After Reading* and October's *Changeling*, the Clint Eastwood film in which he plays Gustav Briegleb, the real-life 1920s minister who helps a Los Angeles woman (played by Angelina Jolie) in the search for her missing son. "I took the role for two reasons," he says. "The first is that Briegleb isn't taking money on the side, or the leader of a pedophile gang, or some insane hypocrite. He's just good. It's rare to have a religious character in a Hollywood film drawn like that." Then, perhaps mindful of the version of himself that comes encased in quotes, Malkovich adds, "It's even rarer for me to play one."
—ANDREW CORSELLO

JOHN MALKOVICH
Mad Genius

THE YEAR IN CULTURE | THEATER | ART | TV | ARCHITECTURE | BOOKS | POP | CLASSICAL + DANCE

MOVIES

The Case for Over-the-Top

It's a phrase that gets applied to performances too easily—as if a large-scale, extravagant star turn from an actor is simply a matter of letting every bigger-is-better impulse pour onto the screen unchecked by fear, timidity, or taste. So let us now praise Robert Downey Jr. in *Tropic Thunder* and Heath Ledger in *The Dark Knight* by saying that we were thrilled to witness perfectly controlled pieces of work by actors who knew exactly how to calibrate what they were doing. Lesser talents would have let the blackface and the whiteface do their job for them, but for these two, good makeup was just a tool of the trade, a starting point for their intelligence and imagination. While we're delighted to applaud the prodigiously talented Downey in his comeback year, we wish we could end 2008 by heralding Ledger's breakthrough to the first rank of young actors instead of by memorializing him. As *The Dark Knight* searingly demonstrated, he always seemed to know how much was too much. How sad and paradoxical that he left us wanting more.

Ledger (top) as the Joker; Downey Jr. as Kirk Lazarus.

THE YEAR IN SUPERLATIVES

BEST SCRIPT REPRISE
Who knew the next-best Charlie Kaufman would actually be two guys from Norway? Joachim Trier and Eskil Vogt's screenplay for *Reprise* begins with a pair of dizzying flash-forwards, then zigs and zags with the brash, spiraling energy of the two young writers it follows. As a whole, the script is a show-off showcase of postmodern tricks, mirroring its literary protagonists, but each individual line rings true.

BEST CINEMATOGRAPHY, SCORE, AND EDITING SLUMDOG MILLIONAIRE
Slumdog's cinematographer,

Anthony Dod Mantle, worked with one-twelfth the budget of *The Dark Knight* and still managed to capture the frantic, violent, hurly-burly pulse and rhythm of Mumbai, while embracing the digital, polyglot future. Superstar Indian composer A. R. Rahman provided the propulsive backbeat, mixing his own symphonic sound with the pounding global pop of collaborators like M.I.A. And editor Chris Dickens stitched it all together, producing director Danny Boyle's shamelessly flashy and gimmicky, sometimes contrived, impossibly romantic, and utterly irresistible vision.

BEST MOVIE YOU DIDN'T SEE GHOST TOWN
Precisely the sort of smart, emotional, well-acted comedy for grown-ups that we've been begging Hollywood for. Needless to say, it finished eighth at the box office its opening weekend.

BEST PERFORMANCE BY AN ACTOR KATE WINSLET
Early in her career, Winslet gave the impression of being a frail, neurasthenic thing. No more. In her husband Sam Mendes's film of Richard Yates's *Revolutionary Road*, she portrays a suburban mother desperately afraid of losing her openness, her self.

42 NEW YORK | DECEMBER 15, 2008

Photograph by Brigitte Lacombe

Kate Winslet in makeup for her other starring role of 2008, *The Reader*, in which she plays a German on trial for war crimes.

/449/ **GQ**
DESIGN DIRECTOR: FRED WOODWARD
DESIGNER: ANTON IOUKHNOVETS
DIRECTOR OF PHOTOGRAPHY: DORA SOMOSI
PHOTOGRAPHER: MARK SELIGER
EDITOR-IN-CHIEF: JIM NELSON
PUBLISHER: CONDÉ NAST PUBLICATIONS INC.
ISSUE: DECEMBER 2008
CATEGORY: PHOTO: FEATURE:
CELEBRITY/ENTERTAINMENT
PROFILE (SINGLE/SPREAD)

/450/ **NEW YORK**
DESIGN DIRECTOR: CHRIS DIXON
DIRECTOR OF PHOTOGRAPHY: JODY QUON
PHOTOGRAPHER: BRIGITTE LACOMBE
EDITOR-IN-CHIEF: ADAM MOSS
PUBLISHER: NEW YORK MAGAZINE HOLDINGS, LLC
ISSUE: DECEMBER 15, 2008
CATEGORY: PHOTO: FEATURE:
CELEBRITY/ENTERTAINMENT PROFILE (SINGLE/SPREAD)

451

452

453

/451/ ROLLING STONE
ART DIRECTOR: JOSEPH HUTCHINSON
DESIGNER: JOSEPH HUTCHINSON
DIRECTOR OF PHOTOGRAPHY: JODI PECKMAN
PHOTOGRAPHER: NADAV KANDER
PUBLISHER: WENNER MEDIA
ISSUE: DECEMBER 25, 2008 - JANUARY 8, 2009
CATEGORY: PHOTO: FEATURE: CELEBRITY/
ENTERTAINMENT PROFILE (SINGLE/SPREAD)

/452/ PLAY, THE NEW YORK TIMES SPORT MAGAZINE
CREATIVE DIRECTOR: JANET FROELICH
ART DIRECTOR: ROB HEWITT
DESIGNER: ROB HEWITT
DIRECTOR OF PHOTOGRAPHY: KATHY RYAN
PHOTO EDITOR: KIRA POLLACK
PHOTOGRAPHER: FINLAY MACKAY
EDITOR-IN-CHIEF: MARK BRYANT
PUBLISHER: THE NEW YORK TIMES
ISSUE: AUGUST 2008
CATEGORY: PHOTO: FEATURE: CELEBRITY/
ENTERTAINMENT PROFILE (SINGLE/SPREAD)

/453/ NEW YORK
DESIGN DIRECTOR: CHRIS DIXON
DIRECTOR OF PHOTOGRAPHY: JODY QUON
PHOTO EDITOR: LEA GOLIS
PHOTOGRAPHER: EDWARD KEATING
EDITOR-IN-CHIEF: ADAM MOSS
PUBLISHER: NEW YORK MAGAZINE HOLDINGS, LLC
ISSUE: OCTOBER 20, 2008
CATEGORY: PHOTO: FEATURE: CELEBRITY/
ENTERTAINMENT PROFILE (SINGLE/SPREAD)

By RAMIN SETOODEH

ANNE HATHAWAY IS TRYING TO TALK ABOUT HER NEW MOVIE, "RACHEL GETTING Married," in which she plays Kym, a recovering drug addict who cuts out of rehab in time for her sister's wedding. It's a hard-edged, powerful performance that's earning Hathaway Oscar buzz for the first time in her career. But Hathaway keeps getting interrupted. She's sitting on the patio of a New York hotel; five or six stories up, her dog, Esmeralda, keeps whimpering from the balcony window. "Hi, baby!" Hathaway calls back. "If she starts barking, I might have to go up. I'm totally wrapped around her finger." Esmeralda was in New Jersey for the summer with Hathaway's parents while the actress did press for "Get Smart," and last night the whole family celebrated Anne's visit to New York with hamburgers and reruns of "The Office." Esmeralda cries louder. "She's so pretty. Ahh, it's heartbreaking. So heartbreaking. She's looking right at me." And with that, Hathaway dashes upstairs.

MOVIES

The Rehabilitation *of* Anne Hathaway

She was a Hollywood princess, and then her real-life prince turned into a frog. Now the actress hopes a dark new film will make us all forget her past.

Esmeralda, a 70-pound chocolate Labrador, was a present from Raffaello Follieri, Hathaway's ex-boyfriend. You remember him, don't you? Hathaway was splashed across the tabloids in June when he was arrested on charges of money laundering and fraud. The Italian businessman pretended to have connections with the Vatican so he could dupe his wealthy clients, including billionaire Ron Burkle, into investing with him. Hathaway doesn't want to talk about Follieri—there have been reports that the FBI, as part of its investigation, has confiscated some of her jewels and diaries. In that sense, "Rachel Getting Married" comes at a perfect time. It gives Hathaway something new, and very different, to focus on. There are times when she almost sounds like someone who is coming out of rehab herself. "I'm curious again," Hathaway says. "I'm thinking about life as an adventure. I'm just in love

with that word right now. Every time I see it in my head, it's in the slanted 'Indiana Jones' font, and I get happy thinking about it: *This is an adventure, this is an adventure, this is an adventure.*" But the past can loom over life like a shadow. The day we meet Esmeralda happens to be the same day that Follieri pleads guilty a few miles away in a Manhattan courthouse.

Hathaway might have had to grow up a lot this year, but she pegs the onset of her adulthood to Nov. 12, 2007, the day she turned 25. "I woke up and I was a little bit nervous," she says. "I realized I would never be precocious again. The good things that happened to me and the bad things, I can own them and earn them." She attributes a lot of that change to "Rachel," which she finished filming last fall. At least physically, you can see the transformation on screen. Hathaway chopped her hair short and she started smoking, a habit she hasn't

kicked yet but she promises she will in two more days. She lived on a diet of pasta, pretzels and bread. "It had a nice bloating effect on my body," she says. Hathaway even started dressing like her character, shopping at Target for clothes. "I'd wind up buying a Hanes men's T shirt and some cruddy underwear. And I felt like I got that nomad feeling that Kym had—never quite being settled anywhere."

Hathaway says she and Kym clicked immediately—"almost like a medieval lock"— but their personalities couldn't be more different. The actress is friendly and courteous, and a bit of a klutz. At a dinner during the Toronto film festival, she accidentally sits on her own diamond ring when she tries to get up. She carries an old, bulky BlackBerry because she spilled sunscreen on the last one. "She has a bad record with phones," says her older brother Michael. "She loses them pretty frequently." But like

GIRL, INTERRUPTED: *Hathaway follows up her dark summer with an even darker role in 'Rachel Getting Married.' But she's back on track now.*

PHOTOGRAPH BY ANDREA MODICA FOR NEWSWEEK   SEPTEMBER 29, 2008 | NEWSWEEK **57**

454

Photograph by Jeff Riedel

The Vampire Empire

Five years ago, Stephenie Meyer was a 29-year-old Mormon housewife. Now, she's about to publish the breathlessly awaited finale to her best-selling 'Twilight' saga—and Hollywood is bringing her beloved undead to life. An intimate chat with the woman who just might be the next J.K. Rowling.

● By Karen Valby

455

THEATER

Let Me Be Entertained
A *Gypsy* skeptic takes stock of Rose's return.
BY JEREMY McCARTER

Photograph by Amy Arbus.

456

/454/ NEWSWEEK
DESIGN DIRECTOR: AMID CAPECI
ART DIRECTOR: PATTY ALVAREZ
DIRECTOR OF PHOTOGRAPHY: SIMON BARNETT
PHOTO EDITOR: PAUL MOAKLEY
PHOTOGRAPHER: ANDREA MODICA — FOR NEWSWEEK
PUBLISHER: THE WASHINGTON POST CO.
ISSUE: SEPTEMBER 29, 2008
CATEGORY: PHOTO: FEATURE: CELEBRITY/
ENTERTAINMENT PROFILE (SINGLE/SPREAD)

/455/ ENTERTAINMENT WEEKLY
DESIGN DIRECTORL: BRIAN ANSTEY
DEPUTY ART DIRECTOR: ERIC PAUL
DIRECTOR OF PHOTOGRAPHY: FIONA MCDONAGH
PHOTO EDITOR: FREYDA TAVIN
PHOTOGRAPHER: JEFF RIEDEL
MANAGING EDITOR: RICK TETZELI
PUBLISHER: TIME INC.
ISSUE: JULY 18, 2008
CATEGORY: PHOTO: FEATURE: CELEBRITY/
ENTERTAINMENT PROFILE (SINGLE/SPREAD)

/456/ NEW YORK
DESIGN DIRECTOR: CHRIS DIXON
DIRECTOR OF PHOTOGRAPHY: JODY QUON
PHOTO EDITOR: LEA GOLIS
PHOTOGRAPHER: AMY ARBUS
EDITOR-IN-CHIEF: ADAM MOSS
PUBLISHER: NEW YORK MAGAZINE HOLDINGS, LLC
ISSUE: APRIL 7, 2008
CATEGORY: PHOTO: FEATURE: CELEBRITY/
ENTERTAINMENT PROFILE (SINGLE/SPREAD)

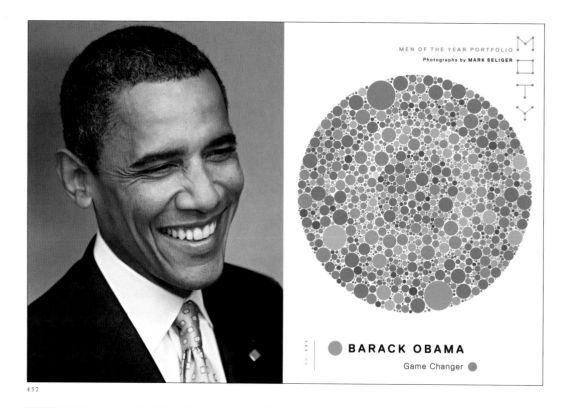

457

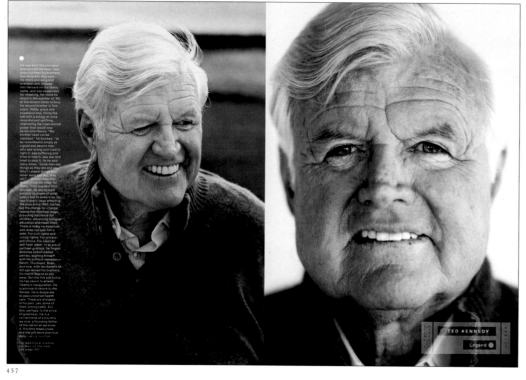

457

/457/ **GQ**
DESIGN DIRECTOR: FRED WOODWARD
DESIGNER: ANTON IOUKHNOVETS
DIRECTOR OF PHOTOGRAPHY: DORA SOMOSI
PHOTOGRAPHER: MARK SELIGER
EDITOR-IN-CHIEF: JIM NELSON
PUBLISHER: CONDÉ NAST PUBLICATIONS INC.
ISSUE: DECEMBER 2008
CATEGORY: PHOTO: FEATURE:
CELEBRITY/ENTERTAINMENT PROFILE (STORY)

/458/ **GLAMOUR**
DESIGN DIRECTOR: GERALDINE HESSLER
ART DIRECTOR: THERESA GRIGGS
DIRECTOR OF PHOTOGRAPHY: SUZANNE DONALDSON
PHOTOGRAPHERS: PATRICK DEMARCHELIER, RON HAVIV,
NORMAN JEAN ROY, EVELYN HOCKSTEIN
PUBLISHER: CONDÉ NAST PUBLICATIONS INC.
ISSUE: DECEMBER 2008
CATEGORY: PHOTO: FEATURE:
CELEBRITY/ENTERTAINMENT PROFILE (STORY)

• *The Olympians*

MISTY MAY-TREANOR & KERRI WALSH

MISTY MAY-TREANOR AND KERRI WALSH ARE WOMEN OF THE YEAR BECAUSE:
They are two of the greatest athletes—male or female—of all time."
—*Gabrielle Reece, former pro beach volleyball star*

"**WE HAVE SEEN** the future. It wears a bikini." That's what one thunderstruck reporter wrote after Kerri Walsh and Misty May-Treanor, two California girls, vanquished the Chinese beach volleyball team to win Olympic gold in Beijing.

The women met as teenagers, when Walsh asked her idol, May, for an autograph. In 2001 they decided to team up, and since then they have not only reached the top of the sport— they've taken it to a new level. Walsh, 30, and May-Treanor, 31, are the only beach volleyball players to win back-to-back gold medals, in Athens and Beijing, and did so without losing a single set. They also made history by racking up 112 straight wins. Says Marjorie A. Snyder, Ph.D., of the Women's Sports Foundation: "Kerri and Misty are in that echelon of all-time great athletes."

The sports elite are fans too. "[WNBA star] Lisa Leslie said how inspired she was watching us," says Walsh. "And the other day on the beach, I heard someone chanting, 'U-S-A! U-S-A!' It was [soccer great] Mia Hamm. To have these strong women cheering you on is so cool."

How do they do it? "Kerri and I have the mind-set that we *will* win," says May-Treanor. Actually being friends helps too: After their victory in Beijing, Walsh says, "we were suddenly doing 10-year-old-girl things—rolling in the sand. The most important thing was to get that hug and hold on to each other—because we *did* it." —*Shaun Dreisbach*

May-Treanor (far left) and Walsh, photographed by Norman Jean Roy in Hermosa Beach, California

---

"**MAYA ANGELOU** told me I should go into politics," Tyra Banks, 35, says. "I was like, 'Child, I have one too many swimsuit pictures out there!'" But TV's fiercest female-power icon probably has more pull than most politicians anyway. She draws about 3.8 million viewers for *America's Next Top Model*, now in its sixth year, and 1.4 million for the *Tyra Show*, a chat fest that makes headlines with episodes about topics like breast implants, gay teens and weight discrimination (she donned a fat suit for that one). When tabloids criticized her un-skinny figure, she went on air in a swimsuit and told them to "kiss my fat ass."

Body confidence isn't new to Banks. She started modeling on fashion runways, but when her curvy frame threatened her career, she asked her mother's advice. The two went out for pizza and devised a new strategy: working with what Banks *had*. She soon found commercial success as the first solo African American cover girl on magazines like *GQ* and *Sports Illustrated*'s Swimsuit Issue.

Today a bona fide TV titan, Banks draws comparisons to the queen of talk. "If Oprah is America's mommy," an MSNBC writer quipped, "Tyra is the cool big sister." In that role, she runs the TZONE Foundation, which raises funds for groups that empower young women and girls. "I can't change society," Banks says. "[Right now] zero is the most attractive size. But I can help women feel good about themselves." —*Laurie Sandell*

Photographed by Norman Jean Roy outside Banks' studio in New York City

The Media Mogul

TYRA BANKS

TYRA BANKS IS A WOMAN OF THE YEAR BECAUSE:
She's a TV powerhouse in terms of genuinely connecting to young women who see her as a real inspiration. That kind of authenticity is hard to find."
—*Soledad O'Brien, CNN anchor*

222

/459/ **ESPN THE MAGAZINE**
CREATIVE DIRECTOR: SIUNG TJIA
DIRECTOR OF PHOTOGRAPHY: CATRIONA NI AOLAIN
PHOTO EDITORS: JULIE CLAIRE, MAISIE TODD
PHOTOGRAPHER: PATRIK GIARDINO
EDITOR-IN-CHIEF: GARY BELSKY
PUBLISHER: ESPN, INC.
CATEGORY: PHOTO: FEATURE: CELEBRITY/
ENTERTAINMENT PROFILE (STORY)

460

460

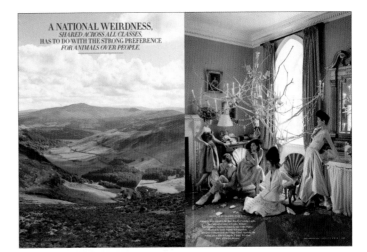

461

461

462

462

/460/ **SPIN**
DESIGN DIRECTOR: DEVIN PEDZWATER
ART DIRECTOR: IAN ROBINSON
DESIGNER: LIZ MACFARLANE
DIRECTOR OF PHOTOGRAPHY: MICHELLE EGIZIANO
PHOTO EDITORS: GAVIN STEVENS,
JENNIFER EDMONDSON
PHOTOGRAPHER: NICK HAYMES
PUBLISHER: SPIN MEDIA LLC
ISSUE: SEPTEMBER 2008
CATEGORY: PHOTO: FEATURE:
CELEBRITY/ENTERTAINMENT PROFILE (STORY)

/461/ **VANITY FAIR**
DESIGN DIRECTOR: DAVID HARRIS
ART DIRECTORS: JULIE WEISS, CHRIS MUELLER
DIRECTOR OF PHOTOGRAPHY: SUSAN WHITE
PHOTOGRAPHER: TIM WALKER
EDITOR-IN-CHIEF: GRAYDON CARTER
PUBLISHER: CONDÉ NAST PUBLICATIONS INC.
ISSUE: JANUARY 2008
CATEGORY: PHOTO: FEATURE:
CELEBRITY/ENTERTAINMENT PROFILE (STORY)

/462/ **ROLLING STONE**
ART DIRECTOR: JOSEPH HUTCHINSON
DESIGNER: JOSEPH HUTCHINSON
DIRECTOR OF PHOTOGRAPHY: JODI PECKMAN
PHOTOGRAPHER: PEGGY SIROTA
PUBLISHER: WENNER MEDIA
ISSUE: DECEMBER 11, 2008
CATEGORY: PHOTO: FEATURE:
CELEBRITY/ENTERTAINMENT PROFILE (STORY)

466

466

/466/ **VANITY FAIR**
DESIGN DIRECTOR: DAVID HARRIS
ART DIRECTORS: JULIE WEISS, CHRIS MUELLER
DIRECTOR OF PHOTOGRAPHY: SUSAN WHITE
PHOTOGRAPHER: ANNIE LEIBOVITZ
DIRECTOR OF PHOTOGRAHY: KATHRYN MACLEOD
EDITOR-IN-CHIEF: GRAYDON CARTER
PUBLISHER: CONDÉ NAST PUBLICATIONS INC.
ISSUE: DECEMBER 2008
CATEGORY: PHOTO: FEATURE: CELEBRITY/ENTERTAINMENT
PROFILE (STORY)

467

467

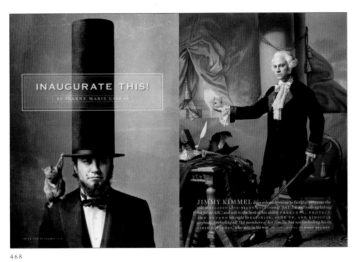

468

468

ANGELINA JOLIE BRAD PITT

469

469

/467/ **NEW YORK**
DESIGN DIRECTOR: CHRIS DIXON
DIRECTOR OF PHOTOGRAPHY: JODY QUON
PHOTO EDITOR: LEA GOLIS
PHOTOGRAPHER: BERT STERN
EDITOR-IN-CHIEF: ADAM MOSS
PUBLISHER: NEW YORK MAGAZINE HOLDINGS, LLC
ISSUE: FEBRUARY 25, 2008
CATEGORY: PHOTO: FEATURE: CELEBRITY/
ENTERTAINMENT PROFILE (STORY)

/468/ **GQ**
DESIGN DIRECTOR: FRED WOODWARD
ART DIRECTOR: ANTON IOUKHNOVETS
DIRECTOR OF PHOTOGRAPHY: DORA SOMOSI
PHOTOGRAPHER: MARK SELIGER
EDITOR-IN-CHIEF: JIM NELSON
PUBLISHER: CONDÉ NAST PUBLICATIONS INC.
ISSUE: NOVEMBER 2008
CATEGORY: PHOTO: FEATURE: CELEBRITY/
ENTERTAINMENT PROFILE (STORY)

/469/ **W**
CREATIVE DIRECTOR: DENNIS FREEDMAN
DESIGN DIRECTOR: EDWARD LEIDA
ART DIRECTOR: NATHALIE KIRSHEH
DESIGNER: EDWARD LEIDA
PHOTOGRAPHER: BRAD PITT
PUBLISHER: CONDÉ NAST PUBLICATIONS INC.
ISSUE: NOVEMBER 2008
CATEGORY: PHOTO: FEATURE: CELEBRITY/
ENTERTAINMENT PROFILE (STORY)

HOW DO YOU BUILD THE WORLD'S BIGGEST BOAT?

BY JEFF WISE + PHOTOGRAPHS BY DAN WINTERS

91
OCTOBER 2008
POPULARMECHANICS.COM

At Aker Yards in Finland, massive metal shapes fit together to form complete ships. This section, a part of the keel called a skeg, aids a cruise ship by helping it move linearly and by protecting its propeller and rudder.

470

471   472

/470/ **POPULAR MECHANICS**
DESIGN DIRECTOR: MICHAEL LAWTON
DESIGNER: STRAVINSKI PIERRE
DIRECTOR OF PHOTOGRAPHY: ALLYSON TORRISI
PHOTOGRAPHER: DAN WINTERS
EDITOR-IN-CHIEF: JAMES B. MEIGS
PUBLISHER: THE HEARST CORPORATION-
MAGAZINES DIVISION
ISSUE: OCTOBER 2008
CATEGORY: PHOTO: FEATURE:
NEWS/REPORTAGE (SINGLE/SPREAD)

/471/ **FORTUNE**
DESIGN DIRECTOR: ROBERT PERINO
DIRECTOR OF PHOTOGRAPHY: GREG POND
PHOTO EDITOR: MIA DIEHL
PHOTOGRAPHER: ROBERT POLIDORI
PUBLISHER: TIME INC.
ISSUE: FEBRUARY 18, 2008
CATEGORY: PHOTO: FEATURE:
NEWS/REPORTAGE (SINGLE/SPREAD)

/472/ **NEWSWEEK**
DESIGN DIRECTOR: AMID CAPECI
ART DIRECTOR: DAN REVITTE
DIRECTOR OF PHOTOGRAPHY: SIMON BARNETT
PHOTO EDITOR: JAMES WELLFORD
PHOTOGRAPHER: ALEX MAJOLI —
MAGNUM FOR NEWSWEEK
PUBLISHER: THE WASHINGTON POST CO.
ISSUE: SEPTEMBER 8, 2008
CATEGORY: PHOTO: FEATURE:
NEWS/REPORTAGE (SINGLE/SPREAD)

2008 OLYMPICS | *Swimming*

To the naked eye, it appeared that Cavic had touched first.
"HE GOT HIM,"
Phelps's coach, Bowman, said. But . . . . No!

TIPPING POINT
In the 100 butterfly Cavic (right in all photos) had Phelps beat but made the mistake of lifting his head too early. For complete details of how these photos were shot, including an interview with the photographer, go to **SI.COM/OLYMPICS**

Photographs by
Heinz Kluetmeier
with Jeff Kavanaugh

473

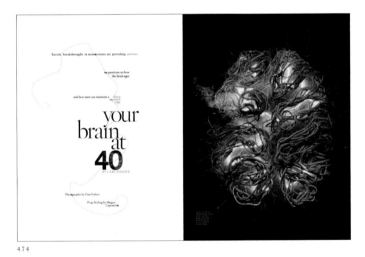

474

475

/473/ SPORTS ILLUSTRATED
CREATIVE DIRECTOR: STEVE HOFFMAN
ART DIRECTOR: CHRIS HERCIK
PHOTOGRAPHER: HEINZ KLUETMEIER
PUBLISHER: TIME INC.
ISSUE: AUGUST 25, 2008
CATEGORY: PHOTO: FEATURE:
NEWS/REPORTAGE (SINGLE/SPREAD)

/474/ BEST LIFE
DESIGN DIRECTOR: BRANDON KAVULLA
DESIGNER: HEATHER JONES
DIRECTOR OF PHOTOGRAPHY: RYAN CADIZ
PHOTOGRAPHER: DAN FORBES
PUBLISHER: RODALE INC.
ISSUE: DECEMBER 2008
CATEGORY: PHOTO: FEATURE:
NEWS/REPORTAGE (SINGLE/SPREAD)

/475/ TIME
ART DIRECTOR: ARTHUR HOCHSTEIN
DEPUTY ART DIRECTOR: D. W. PINE
DIRECTOR OF PHOTOGRAPHY: MARYANNE GOLON
CHIEF PICTURE EDITOR: ALICE GABRINER
ASSOCIATE PICTURE EDITOR: LESLIE DELA VEGA
PHOTOGRAPHER: CALLIE SHELL — AURORA
EDITOR-IN-CHIEF: JOHN HUEY
PUBLISHER: TIME INC.
ISSUE: MARCH 17, 2008
CATEGORY: PHOTO: FEATURE:
NEWS/REPORTAGE (SINGLE/SPREAD)

WORLD

Crazy for Gold

Determined to knock the U.S.
off the top of the Olympics
podium, China's state-run
sports schools are pushing their
young students to the limit.
Inside the medal machine

BY HANNAH BEECH/WEIFANG

Ping-Pong supremacy *China is one of the few countries in the world with academies dedicated to what many consider a rec-room pastime; at the Luneng Table-Tennis School, wannabe champions practice in a gymnasium set up with 80 tables*

Photographs for TIME by Ian Teh—Panos

476

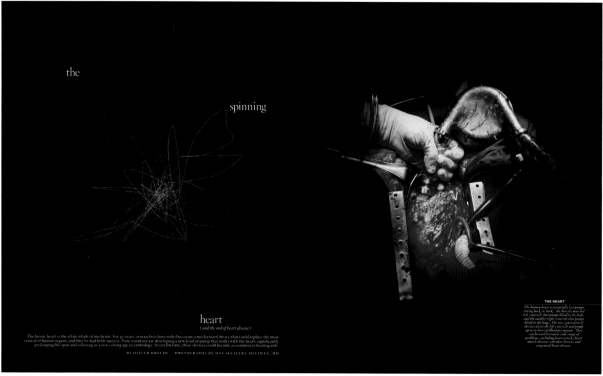

the

spinning

heart
(and the end of heart disease)

THE HEART
The human heart is essentially two pumps sitting back to back, the larger, muscled left ventricle that pumps blood to the body, and the smaller right ventricle that pumps blood to the lungs. The new generation of devices assist the left ventricle and pump up to 10 liters of blood per minute. They can be used to treat a wide range of problems, including heart attack, heart muscle disease, valvular disease, and congenital heart disease.

The bionic heart is the white whale of medicine: For 40 years, researchers have toiled to create a mechanized device that could replace the most critical of human organs, and they've had little success. Now, scientists are developing a new kind of pump that works with the heart, significantly prolonging life span and ushering in a new cyborg age in cardiology. In our lifetime, these devices could become as common as hearing aids.

BY OLIVER BROUDY · PHOTOGRAPHS BY MAX AGUILERA-HELLWEG, MD

477

/476/ **TIME**
ART DIRECTOR: ARTHUR HOCHSTEIN
DEPUTY ART DIRECTOR: CYNTHIA A. HOFFMAN
CHIEF PICTURE EDITOR: ALICE GABRINER
PHOTOGRAPHER: IAN TEH-PANOS
EDITOR-IN-CHIEF: JOHN HUEY
PUBLISHER: TIME INC.
ISSUE: JUNE 6, 2008
CATEGORY: PHOTO: FEATURE:
NEWS/REPORTAGE (SINGLE/SPREAD)

/477/ **BEST LIFE**
DESIGN DIRECTOR: BRANDON KAVULLA
DESIGNER: BRANDON KAVULLA
DIRECTOR OF PHOTOGRAPHY: RYAN CADIZ
PHOTO EDITOR: JEANNE GRAVES
PHOTOGRAPHER: MAX AGUILERA-HELLWEG
PUBLISHER: RODALE INC.
ISSUE: MARCH 2008
CATEGORY: PHOTO: FEATURE:
NEWS/REPORTAGE (SINGLE/SPREAD)

478

480

481

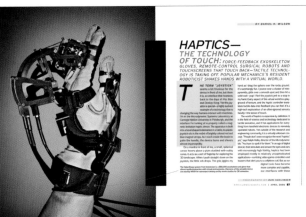

479

482

/478/ **BUSINESS WEEK**
CREATIVE DIRECTOR: ANDREW HORTON
DESIGNER: RON PLYMAN
DIRECTOR OF PHOTOGRAPHY: RONNIE WEIL
PHOTO EDITOR: SARAH MORSE
PHOTOGRAPHER: JEFFREY SALTER
PUBLISHER: MCGRAW-HILL COMPANIES
ISSUE: JUNE 16, 2008
CATEGORY: PHOTO: FEATURE:
NEWS/REPORTAGE (SINGLE/SPREAD)

/479/ **POPULAR MECHANICS**
DESIGN DIRECTOR: MICHAEL LAWTON
DIRECTOR OF PHOTOGRAPHY: ALLYSON TORRISI
PHOTOGRAPHER: DAN SAELINGER
EDITOR-IN-CHIEF: JAMES B. MEIGS
PUBLISHER: THE HEARST CORPORATION-
MAGAZINES DIVISION
ISSUE: APRIL 2008
CATEGORY: PHOTO: FEATURE:
NEWS/REPORTAGE (SINGLE/SPREAD)

/480/ **PEOPLE**
DESIGN DIRECTOR: SARA WILLIAMS
DESIGNER: DAVID SCHLOW
DIRECTOR OF PHOTOGRAPHY: CHRIS DOUGHERTY
PHOTO EDITOR: DEBBE EDELSTEIN
PHOTOGRAPHER: DAVID BUTOW
EDITOR-IN-CHIEF: LARRY HACKETT
PUBLISHER: TIME INC.
ISSUE: SEPTEMBER 22, 2008
CATEGORY: PHOTO: FEATURE:
NEWS/REPORTAGE (SINGLE/SPREAD)

/481/ **KEY, THE NEW YORK TIMES
REAL ESTATE MAGAZINE**
CREATIVE DIRECTOR: JANET FROELICH
ART DIRECTOR: JEFF GLENDENNING
DESIGNER: JULIA MOBURG
DIRECTOR OF PHOTOGRAPHY: KATHY RYAN
PHOTO EDITOR: JOANNA MILTER
PHOTOGRAPHER: PAUL GRAHAM
EDITOR-IN-CHIEF: GERRY MARZORATI
PUBLISHER: THE NEW YORK TIMES
ISSUE: SPRING 2008
CATEGORY: PHOTO: FEATURE:
NEWS/REPORTAGE (SINGLE/SPREAD)

/482/ **BEST LIFE**
DESIGN DIRECTOR: BRANDON KAVULLA
DESIGNER: BRANDON KAVULLA
DIRECTOR OF PHOTOGRAPHY: RYAN CADIZ
PHOTO EDITOR: JEANNE GRAVES
PHOTOGRAPHER: GUIDO VITTI
PUBLISHER: RODALE INC.
ISSUE: OCTOBER 2008
CATEGORY: PHOTO: FEATURE:
NEWS/REPORTAGE (SINGLE/SPREAD)

483

483

484

484

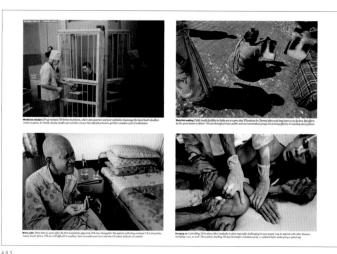

485

485

/483/ **NATIONAL GEOGRAPHIC**
DESIGN DIRECTOR: DAVID WHITMORE
DESIGNER: DAVID WHITMORE
DIRECTOR OF PHOTOGRAPHY: DAVID GRIFFIN
PHOTO EDITOR: KATHY MORAN
PHOTOGRAPHER: MICHAEL NICHOLS
EDITOR-IN-CHIEF: CHRIS JOHNS
PUBLISHER: NATIONAL GEOGRAPHIC SOCIETY
ISSUE: SEPTEMBER 2008
CATEGORY: PHOTO: FEATURE:
NEWS/REPORTAGE (STORY)

/484/ **WIRED**
CREATIVE DIRECTOR: SCOTT DADICH
DESIGN DIRECTOR: WYATT MITCHELL
DESIGNERS: SCOTT DADICH, CHRISTY SHEPPARD
PHOTO EDITOR: ZANA WOODS
PHOTOGRAPHER: NICK WAPLINGTON
PUBLISHER: CONDÉ NAST PUBLICATIONS, INC.
ISSUE: APRIL 2008
CATEGORY: PHOTO: FEATURE:
NEWS/REPORTAGE (STORY)

/485/ **TIME**
ART DIRECTOR: ARTHUR HOCHSTEIN
DEPUTY ART DIRECTOR: CYNTHIA A. HOFFMAN
CHIEF PICTURE EDITOR: ALICE GABRINER
ASSOCIATE PICTURE EDITOR: LESLIE DELA VEGA
PHOTOGRAPHER: JAMES NACHTWEY — VII
EDITOR-IN-CHIEF: JOHN HUEY
PUBLISHER: TIME INC.
ISSUE: OCTOBER 13, 2008
CATEGORY: PHOTO: FEATURE:
NEWS/REPORTAGE (STORY)

486

486

A NIGHT ON THE STREETS

487

487

PROM NIGHT

488

488

/486/ GQ
DESIGN DIRECTOR: FRED WOODWARD
ART DIRECTOR: ANTON IOUKHNOVETS
DIRECTOR OF PHOTOGRAPHY: DORA SOMOSI
PHOTO EDITOR: KRISTA PRESTEK
PHOTOGRAPHER: JEFF RIEDEL
EDITOR-IN-CHIEF: JIM NELSON
PUBLISHER: CONDÉ NAST PUBLICATIONS INC.
ISSUE: NOVEMBER 2008
CATEGORY: PHOTO: FEATURE:
NEWS/REPORTAGE (STORY)

/487/ NEW YORK
DESIGN DIRECTOR: CHRIS DIXON
DIRECTOR OF PHOTOGRAPHY: JODY QUON
PHOTO EDITOR: LEANA ALAGIA
PHOTOGRAPHER: JEFF RIEDEL
EDITOR-IN-CHIEF: ADAM MOSS
PUBLISHER: NEW YORK MAGAZINE HOLDINGS, LLC
ISSUE: MARCH 24, 2008
CATEGORY: PHOTO: FEATURE:
NEWS/REPORTAGE (STORY)

/488/ PEOPLE
DESIGN DIRECTOR: SARA WILLIAMS
DESIGNER: DAVID SCHLOW
DIRECTOR OF PHOTOGRAPHY: CHRIS DOUGHERTY
PHOTO EDITOR: DEBBE EDELSTEIN
PHOTOGRAPHER: MARY ELLEN MARK
EDITOR-IN-CHIEF: LARRY HACKETT
PUBLISHER: TIME INC.
ISSUE: JUNE 16, 2008
CATEGORY: PHOTO: FEATURE:
NEWS/REPORTAGE (STORY)

CAROLINA HERNANDEZ, 37th Avenue and Junction Boulevard, Elmhurst. On August 16, 2007, Hernandez was riding to a mall when she was struck and killed by a Chevy truck. The driver pled guilty to driving with a suspended license.

489

PICTURES THAT MATTERED | 2008

By year's end, American automakers, battered by the financial tumult and economic slowdown, teetered on the brink of collapse

DONDRIC WELLS, 15 YEARS ON THE JOB   SHEILA MARLA, 12 YEARS

JOANNE PRINCE, 14 YEARS   TONY BRANDT, 12 YEARS

Jobs on the line *General Motors employees at two Michigan assembly plants—Lansing Delta Township and Lansing Grand River—are unsure of their company's fate*   **Photographs for TIME by Christopher Morris—VII**

122

490

489

490

/489/ **NEW YORK**
DESIGN DIRECTOR: CHRIS DIXON
DIRECTOR OF PHOTOGRAPHY: JODY QUON
PHOTO EDITOR: ALEX POLLACK
PHOTOGRAPHER: CHRISTOPHER GRIFFITH
EDITOR-IN-CHIEF: ADAM MOSS
PUBLISHER: NEW YORK MAGAZINE HOLDINGS, LLC
ISSUE: JUNE 23, 2008
CATEGORY: PHOTO: FEATURE:
NEWS/REPORTAGE (STORY)

/490/ **TIME**
ART DIRECTOR: ARTHUR HOCHSTEIN
DEPUTY ART DIRECTOR: CYNTHIA A. HOFFMAN
CHIEF PICTURE EDITOR: ALICE GABRINER
ASSOCIATE PICTURE EDITORS: LESLIE DELA VEGA, CRARY PULLEN
SUPPORTING PICTURE EDITOR: DEIRDRE READ
PHOTOGRAPHERS: CHRISTOPHER MORRIS-VII, YURI KOZYREV — NOOR,
JAMES NACHTWEY — VII, LIVIA CORONA, BROOKS KRAFT — CORBIS
EDITOR-IN-CHIEF: JOHN HUEY / PUBLISHER: TIME INC.
ISSUE: DECEMBER 29, 2008 / CATEGORY: PHOTO: FEATURE:
NEWS/REPORTAGE (STORY)

In the early 20th century, railroads lured settlers into North Dakota with promises of homesteads. Towns were planted everywhere. Houses rose from the sweep of the plains, many, like this one, with a story no one can trace. People believed rain would follow the plow. But they were wrong.

BY CHARLES BOWDEN

PHOTOGRAPHS
BY EUGENE RICHARDS

the emptied prairie

MOTT, N. D. The floors of this house are strewn with the detritus of lives let go, ankle deep with abandoned possessions. Except in this room, left orderly and arranged with care like a museum of a vanished loved one. The red hat is part of the uniform for the town's marching band.

491

491

OPEN SPACE Locals call them space capsules. For $14 a night, the beechbol-striped cabins sheltered Ma Shengying (at right) and city friends from Xining, 80 miles away, on a visit to Qinghai's Kanbula National Geopark. As their personal incomes grow, Chinese are traveling more.

492

HERDERS FAREWELL The Malso horse festival in Gansu Province—part race, part county fair—draws nomads into town, briefly. The Sahe Nomads New Village (background) was built by the government to house ethnic Tibetans relocated from grasslands they have long used to pasture livestock.

492

/491/ NATIONAL GEOGRAPHIC
DESIGN DIRECTOR: DAVID WHITMORE
DESIGNER: DAVID WHITMORE
DIRECTOR OF PHOTOGRAPHY: DAVID GRIFFIN
PHOTO EDITOR: SUSAN WELCHMAN
PHOTOGRAPHER: EUGENE RICHARDS
EDITOR-IN-CHIEF: CHRIS JOHNS
PUBLISHER: NATIONAL GEOGRAPHIC SOCIETY
ISSUE: JANUARY 2008
CATEGORY: PHOTO: FEATURE:
NEWS/REPORTAGE (STORY)

/492/ NATIONAL GEOGRAPHIC
DESIGN DIRECTOR: DAVID WHITMORE
DESIGNER: DAVID WHITMORE
DIRECTOR OF PHOTOGRAPHY: DAVID GRIFFIN
PHOTO EDITOR: SARAH LEEN
PHOTOGRAPHERS: FRITZ HOFFMANN, GEORGE STEINMETZ
EDITOR-IN-CHIEF: CHRIS JOHNS
PUBLISHER: NATIONAL GEOGRAPHIC SOCIETY
ISSUE: MAY 2008
CATEGORY: PHOTO: FEATURE:
NEWS/REPORTAGE (STORY)

493

ALTIPLANO

WHERE BOLIVIA MEETS THE SKY

PHOTOGRAPHS BY GEORGE STEINMETZ

The cloud-scraping plateau of the Andes is an otherworldly realm where flamingos lift off from a lagoon warmed by hot springs and colored carnelian by algae (above), where wind erodes rock into a modernist shape perched on a narrow base (left), and vehicles seem to float on a shimmering salt flat flooded by summer rains (previous pages). 71

493

/493/ **NATIONAL GEOGRAPHIC**
DESIGN DIRECTOR: DAVID WHITMORE
DESIGNER: DAVID WHITMORE
DIRECTOR OF PHOTOGRAPHY: DAVID GRIFFIN
PHOTO EDITOR: KEN GEIGER
PHOTOGRAPHER: GEORGE STEINMETZ
EDITOR-IN-CHIEF: CHRIS JOHNS
PUBLISHER: NATIONAL GEOGRAPHIC SOCIETY
ISSUE: JULY 2008
CATEGORY: PHOTO: FEATURE: NEWS/REPORTAGE (STORY)

CHINA

The Sichuan earthquake could change the way Chinese see their leaders.

By MARY HENNOCK *and* MELINDA LIU

HU RONG, 43, WATCHES emergency crews erect a mile-long tent city along Happiness Avenue. Since a magnitude 7.9 earthquake hit Sichuan province on May 12, her home in the city of Dujiangyan has been a small tarpaulin, a couple of planks and one bamboo chair by the road. Times were bad already; Hu hasn't had regular work since the uranium mine went out of business in 1994. Still, her week had one bright spot: soon after the quake, Chinese Prime Minister Wen Jiabao visited an aid station nearby. Hu raced over. "I wanted to see for myself that the prime minister had really come here and that he came so fast," she says, with steady pride. "We were very moved."

An unbelievable tragedy, the Sichuan earthquake has nevertheless given China's leaders a chance to repair the country's battered image, and they're determined not to blow it. Many survivors told of seeing Wen in person as he toured the disaster zone, and TV newscasts showed him wielding a bullhorn and begging exhausted rescue teams not to give up: "Every second lost could mean lives lost!" An estimated 10 percent of Dujiangyan's buildings were destroyed, including a high school where some 900 students were attending their midafternoon classes. Chen Gang, a volunteer helping with crowd control at a collapsed market, says Wen's visit made a huge difference. "He is so much worried. You can see it in his eyes," says the 49-year-old executive. Late in the week President Hu Jintao made his own televised tour of the area, clasping hands with survivors in one of the hardest-hit spots, the little mountain-valley city of Beichuan, where a few untoppled buildings poke out at crazy an-

The earth moved: *As thousands of People's Liberation Army troops poured into the quake zone, relatives clambered through the rubble themselves looking for loved ones— and all too often finding they had been killed*

22 NEWSWEEK | MAY 26, 2008

gles from landslides that smashed entire apartment blocks.

China took a beating for its hamhanded response to the Tibetan riots in March. But this crisis is different. For one thing, it's exactly the kind of problem at which the Beijing leadership excels: a test of mass mobilization and logistics. At the weekend more than 22,000 were confirmed dead, although the government said the final toll might run as high as 50,000, and 4 million homes had been damaged or destroyed. In response, 130,000 soldiers and 97 helicopters were sent to comb the wreckage for survivors. Officials emphasized emergency shipments to places like Aba prefecture, a scene of ethnic Tibetan violence in March. And Beijing's handling of the quake was even more impressive next to the horror in Burma, where the official death toll from Cyclone Nargis is likely to keep climbing far past 78,000, worsened only by the junta's lackadaisical attitude toward survivors.

Moderates like Wen seem to have learned from the Burmese example, as well as Beijing's own mistakes. Shi Anbin, professor of media studies at Tsinghua University, cites three basic rules for public communications in a crisis: "Tell the truth, tell it fast and tell it first." China's authorities neglected those principles in Tibet, he says. "Their earthquake response is the very first time they've lived up to international standards."

The results are unpredictable. The shocking immediacy of the news coverage touched off an explosion of civic action. On the outskirts of shattered towns like Hanwang, police set up checkpoints where people from outside could drop off their contributions. Deng Zhigang, a Red Cross medic there, says volunteers are driving from as far away as Beijing, Shanghai and Hangzhou with donations of food, medicine and clothing. "The government can call up more people, but we don't need that call," says Mu Jin, an economics student from Chengdu Normal University. "We came anyway."

Such enthusiasm can turn quickly. Government-run reconstruction programs can't hope to match such an unprecedented display of personal generosity. As days drag into months, people are sure to grow impatient and angry that the cleanup isn't happening faster, and to question shoddy construction in the area. That would make a perfect opportunity to attack official corruption at the roots—and to wrest some good from a monstrous tragedy.

With JONATHAN ANSFIELD *in Beijing*

PHOTOGRAPHS BY ALAN CHIN FOR NEWSWEEK

494

PHOTO ESSAY

IMAGES OF AN UNRESOLVED WAR

495

495

/494/ **NEWSWEEK**
DESIGN DIRECTOR: AMID CAPECI
ART DIRECTOR: PATTY ALVAREZ
DIRECTOR OF PHOTOGRAPHY: SIMON BARNETT
PHOTO EDITOR: JAMES WELLFORD
PHOTOGRAPHER: ALAN CHIN — FOR NEWSWEEK
PUBLISHER: THE WASHINGTON POST CO.
ISSUE: MAY 26, 2008
CATEGORY: PHOTO: FEATURE:
NEWS/REPORTAGE (STORY)

/495/ **NEWSWEEK**
DESIGN DIRECTOR: AMID CAPECI
ART DIRECTOR: LEAH PURCELL
DIRECTOR OF PHOTOGRAPHY: SIMON BARNETT
PHOTO EDITOR: AMY PEREIRA
PHOTOGRAPHERS: BILL BURKE,
HOWARD GREENBERG GALLERY, NEW YORK
PUBLISHER: THE WASHINGTON POST CO.
ISSUE: MARCH 17, 2008
CATEGORY: PHOTO: FEATURE:
NEWS/REPORTAGE (STORY)

To Die For

Our chief
restaurant
critic travels
to Tokyo
to eat the
world's most
dangerous
meal. So what
does fugu
taste like?
And what's
that funny
tingling
in his throat?

By **Adam Platt**
Photograph by James Wojcik

39

496

Beyond The Glitz

**FORGET SHOPPING. AN EDGY
ALTERNATIVE CULTURE IS
SPRINGING UP IN DUBAI.**

By SAMEER REDDY

THE SUNLIGHT IN DUBAI IS blinding, a layer of searing white that blankets the landscape, best encountered from behind deeply tinted glasses. It is the most notable natural feature in an almost entirely man-made environment, one of the few things in this tiny, but technologically advanced emirate that cannot be controlled. In the glare, differences between the newly erected towers are obscured—postmodern, ultramodern, 50, 70 or

SAIL AWAY: *The Burj tower-the world's tallest building-appears to be blowing in the wind*

PHOTOGRAPH BY AMBROISE TÉZENAS FOR NEWSWEEK

497

/496/ **NEW YORK**
DESIGN DIRECTOR: CHRIS DIXON
DIRECTOR OF PHOTOGRAPHY: JODY QUON
PHOTO EDITOR: CAROLINE SMITH
PHOTOGRAPHER: JAMES WOJCIK
EDITOR-IN-CHIEF: ADAM MOSS
PUBLISHER: NEW YORK MAGAZINE HOLDINGS, LLC
ISSUE: MAY 5, 2008
CATEGORY: PHOTO: FEATURE:
TRAVEL/FOOD/STILL LIFE (SINGLE/SPREAD)

/497/ **NEWSWEEK**
DESIGN DIRECTOR: AMID CAPECI
ART DIRECTOR: LEAH PURCELL
DIRECTOR OF PHOTOGRAPHY: SIMON BARNETT
PHOTO EDITOR: MARION DURAND
PHOTOGRAPHER: AMBROISE TÉZENAS — FOR NEWSWEEK
PUBLISHER: THE WASHINGTON POST CO.
ISSUE: APRIL 21-28, 2008
CATEGORY: PHOTO: FEATURE:
TRAVEL/FOOD/STILL LIFE (SINGLE/SPREAD)

498

499

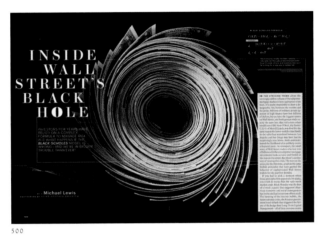

500

501

502

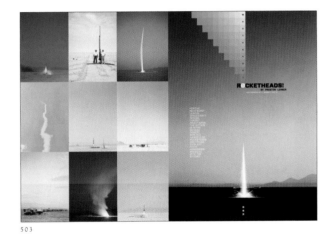

503

/498/ GOURMET
CREATIVE DIRECTOR: RICHARD FERRETTI
DESIGNER: ERIKA OLIVEIRA
PHOTO EDITOR: AMY KOBLENZER
PHOTOGRAPHER: BROWN W. CANNON III
EDITOR-IN-CHIEF: RUTH REICHL
PUBLISHER: CONDÉ NAST PUBLICATIONS, INC.
ISSUE: MARCH 2008
CATEGORY: PHOTO: FEATURE:
TRAVEL/FOOD/STILL LIFE (SINGLE/SPREAD)

/499/ GOURMET
CREATIVE DIRECTOR: RICHARD FERRETTI
DESIGNER: ERIKA OLIVEIRA
PHOTO EDITOR: AMY KOBLENZER
PHOTOGRAPHER: ORIE ICHIHASHI
EDITOR-IN-CHIEF: RUTH REICHL
PUBLISHER: CONDÉ NAST PUBLICATIONS, INC.
ISSUE: DECEMBER 2008
CATEGORY: PHOTO: FEATURE:
TRAVEL/FOOD/STILL LIFE (SINGLE/SPREAD)

/500/ CONDÉ NAST PORTFOLIO
DESIGN DIRECTOR: ROBERT PRIEST
ART DIRECTOR: GRACE LEE
DESIGNER: GRACE LEE
DIRECTOR OF PHOTOGRAPHY: LISA BERMAN
PHOTO EDITOR: SARAH WEISSMAN
PHOTOGRAPHER: CHRISTOPHER GRIFFITH
EDITOR-IN-CHIEF: JOANNE LIPMAN
PUBLISHER: CONDÉ NAST PUBLICATIONS INC.
ISSUE: MARCH 2008
CATEGORY: PHOTO: FEATURE:
TRAVEL/FOOD/STILL LIFE (SINGLE/SPREAD)

/501/ BEST LIFE
DESIGN DIRECTOR: BRANDON KAVULLA
DESIGNER: BRANDON KAVULLA
DIRECTOR OF PHOTOGRAPHY: RYAN CADIZ
PHOTO EDITOR: JEANNE GRAVES
PHOTOGRAPHER: GUIDO VITTI
PUBLISHER: RODALE INC.
ISSUE: OCTOBER 2008
CATEGORY: PHOTO: FEATURE:
TRAVEL/FOOD/STILL LIFE (SINGLE/SPREAD)

/502/ GOURMET
CREATIVE DIRECTOR: RICHARD FERRETTI
ART DIRECTOR: ERIKA OLIVEIRA
DESIGNER: ERIKA OLIVEIRA
PHOTO EDITOR: AMY KOBLENZER
PHOTOGRAPHER: ROMULO YANES
EDITOR-IN-CHIEF: RUTH REICHL
PUBLISHER: CONDÉ NAST PUBLICATIONS, INC.
ISSUE: DECEMBER 2008
CATEGORY: PHOTO: FEATURE:
TRAVEL/FOOD/STILL LIFE (SINGLE/SPREAD)

/503/ WIRED
CREATIVE DIRECTOR: SCOTT DADICH
DESIGN DIRECTOR: WYATT MITCHELL
ART DIRECTOR: CARL DETORRES
DESIGNER: WALTER C. BAUMANN
PHOTO EDITOR: CAROLYN RAUCH
PHOTOGRAPHER: JOHN BENNETT FITTS
PUBLISHER: CONDÉ NAST PUBLICATIONS, INC.
ISSUE: NOVEMBER 2008
CATEGORY: PHOTO: FEATURE:
TRAVEL/FOOD/STILL LIFE (SINGLE/SPREAD)

504

506

505

507

/504/ **NEW YORK**
DESIGN DIRECTOR: CHRIS DIXON
DIRECTOR OF PHOTOGRAPHY: JODY QUON
PHOTO EDITOR: ALEX POLLACK
PHOTOGRAPHER: JAMIE CHUNG
EDITOR-IN-CHIEF: ADAM MOSS
PUBLISHER: NEW YORK MAGAZINE HOLDINGS, LLC
ISSUE: MARCH 10, 2008
CATEGORY: PHOTO: FEATURE:
TRAVEL/FOOD/STILL LIFE (SINGLE/SPREAD)

/505/ **INSTYLE**
CREATIVE DIRECTOR: RINA STONE
ART DIRECTOR: JENIFER WALTER
DESIGNER: JENIFER WALTER
DIRECTOR OF PHOTOGRAPHY: MARIE SUTER
PHOTO EDITOR: MICHELLE THOMAS-CHIARAVALLE
PHOTOGRAPHER: RYANN COOLEY
MANAGING EDITOR: ARIEL FOXMAN
PUBLISHER: TIME INC.
ISSUE: NOVEMBER 2008
CATEGORY: PHOTO: FEATURE:
TRAVEL/FOOD/STILL LIFE (SINGLE/SPREAD)

/506/ **SAMVIRKE**
CREATIVE DIRECTOR: CHRISTEL FRYDKJÆR
ART DIRECTOR: CHRISTEL FRYDKJÆR
PHOTOGRAPHER: JAKOB CARLSEN
EDITOR-IN-CHIEF: PIA THORSEN JACOBSEN
PUBLISHER: SAMVIRKE / FDB
ISSUE: DECEMBER 2008
CATEGORY: PHOTO: FEATURE:
TRAVEL/FOOD/STILL LIFE (SINGLE/SPREAD)

/507/ **T, THE NEW YORK TIMES STYLE MAGAZINE**
CREATIVE DIRECTOR: JANET FROELICH
SENIOR ART DIRECTOR: DAVID SEBBAH
ART DIRECTOR: CHRISTOPHER MARTINEZ
SENIOR DESIGNER: ELIZABETH SPIRIDAKIS
DIRECTOR OF PHOTOGRAPHY: KATHY RYAN
SENIOR PHOTO EDITOR: JUDITH PUCKETT-RINELLA
PHOTOGRAPHER: NADAV KANDER
EDITOR-IN-CHIEF: STEFANO TONCHI
PUBLISHER: THE NEW YORK TIMES
ISSUE: MAY 18, 2008
CATEGORY: PHOTO: FEATURE:
TRAVEL/FOOD/STILL LIFE (SINGLE/SPREAD)

508

509

510

511

512

/508/ REAL SIMPLE
DESIGN DIRECTOR: ELLENE WUNDROK
ART DIRECTOR: HEATH BROCKWELL
DIRECTOR OF PHOTOGRAPHY: CASEY TIERNEY
PHOTO EDITOR: LINDSAY DOUGHERTY
PHOTOGRAPHER: ANNA WILLIAMS
PUBLISHER: TIME INC.
ISSUE: OCTOBER 2008
CATEGORY: PHOTO: FEATURE:
TRAVEL/FOOD/STILL LIFE (SINGLE/SPREAD)

/509/ GARDEN & GUN
ART DIRECTOR: MARSHALL MCKINNEY
DESIGNER: RICHIE SWANN
DIRECTOR OF PHOTOGRAPHY:
MAGGIE BRETT KENNEDY
PHOTOGRAPHER: PETER FRANK EDWARDS
ISSUE: SEPTEMBER/OCTOBER 2008
CATEGORY: PHOTO: FEATURE:
TRAVEL/FOOD/STILL LIFE (SINGLE/SPREAD)

/510/ MEN'S HEALTH
DESIGN DIRECTOR: GEORGE KARABOTSOS
ART DIRECTORS: GEORGE KARABOTSOS, JOHN DIXON
DESIGNERS: GEORGE KARABOTSOS, JOHN DIXON
DIRECTOR OF PHOTOGRAPHY: BRENDA MILLIS
PHOTO EDITOR: BRENDA MILLIS
PHOTOGRAPHER: NIGEL COX
PUBLISHER: RODALE INC.
ISSUE: SEPTEMBER 2008
CATEGORY: PHOTO: FEATURE:
TRAVEL/FOOD/STILL LIFE (SINGLE/SPREAD)

/511/ CONDÉ NAST PORTFOLIO
DESIGN DIRECTOR: ROBERT PRIEST
ART DIRECTOR: GRACE LEE
DESIGNER: GRACE LEE
DIRECTOR OF PHOTOGRAPHY: LISA BERMAN
PHOTO EDITOR: JOHN TOOLAN
PHOTOGRAPHER: SUE TALLON
EDITOR-IN-CHIEF: JOANNE LIPMAN
PUBLISHER: CONDÉ NAST PUBLICATIONS INC.
ISSUE: FEBRUARY 2008
CATEGORY: PHOTO: FEATURE:
TRAVEL/FOOD/STILL LIFE (SINGLE/SPREAD)

/512/ COOKIE
DESIGN DIRECTOR: KIRBY RODRIGUEZ
ART DIRECTOR: ALEX GROSSMAN
DESIGNERS: NICOLETTE BERTHELOT,
SHANNA GREENBERG
PHOTO EDITOR: DARRICK HARRIS
ASSOCIATE PHOTO EDITOR: LINDA DENAHAN
ASSISTANT PHOTO EDITOR: AJA NUZZI
PHOTOGRAPHER: MIKKEL VANG
PUBLISHER: CONDÉ NAST PUBLICATIONS INC.
ISSUE: DECEMBER 2008/JANUARY 2009
CATEGORY: PHOTO: FEATURE:
TRAVEL/FOOD/STILL LIFE (SINGLE/SPREAD)

513

513

/513/ **BARCELONA**
CREATIVE DIRECTORS: LOUIS-CHARLES TIAR, DIANA KLEIN / DESIGNER: QUIQUE CIRIA / PHOTOGRAPHER: J.C. DE MARCOS / EDITOR-IN-CHIEF: MÓNICA ESCUDERO
PUBLISHER: REVISTAS EXCLUSIVAS S.L. / ISSUE: FALL 2008/WINTER 2009 / CATEGORY: PHOTO: FEATURE: TRAVEL/FOOD/STILL LIFE (STORY)

FLYING

Kodak 100TMX

A QUEEN IN FLIGHT, MAGNIFICATION 16X.

AWAY

I'VE LOVED HONEYBEES SINCE I WAS NINE, WHEN I BOUGHT MY VERY
FIRST HIVE. LITTLE DID I KNOW THAT ONE DAY I'D WITNESS THE SUDDEN AND CATASTROPHIC
DISAPPEARANCE OF THESE TREASURED INSECTS.

TEXT AND PHOTOGRAPHS BY DAN WINTERS

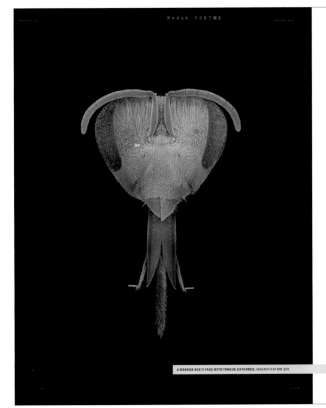

Kodak 100TMX

A WORKER BEE'S FACE WITH TONGUE EXTENDED, MAGNIFICATION 22X.

H oneybees are one of the most important pollinators on the planet. Their labor singularly accounts for up to one third of our nation's annual food supply, contributing about $15 billion in added value to vegetable, fruit, fiber, and nut harvests. In Texas, about ninety crops— melons, cucumbers, apples, cotton, canola, citrus, among others—owe their well-being to the honeybee. For commercial beekeepers, who truck their colonies thousands of miles cross-country, it's this pollination process, much more than honey harvesting, that constitutes their livelihood: A beekeeper can earn upward of $150 per hive for leaving his bees at a farm or orchard for six weeks to pollinate the crops.

But recently our agriculture and apiary industries have been hit with a true crisis: The bees are leaving. Entire colonies across the U.S. started vanishing as early as 2006—commercial operations in more than 22 states have reported losses of as much as 75 percent of their hives—and no one has an explanation. The phenomenon, dubbed colony collapse disorder, occurs when the female worker bees of a seemingly healthy hive abruptly disappear. There are competing theories about what causes CCD: malnutrition, pesticides, modern beekeeping practices (such as long-distance transportation of bees and the administering of antibiotics to the hives), genetically modified crops, mites. But the truth is that no one knows. The scientific community is aggressively searching for clues, and in May, Congress finally set aside some money for CCD research in its farm bill. With no solution in sight, the consequences to the country's food production could well be devastating.

Texas's commercial beekeepers—there are about 250 of them—have been affected too, and it's against this dire backdrop that I decided to focus my photographic energies on the honeybee. I have a personal connection to bees: I began raising them at age nine as one of my 4-H projects. I paid $10 for my first hive in 1971, and by the time I graduated from high school, I had an apiary of a dozen or so hives. I raised my bees purely for honey and usually placed the hives among the citrus groves of my native Southern California. In the winter, as their food supply dwindled, I'd feed the colonies sugar water to sustain them until spring.

I'll never forget the thrill of inspecting my hive boxes and finding the queen, distinguishable by her long abdomen, surrounded by workers who tended to her every need while she tirelessly laid eggs to keep the colony alive. While a worker bee's life span ranges from four weeks to six months, a queen can live for five years or more. She can lay as many as 2,500 eggs a day, or 2 million in her lifetime. A healthy hive has a population of approximately 60,000 bees, all female, save for a few hundred males, called drones. The drones are much larger than the workers, and their sole purpose is to fertilize the queen. Rather than forage for food, they live off the honey produced by the workers. Once their duties are done, they are often evicted from the hive to die alone (those who refuse to leave may be stung to death).

I have a deep admiration and respect for honeybees, as well as insects in general. In fact, had my love of photography not won out, I would have pursued a career in entomology. This series of photographs combines these two passions. Working under the guidance of biologist Dwight Romanovicz, and with specimens I bought from a Georgia beekeeper, I made the images in June and July of this year using a scanning electron microscope at the Institute for Cellular and Molecular Biology, at the University of Texas at Austin. After soaking the bees in ethanol, I employed magnification and micromanipulators—and often as many as twenty pins—to mount them; I then painted each tiny insect with a thin layer of platinum so that it could withstand the microscope's powerful electron beam. This coating is what gives the bees their luminous appearance.

Given both the technology and the specimens' fragility, the project required hundreds of hours to complete. But they were hours well spent; our honeybees deserve such full attention.

October 2008 | **149**

/514/ **TEXAS MONTHLY**
ART DIRECTOR: T.J. TUCKER / DESIGNER: T.J. TUCKER / PHOTO EDITOR: LESLIE BALDWIN / PHOTOGRAPHER: DAN WINTERS / PUBLISHER: EMMIS COMMUNICATIONS CORP.
ISSUE: OCTOBER 2008 / CATEGORY: PHOTO: FEATURE: TRAVEL/FOOD/STILL LIFE (STORY)

515

515

516

516

517

517

/515/ **INTERIOR DESIGN**
CREATIVE DIRECTOR: CINDY ALLEN
ART DIRECTOR: MARINO ZULLICH
DESIGNERS: ZIGENG LI, KARLA LIMA,
GIANNINA MACIAS
PHOTO EDITOR: HELENE OBERMAN
PUBLISHER: REED BUSINESS INFORMATION
ISSUE: DECEMBER 2008
CATEGORY: PHOTO: FEATURE:
TRAVEL/FOOD/STILL LIFE (STORY)

/516/ **BON APPÉTIT**
DESIGN DIRECTOR: MATTHEW LENNING
ART DIRECTOR: ROBERT FESTINO
PHOTO EDITOR: LIZ MATHEWS
PHOTOGRAPHER: JAMES WOJCIK
EDITOR-IN-CHIEF: BARBARA FAIRCHILD
PUBLISHER: CONDÉ NAST PUBLICATIONS, INC.
ISSUE: JULY 2008
CATEGORY: PHOTO: FEATURE:
TRAVEL/FOOD/STILL LIFE (STORY)

/517/ **T, THE NEW YORK TIMES STYLE MAGAZINE**
CREATIVE DIRECTOR: JANET FROELICH
SENIOR ART DIRECTOR: DAVID SEBBAH
ART DIRECTOR: CHRISTOPHER MARTINEZ
SENIOR DESIGNER: ELIZABETH SPIRIDAKIS
DIRECTOR OF PHOTOGRAPHY: KATHY RYAN
PHOTO EDITOR: JENNIFER PASTORE
PHOTOGRAPHER: OLAF OTTO BECKER
EDITOR-IN-CHIEF: STEFANO TONCHI
PUBLISHER: THE NEW YORK TIMES
ISSUE: SEPTEMBER 21, 2008
CATEGORY: PHOTO: FEATURE: TRAVEL/FOOD/STILL
LIFE (STORY)

518

518

519

519

520

520

/518/ **FOUR SEASONS MAGAZINE**
DESIGN DIRECTOR: JAIMEY EASLER
ART DIRECTOR: JEFF BEAMER
DESIGNER: JAIMEY EASLER
PHOTOGRAPHER: JOSON
STUDIO: PACE COMMUNICATIONS
PUBLISHER: PACE COMMUNICATIONS
CLIENT: FOUR SEASONS HOTELS AND RESORTS
ISSUE: SPRING 2008
CATEGORY: PHOTO: FEATURE:
TRAVEL/FOOD/STILL LIFE (STORY)

/519/ **GOURMET**
CREATIVE DIRECTOR: RICHARD FERRETTI
ART DIRECTOR: ERIKA OLIVEIRA
DESIGNER: ERIKA OLIVEIRA
PHOTO EDITOR: AMY KOBLENZER
PHOTOGRAPHER: JOHN KERNICK
EDITOR-IN-CHIEF: RUTH REICHL
PUBLISHER: CONDÉ NAST PUBLICATIONS, INC.
ISSUE: OCTOBER 2008
CATEGORY: PHOTO: FEATURE:
TRAVEL/FOOD/STILL LIFE (STORY)

/520/ **LIFE & STYLE**
CREATIVE DIRECTOR: GUILLERMO CABALLERO
ART DIRECTOR: JULIO CONTRERAS
DESIGNERS: MANUELA SÁNCHEZ, IXEL OSARIO,
MARA LILIANA GONZÁLEZ
PHOTO EDITOR: JACOBO BRAUN
PHOTOGRAPHER: AGNÈS DHERBEYS
PUBLISHER: GRUPO EDITORIAL EXPANSIÓN
ISSUE: JUNE 2008
CATEGORY: PHOTO: FEATURE:
TRAVEL/FOOD/STILL LIFE (STORY)

521

521

/521/ **GOURMET**
CREATIVE DIRECTOR: RICHARD FERRETTI
ART DIRECTORS: RICHARD FERRETTI,
ERIKA OLIVEIRA
DESIGNER: ERIKA OLIVEIRA
PHOTO EDITOR: AMY KOBLENZER
PHOTOGRAPHER: WILLIAM ABRANOWICZ
EDITOR-IN-CHIEF: RUTH REICHL
PUBLISHER: CONDÉ NAST PUBLICATIONS, INC.
ISSUE: FEBRUARY 2008
CATEGORY: PHOTO: FEATURE:
TRAVEL/FOOD/STILL LIFE (STORY)

522

522

523

523

524

/522/ **DETAILS**
CREATIVE DIRECTOR: ROCKWELL HARWOOD
ART DIRECTOR: ANDRE JOINTE
DESIGNER: CHRIS SEGEDY
SENIOR PHOTO EDITOR: HALI TARA FELDMAN
PHOTO EDITORS: CHANDRA GLICK, ALEX GHEZ
PHOTOGRAPHER: JULIANA SOHN
EDITOR-IN-CHIEF: DANIEL PERES
PUBLISHER: CONDÉ NAST PUBLICATIONS
ISSUE: OCTOBER 2008
CATEGORY: DESIGN: FEATURE: TRAVEL/FOOD/STILL LIFE (STORY)

/523/ **FOOD & WINE**
CREATIVE DIRECTOR: STEPHEN SCOBLE
ART DIRECTORS: PATRICIA SANCHEZ, COURTNEY WADDELL ECKERSLEY
DESIGNER: SANDRA GARCIA
DIRECTOR OF PHOTOGRAPHY: FREDRIKA STJÄRNE
PHOTOGRAPHER: QUENTIN BACON
PUBLISHER: AMERICAN EXPRESS PUBLISHING
ISSUE: AUGUST 2008
CATEGORY: PHOTO: FEATURE: TRAVEL/FOOD/STILL LIFE (STORY)

/524/ **MORE**
CREATIVE DIRECTOR: DEBRA BISHOP
DESIGNER: DEBRA BISHOP
DIRECTOR OF PHOTOGRAPHY: KAREN FRANK
PHOTO EDITORS: DAISY CAJAS, NATALIE GIALLUCA, ALLISON CHIN
PHOTOGRAPHER: BROWN W. CANNON III
PUBLISHER: MEREDITH CORPORATION
ISSUE: OCTOBER 2008
CATEGORY: PHOTO: FEATURE: TRAVEL/FOOD/STILL LIFE (STORY)

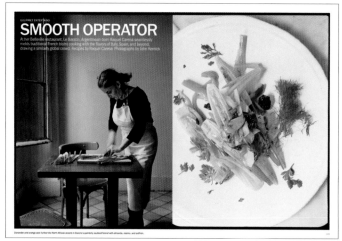

525

525

526

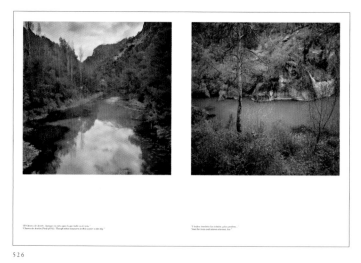

526

527

527

/525/ **GOURMET**
CREATIVE DIRECTOR: RICHARD FERRETTI
ART DIRECTOR: ERIKA OLIVEIRA
DESIGNER: ERIKA OLIVEIRA
PHOTO EDITOR: AMY KOBLENZER
PHOTOGRAPHER: JOHN KERNICK
EDITOR-IN-CHIEF: RUTH REICHL
PUBLISHER: CONDÉ NAST PUBLICATIONS, INC.
ISSUE: SEPTEMBER 2008
CATEGORY: PHOTO: FEATURE:
TRAVEL/FOOD/STILL LIFE (STORY)

/526/ **ROOM**
CREATIVE DIRECTOR: RICARDO FERICHE
ART DIRECTOR: OSCAR ARAGÓN
DESIGNERS: CÉLINE ROBERT, VICENS CASTELLTORT
PHOTO EDITOR: AMPARO ESCOBEDO
PHOTOGRAPHER: JUAN MANUEL CASTRO PRIETO
STUDIO: FERICHE & BLACK
EDITOR-IN-CHIEF: TOÑO ANGULO DANERI
PUBLISHER: LA FABRICA
CLIENT: LA FABRICA
ISSUE: APRIL 2008
CATEGORY: PHOTO: FEATURE:
TRAVEL/FOOD/STILL LIFE (STORY)

/527/ **LIFE & STYLE**
CREATIVE DIRECTOR: GUILLERMO CABALLERO
ART DIRECTOR: JULIO CONTRERAS
DESIGNERS: MANUELA SÁNCHEZ, IXEL OSARIO,
MARA LILIANA GONZÁLEZ
PHOTOGRAPHER: THOMAS KELLNER
PUBLISHER: GRUPO EDITORIAL EXPANSIÓN
ISSUE: AUGUST 2008
CATEGORY: PHOTO: FEATURE:
TRAVEL/FOOD/STILL LIFE (STORY)

+1.000.000m²
SHOPPING
Tekst og foto: Jeppe Carlsen

528

+1.000.000m² shopping

Se flere billeder i soundslide på **Samvirke.dk**

Yiwu har et indbyggertal på 1.000.000. Med så få indbyggere er Yiwu en lille by efter kinesisk målestok, men ikke desto mindre har den markeret sig på det store kinesiske landkort som hovedstaden for handel og eksport, og har i de sidste seks år ligget som nummer et på Kinas top-10-liste over markeder.

En forretningsmand med arabiske træk kigger nøje på en kuglepen i prangende guld, han sukker og lægger den derefter fra sig igen, kun for at fortsætte videre til den næste kuglepennebutik længere nede ad gangen. En højlydt diskussion fra en af de mange butikker bryder stilheden et kort øjeblik, men ingen ænser det.

528

/528/ SAMVIRKE
CREATIVE DIRECTOR: JONATHAN GROES JUNGLØV / ART DIRECTOR: JONATHAN GROES JUNGLØV / PHOTOGRAPHER: JEPPE CARLSEN
EDITOR-IN-CHIEF: PIA THORSEN JACOBSEN / PUBLISHER: SAMVIRKE/FDB / ISSUE: OCTOBER 2008 / CATEGORY: PHOTO: FEATURE: TRAVEL/FOOD/STILL LIFE (STORY)

529

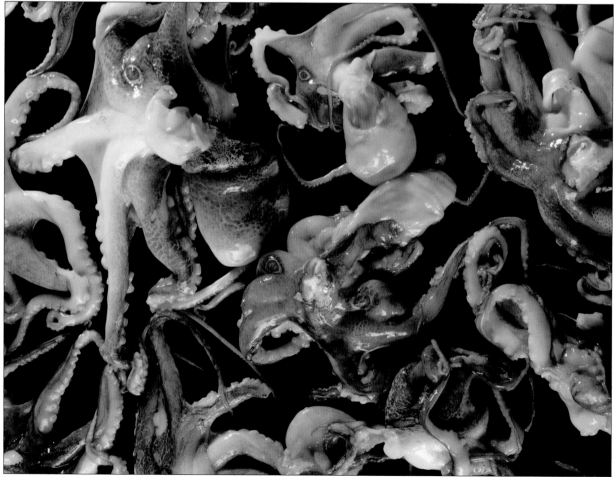

529

THE SEA INSIDE

america's foodiest small town

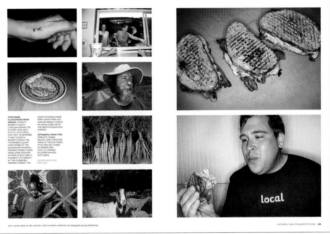

KOSHER

Wars

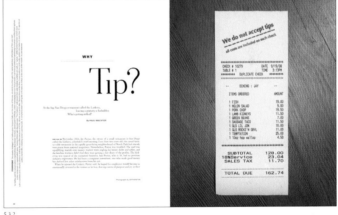

WHY

Tip?

/529/ **(T)HERE**
CREATIVE DIRECTOR: CHRISTOPHER WIELICZKO
DESIGN DIRECTOR: JASON MAKOWSKI
PHOTOGRAPHER: MARCUS BROOKS
PUBLISHER: THERE MEDIA, INC.
ISSUE: VOLUME 10, SPRING 2008
CATEGORY: PHOTO: FEATURE:
TRAVEL/FOOD/STILL LIFE (STORY)

/530/ **T, THE NEW YORK TIMES STYLE MAGAZINE**
CREATIVE DIRECTOR: JANET FROELICH
SENIOR ART DIRECTOR: DAVID SEBBAH
ART DIRECTOR: CHRISTOPHER MARTINEZ
SENIOR DESIGNER: ELIZABETH SPIRIDAKIS
DIRECTOR OF PHOTOGRAPHY: KATHY RYAN
SENIOR PHOTO EDITOR: JUDITH PUCKETT-RINELLA
PHOTOGRAPHER: HARF ZIMMERMAN
EDITOR-IN-CHIEF: STEFANO TONCHI
PUBLISHER: THE NEW YORK TIMES
ISSUE: NOVEMBER 16, 2008
CATEGORY: PHOTO: FEATURE:
TRAVEL/FOOD/STILL LIFE (STORY)

/531/ **BON APPÉTIT**
DESIGN DIRECTOR: MATTHEW LENNING
ART DIRECTORS: ROBERT FESTINO, TOM O'QUINN
PHOTO EDITOR: BAILEY FRANKLIN
PHOTOGRAPHER: SIAN KENNEDY
EDITOR-IN-CHIEF: BARBARA FAIRCHILD
PUBLISHER: CONDÉ NAST PUBLICATIONS, INC.
ISSUE: OCTOBER 2008
CATEGORY: PHOTO: FEATURE:
TRAVEL/FOOD/STILL LIFE (STORY)

/532/ **THE NEW YORK TIMES MAGAZINE**
CREATIVE DIRECTOR: JANET FROELICH
ART DIRECTOR: AREM DUPLESSIS
DEPUTY ART DIRECTOR: GAIL BICHLER
DESIGNERS: CATHERINE GILMORE-BARNES, IAN ALLEN
DIRECTOR OF PHOTOGRAPHY: KATHY RYAN
PHOTO EDITOR: JOANNA MILTER
EDITOR-IN-CHIEF: GERRY MARZORATI
PUBLISHER: THE NEW YORK TIMES
ISSUE: OCTOBER 12, 2008
CATEGORY: PHOTO: FEATURE:
TRAVEL/FOOD/STILL LIFE (STORY)

SARAH SILVERMAN

Age: 37
The Funny Honey

The comic, who dates Jimmy Kimmel (and, um, paired up with Matt Damon), gives insight into her allure.

❝ I grew up in New Hampshire and everyone was very blonde and people would be like, 'Are you from New York?' I was just hairy! I used to bleach my arm hair. And it hurt so much. You don't know suffering for beauty until you're sitting on the floor of your bathroom, weeping, with white cream on your arms.❞

❝ I was a late-developer. I didn't even get my period until I was 17%. I want that in PEOPLE magazine!❞

❝ I'm not a fancy person, but I do always wash my face twice, at night.❞

❝ Thank God for Jimmy, because all the things I don't like about myself are the things that he likes the most. Like my inner thigh fat. He grabs it and he's like, 'I love this!'❞

❝ It sounds corny, but when I'm with my comedian friends, I just feel good. I'm lucky because I feel way more beautiful than I really am.❞

PHOTOGRAPH BY ROBERT TRACHTENBERG

[XIV]

LEFTOVERS

535

535

536

536

537

537

/533/ PEOPLE
DESIGN DIRECTOR: SARA WILLIAMS
DESIGNER: KIER NOVESKY
DIRECTOR OF PHOTOGRAPHY: CHRIS DOUGHERTY
PHOTO EDITOR: BRENNA BRITTON
PHOTOGRAPHER: ROBERT TRACHTENBERG
EDITOR-IN-CHIEF: LARRY HACKETT
PUBLISHER: TIME INC.
ISSUE: MAY 12, 2008
CATEGORY: PHOTO: FEATURE:
FASHION/BEAUTY (SINGLE/SPREAD)

/534/ SHUFTI
CREATIVE DIRECTOR: SEAN KENNEDY SANTOS
ART DIRECTOR: SEAN KENNEDY SANTOS
DESIGNERS: PHIL MORRISON, SI BILLAM, JON BANKS
PHOTOGRAPHER: SEAN KENNEDY SANTOS
EDITOR-IN-CHIEF: MATT AUSTIN
PUBLISHER: VAST AGENCY UK
ISSUE: OCTOBER 2008
CATEGORY: PHOTO: FEATURE:
FASHION/BEAUTY (SINGLE/SPREAD)

/535/ W
CREATIVE DIRECTOR: DENNIS FREEDMAN
DESIGN DIRECTOR: EDWARD LEIDA
ART DIRECTOR: NATHALIE KIRSHEH
DESIGNER: EDWARD LEIDA
PHOTOGRAPHER: MERT ALAS, MARCUS PIGGOTT
PUBLISHER: CONDÉ NAST PUBLICATIONS INC.
ISSUE: AUGUST 2008
CATEGORY: PHOTO: FEATURE:
FASHION/BEAUTY (STORY)

/536/ DETAILS
CREATIVE DIRECTOR: ROCKWELL HARWOOD
ART DIRECTOR: ANDRE JOINTE
SENIOR PHOTO EDITOR: HALI TARA FELDMAN
PHOTOGRAPHER: CASS BIRD
EDITOR-IN-CHIEF: DANIEL PERES
PUBLISHER: CONDÉ NAST PUBLICATIONS
ISSUE: NOVEMBER 2008
CATEGORY: PHOTO: FEATURE:
FASHION/BEAUTY (STORY)

/537/ T, THE NEW YORK TIMES STYLE MAGAZINE
CREATIVE DIRECTOR: JANET FROELICH
SENIOR ART DIRECTOR: DAVID SEBBAH
ART DIRECTOR: CHRISTOPHER MARTINEZ
SENIOR DESIGNER: ELIZABETH SPIRIDAKIS
DIRECTOR OF PHOTOGRAPHY: KATHY RYAN
PHOTO EDITOR: JENNIFER PASTORE
PHOTOGRAPHER: HORACIO SALINAS
EDITOR-IN-CHIEF: STEFANO TONCHI
PUBLISHER: THE NEW YORK TIMES
ISSUE: SEPTEMBER 7, 2008
CATEGORY: PHOTO: FEATURE:
FASHION/BEAUTY (STORY)

538

538

539

539

540

540

/538/ **T, THE NEW YORK TIMES STYLE MAGAZINE**
CREATIVE DIRECTOR: JANET FROELICH
SENIOR ART DIRECTOR: DAVID SEBBAH
ART DIRECTOR: CHRISTOPHER MARTINEZ
SENIOR DESIGNER: ELIZABETH SPIRIDAKIS
DIRECTOR OF PHOTOGRAPHY: KATHY RYAN
SENIOR PHOTO EDITOR: JUDITH PUCKETT-RINELLA
PHOTOGRAPHER: FABIEN BARON
EDITOR-IN-CHIEF: STEFANO TONCHI
PUBLISHER: THE NEW YORK TIMES
ISSUE: FEBRUARY 24, 2008
CATEGORY: PHOTO: FEATURE:
FASHION/BEAUTY (STORY)

/539/ **W**
CREATIVE DIRECTOR: DENNIS FREEDMAN
DESIGN DIRECTOR: EDWARD LEIDA
ART DIRECTOR: NATHALIE KIRSHEH
PHOTOGRAPHERS: MERT ALAS, MARCUS PIGGOTT
PUBLISHER: CONDÉ NAST PUBLICATIONS INC.
ISSUE: SEPTEMBER 2008
CATEGORY: PHOTO: FEATURE:
FASHION/BEAUTY (STORY)

/540/ **W**
CREATIVE DIRECTOR: DENNIS FREEDMAN
DESIGN DIRECTOR: EDWARD LEIDA
ART DIRECTOR: NATHALIE KIRSHEH
DESIGNER: NATHALIE KIRSHEH
PHOTOGRAPHER: BRUCE WEBER
PUBLISHER: CONDÉ NAST PUBLICATIONS INC.
ISSUE: JULY 2008
CATEGORY: PHOTO: FEATURE:
FASHION/BEAUTY (STORY)

541

541

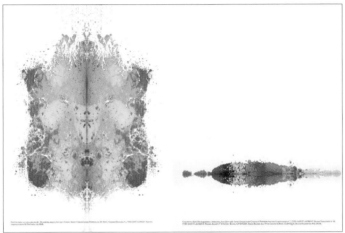

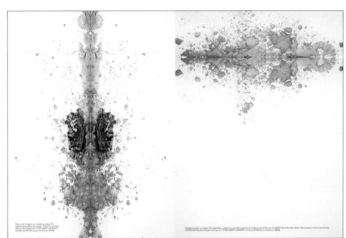

542

542

543

543

/541/ T, THE NEW YORK TIMES STYLE MAGAZINE
CREATIVE DIRECTOR: JANET FROELICH
SENIOR ART DIRECTOR: DAVID SEBBAH
ART DIRECTOR: CHRISTOPHER MARTINEZ
SENIOR DESIGNER: ELIZABETH SPIRIDAKIS
DIRECTOR OF PHOTOGRAPHY: KATHY RYAN
SENIOR PHOTO EDITOR: JUDITH PUCKETT-RINELLA
PHOTOGRAPHER: RAYMOND MEIER
EDITOR-IN-CHIEF: STEFANO TONCHI
PUBLISHER: THE NEW YORK TIMES
ISSUE: SEPTEMBER 21, 2008
CATEGORY: PHOTO: FEATURE:
FASHION/BEAUTY (STORY)

/542/ MADRIZ
CREATIVE DIRECTOR: LOUIS-CHARLES TIAR
DESIGNERS: ABRIL Y DE LA CARRERA,
GRACIELA ARTIGA
PHOTOGRAPHER: KENJI TOMA
PUBLISHER: REVISTAS EXCLUSIVAS S.L.
ISSUE: FALL 2007 / WINTER 2008
CATEGORY: PHOTO: FEATURE:
FASHION/BEAUTY (STORY)

/543/ BARCELONA
CREATIVE DIRECTORS:
LOUIS-CHARLES TIAR, DIANA KLEIN
DESIGNER: QUIQUE CIRIA
PHOTOGRAPHER: KENJI TOMA
EDITOR-IN-CHIEF: MÓNICA ESCUDERO
PUBLISHER: REVISTAS EXCLUSIVAS S.L.
ISSUE: FALL 2008 / WINTER 2009
CATEGORY: PHOTO: FEATURE:
FASHION/BEAUTY (STORY)

544

544

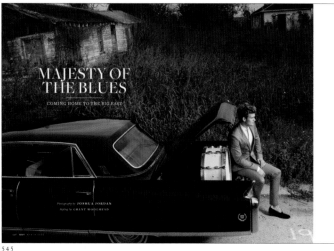

545

545

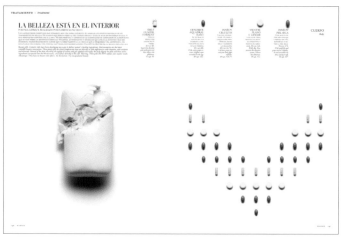

546

546

/544/ **GQ**
DESIGN DIRECTOR: FRED WOODWARD
ART DIRECTOR: ANTON IOUKHNOVETS
DESIGNER: ANTON IOUKHNOVETS
DIRECTOR OF PHOTOGRAPHY: DORA SOMOSI
PHOTOGRAPHER: PEGGY SIROTA
CREATIVE DIRECTOR, FASHION: JIM MOORE
EDITOR-IN-CHIEF: JIM NELSON
PUBLISHER: CONDÉ NAST PUBLICATIONS INC.
ISSUE: JANUARY 2008
CATEGORY: PHOTO: FEATURE:
FASHION/BEAUTY (STORY)

/545/ **OUT**
CREATIVE DIRECTOR: DAVID GRAY
ART DIRECTOR: NICK VOGELSON
DESIGNER: JASON SELDON
DIRECTOR OF PHOTOGRAPHY: JO-EY TANG
PHOTO EDITOR: JULIEN TOMASELLO
PHOTOGRAPHER: JOSHUA JORDAN
STYLIST: BRANT WOOLHEAD
EDITOR-IN-CHIEF: AARON HICKLIN
PUBLISHER: REGENT MEDIA
ISSUE: MARCH 2008
CATEGORY: PHOTO: FEATURE:
FASHION/BEAUTY (STORY)

/546/ **MADRIZ**
CREATIVE DIRECTOR: LOUIS-CHARLES TIAR
ART DIRECTOR: SONIA BILBAO
PHOTOGRAPHER: PAUL LEPREUX
PUBLISHER: REVISTAS EXCLUSIVAS S.L.
ISSUE: FALL 2008/WINTER 2009
CATEGORY: PHOTO: FEATURE:
FASHION/BEAUTY (STORY)

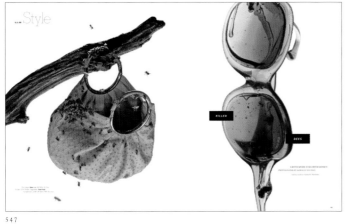

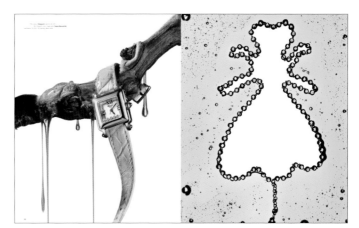

547

547

548

548

/547/ **THE NEW YORK TIMES MAGAZINE**
CREATIVE DIRECTOR: JANET FROELICH
ART DIRECTOR: AREM DUPLESSIS
DEPUTY ART DIRECTOR: GAIL BICHLER
DESIGNER: GAIL BICHLER
PHOTOGRAPHER: HORACIO SALINAS
FASHION EDITOR: KARLA M. MARTINEZ
EDITOR-IN-CHIEF: GERRY MARZORATI
PUBLISHER: THE NEW YORK TIMES
ISSUE: MAY 11, 2008
CATEGORY: PHOTO: FEATURE:
FASHION/BEAUTY (STORY)

/548/ **THE NEW YORK TIMES MAGAZINE**
CREATIVE DIRECTOR: JANET FROELICH
ART DIRECTOR: AREM DUPLESSIS
DEPUTY ART DIRECTOR: GAIL BICHLER
DESIGNER: NANCY HARRIS ROUEMY
PHOTOGRAPHER: JEAN-BAPTISTE MONDINO
FASHION EDITOR: ANNE CHRISTENSEN
EDITOR-IN-CHIEF: GERRY MARZORATI
PUBLISHER: THE NEW YORK TIMES
ISSUE: AUGUST 10, 2008
CATEGORY: PHOTO: FEATURE:
FASHION/BEAUTY (STORY)

549

549

550

550

551

551

/549/ LATINA
CREATIVE DIRECTOR: FLORIAN BACHLEDA
DESIGN DIRECTOR: DENISE SEE
DESIGNER: PHOEBE FLYNN RICH
DIRECTOR OF PHOTOGRAPHY: GEORGE PITTS
PHOTO EDITOR: JENNIFER SARGENT
PHOTOGRAPHER: DAVID ROEMER
STUDIO: FB DESIGN
EDITOR-IN-CHIEF: MIMI VALDÉS RYAN
PUBLISHER: LATINA MEDIA VENTURES
ISSUE: OCTOBER 2008
CATEGORY: PHOTO: FEATURE:
FASHION/BEAUTY (STORY)

/550/ COOKIE
DESIGN DIRECTOR: KIRBY RODRIGUEZ
ART DIRECTOR: ALEX GROSSMAN
DESIGNERS: NICOLETTE BERTHELOT,
SHANNA GREENBERG
PHOTO EDITOR: DARRICK HARRIS
ASSOCIATE PHOTO EDITOR: LINDA DENAHAN
ASSISTANT PHOTO EDITOR: AJA NUZZI
PHOTOGRAPHER: NICK AND CHLOE
PUBLISHER: CONDÉ NAST PUBLICATIONS INC.
ISSUE: SEPTEMBER 2008
CATEGORY: PHOTO: FEATURE:
FASHION/BEAUTY (STORY)

/551/ NEW YORK
DESIGN DIRECTOR: CHRIS DIXON
DIRECTOR OF PHOTOGRAPHY: JODY QUON
PHOTOGRAPHER: HORACIO SALINAS
FASHION EDITOR: HARRIET MAYS POWELL
EDITOR-IN-CHIEF: ADAM MOSS
PUBLISHER: NEW YORK MAGAZINE HOLDINGS, LLC
ISSUE: AUGUST 25, 2008
CATEGORY: PHOTO: FEATURE:
FASHION/BEAUTY (STORY)

552

552

553

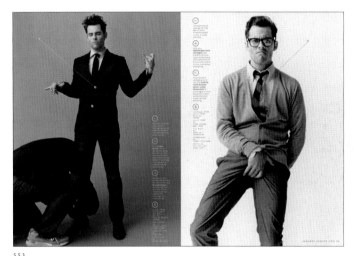

553

554

554

/552/ GQ
DESIGN DIRECTOR: FRED WOODWARD
ART DIRECTOR: ANTON IOUKHNOVETS
DIRECTOR OF PHOTOGRAPHY: DORA SOMOSI
PHOTOGRAPHER: PEGGY SIROTA
CREATIVE DIRECTOR, FASHION: JIM MOORE
EDITOR-IN-CHIEF: JIM NELSON
PUBLISHER: CONDÉ NAST PUBLICATIONS INC.
ISSUE: AUGUST 2008
CATEGORY: PHOTO: FEATURE:
FASHION/BEAUTY (STORY)

/553/ GQ
DESIGN DIRECTOR: FRED WOODWARD
ART DIRECTOR: ANTON IOUKHNOVETS
DIRECTOR OF PHOTOGRAPHY: DORA SOMOSI
PHOTOGRAPHER: PEGGY SIROTA
CREATIVE DIRECTOR, FASHION: JIM MOORE
EDITOR-IN-CHIEF: JIM NELSON
PUBLISHER: CONDÉ NAST PUBLICATIONS INC.
ISSUE: JANUARY 2008
CATEGORY: PHOTO: FEATURE:
FASHION/BEAUTY (STORY)

/554/ T, THE NEW YORK TIMES STYLE MAGAZINE
CREATIVE DIRECTOR: JANET FROELICH
SENIOR ART DIRECTOR: DAVID SEBBAH
ART DIRECTOR: CHRISTOPHER MARTINEZ
SENIOR DESIGNER: ELIZABETH SPIRIDAKIS
DIRECTOR OF PHOTOGRAPHY: KATHY RYAN
SENIOR PHOTO EDITOR: JUDITH PUCKETT-RINELLA
PHOTOGRAPHER: RAYMOND MEIER
EDITOR-IN-CHIEF: STEFANO TONCHI
PUBLISHER: THE NEW YORK TIMES
ISSUE: NOVEMBER 16, 2008
CATEGORY: PHOTO: FEATURE:
FASHION/BEAUTY (STORY)

555

555

556

556

557

557

/555/ **GQ**
DESIGN DIRECTOR: FRED WOODWARD
ART DIRECTOR: ANTON IOUKHNOVETS
DIRECTOR OF PHOTOGRAPHY: DORA SOMOSI
PHOTOGRAPHER: CARTER SMITH
EDITOR-IN-CHIEF: JIM NELSON
PUBLISHER: CONDÉ NAST PUBLICATIONS INC.
ISSUE: AUGUST 2008
CATEGORY: PHOTO: FEATURE:
FASHION/BEAUTY (STORY)

/556/ **W**
CREATIVE DIRECTOR: DENNIS FREEDMAN
DESIGN DIRECTOR: EDWARD LEIDA
ART DIRECTOR: NATHALIE KIRSHEH
PHOTOGRAPHER: JEURGEN TELLER
PUBLISHER: CONDÉ NAST PUBLICATIONS INC.
ISSUE: SEPTEMBER 2008
CATEGORY: PHOTO: FEATURE:
FASHION/BEAUTY (STORY)

/557/ **MEN'S JOURNAL**
CREATIVE DIRECTOR: PAUL MARTINEZ
DESIGNER: PAUL MARTINEZ
DIRECTOR OF PHOTOGRAPHY: MICHELLE WOLFE
PHOTOGRAPHER: ALAN MAHON
EDITOR-IN-CHIEF: JANN S. WENNER
PUBLISHER: WENNER MEDIA LLC
ISSUE: APRIL 2008
CATEGORY: PHOTO: FEATURE:
FASHION/BEAUTY (STORY)

/558/ **LATINA**
CREATIVE DIRECTOR: FLORIAN BACHLEDA
DESIGN DIRECTOR: DENISE SEE
DESIGNERS: PHOEBE FLYNN RICH, GRACE MARTINEZ
DIRECTOR OF PHOTOGRAPHY: GEORGE PITTS
PHOTO EDITOR: JENNIFER SARGENT
PHOTOGRAPHERS: ELIZABETH YOUNG, MAN,
CLARE CHONG, RONY SHRAM
STUDIO: FB DESIGN
EDITOR-IN-CHIEF: MIMI VALDÉS RYAN
PUBLISHER: LATINA MEDIA VENTURES
CATEGORY: PHOTO: FEATURE:
FASHION/BEAUTY (STORY)

/559/ **NOX**
DESIGN DIRECTOR: OSCAR ARAGÓN
ART DIRECTOR: RICARDO FERICHE
DESIGNERS: CÉLINE ROBERT, VICENS CASTELLTORT
PHOTOGRAPHER: JOSE MANUEL FERRATER
STUDIO: FERICHE & BLACK
EDITOR-IN-CHIEF: JOSÉ MARIA DE PABLO
PUBLISHER: FOCUS EDICIONES
CLIENT: FOCUS EDICIONES
ISSUE: FALL 2008 / WINTER 2009
CATEGORY: PHOTO: FEATURE:
FASHION/BEAUTY (STORY)

/560/ **LOOK NEW YORK**
DESIGN DIRECTOR: CHRIS DIXON
ART DIRECTOR: RANDY MINOR
DIRECTOR OF PHOTOGRAPHY: JODY QUON
PHOTO EDITOR: NADIA LACHANCE
PHOTOGRAPHER: BENJAMIN LOWY
EDITOR-IN-CHIEF: ADAM MOSS
PUBLISHER: NEW YORK MAGAZINE HOLDINGS, LLC
ISSUE: FALL 2008 / CATEGORY:
PHOTO: FEATURE: FASHION/BEAUTY (STORY)

Intense

Some call you emotional, but you know better. It's your innate ability to feel things deeply, to know exactly what you want and how you need to get it. Your motives are clear—and you never back down.

LATINA
OCTOBER 2008

558

LATINA
NOVEMBER 2008

Bold

From the time you were a little girl, whether hiding behind Mami's skirt or walking up to strangers, you knew just how to get what you wanted. Shrewd, savvy and willing to fail, you never take "no" for an answer.

558

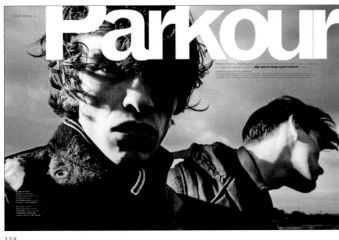

559

559

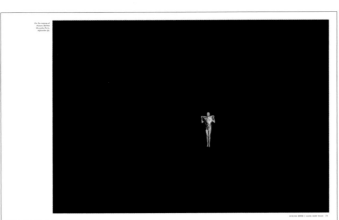

560

2

DOCUMENTARY

SIDESHOWS

Photographs by
BENJAMIN LOWY

560

561

563

562

564

/561/ **BEST LIFE**
DESIGN DIRECTOR: BRANDON KAVULLA
DESIGNER: DENA VERDESCA
DIRECTOR OF PHOTOGRAPHY: RYAN CADIZ
PHOTO EDITOR: JEANNE GRAVES
PHOTOGRAPHER: MARC ASNIN
PUBLISHER: RODALE INC.
ISSUE: JUNE 2008
CATEGORY: PHOTO: SECTION (SINGLE/SPREAD)

/562/ **SPIN**
DESIGN DIRECTOR: DEVIN PEDZWATER
ART DIRECTOR: IAN ROBINSON
DESIGNER: LIZ MACFARLANE
DIRECTOR OF PHOTOGRAPHY: MICHELLE EGIZIANO
PHOTO EDITORS: GAVIN STEVENS,
JENNIFER EDMONDSON
PHOTOGRAPHER: REBECCA SMEYNE
PUBLISHER: SPIN MEDIA LLC
ISSUE: JANUARY 2008
CATEGORY: PHOTO: SECTION (SINGLE/SPREAD)

/563/ **FIELD & STREAM**
ART DIRECTOR: NEIL JAMIESON
DESIGNERS: MIKE LEY, CATHERINE HAWTHORN
DIRECTOR OF PHOTOGRAPHY: AMY BERKLEY
PHOTOGRAPHER: DAN SAELINGER
ASSOCIATE PHOTO EDITOR: CAITLIN PETERS
STYLED BY: LAUREN SHIELDS
PUBLISHER: BONNIER CORPORATION
ISSUE: DECEMBER 2008
CATEGORY: PHOTO: SECTION (SINGLE/SPREAD)

/564/ **ESPN THE MAGAZINE**
CREATIVE DIRECTOR: SIUNG TJIA
DIRECTOR OF PHOTOGRAPHY: CATRIONA NI AOLAIN
PHOTO EDITORS: JIM SURBER, AMY MCNULTY
PHOTOGRAPHER: ROB TRINGALI
EDITOR-IN-CHIEF: GARY BELSKY
PUBLISHER: ESPN, INC.
CATEGORY: PHOTO: SECTION (SINGLE/SPREAD)

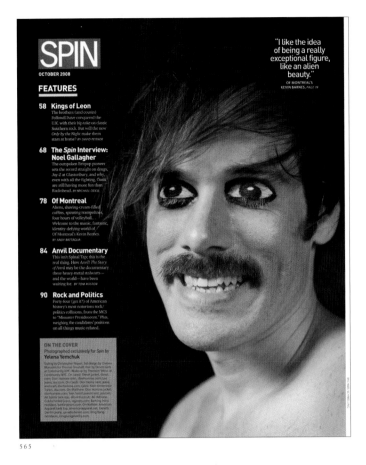

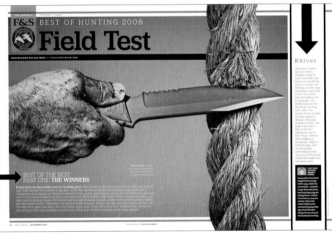

565

567

566

568

/565/ **SPIN**
DESIGN DIRECTOR: DEVIN PEDZWATER
ART DIRECTOR: IAN ROBINSON
DESIGNER: LIZ MACFARLANE
DIRECTOR OF PHOTOGRAPHY: MICHELLE EGIZIANO
PHOTO EDITORS: GAVIN STEVENS,
JENNIFER EDMONDSON
PHOTOGRAPHER: MICHAEL SCHMELLING
PUBLISHER: SPIN MEDIA LLC
ISSUE: OCTOBER 2008
CATEGORY: PHOTO: SECTION (SINGLE/SPREAD)

/566/ **FIELD & STREAM**
ART DIRECTOR: NEIL JAMIESON
DESIGNERS: MIKE LEY, IAN BROWN
DIRECTOR OF PHOTOGRAPHY: AMY BERKLEY
PHOTOGRAPHER: DAN SAELINGER
ASSOCIATE PHOTO EDITOR: CAITLIN PETERS
PUBLISHER: BONNIER CORPORATION
ISSUE: SEPTEMBER 2008
CATEGORY: PHOTO: SECTION (SINGLE/SPREAD)

/567/ **SPIN**
DESIGN DIRECTOR: DEVIN PEDZWATER
ART DIRECTOR: IAN ROBINSON
DESIGNER: LIZ MACFARLANE
DIRECTOR OF PHOTOGRAPHY: MICHELLE EGIZIANO
PHOTO EDITORS: GAVIN STEVENS, JENNIFER EDMONDSON
PHOTOGRAPHER: GREG KADEL
PUBLISHER: SPIN MEDIA LLC
ISSUE: APRIL 2008
CATEGORY: PHOTO: SECTION (SINGLE/SPREAD)

/568/ **GQ**
DESIGN DIRECTOR: FRED WOODWARD
DIRECTOR OF PHOTOGRAPHY: DORA SOMOSI
PHOTO EDITOR: KRISTA PRESTEK
PHOTOGRAPHER: GEOF KERN
EDITOR-IN-CHIEF: JIM NELSON
PUBLISHER: CONDÉ NAST PUBLICATIONS INC.
ISSUE: JULY 2008
CATEGORY: PHOTO: SECTION (SINGLE/SPREAD)

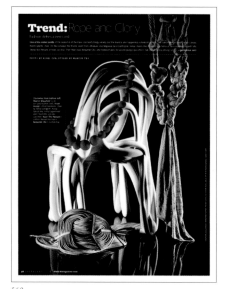

569

570

571

572

/569/ **W**
DESIGN DIRECTOR: EDWARD LEIDA
ART DIRECTOR: NATHALIE KIRSHEH
DESIGNERS: GINA MANISCALCO, LAURA KONRAD
PHOTOGRAPHER: NIGEL COX
PUBLISHER: CONDÉ NAST PUBLICATIONS INC.
ISSUE: FEBRUARY 2008
CATEGORY: PHOTO: SECTION (SINGLE/SPREAD)

/570/ **SELF**
CREATIVE DIRECTOR: CYNTHIA SEARIGHT
ART DIRECTOR: PETRA KOBAYASHI
PHOTO EDITOR: KRISTEN MULVIHILL
SENIOR PHOTO EDITOR: JEAN CABACUNGAN-JARVIS
PHOTO SITTINGS: EDITOR ROBIN PAGE
PHOTOGRAPHER: STEPHANIE RAUSSER
EDITOR-IN-CHIEF: LUCY DANZIGER
PUBLISHER: CONDÉ NAST PUBLICATIONS INC.
ISSUE: NOVEMBER 2008
CATEGORY: PHOTO: SECTION (SINGLE/SPREAD)

/571/ **COOKIE**
DESIGN DIRECTOR: KIRBY RODRIGUEZ
ART DIRECTOR: ALEX GROSSMAN
DESIGNERS: NICOLETTE BERTHELOT, SHANNA GREENBERG
PHOTO EDITOR: DARRICK HARRIS
ASSOCIATE PHOTO EDITOR: LINDA DENAHAN
ASSISTANT PHOTO EDITOR: AJA NUZZI
PHOTOGRAPHER: CRAIG CUTLER
PUBLISHER: CONDÉ NAST PUBLICATIONS INC.
ISSUE: NOVEMBER 2008
CATEGORY: PHOTO: SECTION (SINGLE/SPREAD)

/572/ **FORTUNE**
DESIGN DIRECTOR: ROBERT PERINO
DIRECTOR OF PHOTOGRAPHY: GREG POND
PHOTO EDITOR: ARMIN HARRIS
PHOTOGRAPHER: GREGG SEGAL
PUBLISHER: TIME INC.
ISSUE: MAY 12, 2008
CATEGORY: PHOTO: SECTION (SINGLE/SPREAD)

573

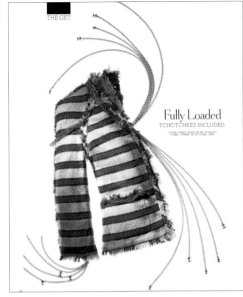

575

574

575

/573/ INTERIOR DESIGN
CREATIVE DIRECTOR: CINDY ALLEN
ART DIRECTOR: MARINO ZULLICH
DESIGNERS: ZIGENG LI, KARLA LIMA,
GIANNINA MACIAS
PHOTO EDITOR: HELENE OBERMAN
PHOTOGRAPHER: MICHELLE LITVIN
PUBLISHER: REED BUSINESS INFORMATION
ISSUE: NOVEMBER 2008
CATEGORY: PHOTO: SECTION (SINGLE/SPREAD)

/574/ RUNNER'S WORLD
DESIGN DIRECTOR: KORY KENNEDY
DEPUTY ART DIRECTOR: MARC KAUFMAN
ASSISTANT ART DIRECTOR: LEE WILLIAMS
PHOTO EDITOR: ANDREA MAURIO
ASSOCIATE PHOTO EDITOR: NICK GALAC
PHOTOGRAPHER: KEITH LADZINSKI
ART PRODUCTION: COORDINATOR TARA MAIDA
PUBLISHER: RODALE INC.
ISSUE: SEPTEMBER 2008
CATEGORY: PHOTO: SECTION (SINGLE/SPREAD)

/575/ T, THE NEW YORK TIMES STYLE MAGAZINE
CREATIVE DIRECTOR: JANET FROELICH
SENIOR ART DIRECTOR: DAVID SEBBAH
ART DIRECTOR: CHRISTOPHER MARTINEZ
SENIOR DESIGNER: ELIZABETH SPIRIDAKIS
DESIGNER: JAMIE BARTOLACCI
DIRECTOR OF PHOTOGRAPHY: KATHY RYAN
PHOTO EDITOR: SCOTT HALL
PHOTOGRAPHER: ILAN RUBIN
EDITOR-IN-CHIEF: STEFANO TONCHI
PUBLISHER: THE NEW YORK TIMES
ISSUE: FEBRUARY 24, 2008
CATEGORY: PHOTO: SECTION (SERIES OF PAGES)

576

576

577

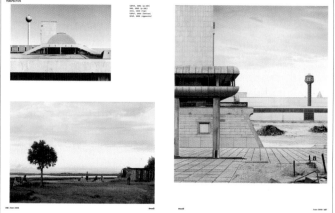

577

/576/ **W**
DESIGN DIRECTOR: EDWARD LEIDA
ART DIRECTOR: NATHALIE KIRSHEH
DESIGNER: LAURA KONRAD
PHOTOGRAPHER: TOBY MCFARLAN POND
PUBLISHER: CONDÉ NAST PUBLICATIONS INC.
ISSUE: MAY 2008
CATEGORY: PHOTO: SECTION (SERIES OF PAGES)

/577/ **DWELL**
DESIGN DIRECTOR: KYLE BLUE
DESIGNERS: BRENDAN CALLAHAN, GEOFF HALBER
DIRECTOR OF PHOTOGRAPHY: KATE STONE FOSS
PHOTO EDITORS: AMY SILBERMAN,
ANDREA LAWSON, ALEXIS TJIAN
PHOTOGRAPHER: BEATE GÜTSCHOW
DESIGN PRODUCTION MANAGER: KATHRYN HANSON
PUBLISHER: DWELL LLC
ISSUE: JUNE 2008
CATEGORY: PHOTO: SECTION (SERIES OF PAGES)

578

579

580

578

581

/578/ BLENDER
CREATIVE DIRECTOR: DIRK BARNETT
DESIGNER: DIRK BARNETT
DIRECTOR OF PHOTOGRAPHY: AMY HOPPY
PHOTO EDITOR: RORY WALSH
PHOTOGRAPHER: ANTONIN KRATOCHVIL
EDITOR-IN-CHIEF: JOE LEVY
PUBLISHER: ALPHAMEDIA GROUP
ISSUE: AUGUST 2008
CATEGORY: PHOTO: SECTION (SERIES OF PAGES)

/579/ SELF
CREATIVE DIRECTOR: CYNTHIA SEARIGHT
ART DIRECTOR: PETRA KOBAYASHI
DESIGNER: JOHN LIN
SENIOR PHOTO EDITOR: JEAN CABACUNGAN-JARVIS
PHOTO EDITOR: FABIENNE LEROUX
PHOTO SITTINGS EDITOR: LIDA MOORE MUSSO
PHOTOGRAPHER: NICOLA MAJOCCHI
EDITOR-IN-CHIEF: LUCY DANZIGER
PUBLISHER: CONDÉ NAST PUBLICATIONS INC.
ISSUE: JULY 2008
CATEGORY: PHOTO: SECTION (SERIES OF PAGES)

/580/ SELF
CREATIVE DIRECTOR: CYNTHIA SEARIGHT
ART DIRECTOR: PETRA KOBAYASHI
DESIGNER: PETRA KOBAYASHI
PHOTO EDITOR: KRISTEN MULVIHILL
SENIOR PHOTO EDITOR: JEAN CABACUNGAN-JARVIS
PHOTOGRAPHER: TOM SCHIERLITZ
EDITOR-IN-CHIEF: LUCY DANZIGER
PUBLISHER: CONDÉ NAST PUBLICATIONS INC.
ISSUE: AUGUST 2008
CATEGORY: PHOTO: SECTION (SERIES OF PAGES)

/581/ GQ
DESIGN DIRECTOR: FRED WOODWARD
ART DIRECTOR: ANTON IOUKHNOVETS
DIRECTOR OF PHOTOGRAPHY: DORA SOMOSI
PHOTO EDITORS: JUSTIN O'NEILL, JESSE LEE
PHOTOGRAPHER: PLAMEN PETKOV
EDITOR-IN-CHIEF: JIM NELSON
PUBLISHER: CONDÉ NAST PUBLICATIONS INC.
ISSUE: NOVEMBER 2008
CATEGORY: PHOTO: SECTION (SERIES OF PAGES)

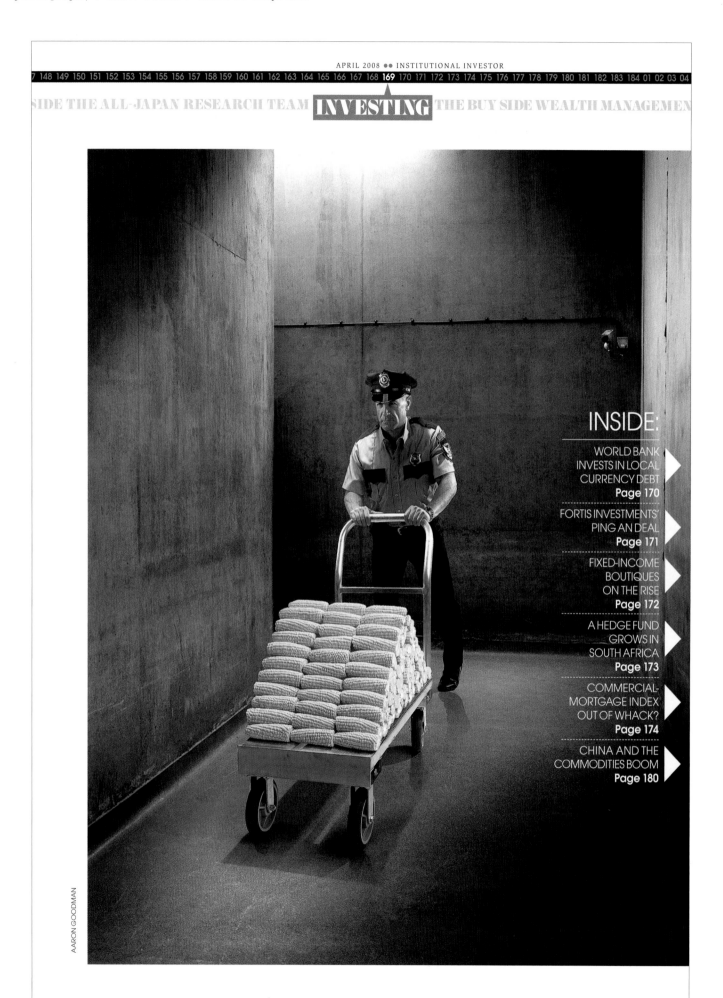

APRIL 2008 ●● INSTITUTIONAL INVESTOR

7 148 149 150 151 152 153 154 155 156 157 158 159 160 161 162 163 164 165 166 167 168 **169** 170 171 172 173 174 175 176 177 178 179 180 181 182 183 184 01 02 03 04

SIDE THE ALL-JAPAN RESEARCH TEAM **INVESTING** THE BUY SIDE WEALTH MANAGEMEN

INSIDE:

WORLD BANK
INVESTS IN LOCAL
CURRENCY DEBT
Page 170

FORTIS INVESTMENTS'
PING AN DEAL
Page 171

FIXED-INCOME
BOUTIQUES
ON THE RISE
Page 172

A HEDGE FUND
GROWS IN
SOUTH AFRICA
Page 173

COMMERCIAL-
MORTGAGE INDEX
OUT OF WHACK?
Page 174

CHINA AND THE
COMMODITIES BOOM
Page 180

AARON GOODMAN

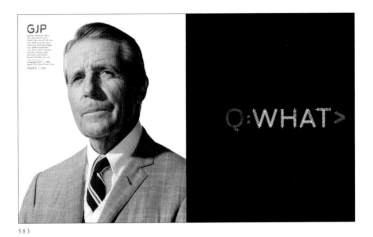

583

583

584

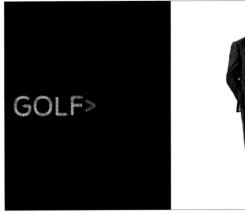

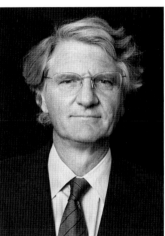

585

586

/582/ INSTITUTIONAL INVESTOR
ART DIRECTOR: NATHAN SINCLAIR
DESIGNER: LEE WILSON
PHOTO EDITOR: DANIELLA NILVA
PHOTOGRAPHER: AARON GOODMAN
PUBLISHER: EUROMONEY INSTITUTIONAL INVESTOR
ISSUE: APRIL 2008
CATEGORY: PHOTO: SINGLE/SPREAD/STORY

/583/ GOLF DIGEST INDEX
DESIGN DIRECTOR: KEN DELAGO
DESIGNER: MARNE MAYER
PHOTO EDITOR: RYAN CLINE
PHOTOGRAPHER: ART STREIBER
PUBLISHER: CONDÉ NAST PUBLICATIONS INC.
ISSUE: SPRING 2008
CATEGORY: PHOTO: SINGLE/SPREAD/STORY

/584/ GOLF DIGEST INDEX
DESIGN DIRECTOR: KEN DELAGO
DESIGNER: WENDY REINGOLD
PHOTO EDITOR: CHRISTIAN IOOSS
PHOTOGRAPHER: HUGH KRETSCHMER
PUBLISHER: CONDÉ NAST PUBLICATIONS INC.
ISSUE: FALL 2008
CATEGORY: PHOTO: SINGLE/SPREAD/STORY

/585/ INSTITUTIONAL INVESTOR
ART DIRECTOR: NATHAN SINCLAIR
DESIGNER: NATHAN SINCLAIR
PHOTO EDITOR: KATIE CONSTANS
PHOTOGRAPHER: STEPHANE GIZARD
PUBLISHER: EUROMONEY INSTITUTIONAL INVESTOR
ISSUE: OCTOBER 2008
CATEGORY: PHOTO: SINGLE/SPREAD/STORY

/586/ GOLF DIGEST INDEX
DESIGN DIRECTOR: KEN DELAGO
DESIGNER: TIM OLIVER
PHOTO EDITOR: RYAN CLINE
PHOTOGRAPHER: MASSIMO GAMMACURTA
PUBLISHER: CONDÉ NAST PUBLICATIONS INC.
ISSUE: FALL 2008
CATEGORY: PHOTO: SINGLE/SPREAD/STORY

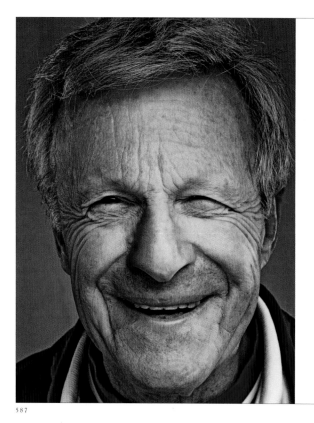

587

588

/587/ **STANFORD MAGAZINE**
ART DIRECTOR: AMY SHROADS
ASSOCIATE ART DIRECTOR: CAROLYN PEROT
DESIGNER: CAROLYN PEROT
PHOTOGRAPHER: MICHAEL SUGRUE
EDITOR-IN-CHIEF: KEVIN COOL
PUBLISHER: STANFORD UNIVERSITY
ISSUE: JANUARY/FEBRUARY 2008
CATEGORY: PHOTO: SINGLE/SPREAD/STORY

/588/ **STANFORD MAGAZINE**
ART DIRECTOR: AMY SHROADS
ASSOCIATE ART DIRECTOR: CAROLYN PEROT
DESIGNER: AMY SHROADS
PHOTOGRAPHERS: MANUELLO PAGANELLI,
GLENN MATSUMURA
EDITOR-IN-CHIEF: KEVIN COOL
PUBLISHER: STANFORD UNIVERSITY
ISSUE: JULY/AUGUST 2008
CATEGORY: PHOTO: SINGLE/SPREAD/STORY

589

589

590

THE SECRETS TO FINDING
A GREAT-FITTING BRA

You count on them for support, but odds are your bras
are not your bosom buddies. If you're like most women,
you think the pinching and slipping are normal and
unavoidable. And you'd probably never dream that a bra
could make your clothes look amazing. But the truth is,
a good bra is the foundation for everything else you put
on. Pick the right one, and you won't even know it's
there—except for the fact that your sweaters and dresses
will sit better, and your T-shirts will look neater. So what's
the secret to finding the perfect bra? Fit is key, obviously,
and it turns out that 47 percent of us have trouble finding
our size in the bra we want. But style, color, and shape
count too. Read on to find out how to get a perfect fit,
pick the right shape for your body, and adjust the straps
and bands so they're supportive and comfy. We'll also tell
you how to keep your bras in good shape. Plus, check out
the latest in bra technology and whether or not an
expensive bra is really worth the splurge.

22%
of women in our
exclusive survey say
they always or often
regret bra purchases.

www.ShopSmartmag.org APRIL/MAY 2008 **23**

/589/ **REAL SIMPLE**
DESIGN DIRECTOR: ELLENE WUNDROK
ART DIRECTOR: HEATH BROCKWELL
ILLUSTRATOR: MATTHEW SPORZYNSKI
DIRECTOR OF PHOTOGRAPHY: CASEY TIERNEY
PHOTO EDITOR: SUSAN GETZENDANNER
PHOTOGRAPHER: MONICA BUCK
PUBLISHER: TIME INC.
ISSUE: NOVEMBER 2008
CATEGORY: PHOTO-ILLUSTRATION:
SINGLE/SPREAD/STORY

/590/ **SHOPSMART**
CREATIVE DIRECTOR: TIM LAPALME
DESIGN DIRECTOR: GEORGE ARTHUR
ART DIRECTORS: MELISSA PATERNO PLONCHAK,
TAMMY MORTON FERNANDEZ
DESIGNER: TAMMY MORTON FERNANDEZ
PHOTO EDITOR: KAREN SHINBAUM
PHOTOGRAPHER: WENDELL WEBBER
CONSTRUCTIONIST: JEFF STYLES
EDITOR-IN-CHIEF: LISA LEE FREEMAN
PUBLISHER: CONSUMERS UNION
ISSUE: APRIL/MAY 2008
CATEGORY: PHOTO-ILLUSTRATION: SINGLE/SPREAD/STORY

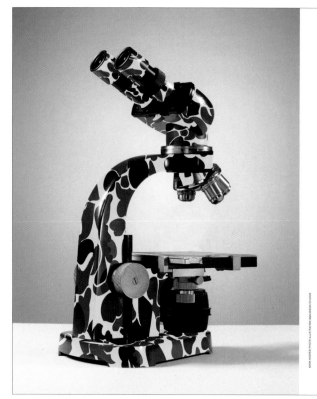

BIOLOGY BOOT CAMP

BASIC TRAINING FOR NEW RECRUITS TO THE LIFE SCIENCES

BY SALLY POBOJEWSKI

25

591

DARK KNIGHT RISING

FROM *BATMAN* TO *SIN CITY* TO *300*, GEEK GOD FRANK MILLER IS FAST BECOMING HOLLYWOOD'S PRINCE OF DARKNESS.

BY LOGAN HILL PHOTOGRAPHS BY FRANK W. OCKENFELS 3 ILLUSTRATIONS BY BILL SIENKIEWICZ

"HE IS THE HERO. HE IS EVERYTHING." The man speaking sounds and looks like an evil archnemesis, the kind of nutso-obsessive who sits at the head of a long conference table like this one and calls for the head of Superman. "I am absolutely dedicated to finding him," he says. Dressed in bad-guy black from the tip of his fedora to the toe of his scuffed sneakers, he is skeletally gaunt and pale, with a scraggly gravedigger's beard. He gestures with long fingers so bony and crooked you'd fear they might shoot off electric sparks. "My whole career is built around my search for the hero," he says, arching one eyebrow comically high over a bugged-out, bloodshot eye. "I'm dedicated to figuring out what a hero is."

Intense? Absolutely. Disturbing? Sure. But he's on our side—as dark a knight as Bruce Wayne. After all, Frank Miller is the comics icon who forced Batman to become, as he puts it, "the badass son of a bitch he always should have been" in *Batman: The Dark Knight Returns*. ("They finally got the title right," he says of Warner Bros.' new movie.) Stephen King called Miller's über-influential deconstruction of *Batman* "probably the finest piece of comic art ever published."

That was 22 years ago, when Miller, along with *Watchmen* creator Alan Moore, changed the course of comics forever. But he was just getting warmed up.

Sitting in the heart of Miller's not-so-secret Hollywood lair at Odd Lot Entertainment—a few yards away from a startlingly realistic copy of his own severed head—the artist-writer-director-auteur repeats his favorite Raymond Chandler quote: "He is the hero. He is everything." Miller likes to sum up every project in one line. *Sin City's* was "Conan in a trench coat." This quote distills his upcoming solo directing debut, *The Spirit*, a stylized update of the 1940s Will Eisner comic about a detective who seemingly comes back from the dead. It says as much about Miller's monomaniacal hero-worshiping career.

In 1979, Miller rebooted the neglected Daredevil, then invented the red-hot ninja Elektra in 1981, and rehabbed Batman in 1986 as a terrifyingly bleak Greek god of vengeance - a vision that heavily informed both Tim Burton's stylized take and, more obviously, Christopher Nolan's dark psychodrama, which is once again storming cineplexes this month. In the 1990s his rough, hyperviolent comics *Hard Boiled* and *Sin City* were

> **MY WHOLE CAREER IS BUILT AROUND MY SEARCH FOR THE HERO.**

adults-only wrecking balls whose plug-ugly thugs and dominatrix babes crashed into comics' kid-friendly facade. Recently, blockbusters based on Miller's *Sin City* and especially the blood-soaked Spartans epic *300* blindsided Hollywood pundits who swore R-rated comic book movies would never work. Then, when *300* grossed $457 million worldwide, Frank Miller went from Comic-Con rock star to Hollywood heavy.

"There's been a massive failure on the part of entertainment to come up with a new generation of heroes," Miller snarls. "Guys are so busy trying hard not to be guys...Right now there's a lot of boys out there.

"All that teen pretty-boy stuff. *The 40-Year-Old Virgin*, it's just not my world," he continues. "Lately there's been a real lack of that Robert Mitchum masculine force in film. You get these guys who are petty and vengeful. Or just...impotent."

Maybe that's why studios are calling heroes back from retirement, from Rambo and Rocky to Indiana Jones and James Bond. There aren't many young contenders who can knock out the old champs. "That's why Bruce Willis could come back with *Live Free or Die Hard*," says Miller, "to show these puppies what a real hero can do."

Miller's men have struck a nerve—pissing off knee-jerk feminists and antiwar liberals, thrilling fanboys, and making millions—because he's one of a few storytellers who's figured out a way to create badass sons of bitches for the new millennium. And in a summer movie season dominated by Robert Downey Jr.'s alcoholic Iron Man, Ron Perlman's brutish Hellboy, Edward Norton's raging Hulk, Will Smith's down-on-his luck Hancock, and especially Christian Bale's tortured Dark Knight, Miller's aesthetic reigns supreme. In *300*, *Sin City*, and *The Dark Knight Returns*, Miller took throwback men's men and made them brutally new. "Right now," he says, grinning like an evil genius hatching a dastardly plan, "I'm the perfect guy in the perfect position."

Welcome to the era of the Frank Miller man. Just as Mickey Spillane, John Wayne, and Sam Peckinpah each ushered in a new kind of American man, Miller has bred his own new, hard-boiled hero. Since we're on the verge of a new era, it's time to define who the hero is.

"Is there a Frank Miller man?" Miller asks. "Yes," he finally answers. "It's my search for a hero, from my Batman, where he was this obses- ➤➤

592

/591/ MEDICINE AT MICHIGAN
ART DIRECTORS: TIM BALDWIN, JOHN GORYL
DESIGNER: TONY MARRO
ILLUSTRATOR: B&G DESIGN STUDIOS
STUDIO: B&G DESIGN STUDIOS
PUBLISHER: UNIVERSITY OF MICHIGAN
CLIENT: MEDICINE AT MICHIGAN
ISSUE: FALL 2008
CATEGORY: PHOTO-ILLUSTRATION:
SINGLE/SPREAD/STORY

/592/ MAXIM
CREATIVE DIRECTOR: DAVID HILTON
ART DIRECTORS: BILLY SORRENTINO,
SEAN JOHNSTON
DESIGNER: CHANDRA ILLICK
ILLUSTRATOR: BILL SIENKIEWICZ
DIRECTOR OF PHOTOGRAPHY: REBECCA HORN
PHOTOGRAPHER: FRANK W OCKENFELS 3
PUBLISHER: ALPHAMEDIA GROUP
ISSUE: JULY 2008
CATEGORY: PHOTO-ILLUSTRATION:
SINGLE/SPREAD/STORY

As a federal corruption probe circles closer to his office, Governor Rod Blagojevich finds himself at war with state lawmakers and abandoned by political allies. Once a rising star with presidential aspirations, now he may be the most unpopular governor in the country. A look at how things fell so utterly apart

Mr. Un-Popularity

by David Bernstein

593

HEALTH WISE / FRENCH WOMEN DO DRINK WINE

She taught us why French women don't get fat. Now she takes a look at the role of wine as part of a healthy—and pleasurable—lifestyle. BY MIREILLE GUILIANO   PHOTOGRAPHY BY MAURICIO ALEJO

I N BORDEAUX back in the 1980s, I was introduced to the reputed oldest man in the Médoc. When asked the secret to his longevity, this spirited 98-year-old—who had spent his entire life tending vineyards—replied, "I drink a glass of wine every day, *bien sûr.*" But what about the so-called essence of life, water? Without hesitation, he answered, "Water is for ducks."

This encounter was memorable because my father used the same French cliché—water is for ducks—and he also drank a glass of wine each day with his lunch. So did most people I knew growing up in France.

Today, French women have one of the longest life expectancies in the world. And by 1991, we knew why. It's called the "French Paradox." The French can eat butter, eggs, and cheese and still have a low rate of heart disease because they also drink wine—specifically red wine. The antioxidants in red wine, when it is consumed in moderation, have been found to reduce blood clots and "bad" cholesterol production. Wine also is good for the circulatory system, and it slows the body's aging.

Even without biochemistry, the ancient Greeks and Romans were aware of wine's healthful properties. They used it as a disinfectant, a wound dressing, a diuretic, and an analgesic. We know now that it also helps prevent coronary disease and cancer and reduces ulcer-causing bacteria. Wine is a mild tranquilizer that /»

82/ bonappetit.com/ june 2008

594

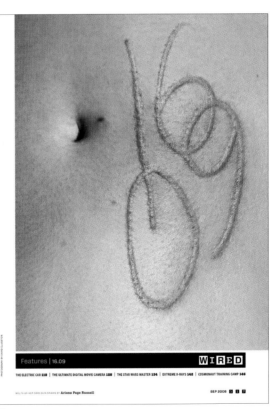

Features | 16.09

WIRED

THE ELECTRIC CAR 118 | THE ULTIMATE DIGITAL MOVIE CAMERA 128 | THE STAR WARS MASTER 134 | EXTREME X-RAYS 142 | COSMONAUT TRAINING CAMP 148

WELTS ON HER OWN SKIN DRAWN BY **Ariana Page Russell**   SEP 2008

595

/593/ **CHICAGO**
ART DIRECTOR: JENNIFER MOORE
DESIGNER: JENNIFER MOORE
ILLUSTRATOR: VIBRACOBRADESIGN/JOSE RIVERA
PHOTO EDITOR: BRITTNEY BLAIR
PHOTOGRAPHERS: JAN STROMME/GETTY IMAGES,
JEFF SCIORTINO
EDITOR-IN-CHIEF: RICHARD BABCOCK
PUBLISHER: CHICAGOLAND PUBLISHING
ISSUE: FEBRUARY 2008
CATEGORY: PHOTO-ILLUSTRATION:
SINGLE/SPREAD/STORY

/594/ **BON APPÉTIT**
DESIGN DIRECTOR: MATTHEW LENNING
ART DIRECTOR: ROBERT FESTINO
PHOTO EDITOR: BAILEY FRANKLIN
PHOTOGRAPHER: MAURICIO ALEJO
EDITOR-IN-CHIEF: BARBARA FAIRCHILD
PUBLISHER: CONDÉ NAST PUBLICATIONS, INC.
ISSUE: JUNE 2008
CATEGORY: PHOTO-ILLUSTRATION:
SINGLE/SPREAD/STORY

/595/ **WIRED**
CREATIVE DIRECTOR: SCOTT DADICH
DESIGN DIRECTOR: WYATT MITCHELL
DESIGNER: MALI HOLIMAN
ILLUSTRATOR: ARIANA PAGE RUSSELL
PHOTO EDITOR: CAROLYN RAUCH
PHOTOGRAPHER: DAVID CLUGSTON
PUBLISHER: CONDÉ NAST PUBLICATIONS, INC.
ISSUE: SEPTEMBER 2008
CATEGORY: PHOTO-ILLUSTRATION:
SINGLE/SPREAD/STORY

ROB HEWITT
ROBERT BEST
ROBERT FESTINO
ROBERT PERINO
ROBERT PRIEST

RODRIGO CORRAL

SAM WEBER

SCOTT DADICH

SEP KAMVAR

SHAWN GREENBERG

SIUNG TJIA

SPLASHLIGHT

LUCAS ALLEN

MAIRA KALMAN

MARTHA RICH

MATTHEW COOK
MATTHEW LENNING

MELINDA BECK

MICHELLE STARK
MICHIKO TOKI

JACK UNRUH

JACQUELINE MUNZ

JANET FROELICH

JASON SALAVON

JEE LEE

JESSICA NELSON
JILLIAN TAMAKI
JODY QUON

JOHN DIXON

DALE STEPHANOS

DANA PRITTS
DANIEL ADEL

DAVIA SMITH

DAVID HARRIS

DAVID MCKENNA
DAVID SEBBAH

DAVID ZAMDMER

DEANNA LOWE

DIENSTSTELLE 75
DIRK BARNETT

EDWARD LEVINE
ELEANOR WILLIAMSON
ELIZABETH SPIRIDAKIS
ELLENE WUNDROK
ELSA MEHARY
EMILY CRAWFORD

/CONTRIBUTORS/
AARON KOBLIN

ADAM BOOKBINDER
ADAM SIMPSON

ALEX GROSSMAN

ALICE CHO

AMID CAPECI

AMY ROSENFELD

ANDREA VENTURA

ANDRZEJ JANERKA
ANDY FRIEDMAN
ANDY OMEL
ANKE STOHLMANN

ANTON IOUKHNOVETS
AREM DUPLESSIS

BALINT ZSAKO
BARRY BLITT

BERNARD SCHARF

WIRED
UD &SE
VANITY FAIR

THIS OLD HOUSE

THE NEW YORK TIMES BOOK REVIEW
THE NEW YORK TIMES MAGAZINE

T
TEXAS MONTHLY

SKI

SEED

PSYCHOLOGY TODAY
REAL SIMPLE

NATIONAL GEOGRAPHIC ADVENTURE
NEW YORK
NEWSWEEK

MINNESOTA MONTHLY
MONEY

MEN'S HEALTH

SUSANA SOARES
T.J. TUCKER
TAVIS COBURN
THOMAS ALBERTY
THOMAS FUCHS
TINA-LYNN CORTEZ TABIBI
TODD ALBERTSON
TYLER LANG
VIK MUNIZ
VIKKI NESTICO
WARD SCHUMAKER
WILBERT GUTIÉRREZ
WYATT MITCHELL
ZOHAR LAZAR

NAI LEE LUM
NATE VAN DYKE
NATHAN FOX
NICHOLAS BLECHMAN
NICK AND CHLOE
NICOLETTE BERTHELOT
NIGEL PARRY
PAUL PRUDENCE
PAUL SCIRECALABRISOTTO
R. KIKUO JOHNSON
RALPH STEADMAN
RANDY MINOR

JONATHAN HARRIS
JONATHAN ROSEN
JOON MO KANG
JOSH KLENERT
JULES ARTHUR
JULIE WEISS
KAT MACLEOD
KATHERINE BIGELOW
KEN DELAGO
KIRBY RODRIGUEZ
LAURA CARLIN
LEANNE SHAPTON
LEO JUNG
LISA BERMAN
LORENZO PETRANTONI
LOU CORREDOR

EVAN CUBERNICK
FRANÇOIS BERTHOUD
FRANK STOCKTON
FRED WOODWARD
GABRIELA HASBUN
GAIL BICHLER
GEORGE KARABOTSOS
GINA TOOLE SAUNDERS
GRACE LEE
GREG GRABOWY
GREG POND
HENRY JANSEN
HILARY GREENBAUM
HOLLY GRESSLEY
HOPE GANGLOFF

BRENDA MILLIS
BRIAN ANSTEY
BRIAN CRONIN
BRUCE RAMSAY
BRYAN CHRISTIE DESIGN
CAHAN AND ASSOCIATES
CALEB BENNETT
CARL DETORRES
CAROLYN RAUCH
CATHERINE GILMORE-BARNES
CHRIS CRISTIANO
CHRIS DIXON
CHRIS MUELLER
CHRISTINE BOWER-WRIGHT
CHRISTOPH NIEMANN
CHRISTOPHER MARTINEZ

GQ
GOLF DIGEST
FORTUNE
ENTERTAINMENT WEEKLY
ESPN THE MAGAZINE
DEPARTURES
CULTURE + TRAVEL
COOKIE
CONTRIBUTE
CONDÉ NAST TRAVELER
CONDÉ NAST PORTFOLIO
CALIFORNIA
BON APPÉTIT
BLENDER
BLACK INK
BILLBOARD
AARP THE MAGAZINE
AARP SEGUNDA JUVENTUD
/PUBLICATIONS/

MAY/JUNE 2008: The Group of Insanely Talented Artists Near the Vienna Woods   Madrid's Best Soccer Team, and Why Half the City Hates It   Death Becomes Them: Puccini's Divas Don't Look a Day Over 150   What Were the Pope and Abe Lincoln Doing in a Scottish Castle?   King Gorilla Eucalyptus and his Underground World in Piedmont

CULTURE +TRAVEL

EUROPE

PAGE 110: "AS MARIA CALLAS BENT OVER TO REACH FOR A KNIFE THAT WAS NEXT TO A CANDLE, HER WIG CAUGHT ON FIRE."

596

/596/ **CULTURE + TRAVEL**
CREATIVE DIRECTOR: EMILY CRAWFORD / DESIGNER: EMILY CRAWFORD
ILLUSTRATOR: BALINT ZSAKO / PUBLISHER: LOUISE BLOUIN MEDIA
ISSUE: MAY/JUNE 2008 / CATEGORY: ILLO: COVER

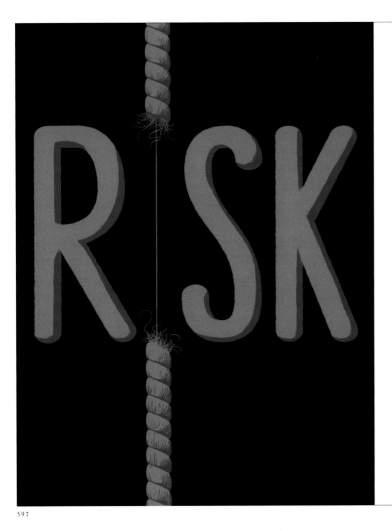

How to
Keep Your Cool
in
a
Dangerous
Market

With every dip in the Dow, that inner voice urging you to sell gets louder. Here are four reasons you shouldn't listen.

BY JANICE REVELL
ILLUSTRATION BY CHRISTOPH NIEMANN

JUST A FEW SHORT MONTHS AGO, when you looked at your 401(k) you probably felt quite at peace with the risks you were taking. Sure, you knew your stock funds would hit some rough patches, but after every bump they seemed to rebound higher. You could handle that.

Today your attitude is likely to be decidedly less calm. You're not so sure you signed up for a market exposed to recession *and* inflation *and* a credit crisis *and* 300-point plunges on any random market session. The urge to do something—anything!—to stop the pain gets more insistent by the day.

Let's be clear: If you have a reasonable asset allocation (check yours against the charts on page 77), you should not change a thing. Yes, your gut tells you risk is everywhere. But on the next few pages you'll find four reasons, drawn from market history and investment psychology, why you probably shouldn't go with your gut at a time like this. So what *should* you do? Start with our five tips for avoiding a panicky misstep (page 76), and then keep your eye on the only factors that should drive your decisions in any market: your long-term goals.

Money April 2008 75

597

598

191

/597/ MONEY
ART DIRECTOR: DAVIA SMITH / DESIGNER: DAVIA SMITH
ILLUSTRATOR: CHRISTOPH NIEMANN / EDITOR-IN-CHIEF: ERIC SCHURENBERG
PUBLISHER: TIME INC. / ISSUE: APRIL 2008 / CATEGORY: ILLO: SINGLE/SPREAD

/598/ THE NEW YORK TIMES MAGAZINE
CREATIVE DIRECTOR: JANET FROELICH / ART DIRECTOR: AREM DUPLESSIS
DEPUTY ART DIRECTOR: GAIL BICHLER / DESIGNER: GAIL BICHLER
ILLUSTRATOR: EDWARD DEL ROSARIO / EDITOR-IN-CHIEF: GERRY MARZORATI
PUBLISHER: THE NEW YORK TIMES / ISSUE: JUNE 29, 2008
CATEGORY: ILLO: STORY

/599/ **NEWSWEEK**
DESIGN DIRECTOR: AMID CAPECI / DIRECTOR OF COVERS: BRUCE RAMSAY / ART DIRECTOR: BRUCE RAMSAY / ILLUSTRATOR: LORENZO PETRANTONI — FOR NEWSWEEK
DIRECTOR OF PHOTOGRAPHY: SIMON BARNETT / PHOTO EDITOR: MICHELLE MOLLOY / PHOTOGRAPHER: NIGEL PARRY — CPI FOR NEWSWEEK
PUBLISHER: THE WASHINGTON POST CO. / ISSUE: DECEMBER 29, 2008 - JANUARY 5, 2009 / CATEGORY: ILLO: COVER

Gang of Four

COMME DES GARÇONS IS AN EXTENSION OF REI KAWAKUBO'S BRAIN. A KIND OF ZEN MASTER, SHE ALLOWS HER PROTÉGÉS TOTAL FREEDOM. AND THAT'S TOUGH. BY CATHY HORYN *Illustration by François Berthoud*

Peoples' eyes constantly deceive them, and that was certainly true in Paris in the fall of 1996, when Rei Kawakubo, the designer behind Comme des Garçons, presented a collection of dresses swollen with huge lumps. In profile, the models looked like hunchbacks or camels tipped onto their sides. There were smaller, kidney-shaped masses on shoulders and arms, most covered in cheerful gingham. The clothes confounded critics, even those used to Kawakubo's abstract methods. Amy Spindler wrote in The New York Times that Kawakubo had "invented whole new deformities for women." During the show, which was conducted in silence, one photographer muttered, "Quasimodo."

"Lumps and Bumps," as the collection came to be called, illustrates the difficulties for a designer of being not merely original but also a modernist. Kawakubo said she was interested in exploring "volume and space." If you begin with the outline made by her shapes (the classic "silhouette") and then pull back — moving away, as it were, from the confinements of fashion — you realize that Kawakubo has in fact recreated a reality of the late 20th century: the individual seemingly joined to her backpack and her burdens; even the act of talking on a cellphone assumes a spatial connection, producing what appears in the abstract to be a growth. Kawakubo's objective was not to distort the female body but rather to express a thought that probably, for her, began with a gesture or a glimpse. Some designers, like Alber Elbaz of Lanvin and Azzedine Alaïa, solve problems of dressmaking — putting darts in a skirt to give it softer volume. Kawakubo, working more in the spirit of an artist than any designer today, attacks the problems of consciousness.

Kawakubo has been making clothes for nearly 40 years, always under the label Comme des Garçons, which means "like some boys" and in a way suggests a gang. In the '80s, this could be seen in the hordes of black-clad women, many of whom considered themselves feminists and

 FOR A SLIDE SHOW OF PAST COMME DES GARÇONS COLLECTIONS, GO TO NYTIMES.COM/TMAGAZINE.

were eager, like the architect Kazuyo Sejima, whose firm recently completed the New Museum in Lower Manhattan, to express themselves radically. In 1992, Kawakubo decided to branch out and gave a young patternmaker, Junya Watanabe, his own label, a move that revealed her to be an innovative businesswoman as well. By the end of the '90s, "multibrands" had taken over the industry. Since then, she has added Tao by Tao Kurihara and, more recently, a youth-oriented label called Ganryu, by the baby-faced Fumito Ganryu, 31, who has been with the company for four years. Kawakubo and her husband, Adrian Joffe, also operate the eclectic Dover Street Market in London, giving the Comme des Garçons company another way to burnish its avant-garde image while continuing to grow. These new ventures now account for 22 percent of the company's annual sales, which in 2007 were $180 million, said Joffe.

Editors still follow Kawakubo's shows with rapt interest. But more and more you wonder why they go. What do they expect to learn from this small, dour woman whose gnomic pronouncements ("Red is the new black") would surely qualify as Gumpsms if they hadn't been issued before we found such things funny? As it is, hardly any of the editors wear her clothes nowadays — and that's also true in Tokyo, said Kazuhiro Saito, the editor in chief of Japanese Vogue. "Even five years ago, Comme des Garçons was kind of part of the national wardrobe," said Tiffany Godoy, a writer who has followed Tokyo fashion for a decade and who has recently published a book on Harajuku street style. "But that's not the case anymore." And while Kawakubo offers women the possibility to own a runway garment for $1,500 — largely because she doesn't spend a lot of money on marketing and because she uses the same mills and factories she has always used — young Japanese women prefer European brands at more than twice the price. "They want to look like celebrities," Godoy pointed out.

Kawakubo's influence, then, on the self-perceptions of women, on

/600/ T, THE NEW YORK TIMES STYLE MAGAZINE
CREATIVE DIRECTOR: JANET FROELICH / SENIOR ART DIRECTOR: DAVID SEBBAH
ART DIRECTOR: CHRISTOPHER MARTINEZ
SENIOR DESIGNER: ELIZABETH SPIRIDAKIS / ILLUSTRATOR: FRANÇOIS BERTHOUD
EDITOR-IN-CHIEF: STEFANO TONCHI / PUBLISHER: THE NEW YORK TIMES
ISSUE: FEBRUARY 24, 2008 / CATEGORY: ILLO: SINGLE/SPREAD

/601/ DEPARTURES
CREATIVE DIRECTOR: BERNARD SCHARF
ART DIRECTOR: ADAM BOOKBINDER / DESIGNER: LOU CORREDOR
ILLUSTRATOR: MAIRA KALMAN / PHOTO EDITOR: JESSICA DIMSON
PUBLISHER: AMERICAN EXPRESS PUBLISHING CO.
ISSUE: MAY/JUNE 2008 / CATEGORY: ILLO: STORY

602

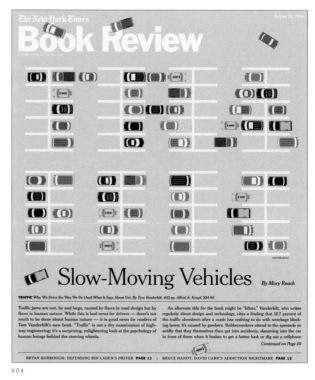

604

603

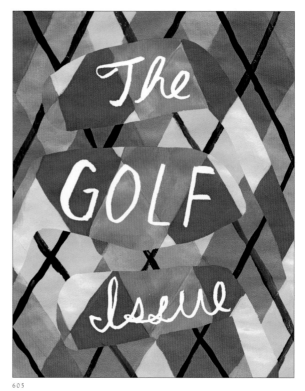

605

/602/ **THE NEW YORK TIMES BOOK REVIEW**
ART DIRECTORS: NICHOLAS BLECHMAN, ANKE STOHLMANN
ILLUSTRATOR: TAVIS COBURN / ASSISTANT MANAGING EDITOR: TOM BODKIN
PUBLISHER: THE NEW YORK TIMES / ISSUE: OCTOBER 12, 2008
CATEGORY: ILLO: COVER

/603/ **THE NEW YORK TIMES MAGAZINE**
CREATIVE DIRECTOR: JANET FROELICH / ART DIRECTOR: AREM DUPLESSIS
DEPUTY ART DIRECTOR: GAIL BICHLER / DESIGNER: GAIL BICHLER
ILLUSTRATOR: EDWARD DEL ROSARIO / EDITOR-IN-CHIEF: GERRY MARZORATI
PUBLISHER: THE NEW YORK TIMES / ISSUE: JUNE 29, 2008 CATEGORY: ILLO: COVER

/604/ **THE NEW YORK TIMES BOOK REVIEW**
ART DIRECTOR: NICHOLAS BLECHMAN / ILLUSTRATOR: JOON MO KANG
ASSISTANT MANAGING EDITOR: TOM BODKIN / PUBLISHER: THE NEW YORK TIMES
ISSUE: AUGUST 10, 2008 / CATEGORY: ILLO: COVER

/605/ **BLACK INK**
CREATIVE DIRECTOR: BERNARD SHARF / ART DIRECTOR: ADAM BOOKBINDER
DESIGNER: LOU CORREDOR / ILLUSTRATOR: LEANNE SHAPTON
PHOTO EDITOR: JESSICA DIMSON / PUBLISHER: AMERICAN EXPRESS PUBLISHING
ISSUE: SUMMER 2008 / CATEGORY: ILLO: COVER

J.P. MORGAN'S SWAT TEAM

FORTUNE

SEPTEMBER 15, 2008 /// NO.16

THE NEW RUSSIAN THREAT

What Russia's resurgence means for the world economy.
BY BILL POWELL

Prime Minister
Vladimir Putin (left)
and President
Dmitry Medvedev

FORTUNE.COM

/606/ **FORTUNE**
DESIGN DIRECTOR: ROBERT PERINO / ART DIRECTOR: DEANNA LOWE / DESIGNER: NAI LEE LUM / ILLUSTRATOR: ANDREA VENTURA
PUBLISHER: TIME INC. / ISSUE: SEPTEMBER 15, 2008 / CATEGORY: ILLO: COVER

607

608

609

/607/ **MEN'S HEALTH**
DESIGN DIRECTOR: GEORGE KARABOTSOS
ART DIRECTOR: VIKKI NESTICO
DESIGNER: VIKKI NESTICO
ILLUSTRATOR: RALPH STEADMAN
DIRECTOR OF PHOTOGRAPHY: BRENDA MILLIS
PHOTO EDITORS: BRENDA MILLIS, MICHELLE STARK
PUBLISHER: RODALE INC. / ISSUE: OCTOBER 2008
CATEGORY: ILLO: SINGLE/SPREAD

/608/ **SKI**
ART DIRECTOR: ELEANOR WILLIAMSON
DESIGNER: DANA PRITTS
ILLUSTRATOR: JOHN HENDRIX
PHOTO EDITORS: SARAH LAVIGNE, KERI BASCETTA
EDITOR-IN-CHIEF: KENDALL HAMILTON
PUBLISHER: BONNIER CORPORATION
ISSUE: MARCH/APRIL 2008
CATEGORY: ILLO: SINGLE/SPREAD

/609/ **BILLBOARD**
CREATIVE DIRECTOR: JOSH KLENERT
ART DIRECTOR: CHRISTINE BOWER-WRIGHT
ILLUSTRATOR: TAVIS COBURN
PHOTO EDITOR: AMELIA HALVERSON
SENIOR DESIGNER: GREG GRABOWY
PUBLISHER: NIELSEN BUSINESS MEDIA
ISSUE: MARCH 29, 2008
CATEGORY: ILLO: SINGLE/SPREAD

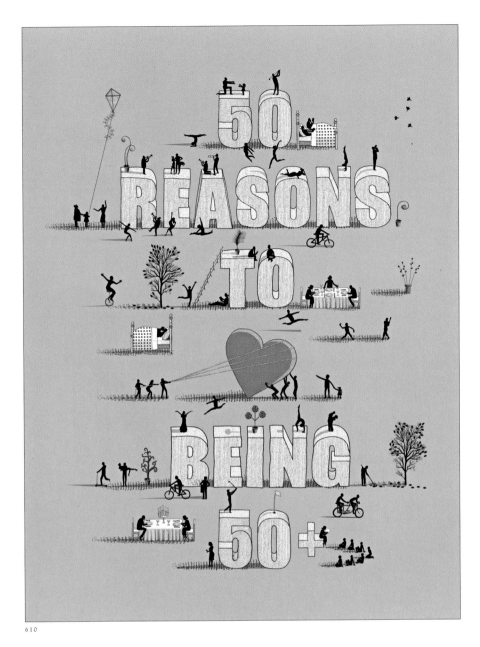

610

611

612

/610/ **AARP THE MAGAZINE**
DESIGN DIRECTOR: ANDRZEJ JANERKA
ART DIRECTOR: TODD ALBERTSON
DESIGNER: TODD ALBERTSON
ILLUSTRATOR: ADAM SIMPSON
EDITOR-IN-CHIEF: STEVEN SLON
PUBLISHER: AARP PUBLICATIONS
ISSUE: SEPTEMBER/OCTOBER 2008
CATEGORY: ILLO: SINGLE/SPREAD

/611/ **VANITY FAIR**
DESIGN DIRECTOR: DAVID HARRIS
ART DIRECTORS: JULIE WEISS, CHRIS MUELLER
ILLUSTRATOR: DANIEL ADEL
EDITOR-IN-CHIEF: GRAYDON CARTER
PUBLISHER: CONDÉ NAST PUBLICATIONS INC.
ISSUE: JUNE 2008
CATEGORY: ILLO: SINGLE/SPREAD

/612/ **VANITY FAIR**
DESIGN DIRECTOR: DAVID HARRIS
ART DIRECTORS: JULIE WEISS, CHRIS MUELLER
ILLUSTRATOR: DANIEL ADEL
EDITOR-IN-CHIEF: GRAYDON CARTER
PUBLISHER: CONDÉ NAST PUBLICATIONS INC.
ISSUE: JULY 2008
CATEGORY: ILLO: SINGLE/SPREAD

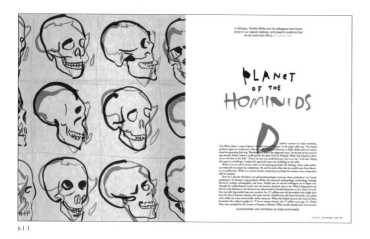

613

616

614

617

615

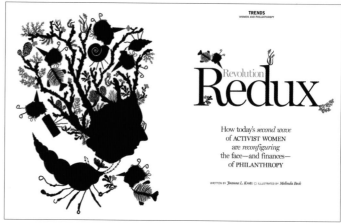

618

/613/ CALIFORNIA
ART DIRECTOR: MICHIKO TOKI
DESIGNER: MICHIKO TOKI
ILLUSTRATOR: WARD SCHUMAKER
STUDIO: TOKI DESIGN
EDITOR-IN-CHIEF: KERRY TREMAIN
PUBLISHER: CALIFORNIA ALUMNI ASSOCIATION
CLIENT: CALIFORNIA
ISSUE: JULY/AUGUST 2008
CATEGORY: ILLO: SINGLE/SPREAD

/614/ THIS OLD HOUSE
DESIGN DIRECTOR: AMY ROSENFELD
ART DIRECTOR: DOUG ADAMS
ILLUSTRATOR: JOHN HENDRIX
PUBLISHER: TIME INC.
ISSUE: JUNE 2008
CATEGORY: ILLO: SINGLE/SPREAD

/615/ ESPN THE MAGAZINE
CREATIVE DIRECTOR: SIUNG TJIA
DESIGNER: SIUNG TJIA
ILLUSTRATORS: JILLIAN TAMAKI, SAM WEBER
EDITOR-IN-CHIEF: GARY BELSKY
PUBLISHER: ESPN, INC.
ISSUE: SEPTEMBER 8, 2008
CATEGORY: ILLO: SINGLE/SPREAD

/616/ ESPN THE MAGAZINE
CREATIVE DIRECTOR: SIUNG TJIA
DESIGNER: SIUNG TJIA
ILLUSTRATOR: JILLIAN TAMAKI
EDITOR-IN-CHIEF: GARY BELSKY
PUBLISHER: ESPN, INC.
ISSUE: MARCH 24, 2008
CATEGORY: ILLO: SINGLE/SPREAD

/617/ AARP SEGUNDA JUVENTUD
ART DIRECTORS: GINA TOOLE SAUNDERS,
TINA-LYNN CORTEZ TABIBI
DESIGNER: TINA-LYNN CORTEZ TABIBI
ILLUSTRATOR: BRIAN CRONIN
PUBLISHER: AARP PUBLICATIONS
ISSUE: SUMMER 2008
CATEGORY: ILLO: SINGLE/SPREAD

/618/ CONTRIBUTE
DESIGN DIRECTOR: MITCH SHOSTAK
ART DIRECTOR: SUSANA SOARES
ILLUSTRATOR: MELINDA BECK
STUDIO: SHOSTAK STUDIOS
EDITOR-IN-CHIEF: MARCIA STEPANEK
PUBLISHER: CONTRIBUTE MEDIA
CLIENT: CONTRIBUTE
ISSUE: JANUARY/FEBRUARY 2008
CATEGORY: ILLO: SINGLE/SPREAD

619

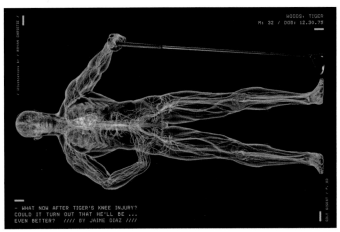

622

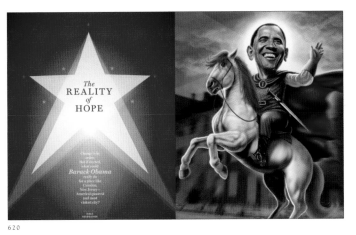

620

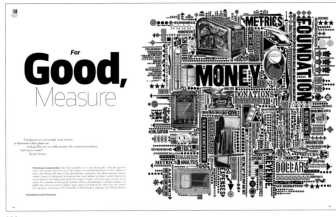

623

621

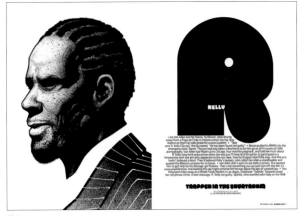

624

/619/ **TEXAS MONTHLY**
ART DIRECTOR: T.J. TUCKER
DESIGNER: CALEB BENNETT
ILLUSTRATOR: CARL DETORRES
PUBLISHER: EMMIS COMMUNICATIONS CORP.
ISSUE: MAY 2008
CATEGORY: ILLO: SINGLE/SPREAD

/620/ **KING**
CREATIVE DIRECTOR: EVAN GUBERNICK
ART DIRECTOR: PAUL SCIRECALABRISOTTO
ASSISTANT ART DIRECTORS: DAVID ZAMDMER,
CHRIS CRISTIANO / DESIGNER: CHRIS CRISTIANO
ILLUSTRATOR: DALE STEPHANOS
EDITOR-IN-CHIEF: JERMAINE HALL
PUBLISHER: HARRIS PUBLICATIONS
ISSUE: NOVEMBER 2008
CATEGORY: ILLO: SINGLE/SPREAD

/621/ **THE NEW YORK TIMES MAGAZINE**
CREATIVE DIRECTOR: JANET FROELICH
ART DIRECTOR: AREM DUPLESSIS
DEPUTY ART DIRECTOR: GAIL BICHLER
DESIGNER: HILARY GREENBAUM
ILLUSTRATOR: MITCH BLUNT
EDITOR-IN-CHIEF: GERRY MARZORATI
PUBLISHER: THE NEW YORK TIMES
ISSUE: SEPTEMBER 21, 2008
CATEGORY: ILLO: SINGLE/SPREAD

/622/ **GOLF DIGEST**
DESIGN DIRECTOR: KEN DELAGO
DESIGNER: KEN DELAGO
ILLUSTRATOR: BRYAN CHRISTIE
PUBLISHER: CONDÉ NAST PUBLICATIONS INC.
ISSUE: SEPTEMBER 2008
CATEGORY: ILLO: SINGLE/SPREAD

/623/ **THE NEW YORK TIMES MAGAZINE**
CREATIVE DIRECTOR: JANET FROELICH
ART DIRECTOR: AREM DUPLESSIS
DEPUTY ART DIRECTOR: GAIL BICHLER
DESIGNER: HOLLY GRESSLEY
ILLUSTRATOR: LORENZO PETRANTONI
EDITOR-IN-CHIEF: GERRY MARZORATI
PUBLISHER: THE NEW YORK TIMES
ISSUE: MARCH 9, 2008
CATEGORY: ILLO: SINGLE/SPREAD

/624/ **BLENDER**
CREATIVE DIRECTOR: DIRK BARNETT
DESIGNER: DIRK BARNETT
ILLUSTRATOR: NATE VAN DYKE
EDITOR-IN-CHIEF: JOE LEVY
PUBLISHER: ALPHAMEDIA GROUP
ISSUE: SEPTEMBER 2008
CATEGORY: ILLO: SINGLE/SPREAD

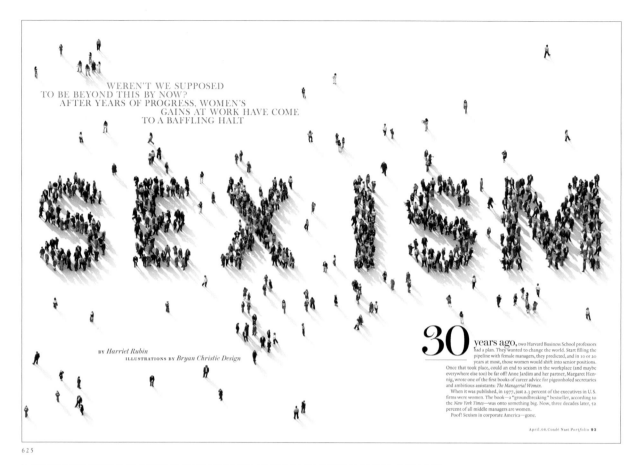

625

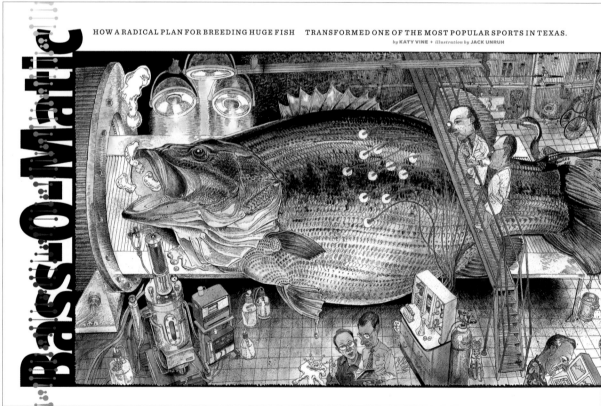

626

/625/ **CONDÉ NAST PORTFOLIO**
DESIGN DIRECTOR: ROBERT PRIEST / ART DIRECTOR: GRACE LEE
DESIGNER: GRACE LEE / ILLUSTRATOR: BRYAN CHRISTIE DESIGN
EDITOR-IN-CHIEF: JOANNE LIPMAN
PUBLISHER: CONDÉ NAST PUBLICATIONS INC.
ISSUE: APRIL 2008 / CATEGORY: ILLO: SINGLE/SPREAD

/626/ **TEXAS MONTHLY**
ART DIRECTOR: T.J. TUCKER / DESIGNER: T.J. TUCKER
ILLUSTRATOR: JACK UNRUH / PUBLISHER: EMMIS COMMUNICATIONS CORP.
ISSUE: AUGUST 2008 / CATEGORY: ILLO: SINGLE/SPREAD

What's on the other side of this dangerous passage? In our 28-page report on the upheaval in the U.S. financial system, Fortune looks at the populist backlash, the new king of banking, the risky business of AIG, and the ticking time bomb that's still out there: derivatives.

FORTUNE

BAILING OUT AMERICA

ILLUSTRATION BY SPLASHLIGHT

THAT SINKING FEELING
With apologies to "Washington Crossing the Delaware," painted by Emanuel Leutze in 1851, we portray the risky passage of Hank Paulson (as Washington), Ben Bernanke (with flag), and Christopher Cox (bailing). Will they make it across?

627

At 2 months old, Livia was a colicky baby who would only stop crying if at my breast or near the loud, rumbling sound of an 18-wheeler. Twenty hours a day, she would cry. My sister, who lived nearby and who was pregnant with her second child, would not visit, so afraid was she that her baby would be like mine. My husband had a teaching job in another state and lived there most of the week. I suffered chronic mastitis that left me sick and with lumps in my breast that needed to be aspirated. The apartment was a mess, my daughter's fingernails were long and scratched her, and I was living on brownies.

AND THEN CAME HEATHER.

BY **MARTHA McPHEE**   ILLUSTRATIONS BY **LAURA CARLIN**

628

/627/ **FORTUNE**
DESIGN DIRECTOR: ROBERT PERINO / ART DIRECTOR: DEANNA LOWE
ILLUSTRATOR: SPLASHLIGHT / DIRECTOR OF PHOTOGRAPHY: GREG POND
PHOTO EDITOR: AMY WOLFF / PUBLISHER: TIME INC.
ISSUE: OCTOBER 13, 2008 / CATEGORY: ILLO: SINGLE/SPREAD

/628/ **COOKIE**
DESIGN DIRECTOR: KIRBY RODRIGUEZ / ART DIRECTOR: ALEX GROSSMAN
DESIGNERS: NICOLETTE BERTHELOT, SHANNA GREENBERG
ILLUSTRATOR: LAURA CARLIN / PHOTO EDITOR: DARRICK HARRIS
ASSOCIATE PHOTO EDITOR: LINDA DENAHAN
ASSISTANT PHOTO EDITOR: AJA NUZZI
PUBLISHER: CONDÉ NAST PUBLICATIONS INC.
ISSUE: NOVEMBER 2008 / CATEGORY: ILLO: SINGLE/SPREAD

629

630

631

/629/ **NATIONAL GEOGRAPHIC ADVENTURE**
ART DIRECTOR: DAVID MCKENNA
ASSISTANT ART DIRECTOR: JACQUELINE MUNZ
ILLUSTRATOR: FRANK STOCKTON
PHOTO EDITORS: SABINE MEYER, CAROLINE HIRSCH
PUBLISHER: NATIONAL GEOGRAPHIC SOCIETY
ISSUE: AUGUST 2008
CATEGORY: ILLO: STORY

/630/ **CONDÉ NAST TRAVELER**
DESIGN DIRECTOR: ROBERT BEST
ART DIRECTOR: ANDY OMEL
DESIGNER: JEE LEE
ILLUSTRATOR: MATTHEW COOK
DIRECTOR OF PHOTOGRAPHY: KATHLEEN KLECH
PUBLISHER: CONDÉ NAST PUBLICATIONS, INC.
ISSUE: OCTOBER 2008
CATEGORY: ILLO: STORY

/631/ **ENTERTAINMENT WEEKLY**
DESIGN DIRECTOR: BRIAN ANSTEY
DEPUTY ART DIRECTOR: ERIC PAUL
ILLUSTRATOR: JILLIAN TAMAKI
DIRECTOR OF PHOTOGRAPHY: LISA BERMAN
MANAGING EDITOR: RICK TETZELI
PUBLISHER: TIME INC.
ISSUE: NOVEMBER 21, 2008
CATEGORY: ILLO: STORY

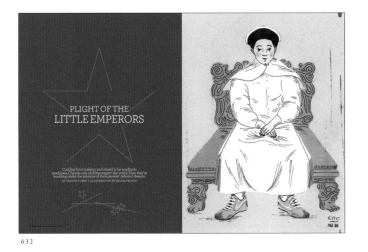

632

632

633

633

634

635

/632/ PSYCHOLOGY TODAY
CREATIVE DIRECTOR: EDWARD LEVINE
ART DIRECTOR: KATHERINE BIGELOW
ILLUSTRATOR: BRIAN CRONIN
STUDIO: LEVINE DESIGN INC.
PUBLISHER: SUSSEX PUBLISHERS
ISSUE: JULY/AUGUST 2008
CATEGORY: ILLO: STORY

/633/ GQ
DESIGN DIRECTOR: FRED WOODWARD
DESIGNER: ANTON IOUKHNOVETS
ILLUSTRATOR: ZOHAR LAZAR
DIRECTOR OF PHOTOGRAPHY: DORA SOMOSI
EDITOR-IN-CHIEF: JIM NELSON
PUBLISHER: CONDÉ NAST PUBLICATIONS INC.
ISSUE: JUNE 2008
CATEGORY: ILLO: STORY

/634/ NEW YORK
DESIGN DIRECTOR: CHRIS DIXON
ART DIRECTOR: RANDY MINOR
DESIGNER: RANDY MINOR
ILLUSTRATORS: RODRIGO CORRAL, JULES ARTHUR,
HENRY JANSEN, DIENSTSTELLE 75
DIRECTOR OF PHOTOGRAPHY: JODY QUON
EDITOR-IN-CHIEF: ADAM MOSS
PUBLISHER: NEW YORK MAGAZINE HOLDINGS, LLC
ISSUE: AUGUST 18, 2008
CATEGORY: ILLO: STORY

636

636

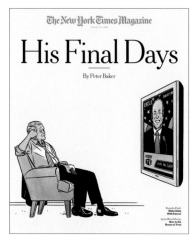

637

637

638

638

/636/ **THE NEW YORK TIMES MAGAZINE**
CREATIVE DIRECTOR: JANET FROELICH
ART DIRECTOR: AREM DUPLESSIS
DEPUTY ART DIRECTOR: GAIL BICHLER
DESIGNER: CATHERINE GILMORE-BARNES
ILLUSTRATOR: NATHAN FOX
EDITOR-IN-CHIEF: GERRY MARZORATI
PUBLISHER: THE NEW YORK TIMES
ISSUE: NOVEMBER 16, 2008
CATEGORY: ILLO: STORY

/637/ **THE NEW YORK TIMES MAGAZINE**
CREATIVE DIRECTOR: JANET FROELICH
ART DIRECTOR: AREM DUPLESSIS
DEPUTY ART DIRECTOR: GAIL BICHLER
DESIGNER: AREM DUPLESSIS
ILLUSTRATOR: R. KIKUO JOHNSON
EDITOR-IN-CHIEF: GERRY MARZORATI
PUBLISHER: THE NEW YORK TIMES
ISSUE: AUGUST 31, 2008
CATEGORY: ILLO: STORY

/638/ **THE NEW YORK TIMES MAGAZINE**
CREATIVE DIRECTOR: JANET FROELICH
ART DIRECTOR: AREM DUPLESSIS
DEPUTY ART DIRECTOR: GAIL BICHLER
DESIGNER: AREM DUPLESSIS
ILLUSTRATOR: ANDY FRIEDMAN
EDITOR-IN-CHIEF: GERRY MARZORATI
PUBLISHER: THE NEW YORK TIMES
ISSUE: MARCH 16, 2008
CATEGORY: ILLO: STORY

Illustration by THOMAS FUCHS

639

Your Privates

THE COMPLETE INSTRUCTIONS

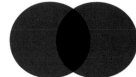

They don't come with an owner's manual,
so we created this ultimate guide to
every man's first—and most powerful—
set of tools

BY JIM THORNTON

639

639

/639/ MEN'S HEALTH
DESIGN DIRECTOR: GEORGE KARABOTSOS
ART DIRECTORS: VIKKI NESTICO, JOHN DIXON
DESIGNER: WILBERT GUTIÉRREZ
ILLUSTRATORS: THOMAS FUCHS, ANDREA DEZSÖ,
JONATHAN ROSEN, CAHAN AND ASSOCIATES
DIRECTOR OF PHOTOGRAPHY: BRENDA MILLIS
PUBLISHER: RODALE INC.
ISSUE: OCTOBER 2008
CATEGORY: ILLO: STORY

Her
idyllic childhood
was shattered by
a violent
civil war.

In Search of a Lost Africa By Helene Cooper

Her return
from exile revealed
what she had, and had not,
left behind.

September 2003

AS I LOOKED DOWN FROM MY FLIGHT onto the dense green rain forest that surrounds
Robertsfield airport, all I could see was bush. From the air, Liberia looked lush and
completely uninhabited. Fierce waves from the Atlantic hurled at the shoreline.
   During my growing-up years in Liberia in the 1970s, I had made the descent to
Robertsfield more than a dozen times, usually when returning home from summer
vacations. I sat so close to the plane window that it clouded from my breath. I would
look down for the landmarks that told me I was home: the rubber trees at Firestone,
the squat, red-clay-tinged whitewash buildings of Schieffelin, the three-headed palm

Illustrations by Laura Carlin

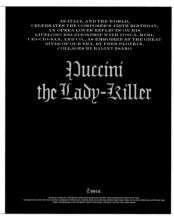

642

642

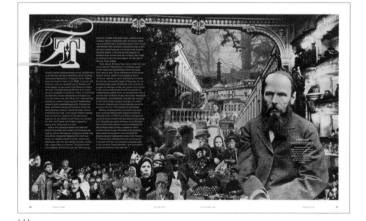

643

643

644

644

/640/ **THE NEW YORK TIMES MAGAZINE**
CREATIVE DIRECTOR: JANET FROELICH / ART DIRECTOR: AREM DUPLESSIS
DEPUTY ART DIRECTOR: GAIL BICHLER / DESIGNER: CATHERINE GILMORE-BARNES
ILLUSTRATOR: LAURA CARLIN / EDITOR-IN-CHIEF: GERRY MARZORATI
PUBLISHER: THE NEW YORK TIMES / ISSUE: APRIL 6, 2008
CATEGORY: ILLO: STORY

/641/ **COOKIE**
DESIGN DIRECTOR: KIRBY RODRIGUEZ / ART DIRECTOR: ALEX GROSSMAN
DESIGNERS: NICOLETTE BERTHELOT, SHANNA GREENBERG
ILLUSTRATOR: JILLIAN TAMAKI / PHOTO EDITOR: DARRICK HARRIS
ASSOCIATE PHOTO EDITOR: LINDA DENAHAN
ASSISTANT PHOTO EDITOR: AJA NUZZI
PUBLISHER: CONDÉ NAST PUBLICATIONS INC.
ISSUE: MARCH 2008 / CATEGORY: ILLO: STORY

/642/ **CULTURE + TRAVEL**
CREATIVE DIRECTOR: EMILY CRAWFORD / DESIGNER: EMILY CRAWFORD
ILLUSTRATOR: BALINT ZSAKO/ PUBLISHER: LOUISE BLOUIN MEDIA
ISSUE: MAY/JUNE 2008 / CATEGORY: ILLO: STORY

/643/ **WIRED**
CREATIVE DIRECTOR: SCOTT DADICH / DESIGN DIRECTOR: WYATT MITCHELL
ART DIRECTOR: CARL DETORRES / DESIGNER: CARL DETORRES
ILLUSTRATORS: AARON KOBLIN, ALEX DRAGELESCU, JASON SALAVON,
PAUL PRUDENCE, CASEY REAS, JONATHAN HARRIS, SEP KAMVAR
DIRECTOR OF PHOTOGRAPHY: CAROLYN RAUCH
PHOTOGRAPHER: GABRIELA HASBUN
PUBLISHER: CONDÉ NAST PUBLICATIONS, INC.
ISSUE: MARCH 2008 / CATEGORY: ILLO: STORY

/644/ **CULTURE + TRAVEL**
CREATIVE DIRECTOR: EMILY CRAWFORD / DESIGNER: EMILY CRAWFORD
ILLUSTRATOR: BALINT ZSAKO / PUBLISHER: LOUISE BLOUIN MEDIA
ISSUE: JANUARY/FEBRUARY 2008 / CATEGORY: ILLO: STORY

645

645

646

646

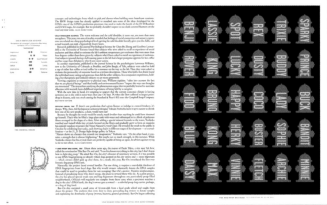

647

647

/645/ **BON APPÉTIT**
DESIGN DIRECTOR: MATTHEW LENNING
ART DIRECTOR: ROBERT FESTINO
ILLUSTRATOR: MARTHA RICH
PHOTOGRAPHER: MARTHA RICH
EDITOR-IN-CHIEF: BARBARA FAIRCHILD
PUBLISHER: CONDÉ NAST PUBLICATIONS, INC.
ISSUE: JULY 2008
CATEGORY: ILLO: STORY

/646/ **NEW YORK**
DESIGN DIRECTOR: CHRIS DIXON
ART DIRECTOR: RANDY MINOR
DESIGNER: CAROL HAYES
ILLUSTRATOR: HOPE GANGLOFF
DIRECTOR OF PHOTOGRAPHY: JODY QUON
EDITOR-IN-CHIEF: ADAM MOSS
PUBLISHER: NEW YORK MAGAZINE HOLDINGS, LLC
ISSUE: DECEMBER 15, 2008
CATEGORY: ILLO: STORY

/647/ **THE NEW YORK TIMES MAGAZINE**
CREATIVE DIRECTOR: JANET FROELICH
ART DIRECTOR: AREM DUPLESSIS
DEPUTY ART DIRECTOR: GAIL BICHLER
DESIGNERS: LEO JUNG, HILARY GREENBAUM
ILLUSTRATOR: VIK MUNIZ
EDITOR-IN-CHIEF: GERRY MARZORATI
PUBLISHER: THE NEW YORK TIMES
ISSUE: DECEMBER 14, 2008
CATEGORY: ILLO: STORY

style

the pants handbook

How to find a pair of trousers that will **fit and flatter your unique shape.**

WRITTEN BY KRISTINA GRISH
ILLUSTRATIONS BY KAT MACLEOD

LETTER FROM CHINA

STEALING WEATHER

In 1946, three G.E. scientists found that seeding clouds with dry ice or silver iodide could affect precipitation. The Pentagon soon had hopes of weaponizing the sky. Now it's the Chinese whose artillery is aimed at controlling the weather

BY WILLIAM LANGEWIESCHE

JAMES WOLCOTT

THE NEWS BLUES

The author has lived through a lot of hair-raising times—nuclear standoffs, assassinations, 9/11, financial meltdown—but now he's *sure* the world is going to hell in a handbasket. And, God knows, the media are only making it worse

---

648

style / PANTS HANDBOOK

Q. I'm curvy and short. Which styles work for me?

Q. Pants pull at my thighs but fit elsewhere. What do I do?

Q. A low rise reveals too much, and a high rise looks dumpy. What's a happy medium?

110

LETTER FROM CHINA

THE XINJIANG REGION HAS
500 ROCKET LAUNCHERS AND 600 TWIN-BARREL, 37-MM, RAPID-FIRE CANNONS FOR SHOOTING AT CLOUDS IN THE HOPES OF PRODUCING RAIN. WE WATCHED THE STORM FRONT APPROACH.

649

WOLCOTT

OUR TRUE GRIT HAS SUCCUMBED TO
DRY ROT AND TOFU. ONCE A VIRILE NATION CAPABLE
OF LANDING ON THE MOON, NOW LOOK AT US. PATHETIC.

650

/648/ REAL SIMPLE
DESIGN DIRECTOR: ELLENE WUNDROK
ART DIRECTOR: ELSA MEHARY
ILLUSTRATOR: KAT MACLEOD
DIRECTOR OF PHOTOGRAPHY: CASEY TIERNEY
PUBLISHER: TIME INC.
ISSUE: NOVEMBER 2008
CATEGORY: ILLO: STORY

/649/ VANITY FAIR
DESIGN DIRECTOR: DAVID HARRIS
ART DIRECTORS: JULIE WEISS, CHRIS MUELLER
ILLUSTRATOR: BRAD HOLLAND
EDITOR-IN-CHIEF: GRAYDON CARTER
PUBLISHER: CONDÉ NAST PUBLICATIONS INC.
ISSUE: MAY 2008
CATEGORY: ILLO: STORY

/650/ VANITY FAIR
DESIGN DIRECTOR: DAVID HARRIS
ART DIRECTORS: JULIE WEISS, CHRIS MUELLER
ILLUSTRATOR: BARRY BLITT
EDITOR-IN-CHIEF: GRAYDON CARTER
PUBLISHER: CONDÉ NAST PUBLICATIONS INC.
ISSUE: NOVEMBER 2008
CATEGORY: ILLO: STORY

/CONTRIBUTORS/

OTHER/

ROBERT PERINO

RYAN THACKER

SCOTT DADICH

SCOTT STOWELL

SERIFCAN OZCAN

MAILI HOLIMAN

MATTHEW ERICSON

JANET FROELICH

JEFF GLENDENNING

JENNIFER MOORE

JILL GREENBERG

DEANNA LOWE

DORA SOMOSI

DRAGOS LEMNEI

EDMUND D. FOUNTAIN

EMILY CRAWFORD

AMANDA COX

ANTON IOUKHNOVETS

ARMIN HARRIS

WIRED

THE NEW YORK TIMES

PLAY

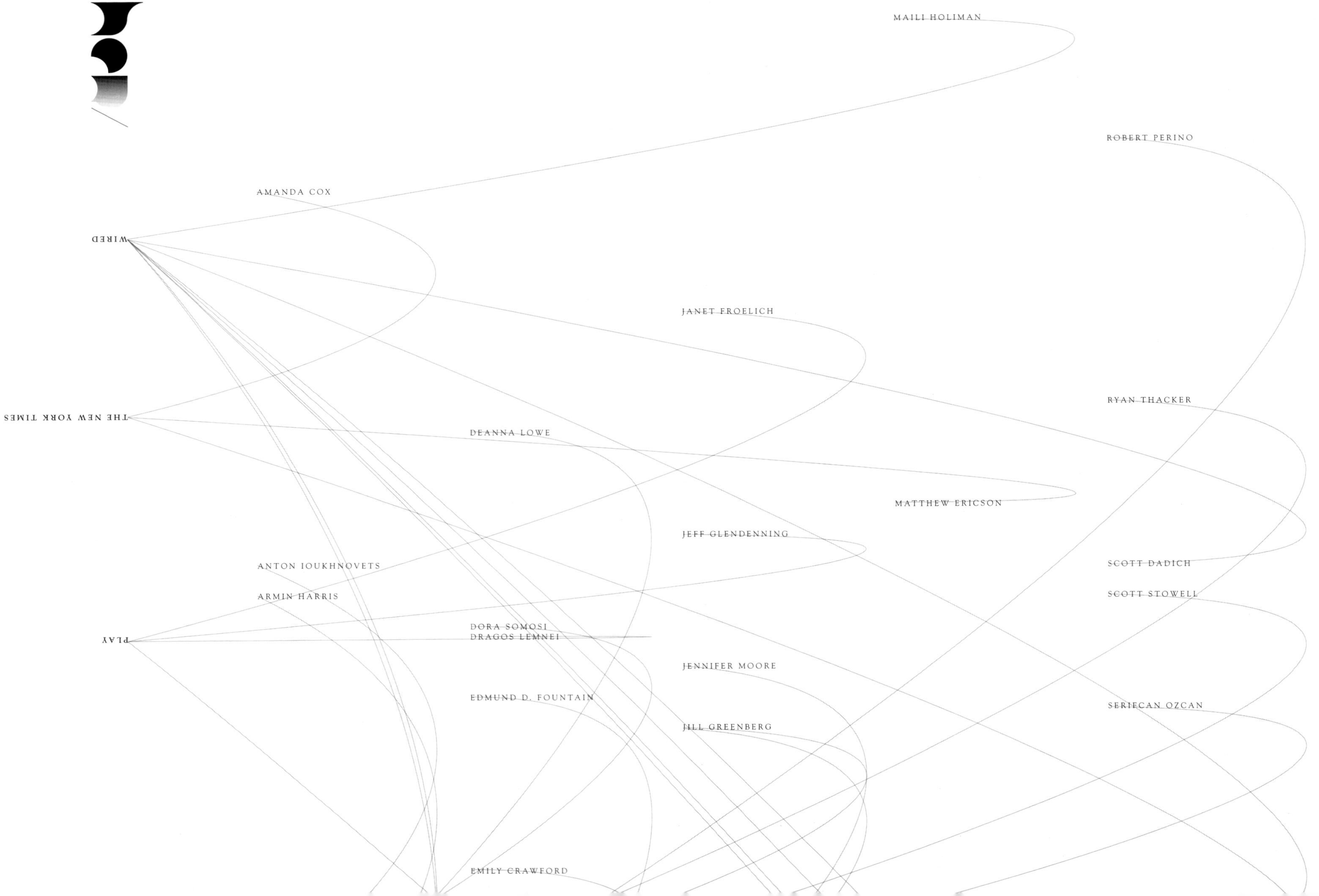

STEVE DUENES

SUZETTE MOYER

NAI LEE LUM

NATALIE MATUTSCHOVSKY

TONY MIKOLAJCZYK

VICTOR KRUMMENACHER

WALTER C. BAUMANN

WYATT MITCHELL

ZACHARY ZAVISLAK

PLUSISM

OPEN

JUSTIN O'NEILL

KEN DELAGO

KEVIN BANNA

FRED WOODWARD

GREG POND

BRITTNEY BLAIR

BRUCE MOYER

BRYAN CHRISTIE DESIGN

CARL DETORRES

CAROLYN RAUCH

CATALOGTREE

CORY JACOBS

GQ

GOOD

GOLF DIGEST

FORTUNE

CULTURE + TRAVEL

CHICAGO

BAY

/PUBLICATIONS/

Feed the World

DEMAND FOR FOOD IS RISING, AND THE WORLD'S FARMERS ARE STRUGGLING TO KEEP UP. IT'S TIME FOR A NEW GREEN REVOLUTION.

FORTY YEARS AGO, we defused the Population Bomb with the Green Revolution. Modern fertilizers, pesticides, and herbicides boosted crop yield and fed an expanding population. But now the chemical age of agriculture is running out of juice. Yields—production per acre—have gone flat while demand is rising faster than ever, as the chart below shows. Fortunately, we can reverse those trends. Biotech and genetics can improve productivity and profitability. Trade reform can ease the flow of food between nations. In the following pages, we present an atlas that shows where the problems lie and what to do about them. The good news: Our capacity for innovation is as limitless as our appetites.

PHOTO ILLUSTRATIONS BY STEPHEN DOYLE + ZACK ZAVISLAK

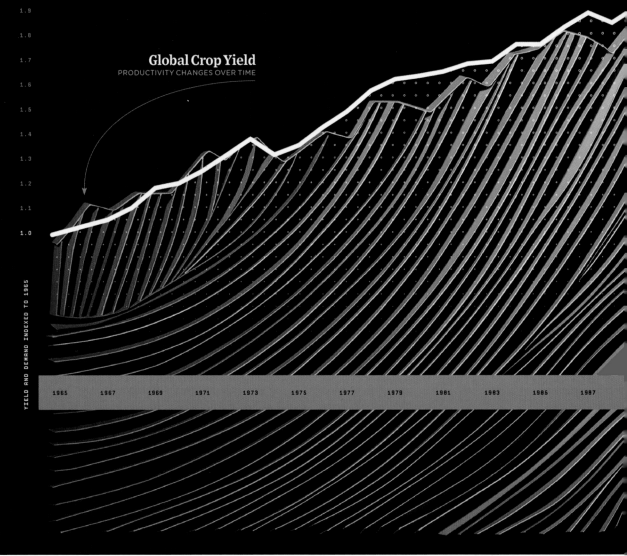

Global Crop Yield
PRODUCTIVITY CHANGES OVER TIME

3.2 3.1 3.0 2.9 2.8 2.7 2.6 2.5 2.4 2.3 2.2 2.1 2.0 1.9 1.8 1.7 1.6 1.5 1.4 1.3 1.2 1.1 1.0

YIELD AND DEMAND INDEXED TO 1965

1965 1967 1969 1971 1973 1975 1977 1979 1981 1983 1985 1987

651

You Are Here
AS FARM YIELD
LEVELS OFF, DEMAND
CONTINUES TO RISE.

Global Demand
CROP PRODUCT CONSUMPTION

Source:
**Goldman Sachs,
March 2007**

/651/ **WIRED**
CREATIVE DIRECTOR: SCOTT DADICH / DESIGN DIRECTOR: WYATT MITCHELL /ART DIRECTORS: CARL DETORRES, MAILI HOLIMAN
DESIGNERS: CARL DETORRES, MAILI HOLIMAN, VICTOR KRUMENNACHER, WALTER C. BAUMANN, SCOTT DADICH
ILLUSTRATOR: STEPHEN DOYLE / PHOTO EDITOR: CAROLYN RAUCH / PHOTOGRAPHER: ZACHARY ZAVISLAK
PUBLISHER: CONDÉ NAST PUBLICATIONS, INC./ ISSUE: NOVEMBER 2008 / CATEGORY: INFOGRAPHICS: SINGLE/SPREAD/STORY

YOU SHOULD VOTE BECAUSE...

184.

Barack Obama and John McCain have raised millions of dollars for their presidential campaigns. In GOOD's second installment of Political NASCAR, we look at the uniforms the two candidates would wear if companies wanted to use their political donations as advertisements, and if running for president ended with the winner doing donuts on the White House lawn.

Finance, Insurance, Real Estate
Lawyers/Lobbyists
Misc. Business
Communications/ Electronics
Health
Construction
Energy/ Natural Resources
Education
Government/ Military

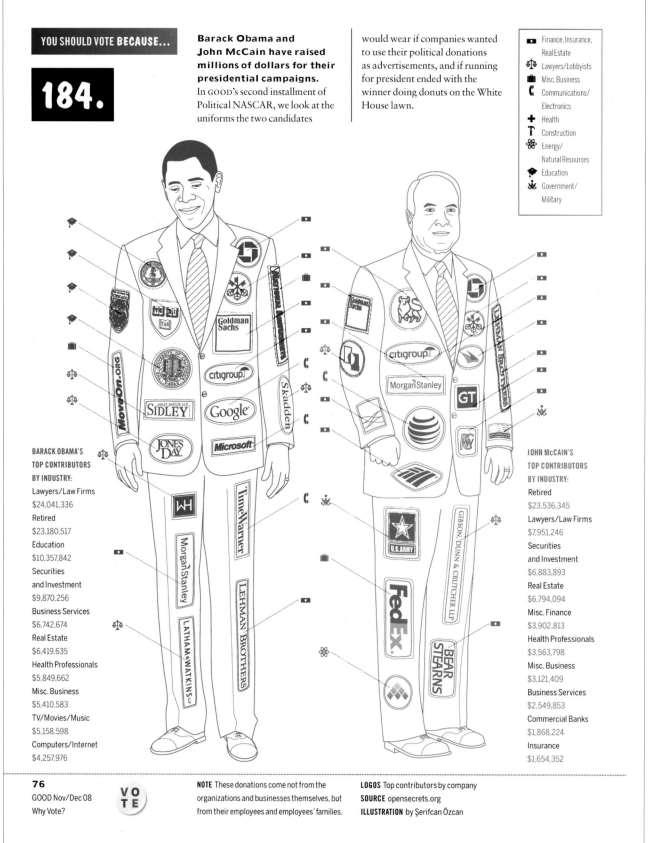

BARACK OBAMA'S TOP CONTRIBUTORS BY INDUSTRY:

Lawyers/Law Firms
$24,041,336
Retired
$23,180,517
Education
$10,357,842
Securities and Investment
$9,870,256
Business Services
$6,742,674
Real Estate
$6,419,635
Health Professionals
$5,849,662
Misc. Business
$5,410,583
TV/Movies/Music
$5,158,598
Computers/Internet
$4,257,976

JOHN McCAIN'S TOP CONTRIBUTORS BY INDUSTRY:

Retired
$23,536,345
Lawyers/Law Firms
$7,951,246
Securities and Investment
$6,883,893
Real Estate
$6,794,094
Misc. Finance
$3,902,813
Health Professionals
$3,563,798
Misc. Business
$3,121,409
Business Services
$2,549,853
Commercial Banks
$1,868,224
Insurance
$1,654,352

76
GOOD Nov/Dec 08
Why Vote?

VOTE

NOTE These donations come not from the organizations and businesses themselves, but from their employees and employees' families.

LOGOS Top contributors by company
SOURCE opensecrets.org
ILLUSTRATION by Şerifcan Özcan

/652/ **GOOD**
DESIGN DIRECTOR: SCOTT STOWELL / DESIGNER: RYAN THACKER / ILLUSTRATOR: SERIFCAN OZCAN / STUDIO: OPEN
PUBLISHER: GOOD WORLDWIDE, INC. / CLIENT: GOOD / ISSUE: NOVEMBER/DECEMBER 2008 / CATEGORY: INFOGRAPHICS: SINGLE/SPREAD/STORY

IKE'S 1,000-PLUS DAYS OF GOLF IN OFFICE

● PRACTICE ● PLAYED AT LEAST ONE ROUND
○ SUFFERED HEART ATTACK (1955)
○ HOSPITALIZED FOR STOMACH AILMENT (1956)
○ SUFFERED SLIGHT STROKE (1957)

1953

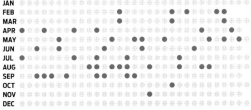

World events: Stalin dies.... Nuclear tests in Nevada....
Soviet Union sends troops to East Berlin.... Spies Ethel and Julius Rosenberg
executed.... Tito becomes president of Yugoslavia.... Korean War ends.

1954

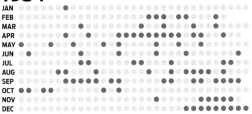

World events: Eisenhower warns against U.S. intervention in
Vietnam.... Mass vaccination against polio.... McCarthy hearings on
communism.... Supreme Court bans racial segregation in public schools.

1955

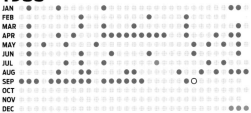

World events: Churchill resigns as prime minister.... Perón
ousted in military coup.... Eisenhower suffers heart attack.... Rosa
Parks arrested after refusing to give up bus seat.... AFL-CIO formed.

1956

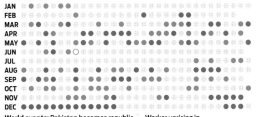

World events: Pakistan becomes republic.... Worker uprising in
Poland.... Hungarian revolution.... Suez Canal crisis....
Eisenhower wins re-election.... Japan becomes member of United Nations.

1957

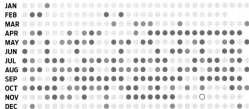

World events: FBI arrests Jimmy Hoffa.... Federal troops sent to enforce
school integration in Little Rock.... Soviet Union launches Sputnik....
First U.S. attempt to launch satellite fails.... First U.S. combat fatality in Vietnam.

1958

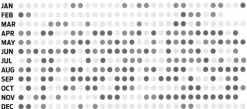

World events: The word "aerospace" is coined.... Khrushchev becomes premier
of Soviet Union.... Castro's army continues attacks in Cuba.... Marines land
in Beirut.... Soviet Union performs nuclear test.... NASA created.

1959

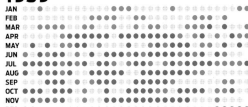

World events: Castro takes power in Cuba after Batista is driven from Havana.
... Alaska and Hawaii become states.... Dalai Lama flees Tibet....
Khrushchev meets with Eisenhower at Camp David.

1960

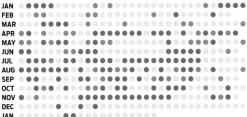

World events: American U-2 spy plane shot down over Soviet Union....
Eisenhower signs Civil Rights Act.... Khrushchev pounds shoe on table at
United Nations.... John F. Kennedy wins presidential election.

HANK WALKER/TIME LIFE PICTURES/GETTY IMAGES

/653/ **GOLF DIGEST**
DESIGN DIRECTOR: KEN DELAGO / DESIGNER: KEN DELAGO / PUBLISHER: CONDÉ NAST PUBLICATIONS INC.
ISSUE: APRIL 2008 / CATEGORY: INFOGRAPHICS: SINGLE/SPREAD/STORY

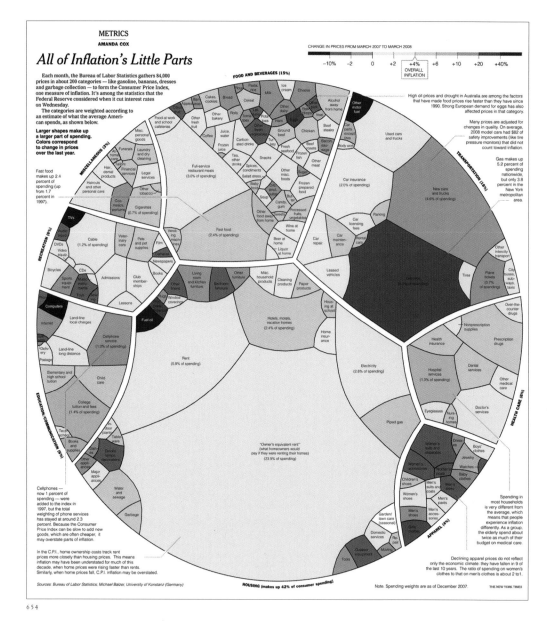

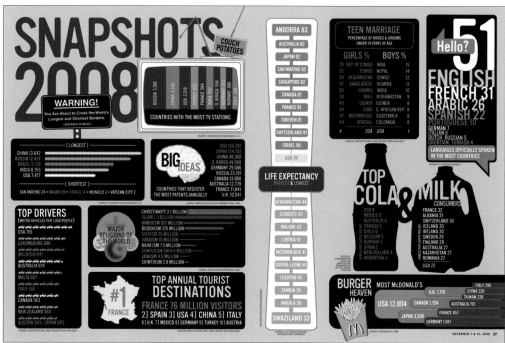

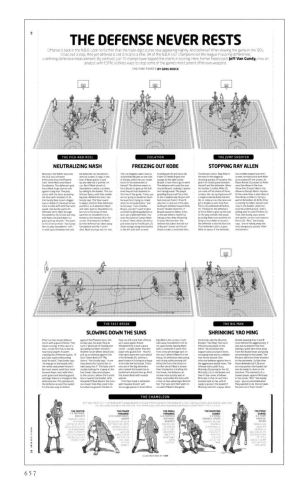

656

657

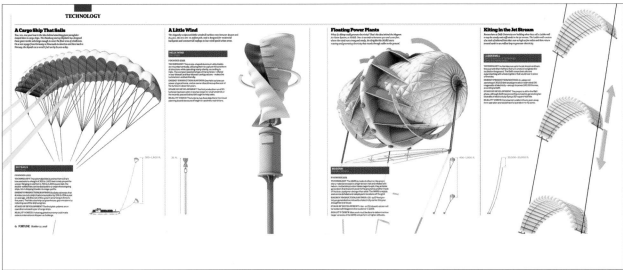

658

GOLD MEDAL
/659/ THE BIG PICTURE
CREATIVE DIRECTOR: ALAN TAYLOR
PUBLISHER: THE NEW YORK TIMES CO.
CATEGORY: ONLINE: PHOTOGRAPHY

SILVER MEDAL
/660/ THE NEW YORK TIMES
DESIGN DIRECTORS: STEVE DUENES,
MATTHEW ERICSON
DESIGNERS: LEE BYRON, AMANDA COX,
MATTHEW ERICSON
PUBLISHER: THE NEW YORK TIMES
CATEGORY: ONLINE: INFORMATION GRAPHICS

/661/ THE NEW YORK TIMES
DESIGN DIRECTORS: STEVE DUENES,
MATTHEW ERICSON
DESIGNERS: MIKA GRÖNDAHL, XAQUÍN G.V.
PUBLISHER: THE NEW YORK TIMES
CATEGORY: ONLINE: INFORMATION GRAPHICS

A Map of Olympic Medals

Circles are sized by the number of medals that countries won in summer Olympic Games. Use the slider to view past Olympics, or click on a country to display a list of its medal winners.

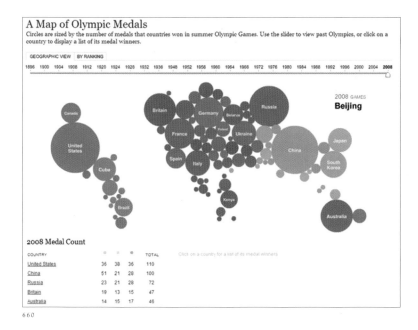

2008 Medal Count

COUNTRY				TOTAL
United States	36	38	36	110
China	51	21	28	100
Russia	23	21	28	72
Britain	19	13	15	47
Australia	14	15	17	46

660

A House of Glass

The cascading public staircase that covers the new TKTS discount booth in Duffy Square is made almost entirely of structural-strength glass: walls, beams, treads and risers. (Related Article)

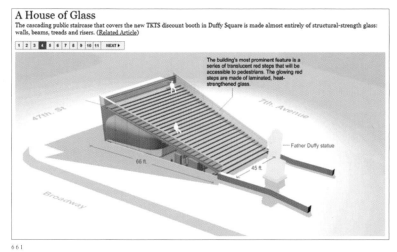

661

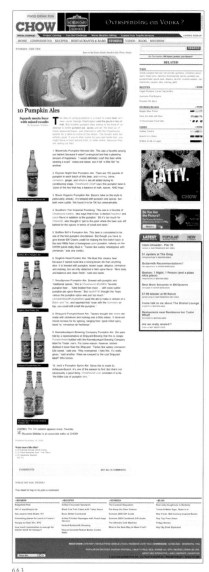

10 Pumpkin Ales

663

Oil Prices Reach a Symbolic Mark

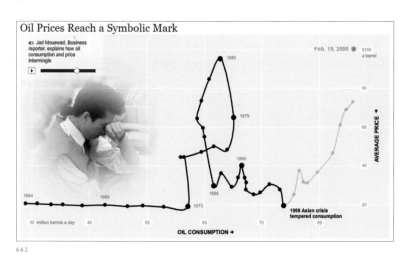

662

President Map

664

/662/ THE NEW YORK TIMES
DESIGN DIRECTORS: STEVE DUENES,
MATTHEW ERICSON
DESIGNERS: AMANDA COX, VU NGUYEN
PUBLISHER: THE NEW YORK TIMES
CATEGORY: ONLINE: INFORMATION GRAPHICS

/663/ CHOW.COM
CREATIVE DIRECTOR: JEREMY LACROIX
DESIGNERS: JACKSON PUFF,
BRENDA BITTERLICH
PHOTOGRAPHER: CHRIS ROCHELLE
FRONT END DEVELOPER: MARISSA MARQUEZ
PUBLISHER: CBS INTERACTIVE
CATEGORY: ONLINE: SERIES OR COLUMN

/664/ THE NEW YORK TIMES
DESIGN DIRECTORS: STEVE DUENES,
MATTHEW ERICSON
DESIGNERS: MATTHEW BLOCH, SHAN CARTER,
MATTHEW ERICSON
PUBLISHER: THE NEW YORK TIMES
CATEGORY: ONLINE: INFORMATION GRAPHICS

/665/ BACKPACKER
DESIGN DIRECTOR: MATTHEW BATES
DESIGNERS: JONATHAN DORN, ANTHONY
CERRETANI, KRIS WAGNER, KATIE HERRELL,
TED ALVAREZ, JACKIE MCCAFFREY
PHOTOGRAPHERS: JULIA VANDENOEVER,
GENNY FULLERTON
PUBLISHER: ACTIVE INTEREST MEDIA
CATEGORY: ONLINE: REDESIGN

/666/ THE DAILY BEAST
CREATIVE DIRECTOR: BRANDON RALPH
DESIGN DIRECTOR: SAPNA GUPTA
ART DIRECTOR: JEREMY DAVIS
FRONT END DEVELOPER: VINCENT TUSCANO
STUDIO: CODE AND THEORY /PUBLISHER: IAC
CLIENT: THE DAILY BEAST / CATEGORY: ONLINE:
SITE INDEPENDENT OF A PRINT PUBLICATION

/667/ THE NEW YORK TIMES
DESIGN DIRECTORS: STEVE DUENES,
MATTHEW ERICSON / DESIGNERS: SHAN CARTER,
GRAHAM ROBERTS, HAEYOUN PARK, JOE WARD,
ARCHIE TSE / PUBLISHER: THE NEW YORK TIMES
CATEGORY: ONLINE: INFORMATION GRAPHICS

/668/ BONAPPETIT.COM
CREATIVE DIRECTOR: SCOTT IRWIN DESIGN
DIRECTOR: MATTHEW LENNING
DESIGNER: GENEVIEVE SOUTHERN
STUDIO: CONDÉ NAST DIGITAL
EDITOR-IN-CHIEF: BARBARA A. FAIRCHILD
PUBLISHER: CONDÉ NAST PUBLICATIONS INC.
CATEGORY: ONLINE: SITE ASSOCIATED WITH A
PRINT PUBLICATION

/669/ THE NEW YORK TIMES
DESIGN DIRECTORS: STEVE DUENES,
MATTHEW ERICSON
DESIGNERS: LEE BYRON, ALICIA DESANTIS,
PHIL PATTON / PUBLISHER: THE NEW YORK TIMES
CATEGORY: ONLINE: INFORMATION GRAPHICS

/670/ THE NEW YORK TIMES
DESIGN DIRECTORS: STEVE DUENES,
MATTHEW ERICSON / DESIGNERS: GRAHAM
ROBERTS, JONATHAN CORUM
PUBLISHER: THE NEW YORK TIMES
CATEGORY: ONLINE: INFORMATION GRAPHICS

665

666

667

668

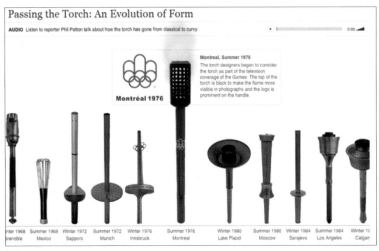

669

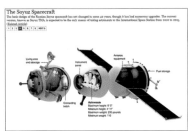

670

/671/ **THE NEW YORK TIMES**
DESIGN DIRECTORS: STEVE DUENES,
MATTHEW ERICSON
DESIGNERS: AMANDA COX, MATTHEW BLOCH
PUBLISHER: THE NEW YORK TIMES
CATEGORY: ONLINE: INFORMATION GRAPHICS

/672/ **GOURMET.COM**
CREATIVE DIRECTORS: RICHARD FERRETTI,
SCOTT IRWIN
DESIGNER: JENNIFER ROSS
ONLINE EDITORIAL DIRECTOR: ADAM HOUGHTALING
STUDIO: CONDÉ NAST DIGITAL
EDITOR-IN-CHIEF: RUTH REICHL
PUBLISHER: CONDÉ NAST PUBLICATIONS INC.
CATEGORY: ONLINE: SITE ASSOCIATED WITH A
PRINT PUBLICATION

/673/ **THE NEW YORK TIMES**
DESIGN DIRECTORS: STEVE DUENES,
MATTHEW ERICSON
DESIGNERS: MATTHEW BLOCH, SHAN CARTER,
GRAHAM ROBERTS, MIKA GRÖNDAHL, ERIN AIGNER,
KEVIN QUEALY
PUBLISHER: THE NEW YORK TIMES
CATEGORY: ONLINE: INFORMATION GRAPHICS

/674/ **T, THE NEW YORK TIMES STYLE MAGAZINE**
CREATIVE DIRECTOR: JANET FROELICH SENIOR
PHOTO EDITOR: JUDITH PUCKETT-RINELLA
ONLINE DIRECTOR: HORACIO SILVA
VISUAL EDITOR: JENNIFER HUNG
EDITOR-IN-CHIEF: STEFANO TONCHI
PUBLISHER: THE NEW YORK TIMES
CATEGORY: ONLINE: VIDEO

/675/ **T, THE NEW YORK TIMES STYLE MAGAZINE**
CREATIVE DIRECTOR: JANET FROELICH
SENIOR PHOTO EDITOR: JUDITH PUCKETT-RINELLA
ONLINE DIRECTOR: HORACIO SILVA
VISUAL EDITOR: JENNIFER HUNG
EDITOR-IN-CHIEF: STEFANO TONCHI
PUBLISHER: THE NEW YORK TIMES
CATEGORY: ONLINE: VIDEO

671

673

675

672

674

676

677

GOLD MEDAL
/676/ **GQ**
DESIGN DIRECTOR: FRED WOODWARD
ART DIRECTOR: ANTON IOUKHNOVETS
DIRECTOR OF PHOTOGRAPHY: DORA SOMOSI
PHOTO EDITOR: JUSTIN O'NEILL
PHOTOGRAPHER: JILL GREENBERG
EDITOR-IN-CHIEF: JIM NELSON
PUBLISHER: CONDÉ NAST PUBLICATIONS INC.
ISSUE: FEBRUARY 2008
CATEGORY: CREATURE FEATURE

/677/ **CHICAGO**
ART DIRECTOR: JENNIFER MOORE
DESIGNER: JENNIFER MOORE
PHOTO EDITOR: BRITTNEY BLAIR
PHOTOGRAPHER: KEVIN BANNA
EDITOR-IN-CHIEF: RICHARD BABCOCK
PUBLISHER: CHICAGOLAND PUBLISHING
ISSUE: JUNE 2008
CATEGORY: CREATURE FEATURE

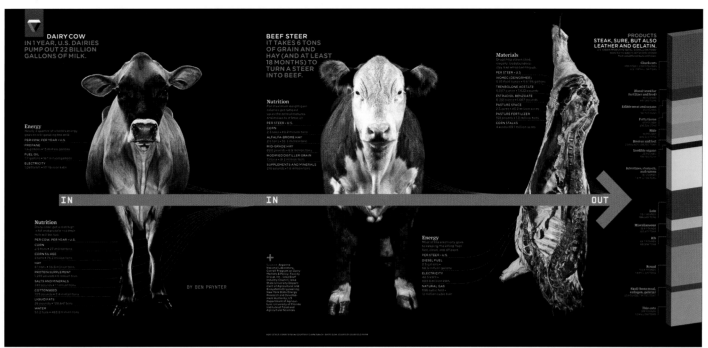

678

679

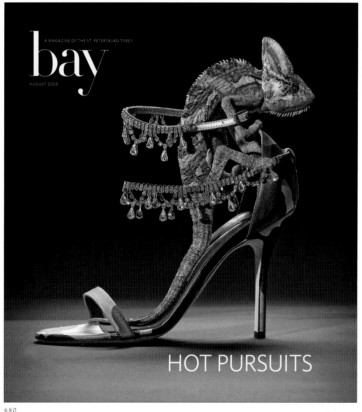

680

/678/ **WIRED**
CREATIVE DIRECTOR: SCOTT DADICH
DESIGN DIRECTOR: WYATT MITCHELL
ART DIRECTORS: MAILI HOLIMAN, CARL DETORRES
DESIGNERS: VICTOR KRUMMENACHER,
WALTER BAUMANN
ILLUSTRATOR: STEPHEN DOYLE
PHOTO EDITOR: CAROLYN RAUCH
PHOTOGRAPHER: ZACHARY ZAVISLAK
PUBLISHER: CONDÉ NAST PUBLICATIONS, INC.
ISSUE: NOVEMBER 2008
CATEGORY: CREATURE FEATURE

/679/ **CULTURE + TRAVEL**
CREATIVE DIRECTOR: EMILY CRAWFORD
DESIGNER: EMILY CRAWFORD
DIRECTOR OF PHOTOGRAPHY: CORY JACOBS
PHOTO EDITOR: NATALIE MATUTSCHOVSKY
PHOTOGRAPHER: JILL GREENBERG
PUBLISHER: LOUISE BLOUIN MEDIA
ISSUE: JANUARY/FEBRUARY 2008
CATEGORY: CREATURE FEATURE

/680/ **BAY**
CREATIVE DIRECTOR: SUZETTE MOYER
DIRECTOR OF PHOTOGRAPHY: BRUCE MOYER
PHOTOGRAPHER: EDMUND D. FOUNTAIN
PUBLISHER: ST. PETERSBURG TIMES
ISSUE: AUGUST 2008
CATEGORY: CREATURE FEATURE

The Student and Sports Competitions

681

681

682

682

683

683

/681/ 1ST PLACE
WINNER OF THE ADOBE SCHOLARSHIP
IN HONOR OF B.W. HONEYCUTT
DESIGNER: MELANIE TEPPICH
TITLE: TIME FOR CHANGE
SCHOOL: SCHOOL OF VISUAL ARTS
INSTRUCTORS: JEFF GLENDENNING, LUISE STAUSS

/682/ 2ND PLACE
DESIGNER: RAUL AGUILA
TITLE: DAFT PUNK
SCHOOL: SCHOOL OF VISUAL ARTS
INSTRUCTOR: JEFF GLENDENNING

/683/ 3RD PLACE
DESIGNER: RAUL AGUILA
TITLE: STILL LAUGHING, JACK BLACK
SCHOOL: SCHOOL OF VISUAL ARTS
INSTRUCTOR: JEFF GLENDENNING

684

684

685

685

686

686

/684/ 1ST HONORABLE MENTION
DESIGNER: ERIC CHANG
TITLE: DEEP SECRETS // MOUNTAIN BIKING
SCHOOL: CITY COLLEGE OF NEW YORK
INSTRUCTOR: LIANA ZAMORA

/685/ 2ND HONORABLE MENTION
DESIGNER: KATIE KINDINGER
TITLE: WHAT MAKES THE LEGO SO GREAT?
SCHOOL: MILWAUKEE INSTITUTE OF ART & DESIGN
INSTRUCTOR: DANIELLE GAGLIANO

/686/ 3RD HONORABLE MENTION
DESIGNER: ANTHONY CRUZ
TITLE: LADY GAGA
SCHOOL: AMERICAN ACADEMY OF ART, CHICAGO
INSTRUCTOR: CAROL LUC

687

688

689

/687/ **1ST PLACE**
DESIGNER: TANNER ELLISON
SCHOOL: THE UNIVERSITY OF NORTH TEXAS

/688/ **2ND PLACE**
DESIGNER: ALYSSA CRAWFORD
SCHOOL: THE UNIVERSITY OF DELAWARE

/689/ **3RD PLACE**
DESIGNER: JOE MARTINEZ
SCHOOL: PORTFOLIO CENTER

690

691

692

693

694

695

696

697

698

699

DISTINCTIVE MERIT

/690/ **JOSH COCHRAN**
TITLE: LOOKING FOR A MIRACLE
DESIGN DIRECTOR: MICHAEL LAWTON
PUBLICATION: POPULAR MECHANICS
PUBLISHER: THE HEARST CORPORATION-
MAGAZINES DIVISION
ISSUE: OCTOBER 2008

/691/ **JOSH COCHRAN**
TITLE: WELCOME TO CRAZYTOWN!
DESIGN DIRECTOR: BRIAN ANSTEY
PUBLICATION: ENTERTAINMENT WEEKLY
PUBLISHER: TIME INC.
ISSUE: OCTOBER 17, 2008

/692/ **GUY BILLOUT**
TITLE: A STRIKE IN THE DARK
ART DIRECTOR: CHRIS CURRY
PUBLICATION: THE NEW YORKER
PUBLISHER: CONDÉ NAST PUBLICATIONS INC.
ISSUE: FEBRUARY 2008

/693/ **CAMERON LAW**
TITLE: POWER CLASSICS: SHARES
AND SHARES ALIKE
ART DIRECTOR: DARREN LONG
PUBLICATION: POWER MAGAZINE
PUBLISHER: INFINITY MEDIA HONG KONG LTD.
ISSUE: OCTOBER 2008

/693/ **JOSH COCHRAN**
TITLE: ASK MILES: LOUD MUSIC
DESIGN DIRECTOR: KORY KENNEDY
ASSISTANT ART DIRECTOR: LEE WILLIAMS
PUBLICATION: RUNNER'S WORLD
PUBLISHER: RODALE INC. / ISSUE: DECEMBER 2008

/695/ **JASON MUNN**
TITLE: TALK, LISTEN, REPEAT
DESIGN DIRECTOR: GEORGE KARABOTSOS
ART DIRECTOR: ELIZABETH NEAL
PUBLICATION: MEN'S HEALTH
PUBLISHER: RODALE INC. / ISSUE: OCTOBER 2008

/696/ **GUY BILLOUT**
TITLE: LIGHTS
ART DIRECTOR: JASON TREAT
PUBLICATION: THE ATLANTIC MONTHLY
PUBLISHER: THE ATLANTIC MONTHLY
ISSUE: NOVEMBER 2008

/697/ **GUY BILLOUT**
TITLE: WHO'S SORRY NOW?
ART DIRECTOR: HERVÉ KWOMO
PUBLICATION: O, THE OPRAH MAGAZINE
PUBLISHER: THE HEARST CORPORATION
-MAGAZINES DIVISION
ISSUE: JULY 2008

/698/ **GUY BILLOUT**
TITLE: STATE SECRETS
ART DIRECTOR: CHRIS CURRY
PUBLICATION: THE NEW YORKER
PUBLISHER: CONDÉ NAST PUBLICATIONS INC.
ISSUE: APRIL 2008

/699/ **JOHN HENDRIX**
TITLE: WHO OWNS THE MOON?
DESIGN DIRECTOR: MICHAEL LAWTON
PUBLICATION: POPULAR MECHANICS
PUBLISHER: THE HEARST CORPORATION-
MAGAZINES DIVISION
ISSUE: JUNE 2008

700

703

701

702

704

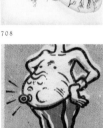

708

707

709

706

705

710

711

712

/700/ **JODY HEWGILL**
TITLE: HOW TO CHANGE SOMEONE'S LIFE
ART DIRECTOR: AMY SHROADS
PUBLICATION: STANFORD / PUBLISHER:
STANFORD UNIVERSITY / ISSUE: MARCH/APRIL 2008

/701/ **RACHEL SOLOMON**
TITLE: DAMNED SPOT!
ART DIRECTOR: ROMAN LUBA
PUBLICATION: PROTO /
PUBLISHER: TIME INC. CONTENT SOLUTIONS
ISSUE: SPRING 2008

/702/ **JODY HEWGILL**
TITLE: MY FAVORITE YEAR: 1994
DESIGN DIRECTOR: BRIAN ANSTEY
ART DIRECTOR: ERIC PAUL   PUBLICATION:
ENTERTAINMENT WEEKLY   PUBLISHER: TIME INC.
ISSUE: JUNE 27 - JULY 4, 2008

/703/ **MARC ROSENTHAL**
TITLE: REMAIN CALM
ART DIRECTOR: SOOJIN BUZELLI
PUBLICATION: PLANADVISER
ISSUE: 2008 YEAR IN REVIEW

/704/ **ALEX NABAUM**
TITLE: ASK THE EXPERTS:
NAUSEOUS AFTER SPEEDWORK
DESIGN DIRECTOR: KORY KENNEDY
DEPUTY ART DIRECTOR: MARC KAUFFMAN
PUBLICATION: RUNNER'S WORLD
PUBLISHER: RODALE INC. / ISSUE: AUGUST 2008

/705/ **JEFFREY DECOSTER**
TITLE: COMING FULL CIRCLE
DESIGN DIRECTOR: KORY KENNEDY
PUBLICATION: RUNNER'S WORLD
PUBLISHER: RODALE INC. / ISSUE: MARCH 2008

/706/ **MARK KAUFMAN**
TITLE: WHAT A HOOT!
ART DIRECTOR: WILLIAM QUINBY
PUBLICATION: SEATTLE METROPOLITAN
ISSUE: DECEMBER 2008

DISTINCTIVE MERIT
/707/ **MARCOS CHIN**
TITLE: RUNNING FREE / DESIGN DIRECTOR:
KORY KENNEDY / PUBLICATION: RUNNER'S WORLD
PUBLISHER: RODALE INC. / ISSUE: MARCH 2008

/708/ **CHRISTOPHER SILAS NEAL**
TITLE: MARRIED TO HEART HEALTH
CREATIVE DIRECTOR: JILL ARMUS
ART DIRECTOR: JESSICA SOKOL
PUBLICATION: PREVENTION
PUBLISHER: RODALE / ISSUE: AUGUST 2008

DISTINCTIVE MERIT
/709/ **GARY TAXALI**
TITLE: FAT BABY
DESIGN DIRECTOR: KORY KENNEDY
DEPUTY ART DIRECTOR: MARC KAUFMANN
PUBLICATION: RUNNER'S WORLD
PUBLISHER: RODALE INC. / ISSUE: APRIL 2008

DISTINCTIVE MERIT
/710/ **IAN KIM**
TITLE: WHO'LL START THE RAIN
DESIGN DIRECTOR: MICHAEL LAWTON
PUBLICATION: POPULAR MECHANICS
PUBLISHER: THE HEARST CORPORATION-
MAGAZINES DIVISION / ISSUE: APRIL 2008

/711/ **RONALD KURNIAWAN**
TITLE: FACING THE MUSIC
DESIGN DIRECTOR: KORY KENNEDY
PUBLICATION: RUNNER'S WORLD
PUBLISHER: RODALE INC. / ISSUE: JULY 2008

/712/ **MARC ROSENTHAL**
TITLE: DISCLOSURE
ART DIRECTOR: SOOJIN BUZELLI
PUBLICATION: PLANSPONSOR / ISSUE: MAY 2008

713

714

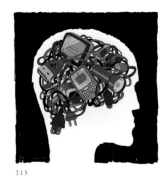

715

716

717

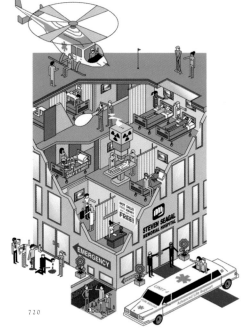

720

718

719

721

723

722

724

/713/ **MARK MATCHO**
TITLE: WALL STREET WHINERS / DESIGN DIRECTOR:
ROBERT PERINO / PUBLICATION: FORTUNE
PUBLISHER: TIME INC. / ISSUE: APRIL 14, 2008

/714/ **PIETARI POSTI**
TITLE: SAILING THROUGH THE STORM
DESIGN DIRECTOR: ROBERT PERINO
PUBLICATION: FORTUNE / PUBLISHER: TIME INC.
ISSUE: SEPTEMBER 15, 2008

/715/ **FRANK STOCKTON**
TITLE: TECHNOLOGY RUN AMOK
DESIGN DIRECTOR: MICHAEL LAWTON
PUBLICATION: POPULAR MECHANICS
PUBLISHER: THE HEARST CORPORATION
-MAGAZINES DIVISION / ISSUE: FEBRUARY 2008

/716/ **HARRY CAMPBELL**
TITLE: FLIP-FLOPPING TO THE WHITE HOUSE
ART DIRECTORS: JOHN GENZO,
EVELYN GOOD, CODY SCHNEIDER, KAM TAI
PUBLICATION: BLOOMBERG MARKETS MAGAZINE
PUBLISHER: BLOOMBERG L.P.
ISSUE: SEPTEMBER 2008

/717/ **THOMAS FUCHS**
TITLE: MIMICKING JAPAN'S WOE
ART DIRECTORS: JOHN GENZO, EVELYN GOOD,
CODY SCHNEIDER, KAM TAI
PUBLICATION: BLOOMBERG MARKETS MAGAZINE
PUBLISHER: BLOOMBERG L.P. / ISSUE: APRIL 2008

/718/ **ANDREW ZBIHLYJ**
TITLE: YOU FAILED. NOW PREVAIL!
DESIGN DIRECTOR: GEORGE KARABOTSOS
ART DIRECTOR: ELIZABETH NEAL
PUBLICATION: MEN'S HEALTH
PUBLISHER: RODALE INC. / ISSUE: JUNE 2008

/719/ **JASON SCHNEIDER**
TITLE: DRIVEN MAD BY BOGGLE
DESIGN DIRECTOR: ROBERT PERINO
PUBLICATION: FORTUNE / PUBLISHER: TIME INC.
ISSUE: SEPTEMBER 15, 2008

/720/ **QUICKHONEY, PETER STEMMLER**
TITLE: CHECK OUT OF HOSPITAL HELL
DESIGN DIRECTOR: GEORGE KARABOTSOS
ART DIRECTOR: VIKKI NESTICO
PUBLICATION: MEN'S HEALTH
PUBLISHER: RODALE INC. / ISSUE: OCTOBER 2008

/721/ **JOHN KASCHT**
TITLE: KEITH RICHARDS
DESIGN DIRECTOR: BRIAN ANSTEY
PUBLICATION: ENTERTAINMENT WEEKLY
PUBLISHER: TIME INC. / ISSUE: APRIL 11, 2008

/722/ **DAVID PLUNKERT**
TITLE: FOR DEFENDANTS ALONE?
ART DIRECTOR: JAY DEA
PUBLICATION: THE AMERICAN LAWYER
PUBLISHER: INCISIVE MEDIA / ISSUE: APRIL 2008

/723/ **CHRISTOPH NIEMANN**
TITLE: BREAK YOUR SLUMP
DESIGN DIRECTOR: GEORGE KARABOTSOS
ART DIRECTOR: ELIZABETH NEAL
PUBLICATION: MEN'S HEALTH PUBLISHER:
RODALE INC. ISSUE: MARCH 2008

/724/ **NICK DEWAR**
TITLE: THE UPSIDE
DESIGN DIRECTOR: ROBERT PERINO
PUBLICATION: FORTUNE
PUBLISHER: TIME INC.

725

726

727

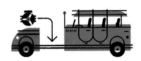

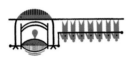

728

729

730

731

DISTINCTIVE MERIT
/725/ CHIP WASS
TITLE: CHIP WASS TOC SERIES
DESIGN DIRECTOR: BRIAN ANSTEY
PUBLICATION: ENTERTAINMENT WEEKLY
PUBLISHER: TIME INC.
ISSUE: JULY 25 / SEPTEMBER 26 / OCTOBER 24 /
DECEMBER 19, 2008

/726/ THOMAS FUCHS
TITLE: A BANKER'S GUIDE
TO WASHINGTON
ART DIRECTORS: JOHN GENZO, EVELYN GOOD,
CODY SCHNEIDER, KAM TAI
PUBLICATION: BLOOMBERG MARKETS MAGAZINE
PUBLISHER: BLOOMBERG L.P.
ISSUE: DECEMBER 2008

/727/ RAYMOND BIESINGER
TITLE: 500 COMPANIES
DESIGN DIRECTOR: ROBERT PERINO
PUBLICATION: FORTUNE
PUBLISHER: TIME INC.
ISSUE: JULY 21, 2008

/728/ DAVID PLUNKERT
TITLE: FREE TRADE HITS A WALL
ART DIRECTORS: JOHN GENZO, EVELYN GOOD,
CODY SCHNEIDER, KAM TAI
PUBLICATION: BLOOMBERG MARKETS MAGAZINE
PUBLISHER: BLOOMBERG L.P.
ISSUE: SEPTEMBER 2008

/729/ DANIEL BEJAR
TITLE: OPEN WOUNDS
ART DIRECTOR: JAY DEA
PUBLICATION: THE AMERICAN LAWYER
PUBLISHER: INCISIVE MEDIA
ISSUE: OCTOBER 2008

/730/ PHILIPPE PETIT-ROULET
TITLE: WRONG BOOK
ART DIRECTOR: CHRIS CURRY
PUBLICATION: THE NEW YORKER
PUBLISHER: CONDÉ NAST PUBLICATIONS INC.
ISSUE: JUNE 9 & 16, 2008

/731/ KIRSTEN ULVE
TITLE: KIRSTEN ULVE TOC SERIES
DESIGN DIRECTOR BRIAN ANSTEY
PUBLICATION: ENTERTAINMENT WEEKLY
PUBLISHER: TIME INC.
ISSUE: JULY 11 / AUGUST 8 / NOVEMBER 7 /
DECEMBER 5, 2008

THE ANNUAL JUDGING TAKES A VILLAGE, AND WOULD NOT BE POSSIBLE WITHOUT AN OUTPOURING OF WORK FROM SO MANY. NATHALIE KIRSHEH, ART DIRECTOR, W, AND JUDITH PUCKETT-RINELLA, SENIOR PHOTO EDITOR, T, THE NEW YORK TIMES STYLE MAGAZINE, (CO-CHAIRS), JEREMY LACROIX, CREATIVE DIRECTOR, CBS INTERACTIVE (ONLINE CHAIR), BRUCE RAMSAY (MAGAZINE OF THE YEAR CHAIR), AND NANCY STAMATOPOULOS (COMPETITION COORDINATOR) EXTEND AN ENORMOUS THANK-YOU ON BEHALF OF SPD TO ALL THE JUDGES AND VOLUNTEERS FOR AN INSPIRING AND REWARDING WEEKEND JUDGING OVER 6,100 ENTRIES AT FIT ON JANUARY 30TH, 31ST AND FEBRUARY 1ST, 2009.

/ MANY THANKS ALSO TO /
MARY OLENICZAK, ANNE ELMER AND THE STAFF IN THE FIT FACILITIES OFFICE.
GAEL TOWEY AND STEPHEN DOYLE FOR OPENING THEIR HOME TO US FOR THE DINNER PARTY DURING THE JUDGING WEEKEND.
HILARY WALSH AND DÉVA LORD OF MAREK AND ASSOCIATES FOR THE PHOTOGRAPHS OF THE JUDGES DURING THE COMPETITION.
TOM WAGNER FOR EVENT PRODUCTION OF THE GALA.
LAURA KONRAD OF W FOR HER DESIGN OF THE CALL FOR ENTRIES AND MANY, MANY OTHER DESIGN CONSULTATIONS THROUGHOUT THE YEAR.
AMERIKOM FOR PRINTING THE CALL FOR ENTRIES POSTER FOR THE STUDENT COMPETITION.
DAVID RHODES AND RICHARD WILDE OF SVA, FOR PROVIDING FREE SUMMER HOUSING FOR THE WINNERS OF THE SPD STUDENT COMPETITION.
TERRY FORTESCUE AND COURTNEY SPAIN OF ADOBE.
FOR INVALUABLE HELP AND SUPPORT IN THROUGHOUT THE YEAR, KEISHA DEAN, MIKE LEY, CLARE MINGES AND LISA VOSPER.

spots

CHAIRS MATTHEW LENNING AND DON MORRIS LED THE 22ND ANNUAL SPOTS COMPETITION, CHAMPIONING THE LITTLE ILLUSTRATIONS THAT SAY SO MUCH. FROM HUNDREDS OF ENTRIES, THE JUDGES SELECTED A CLASS OF ILLUSTRATIONS THAT DO AN EXCELLENT JOB OF AMPLIFYING THE EDITORIAL MESSAGE, FROM A WIDE SPECTRUM OF PUBLICATIONS. WINNERS ARE FEATURED IN A VISUAL INDEX HERE, AND CELEBRATED MORE EXTENSIVELY IN A VERY LIMITED-EDITION BOOK, THE SPOTS BOOK, SHOWCASING BOTH THE ILLUSTRATIONS AND SMALLER VERSIONS OF THE ORIGINAL EDITORIAL PAGES THAT FEATURED THE WORK.

/ SPECIAL THANKS TO THIS YEAR'S JUDGES /
J. R. AREBALO, JR / DESIGN DIRECTOR / AMERICAN WAY
JULIETTE BORDA / ILLUSTRATOR
DAVID CURCURITO / DESIGN DIRECTOR / ESQUIRE
JOHN GENZO / ART DIRECTOR / BLOOMBERG MARKETS
MICHAEL LAWTON / DESIGN DIRECTOR / POPULAR MECHANICS
GRACE LEE / ART DIRECTOR
CHRISTOPHER SILAS NEAL / ILLUSTRATOR
SIUNG TJIA / DESIGN DIRECTOR / ESPN THE MAGAZINE

student competition

THE STUDENT COMPETITION & THE ADOBE SCHOLARSHIP IN HONOR OF B.W. HONEYCUTT / ESTABLISHED IN 1995, THIS COMPETITION HONORS THE LIFE AND WORK OF B.W. HONEYCUTT. IT RECOGNIZES EXCEPTIONAL DESIGN BY STUDENTS WITH AWARDS AND THREE CASH PRIZES: THE ADOBE SCHOLARSHIP IN HONOR OF B.W. HONEYCUTT, THE FIRST-PLACE PRIZE OF $2500; SECOND-PLACE PRIZE OF $1000; AND A THIRD-PLACE PRIZE OF $500. THE TOP FOUR WINNERS ALSO RECEIVED SUMMER INTERNSHIPS AT ESQUIRE, GLAMOUR, INC., AND W. CHAIRED BY IAN DOHERTY AND ROBERT PERINO, THIS JURIED COMPETITION ACKNOWLEDGES THE STUDENT DESIGNER AND THE TEACHERS WHO DEVELOP THEIR UNIQUE TALENTS.

IN RECOGNIZING THE PROMISE OF EACH STUDENT, ADOBE AFFIRMS THE CREATIVE POSSIBILITIES INHERENT IN THE INDIVIDUAL. THROUGHOUT ITS PARTNERSHIP WITH SPD, ADOBE IS HELPING SHAPE THE NEXT GENERATION OF CREATIVE PROFESSIONALS. TOGETHER WE ARE BUILDING THE GROUNDWORK THAT WILL SUSTAIN AND FURTHER ARTISTIC ACCOMPLISHMENTS WITHIN THE EDITORIAL DESIGN COMMUNITY.

/ SPECIAL THANKS TO THE JUDGES /
NEIL JAMIESON / ART DIRECTOR / FIELD & STREAM
TRENT JOHNSON / ART DIRECTOR / GOOD HOUSEKEEPING
BRANDON KAVULLA / DESIGN DIRECTOR / MEN'S HEALTH
DEVIN PEDZWATER / DESIGN DIRECTOR / SPIN
ELLENE WUNDROK / DESIGN DIRECTOR / REAL SIMPLE

THE SOCIETY THANKS OUR PARTNER, ADOBE SYSTEMS, INC. FOR THEIR ONGOING SUPPORT.

THE SPD 44TH PUBLICATION DESIGN ANNUAL WAS DESIGNED AND PRODUCED BY TODD ALBERTSON AND TOM BROWN, WWW.WEAPONOFCHOICE.CA ADDITIONAL DESIGN BY DIAN HOLTON, LESLEY QUITMEIER, AND JENNIFER ROBERTS. SET IN LE TOUR DISPLAY AND GOUDY OLD STYLE. COVER PHOTOGRAPH BY FREDRIK BRODEN.

FIRST PUBLISHED IN THE UNITED STATES OF AMERICA BY:
ROCKPORT PUBLISHERS, INC. / 100 CUMMINGS CENTER, SUITE 406-L
BEVERLY, MA 01915 / TEL: 978.282.9590 / FAX: 978.283.2742